Contents

HEALTH & SOCIAL CARE | LEVEL 3

Book 1 BTEC National

Carolyn Aldworth | Marilyn Billingham
Peter Lawrence | Neil Moonie | Hilary Talman
Series editors: Beryl Stretch | Mary Whitehouse

A PEARSON COMPANY

Published by Pearson Education Limited, a company incorporated in England and Wales, having its registered office at Edinburgh Gate, Harlow, Essex, CM20 2JE. Registered company number: 872828

www.pearsonschoolsandfecolleges.co.uk

Edexcel is a registered trademark of Edexcel Limited
Text © Neil Moonie, Peter Lawrence, Carolyn Aldworth, Beryl Stretch, Mary Whitehouse, Marilyn Billingham, Hilary Talman

First published 2010

16 15

11 10 9

British Library Cataloguing in Publication Data. A catalogue record for this book is available from the British Library.

ISBN 978 1 846907 46 3

Edited by Kelly Davis
Designed by Tony Richardson (Wooden Ark)
Typeset by Phoenix Photosetting, Chatham, Kent
Original illustrations © Pearson Education Limited 2010
Cover design by Pearson Education Limited
Picture research by Pearson Education Limited
Cover photo/illustration © Plainpicture ltd/fStop
Printed in Slovakia by Neografia

Disclaimer

This material has been published on behalf of Edexcel and offers high-quality support for the delivery of Edexcel qualifications. This does not mean that the material is essential to achieve any Edexcel qualification, nor does it mean that it is the only suitable material available to support any Edexcel qualification. Edexcel material will not be used verbatim in setting any Edexcel examination or assessment. Any resource lists produced by Edexcel shall include this and other appropriate resources.

Copies of official specifications for all Edexcel qualifications may be found on the Edexcel website: www.edexcel.com

Acknowledgements

The authors and publisher would like to thank the following organisations for permission to quote, adapt or reproduce their materials:

p.57 Office for National Statistics for Figure 2.2 'Unemployment rates of men: by ethnic group, 2004' from *The Annual Population Survey*; **p. 79, 90, 158, 330** Statistics quoted, or used to produce graphs. Office for National Statistics. Crown Copyright. Reproduced under the terms of the PSI Licence; **p.73, 263** The Nursing and Midwifery Council for their Code of Professional Conduct www.nmc-uk.org, reproduced with permission; **p.90** Figure 3.2 'Deaths related to MRSA in England and Wales 1993–2008'; Extracts from *Social Trends 2004*, Vol. 34, HMSO; **p.149** Crossed Grain Symbol. Reproduced with permission from Coeliac UK, the national charity for people with coeliac disease and dermatitis herpetiformis. You can contact Coeliac UK via their website at www.coeliac.org.uk or by phoning their helpline on 0845 305 2060 (Helpline open 10-4, Mon, Tue, Thu, Fri and 11-4, Wed); **p. 151** Air pollution in the UK. R. Walters (2009) *Crime is in the air: air pollution and regulation in the UK*, Centre for Crime and Justice Studies, Kings College London; **p.244** Pearson Education, Inc. for Figure 6.3 'Kolb's experiential learning cycle' and extract from *Experiential Learning: Experience as a Source of Learning & Development* by David, A. Kolb, p.21, copyright © 1984, Prentice Hall; **p.348** for Figure 8.8 'Maslow's hierarchy of needs' from *Motivation and Personality, 3rd edition* by Abraham H. Maslow, Robert D. Frager and James Fadiman, copyright © 1987, Prentice Hall. Reprinted with the permission of Pearson Education, Inc., Upper Saddle River, NJ; **p.245** Peter Honey Publications Ltd for Table 6.1 'Honey and Mumford's learning styles theory' from *The Manual of Learning Styles* by Honey, P., Mumford, A., 1985, copyright © Peter Honey, Education Development International; **p.323** Child Poverty Action Group for facts and details from www.cpag.org.uk/povertyfacts, copyright © Child Poverty Action Group; **p.329** Figure 7.6 'Expectation of life at birth by sex', Figure 7.7 'Prevalence of cardiovascular disease by household income and sex', **p.330** Figure 7.8 'Unemployment rates of men by ethnic group from *Social Trends 2006*, Vol. 36, HMSO; and extracts *Social Trends 2009*, Vol. 39, HMSO. Crown Copyright material is reproduced with the permission of the Office of Public Sector Information; **p.318** British Library for Figure 7.4 and an extract from the *Report on Social Insurance and Allied Services* by Sir William Beveridge, 1941, copyright © British Library Board, BS Ref 1/1942-43 vi.119 Cmnd 6404; **p.323** Child Poverty Action Group for facts and details from www.cpag.org.uk/povertyfacts, copyright © Child Poverty Action Group; **p. 372** UK90 4 to 18 years charts © Child Growth Foundation, reproduced with permission. Further information and supplies at www.healthforallchildren.co.uk; **p. 373, 385, 386, 387, 397** Values quoted or adapted. Food Standards Agency. Crown Copyright. Reproduced under the terms of the PSI Licence; **p.386** Food Standards Agency for Table 21.5 'Selenium and zinc: functions, sources and characteristics', adapted from Food Standards Agency, www.eatwell.gov.uk; **p.452** Health Protection Agency for Figure 22.8 'Line graph showing changes in annual incidence of measles in England and Wales over a 10 year period' taken from data in the tables between 1998 and 2008 on www.hpa.org.uk/, data courtesy of Health Protection Agency; **throughout the text** Equality and Human Rights Commission for extracts from *Equality and Human Rights Commission Publication Scheme*, February 2009, www.equalityhumanrights.com copyright © Equality and Human Rights Commission; Office of Public Sector Information for extracts from The Human Rights Act of 2000; Health and Safety at Work Act 1974; Manual Handling Operations Regulations 1992; Management of Health and Safety at Work Regulations 1999; Reporting of Injuries, Diseases and Dangerous Occurrences Regulations (RIDDOR) 1995; and Control of Substances Hazardous to Health (COSHH) 2002. © Crown copyright 2002 – 2008.

In some instances we have been unable to trace the owners of copyright material, and we would appreciate any information that would enable us to do so.

Photos
The publisher would like to thank the following for their kind permission to reproduce their photographs:

(Key: b-bottom; c-centre; l-left; r-right; t-top)

1 Shutterstock: Yuri Arcurs.. **3 Shutterstock:** Francesco Ridolfi. **8 Pearson Education Ltd:** Studio 8. Clark Wiseman. **11 Pearson Education Ltd:** Lord and Leverett. **16 Shutterstock:** sa2324. **19 Pearson Education Ltd:** Studio 8. Clark Wiseman. **20 Pearson Education Ltd:** Jules Selmes. **23 Pearson Education Ltd:** Studio 8. Clark Wiseman. **28 Pearson Education Ltd:** Studio 8. Clark Wiseman. **31 Pearson Education Ltd:** Studio 8. Clark Wiseman. **34 Pearson Education Ltd:** Studio 8. Clark Wiseman. **35 Pearson Education Ltd:** Studio 8. Clark Wiseman. **37 Shutterstock:** Galina Barskaya. **45 Shutterstock:** Olly. **47 Pearson Education Ltd:** Jules Selmes. **49 Shutterstock:** Olly. **53 Shutterstock:** Yuri Arcurs. **57 Shutterstock:** Philip Date. **66 Shutterstock:** Andrew Gentry. **85 Pearson Education Ltd:** Studio 8. Clark Wiseman. **87 Pearson Education Ltd:** Studio 8. Clark Wiseman. **92 Alamy Images:** Medical-on-Line. **97 Shutterstock:** Christopher Futcher. **98 Alamy Images:** Justin Kase z10z. **99 Shutterstock:** robcocquyt. **113 Alamy Images:** Medical-on-Line. **116 Pearson Education Ltd:** Studio 8. Clark Wiseman. **129 Image Source Ltd. 131 Pearson Education Ltd:** Jules Selmes. **132 Pearson Education Ltd:** Studio 8. Clark Wiseman. **141 Shutterstock:** Anita Patterson Peppers. **151 PhotoDisc:** Photolink. **152 Pearson Education Ltd:** Jules Selmes (l). **Shutterstock:** Stephen Finn (r). **161 Pearson Education Ltd:** Studio 8. Clark Wiseman. **166 Stockbyte. 167 Pearson Education Ltd:** Jules Selmes. **169 Pearson Education Ltd:** Studio 8. Clark Wiseman. **173 PhotoDisc:** Kevin Peterson. **175 Science Photo Library Ltd:** NATIONAL CANCER INSTITUTE. **177 Alamy Images:** Rubberball. **182 Science Photo Library Ltd:** PASIEKA. **186 Science Photo Library Ltd:** NATIONAL CANCER INSTITUTE. **236 Shutterstock:** Christopher Futcher. **239 Shutterstock:** Sean Nel. **241 Shutterstock:** Studio Foxy. **259 Pearson Education Ltd:** MindStudio. **296 Shutterstock:** PT Images. **301 Shutterstock:** Daniel Gale. **303 Shutterstock:** Monkey Business Images. **314 Corbis:** Stapleton Collection. **316 Alamy Images:** Vstock. **325 Shutterstock:** iofoto. **328 Shutterstock:** Andresr. **335 Alamy Images:** Horizon International Images Limited. **337 Pearson Education Ltd:** Studio 8. Clark Wiseman. **345 Shutterstock:** anyaivanova. **348 Pearson Education Ltd:** Studio 8. Clark Wiseman. **350 Shutterstock:** Losevsky Pavel. **355 Alamy Images:** Allstar Picture Library. **358 Shutterstock:** Yuri Arcurs. **359 Pearson Education Ltd:** Gareth Boden. **367 Shutterstock:** Regien Paassen. **369 Pearson Education Ltd:** Jules Selmes. **378 Shutterstock:** Regien Paassen. **379 Pearson Education Ltd:** Jules Selmes. **391 Alamy Images:** Kumar Sriskandan. **392 Pearson Education Ltd:** Jules Selmes (bl); Jules Selmes (bc); Jules Selmes (br). **Science Photo Library Ltd:** DR P. MARAZZI (cr). **394 Alamy Images:** David Taylor. **399 Alamy Images:** MBI. **401 Shutterstock:** Gabi Moisa. **405 Shutterstock:** Chad McDermott. **407 Pearson Education Ltd:** Studio 8. Clark Wiseman. **411 Shutterstock:** Andre Blais. **426 Shutterstock:** Zsolt Nyulaszi. **433 Getty Images**

Cover images: *Front:* **Plainpicture Ltd:** fStop; *Back:* **Pearson Education Ltd:** MindStudio tl; **Stockbyte:** tr

All other images © Pearson Education

Every effort has been made to trace the copyright holders and we apologise in advance for any unintentional omissions. We would be pleased to insert the appropriate acknowledgement in any subsequent edition of this publication.

About your BTEC Level 3 National Health and Social Care book

Choosing to study for a BTEC Level 3 National Health and Social Care qualification is a great decision to make for lots of reasons. It is an area to work in which gives many varied opportunities for you to make a difference to people's lives in a positive way. At the same time you are gaining skills that you can transfer to other professions later. Working in the health and social care professions can also take you to different parts of the country and overseas. The opportunities are endless.

Your BTEC Level 3 National in Health and Social Care is a **vocational** or **work-related** qualification. This doesn't mean that it will give you all the skills you need to do a job, but it does mean that you'll have the opportunity to gain specific knowledge, understanding and skills that are relevant to your chosen subject or area of work.

What will you be doing?

The qualification is structured into **mandatory units** (ones that you must do) and **optional units** (ones that you can choose to do). How many units you do and which ones you cover depend on the type of qualification you are working towards.

Qualifications	Credits from mandatory units	Credits from optional units	Total credits
Edexcel BTEC Level 3 Certificate in Health and Social Care	10	10 specialist 10 optional	30
Edexcel BTEC Level 3 Subsidiary Diploma in Health and Social Care	30	30	60
Edexcel BTEC Level 3 Diploma in Health and Social Care	80	40	120
Edexcel BTEC Level 3 Diploma in Health and Social Care (Social Care)	100	20	120
Edexcel BTEC Level 3 Diploma in Health and Social Care (Health Sciences)	100	20	120
Edexcel BTEC Level 3 Diploma in Health and Social Care (Health Studies)	100	20	120
Edexcel BTEC Level 3 Extended Diploma in Health and Social Care	80	100	180
Edexcel BTEC Level 3 Extended Diploma in Health and Social Care (Social Care)	110	70	180
Edexcel BTEC Level 3 Extended Diploma in Health and Social Care (Health Studies)	130	50	180
Edexcel BTEC Level 3 Extended Diploma in Health and Social Care (Health Sciences)	110	70	180

You may have chosen a general health and social care qualification or you may be following a more specialist route, and the units you study will reflect this. Whatever your choice, you will need to complete a mix of mandatory units and optional units.

The table below shows how each unit in the book fits into each qualification.

Unit title	Mandatory	Optional
Unit 1 Developing effective communication in health and social care	All levels ~~Completed~~	~~Distinction~~
Unit 2 Equality, diversity and rights in health and social care	All levels except Certificate ~~Completed~~	Specialist optional unit for Certificate ~~Distinction~~
Unit 3 Health, safety and security in health and social care	All levels except Certificate ~~Completed~~	Specialist optional unit for Certificate ~~Distinction~~
Unit 4 Development through the life stages	All Diplomas All Extended Diplomas ~~Completed~~	Certificate H&SC Subsidiary Diploma H&SC ~~Distinction~~
Unit 5 Anatomy and physiology for health and social care	All Diplomas All Extended Diplomas ~~Completed~~	Certificate H&SC Subsidiary Diploma H&SC ~~Distinction~~
Unit 6 Personal and professional development in health and social care	All Diplomas All Extended Diplomas ~~Completed~~	~~Distinction.~~
Unit 7 Sociological perspectives for health and social care	Diploma H&SC All Extended Diplomas ~~Completed~~	Certificate H&SC Subsidiary Diploma H&SC Diploma H&SC (SC) Diploma H&SC (HSt) Diploma H&SC (HSc) ~~Distinction~~
Unit 8 Psychological perspectives for health and social care	Diploma H&SC All Extended Diplomas ~~Completed~~	Certificate H&SC Subsidiary Diploma H&SC Diploma H&SC (SC) Diploma H&SC (HSt) Diploma H&SC (HSc)
Unit 21 Nutrition for health and social care		Certificate H&SC Subsidiary Diploma H&SC All Diplomas All Extended Diplomas
Unit 22 Research methodology for health and social care		All Diplomas All Extended Diplomas

vii

How to use this book

This book is designed to help you through your BTEC Level 3 National Health and Social Care course. It is specifically designed to support you when you are studying for the BTEC Level 3 National qualifications. The book is divided into 10 units to reflect the units in the specification. To make your learning easier we have divided each unit into a series of topics each related to the learning outcomes and content of the qualification.

This book also contains many features that will help you use your skills and knowledge in work-related situations and assist you in getting the most from your course.

We also provide a second book (Book 2) which gives you an additional nine units for study and you will find details of this either from your tutor or at www.pearsonfe.co.uk/btecH&SC.

Credit value: 10

3 Health, safety and security

This unit introduces you to health, safety and security issues in health and social care settings. In the UK health and safety is taken extremely seriously, and we take it for granted that our workplaces will be safe. However, as a practitioner you will have to consider what risks exist, and be able to plan a safe environment. You will need to know what the law requires you to do, and how to carry it out. If you become a manager of a setting, you must make sure that everything possible has been done to keep your staff and the people you care for safe, and that you can prove you have done so.

To be good at health and safety, you need to be creative and innovative, and be able to think ahead and remain calm in an emergency. You will gain a thorough understanding of potential hazards. You will also learn how legislation, policies and procedures work to reduce risk, and the consequences of not following them, both for your safety and your career! You will learn about the health, safety and security responsibilities of employees and employers, and their relevance to you as a student. Finally you will learn how to deal with all sorts of incidents and emergencies that could occur in health and social care settings.

Learning outcomes

After completing this unit you should:

1 understand potential hazards in health and social care
2 know how legislation, policies and procedures promote health, safety and security in health and social care settings
3 be able to implement a risk assessment
4 understand priorities and responses in dealing with incidents and emergencies

Introduction

These introductions give you a snapshot of what to expect from each unit – and what you should be aiming for by the time you finish it!

Assessment and grading criteria

This table explains what you must do to achieve each of the assessment criteria for each unit. For each assessment criterion, shown by the grade button **P1**, there is an assessment activity.

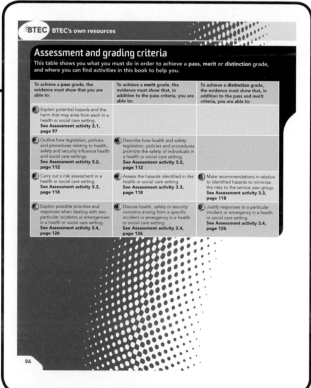

BTEC **BTEC's own resources**

Assessment and grading criteria

This table shows you what you must do in order to achieve a **pass**, **merit** or **distinction** grade, and where you can find activities in this book to help you.

To achieve a pass grade, the evidence must show that you are able to:	To achieve a merit grade, the evidence must show that, in addition to the pass criteria, you are able to:	To achieve a distinction grade, the evidence must show that, in addition to the pass and merit criteria, you are able to:
P1 Explain potential hazards and the harm that may arise from each in a health or social care setting. **See Assessment activity 3.1, page 97**		
P2 Outline how legislation, policies and procedures relating to health, safety and security influence health and social care settings. **See Assessment activity 3.2, page 112**	**M1** Describe how health and safety legislation, policies and procedures promote the safety of individuals in a health or social care setting. **See Assessment activity 3.2, page 112**	
P3 Carry out a risk assessment in a health or social care setting. **See Assessment activity 3.3, page 118**	**M2** Assess the hazards identified in the health or social care setting. **See Assessment activity 3.3, page 118**	**D1** Make recommendations in relation to identified hazards to minimise the risks to the service user group. **See Assessment activity 3.3, page 118**
P4 Explain possible priorities and responses when dealing with two particular incidents or emergencies in a health or social care setting. **See Assessment activity 3.4, page 126**	**M3** Discuss health, safety or security concerns arising from a specific incident or emergency in a health or social care setting. **See Assessment activity 3.4, page 126**	**D2** Justify responses to a particular incident or emergency in a health or social care setting. **See Assessment activity 3.4, page 126**

86

Assessment

Your tutor will set **assignments** throughout your course for you to complete. These may take the form of research, presentations, written work or research assignments. The important thing is that you evidence your skills and knowledge to date.

Stuck for ideas? Daunted by your first assignment? These learners have all been through it before…

Unit 7 Sociological perspectives for health and social care

How you will be assessed

This unit will be assessed by internal assignments that will be marked by the staff at your centre. It may be subject to sampling by your centre's external verifier as part of Edexcel's on-going quality assurance procedures. The assignments will be designed to allow you to show your understanding of the unit learning outcomes. These directly relate to what you should know and be able to do after completing this unit.

Your assignments could be in the form of:

- presentations
- written assignments
- case studies
- essays.

Guidance is included throughout this unit to help you prepare and present your work.

Sam, 18 years old

I've been on placement at a hostel for homeless young people for six weeks so far. Many of the residents at the hostel have very sad life stories. Few of them have any family support. Some have been in care. They have come from poor areas, where unemployment and crime are high and drugs are easily available. They all seem to have had very deprived childhoods. Has this all led to the hostel being their home?

I think of Joe. He was brought up by his grandparents, who were retired and on a very low income. He never knew his dad, and his mum had a drug habit. When he left school he also left home. After that he lived with friends, sometimes in hostels and often on the streets. He has been in hospital at various times with chronic bronchitis, pneumonia and hypothermia. His diet has been very poor – sometimes eating from rubbish bins. He hasn't ever worked. He often seems very depressed. He doesn't seem to talk to anyone very much. His personal hygiene is poor and his self-esteem is low.

This unit helped me to see that guys like Joe are homeless partly because they haven't yet had much of a chance in life. Poverty, little family support, poor housing and poor health seem to have led them to this.

Over to you!

1 Which parts of this unit do you think you will find most interesting?
2 Which other units do you think are linked with the issues covered in this unit?
3 Which parts of this unit will help you better understand the homeless young people at the hostel?

Activities

There are different types of activities for you to do: **Assessment activities** are suggestions for tasks that you might do as part of your assignment and will help you develop your knowledge, skills and understanding. **Grading tips** clearly explain what you need to do in order to achieve a pass, merit or distinction grade.

Assessment activity 6.1

P1 M1 D1 BTEC

Produce a piece of writing that explains influences on the personal learning process of different individuals.

Include an assessment of how different influences in your life have affected your own learning. Consider influences on the development of your knowledge and understanding, skills and abilities. Present your assessment as a personal statement and include a curriculum vitae.

Evaluate how the personal learning and development of health and social care workers can benefit others.

M1 Sketch a timeline to help collect your thoughts about the factors that have influenced your learning from your childhood, school, work and other life experiences. You could put the significant events and experiences (e.g. starting school, moving home) on top of the line and their effects below the line. Use the timeline as a tool to help you construct your personal statement. Research how to present a curriculum vitae.

D1 Before you prepare your evaluation for D1, you could carry out some research about PPD and its benefits in health and social care. You should talk to staff at your placement about how their learning and career backgrounds have helped them in their work. You could also consider how you have used your own learning throughout your life so far to help others.

Grading tips

P1 For P1, you should consider a wide range of influences that may affect people's learning and not just the factors that have influenced your own learning. Remember to explain the possible effects of the influences, applying the theories discussed in this section.

There are also suggestions for **activities** that will give you a broader grasp of the sector, stretch your imagination and deepen your skills.

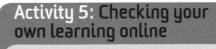

Activity 5: Checking your own learning online

Are your individual learning plan and the records of what you have achieved so far available to you online at your school or college? If so, it probably means that your school or college has its own intranet or virtual learning environment. ICT is an increasingly important tool for study. Becoming familiar with the way it can help you would be valuable preparation for study in higher education. Ask yourself the following questions about your own online learning information:

1 How often do you use it?
2 Do you find it useful?
3 Could you make more or better use of it to support your studies?

Personal, learning and thinking skills

Throughout your BTEC Level 3 National Health and Social Care course, there are lots of opportunities to develop your personal, learning and thinking skills. Look out for these as you progress.

PLTS

Independent enquirer: Processing observed information on complex subjects concisely and clearly will allow you to demonstrate your independent enquiry skills.

Functional skills

It's important that you have good English, maths and ICT skills – you never know when you'll need them, and employers will be looking for evidence that you've got these skills too.

Functional skills

English: In discussing the changes in social development, you will develop your speaking and listening skills and skills of presenting arguments and listening to others. Recording your conclusions will develop your writing skills.

Key terms

Technical words and phrases are easy to spot, and definitions are included. The terms and definitions are also in the glossary at the back of the book.

Key terms

Personal and professional development (PPD) – Learning acquired from experience before qualifying as a professional.

Continuing professional development (CPD) – Learning acquired after qualifying as a professional.

WorkSpace

Case studies provide snapshots of real workplace issues, and show how the skills and knowledge you develop during your course can help you in your career.

There are also mini-case studies throughout the book to help you relate ideas and concepts to real life issues and situations.

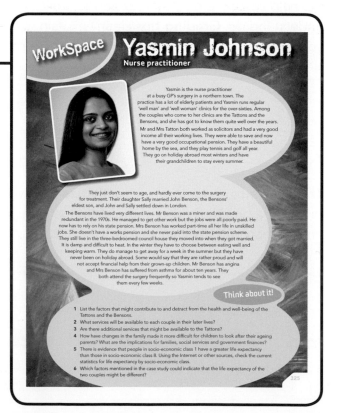

WorkSpace — Yasmin Johnson
Nurse practitioner

Yasmin is the nurse practitioner at a busy GP's surgery in a northern town. The practice has a lot of elderly patients and Yasmin runs regular 'well man' and 'well woman' clinics for the over-sixties. Among the couples who come to her clinics are the Tattons and the Bensons, and she has got to know them quite well over the years. Mr and Mrs Tatton both worked as solicitors and had a very good income all their working lives. They were able to save and now have a very good occupational pension. They have a beautiful home by the sea, and they play tennis and golf all year. They go on holiday abroad most winters and have their grandchildren to stay every summer.

They just don't seem to age, and hardly ever come to the surgery for treatment. Their daughter Sally married John Benson, the Bensons' eldest son, and John and Sally settled down in London.

The Bensons have lived very different lives. Mr Benson was a miner and was made redundant in the 1970s. He managed to get other work but the jobs were all poorly paid. He now has to rely on his state pension. Mrs Benson has worked part-time all her life in unskilled jobs. She doesn't have a works pension and she never paid into the state pension scheme. They still live in the three-bedroomed council house they moved into when they got married. It is damp and difficult to heat. In the winter they have to choose between eating well and keeping warm. They do manage to get away for a week in the summer but they have never been on holiday abroad. Some would say that they are rather proud and will not accept financial help from their grown-up children. Mr Benson has angina and Mrs Benson has suffered from asthma for about ten years. They both attend the surgery frequently so Yasmin tends to see them every few weeks.

Think about it!

1 List the factors that might contribute to and detract from the health and well-being of the Tattons and the Bensons.
2 What services will be available to each couple in their later lives?
3 Are there additional services that might be available to the Tattons?
4 How have changes in the family made it more difficult for children to look after their ageing parents? What are the implications for families, social services and government finances?
5 There is evidence that people in socio-economic class 1 have a greater life expectancy than those in socio-economic class 8. Using the Internet or other sources, check the current statistics for life expectancy by socio-economic class.
6 Which factors mentioned in the case study could indicate that the life expectancy of the two couples might be different?

325

Did you know?

Fascinating facts, figures and information are given, providing you with additional information relating to the ideas and concepts covered.

Did you know?

Aseptic technique is the method used to keep the patient or individual as free from contamination as possible. It is used to prevent micro-organisms entering the body, which could cause infection. You need to use sterile equipment and fluids during invasive medical and nursing procedures, including wound dressings and catheterisation and during operations.

Reflect

These are opportunities for individual reflection on, or group discussions about, your experiences in a health and social care context. They will widen your understanding and help you reflect on issues that impact on health and social care.

Reflect

Reflect on your thoughts on homophobia and be honest! Then reflect on how your thoughts may influence you when you are working with and supporting people in health and social care. This is personal to you, unless you want to discuss it openly.

Further reading and resources

Recommended books, journals and websites to develop your knowledge on the subjects covered in each unit.

Resources and further reading

Argyle, M. (1972) *The Psychology of Interpersonal Behaviour*, second ed. Harmondsworth: Pelican
Burnard, P. (1996) *Acquiring Interpersonal Skills*, second ed. London: Chapman & Hall
Burnard, P., Morrison, P. (1997) *Caring and Communicating* Basingstoke and London: Macmillan Press Ltd
Engebretson, J. (2003) 'Caring presence: a case study' in *Communication, Relationships and Care* Robb, M., Barrett, S., Komaromy, C., Rogers, A. (eds) London & New York: OU & Routledge
Pinker, S. (1994) *The Language Instinct* Harmondsworth: Penguin
Tuckman, B. (1965) 'Development Sequence in Small Groups', *Psychological Bulletin*, Vol. 63, No. 6

Useful websites

Braille www.brailleplus.net
British Sign Language www.bda.org.uk
Makaton www.makaton.org
Signs and finger spelling alphabet
www.british-sign.co.uk
and at www.royaldeaf.org.uk

Just checking

When you see this sort of activity, take stock! These quick activities and questions are there to check your knowledge. You can use them to see how much progress you've made or as a revision tool.

Edexcel's assignment tips

At the end of each chapter, you'll find hints and tips to help you get the best mark you can, such as the best websites to go to, checklists to help you remember processes and really useful facts and figures.

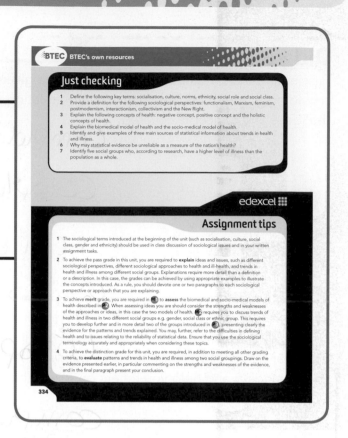

Have you read your **BTEC Level 3 National Study Skills Guide**? It's full of advice on study skills, putting your assignments together and making the most of being a BTEC Health and Social Care student.

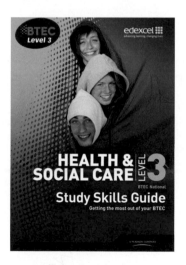

Ask your tutor about extra materials to help you through your course. We also provide **Student Book 2** which gives you even more units for your study. The **Tutor Resource Pack** which accompanies this book contains interesting videos, activities, presentations and information about the Health and Social Care sector.

Your book is just part of the exciting resources from Edexcel to help you succeed in your BTEC course.

Visit:

• www.edexcel.com/BTEC or
• www.pearsonfe.co.uk/BTEC 2010

1 Developing effective communication in health and social care

This unit is designed to help you develop your communication skills. You will explore ways of overcoming barriers to communication and develop your own skills in one-to-one and group interactions.

In order to work with people you must be good at communicating with them. Effective communication requires advanced practical skills in much the same way as driving a car does. Driving a car involves responding to changes in the road ahead, as well as responding to other road users. Effective communication in care involves being sensitive to feedback from others. Sometimes the people you meet may be happy but often they may feel sad, afraid, upset or anxious. You need to be able to recognise and respond appropriately to many different emotional situations. Different contexts will require you to communicate in different ways. Skilled communication requires you to make decisions as to what response would be most effective in the situation you find yourself in. Effective communication involves much more than just giving or receiving information.

Learning outcomes

After completing this unit you should:

1 understand effective communication and interpersonal interaction in health and social care

2 understand factors that influence communication and interpersonal interaction in health and social care environments

3 understand ways to overcome barriers in a health and social care environment

4 be able to communicate and interact effectively in a health or care environment.

Assessment and grading criteria

This table shows you what you must do in order to achieve a **pass**, **merit** or **distinction** grade, and where you can find activities in this book to help you.

To achieve a **pass** grade, the evidence must show that you are able to:	To achieve a **merit** grade, the evidence must show that, in addition to the pass criteria, you are able to:	To achieve a **distinction** grade, the evidence must show that, in addition to the pass and merit criteria, you are able to:
P1 Explain the role of effective communication and interpersonal interaction in a health and social care context. **See Assessment activity 1.1, page 17** *achieved*	**M1** Assess the role of effective communication and interpersonal interaction in health and social care with a reference to theories of communication. **See Assessment activity 1.2, page 21** *achieved*	
P2 Discuss theories of communication. **See Assessment activity 1.2, page 21** *achieved*		**D1** Evaluate strategies used in health and social care environments to overcome barriers to effective communication and interpersonal interactions. **See Assessment activity 1.4, page 40** *achieved*
P3 Explain factors that may influence communication and interpersonal interactions in health and social care environments. **See Assessment activity 1.3, page 28** *achieved*	**M2** Review strategies used in health and social care environments to overcome barriers to effective communication and interpersonal interactions. **See Assessment activity 1.4, page 40** *achieved*	
P4 Explain strategies used in health and social care environments to overcome barriers to effective communication and interpersonal interactions. **See Assessment activity 1.4, page 40** *achieved*		
P5 Participate in a one-to-one interaction in a health and social care context. **See Assessment activity 1.5, page 42** *achieved*	**M3** Assess your communication and interpersonal skills in relation to each interaction. **See Assessment activity 1.5, page 42** *achieved*	**D2** Evaluate factors that influence the effectiveness of each interaction. **See Assessment activity 1.5, page 42** *achieved*
P6 Participate in a group interaction in a health and social care context. **See Assessment activity 1.5, page 42** *achieved*		

How you will be assessed

You will need to produce written evidence of examples of the role of communication and interpersonal interaction in health and social care. You will also need to explain theories of one-to-one and group communication. You will need to demonstrate your own skills both in one-to-one and in group interaction situations. Varied assessment tasks are included throughout this unit to help you prepare your work.

Daniel, 17 years old

This is a very practical unit. Although there's quite a lot of theory, I found that I 'sort of knew' some of the ideas, although I had never put them into words before.

The great thing about studying this unit is that it enables you to explain what's going on in one-to-one and group situations. The unit changes the way you understand conversations and the way people behave when they are in groups. Whenever I see people talking, I start to work out what their body language might mean. I now realise that there are special communication skills that you can use in care work. Sometimes the way you say something can be more important than what you say. There are a lot of barriers in care situations that can stop people from understanding each other. But the unit explains ways of overcoming these problems.

The assignment work is all very practical. To begin with, I had to set up a logbook to record examples of the theory we were studying. We had to study practical examples of the communication cycle and group formation. I went on to explore barriers to communication and how to overcome barriers. I found my supervisor at my practice placement was very helpful in getting me to understand how to overcome barriers. Finally, I had to explore my own skills in one-to-one communication and group situations. I tried analysing several situations that I had experienced before going on to complete my final assignment work.

Over to you!

1   Why is skilled communication so important in health and social care work?

2   Do you think effective group or effective one-to-one communication will be the hardest to demonstrate?

3   What part of the practical work for this unit do you think will be most enjoyable?

1 Understanding effective communication and interpersonal interaction in health and social care

Changing the way you communicate

Imagine that you have to interview people in a youth club in a distant city as part of a project. You do not know the members of this club. The members speak English but they are very different from your friends in your local area. The people you are interviewing don't have to answer your questions.

How would you act to get these people to like you and listen to you?

The way you communicate with other people always depends on the situation or the context you find yourself in. You will have developed effective ways of communicating and interacting with your friends. But if you find yourself in a different context you will need to be able to change the way you act in order to get a good response from people.

1.1 Contexts of communication

One-to-one communication

When you start a conversation with someone you don't know well, you should always try to create the right kind of feeling. It is important to create a positive emotional atmosphere before you go on to discuss complicated issues or give people information. The other person needs to feel relaxed and happy to talk to you. Very often people will start with a greeting such as 'Good morning'. You can help other people to relax by showing that *you* are friendly and relaxed.

Imagine a care worker in a day centre for older people walking around and sharply asking each person: 'You want tea or coffee?' Without any other conversation, this behaviour would probably come across as 'mechanical'. The care worker would just be carrying out a practical task – getting fluid into the bodies of these people. However, some older people might find this behaviour disrespectful, and others might find it cold and unfriendly.

How would you offer a choice of drinks to people in a warm and friendly way?

1. Greeting or warm-up

2. Conversation or information exchange

3. Farewells or winding-down

Fig 1.1: Interaction often involves a three-stage process

Once you have created a good feeling, you can move on to the business – the things you want to talk about. When it is time to finish the conversation, you want to leave the other person with the right kind of emotions so you might say something like 'See you soon' to show that you value them. Formal conversations often follow a three-stage model, with an emotional 'warm-up stage' at the beginning, a 'business' or 'exchange of information' stage in the middle, and a 'winding down stage' at the end.

Group communication

Taking part in a group discussion involves the same issues as one-to-one communication as well as some additional issues.

How does it feel to be in the group?

Group discussion only works well if people want to be involved. Sometimes people feel threatened if they have to speak within a formal group of people, or they might stay quiet because they are worried about other people's reactions. It is important that the group has the right emotional atmosphere. People in groups often use humour or other friendly ways of behaving to create the right group feeling, which encourages people to talk. Creating the right group atmosphere involves 'maintaining' the group so this aspect of group communication is often called group maintenance.

Is there a group leader?

Some groups, such as team meetings or classroom discussions, have a leader or chairperson. Having a leader is very useful because the leader can encourage people to express their ideas and help them to take turns when talking. Group leaders often encourage people to focus on a particular task within a group.

Have you prepared what you are going to say?

When talking in a formal group you will need to think through your points before sharing them with the whole group. Because of this extra preparation, talking to a group can feel very different from talking in a one-to-one situation.

Are you good at taking turns?

Group communication fails if everybody speaks at the same time. It is harder to work out who should be speaking in a group discussion than in a one-to-one conversation. The skill of taking turns involves identifying the following pattern. When a person is

about to finish speaking they usually signal this by lowering their voice tone, slowing their pace of talking and looking around at other people in the group. The next person to talk knows that it is their turn by watching the eyes of other group members. If people fail to notice these patterns then too many people may try to speak at the same time. If everybody is talking then nobody is listening!

Can everybody see each other clearly?

If people sit in a circle then everyone can see everyone else's face. This is very important because positive group feeling and successful turn-taking often depend on people being able to understand the messages in other people's faces. If people sit behind each other or in rows, then some of the group cannot see others' faces. Bad seating or standing positions can make group communication harder.

Activity 1: Record eye contact and turn-taking in group discussion

Get together with five or six colleagues and agree on a current news topic that you would all enjoy discussing for four or five minutes. One of you should use a camcorder to record the eye contact and speech of other group members. Analyse your recording and work out how good people were at taking turns in group discussion.

PLTS

Independent enquirer: This activity will help you demonstrate that you can analyse and evaluate information, judging its relevance and value. The activity may also help to develop team working and participation skills.

Informal communication

We often use informal communication when we know people well – for example, with friends and family. Some friends or family members may use terms that other people would not understand. Local groups from particular places might also have their own ways of speaking. For example, some people in southern England might say things like 'Hiya, mate. How's it goin'?' If you belong to this group, you will appreciate this as a warm, friendly greeting. But different groups of people use different informal language so it can sometimes be hard to understand the informal communication of people from different social groups.

Formal communication

Health and social care work often involves formal communication. For example, if you went to a local authority social services reception desk you might expect to be greeted with the phrase 'Good morning. How can I help you?' This formal communication is understood by a wide range of people. Formal communication also shows respect for others. The degree of formality or informality is called the language 'register'.

Imagine going to the reception desk and being greeted with the phrase 'What *you* after then?' Some people might actually prefer such an informal greeting. It might put them at ease, making them feel that the other person is like them. But in many situations, such informal language could make people feel that they are not being respected. Being 'after something' could be a 'put down'; you might assume that you are being seen as a scrounger. So it is often risky to use informal language unless you are sure that other people expect you to do so. If you are treated informally, you may

interpret this as not being treated seriously, or 'not being respected'.

So is there a correct way to speak to people when you first introduce yourself? After all, if you are too formal you may come across as pretentious or 'posh'. Usually care workers will adjust the way they speak in order to communicate respect for different 'speech communities'.

Communication between colleagues

Family and friends know you well and will usually understand you, even if you communicate poorly or very informally. Communicating with people at work is different because:

- It is important that care workers communicate respect for each other. Colleagues who do not show respect for each other may fail to show respect to the people who use care services.

- You may often have to greet colleagues by asking if they are well and spend time on 'warm-up talk' in order to show that you value them.

- You will need to demonstrate that you are a good listener and can remember details of conversations with your colleagues.

- Colleagues have to develop trust in each other. It is important to demonstrate that you respect the confidentiality of conversation with colleagues.

- Work settings may have their own social expectations about the correct way to communicate thoughts and feelings. These may differ from social expectations when communicating with your friends and family.

Although communication between colleagues may often be informal it is important that care workers use skilled communication in order to develop respect and trust.

Fig 1.2: Informality can be seen as a sign of disrespect

Activity 2: Formal and informal communication

Get together with a small group of colleagues and imagine an introductory meeting between a student and a care manager as part of a work practice placement. One person should act as the manager and another as the student. Work out how the manager would welcome the student and explain the work of the care centre. Then work out what questions the student should ask. After you have performed this simulation or role-play, two other students should undertake exactly the same task, but this time they should pretend that they are close friends chatting about the situation.

The whole group should then discuss the differences between these two simulations.

Functional skills

English: Your discussion activity may also contribute towards English speaking and listening skills.

Communication between professional people and people using services

Professional people, such as doctors and nurses, often work within their own specialised language community. A **language community** is a community of people that has developed its own special words, phrases, social expectations and ways of interacting that set it apart from other groups of people. Professionals are usually well aware of the need to translate technical language into everyday language when they work with people from other professions or people who use services. It is important that professionals check that they are not being misunderstood (see section 2 on the role of feedback).

Communication with professionals

When people who use services communicate with professionals there is always a risk of misunderstanding between people from different language communities. It is important that people check that they are being understood correctly. Professional health and social care staff need to check their understanding of issues with people who are communicating with them.

Multi-agency working

Health and social care professionals often have to communicate with colleagues who work for different organisations. For example, a home care organiser might have to communicate not only with people who use services and care workers but also with community nurses, GPs' surgeries, hospital services, occupational therapists, voluntary groups, day care groups and many other organisations. It is important not to assume that people from different agencies will understand

Key term

Language community – A social community of people that has its own special ways of using language in order to communicate between group members.

Case study: Amber

The following conversation took place between members of the same family:

Mother: How was your day at work?

Amber: OK, didn't do much, walked about a bit. Have to learn where everything is – like.

Mother: Did you enjoy it there?

Amber: Suppose it was all right. I had to listen to a guy going on about stuff but it was boring. Might be better tomorrow. I am going to 'do' the residents tomorrow – they should be more fun!

1 If Amber had spoken to her colleagues like this, would they have assumed that Amber respected and valued them?

2 Can you explain why a conversation like this might be acceptable within a family context but not within a work context?

3 Can you explain how Amber should change her comments if she was describing her first day at work to a professional colleague?

the same terminology. Formal communication may help to convey respect and avoid misunderstandings when interacting with unfamiliar professionals in other agencies.

Multi-professional working

Professionals from different backgrounds often have to work together in order to assess and meet the needs of people who use services. Multi-professional working happens when many different professionals work together. Communication will often need to be formal and carefully planned in order to avoid barriers to understanding.

Reflect

No one has ever written a rule book defining how health and social care workers should behave in all the different contexts listed above. One of the reasons this has not been attempted is that every interaction involves a feedback cycle (see section 2 in this unit). There may not be a single correct way of handling each interaction.

Table 1.1: Degrees of formality in different contexts

Context	Degree of formality	Key issues
Between colleagues	Often informal.	Must demonstrate respect for each other.
Between professionals and people using services	Usually informal.	Professionals must adapt their language (not use technical terms or jargon) in order to be understood.
With professionals	People using services may communicate informally. Professionals may respond formally.	Professionals must take responsibility for checking their understanding.
Multi-agency working	Usually formal – unless workers know each other well.	Important not to make assumptions or use technical terminology.
Multi-professional working	Usually formal – may need formal planning to produce 'agendas' for business.	Different professional people must be careful to check that they are understood.

Case study: Karen

Karen is a home care worker. Here are some statements that people have made about the way she works:

'I always feel better when she visits – she always smiles and cheers me up if I feel down.'

'She makes you feel important – she always listens to you, even when she is very busy.'

'She is so easy to talk to – she takes an interest in you. She is never 'bossy' or 'posh' – she's like one of my family'.

'She makes you feel special – not just one of the crowd.'

'She is very kind and considerate. There aren't very many people like her – it's a sort of magical touch – you feel different when she is around.'

Karen has excellent interpersonal skills – a 'magical touch'. Karen's skills enrich her own life and the lives of other people.

1 Why do some people get on so well with other people?

2 What makes someone good at interpersonal work?

1.2 Forms of communication

Communication between people enables us to exchange ideas and information but it involves much more than simply passing on information to others. Communication helps people to feel safe, to form relationships and to develop self-esteem. Poor communication can make an individual feel vulnerable, worthless or emotionally threatened.

There are many different types of communication as shown in Fig. 1.3 below.

Activity 3: Communicating emotion

Get together with a small group of colleagues and discuss the relative importance of all the different types of communication in Fig. 1.3 when you try to communicate emotions such as feeling happy or sad. Discuss whether or not spoken words are usually the best way to communicate emotion.

PLTS

Creative thinker: This activity will help you demonstrate that you can generate ideas and explore possibilities.

Independent enquirer: The activity may also lead you to identify questions and problems to resolve.

1.3 Types of interpersonal interaction

Speech

Different localities, ethnic groups, professions and work cultures all have their own special words, phrases and speech patterns. These localities and groups may be referred to as different speech communities. Some people may feel threatened or excluded by the kind of language they encounter in these speech communities. However, just using formal language will not solve this problem. The technical terminology used by care workers (often called **jargon**) can also create barriers for people who are not a part of that 'speech community'.

When people from different geographical areas use different words and pronounce words differently they are often using a different **dialect**. Some social groups use **slang** – non-standard words that are understood by other members of a speech community but which cannot usually be found in a dictionary.

Key terms

Jargon – Words used by a particular profession or group that are hard for others to understand.

Dialect – Words and their pronunciation, which are specific to a geographical community. For example, people who live in the north west of England might use a different dialect from Londoners.

Slang – Informal words and phrases that are not usually found in standard dictionaries but which are used within specific social groups and communities.

Fig 1.3: Forms of communication

- One-to-one spoken communication between individuals
- Unspoken communication using facial expressions
- Text messaging using mobile phones
- Artwork, paintings, photographs, sculptures, architecture, ornaments and other objects communicate messages and emotions
- Music and drama have been called the language of emotion. Mime and drama provide powerful ways of communicating
- **Types of communication**
- Communication using information technology, e.g. emails and other technological aids to communication
- Spoken (oral) communication within groups of people
- Written communication
- The use of signed (visual) languages
- Braille communication using raised marks on paper that can be touched

Case study: Professional jargon

The following conversation involves speech from different speech communities.

Relative: If my mother needed care who would pay for it?

Professional: Well the national framework for NHS continuing health care and NHS funded nursing care provides principles and processes for an assessment process that will establish eligibility for NHS continuing health care.

Relative: So the NHS would pay for care?

Professional: No, as I said, the framework provides for guidance that must be followed by all PCTs to result in a national assessment process supported by a checklist tool, decision support tool, and fast track tool which are used to provide clarity, transparency and consistency in the decision-making process for eligibility.

1 Can you work out what the professional is talking about?

2 Can you see how technical and legal terminology can exclude people?

3 Will the relative feel helped and respected by such a technical answer?

Did you know?

Teenagers can be thought of as a speech community with their own slang. Lucy Tobin has published a book called *Pimp your vocab*, which acts as a dictionary for 'teek people' – people who are outside the teenage speech community. This 'teenglish dictionary' enables others to understand teenage terminology.

Many people think the book is great fun, but some critics argue that adolescent language changes so rapidly that it is hard to keep up to date and to be sensitive to local variations.

First language

The author and psychologist Steven Pinker (1994) estimated that there may be about 600 languages in the world that are spoken by more than 100,000 people. There are many more minority languages. Some people grow up in multilingual communities, where they learn several languages from birth. But many people in the UK have grown up using only one language to think and communicate. People who learn a second language later in life often find that they cannot communicate their thoughts as effectively as they might have done using their **first language**. The first language that people have learned to think in usually becomes their preferred language.

Key term

First language – The first language that a person learns to speak is often the language that they will think in. Working with later languages can be difficult, as mental translation between languages may be required.

Non-verbal communication

Within a few seconds of meeting an individual you will usually be able to tell what they are feeling. You will know whether the person is tired, happy, angry, sad, frightened – even before they say anything. You can usually guess what a person feels by studying their non-verbal communication.

Non-verbal means 'without words', so non-verbal communication refers to the messages that we send without using words. We send these messages using our eyes, the tone of our voice, our facial expression, our hands and arms, gestures with our hands and arms, the angle of our head, the way we sit or stand (known as body posture) and the tension in our muscles.

Posture

The way you sit or stand can send messages. Sitting with crossed arms can mean 'I'm not taking any notice'. Leaning back can send the message that you are relaxed or bored. Leaning forward can show interest or intense involvement.

Person 2   Person 1

Fig 1.4: You can see that person 2 is rejecting what person 1 is communicating

The way you move

As well as posture, your body movements will communicate messages. For example, the way you walk, move your head, sit, cross your legs and so on will send messages about whether you are tired, happy, sad, or bored.

Facing other people

The way in which you face other people can also communicate emotional messages. Standing or sitting face-to-face may send a message that you are being formal or angry. A slight angle can create a more relaxed and friendly feeling.

Fig 1.5: Square-on orientation can communicate aggression

Gestures

Gestures are hand and arm movements that can help us to understand what a person is saying. Some gestures carry a common meaning in most communities in the UK.

Fig 1.6: Common gestures for 'good' and 'perfect'

Can you see how a person's emotions can often be interpreted from their facial expression?

Facial expression

Your face often indicates your emotional state. When a person is sad they may signal this emotion by looking down – there may be tension in their face and their mouth will be closed. The muscles in the person's shoulders are likely to be relaxed but their face and neck may show tension. A happy person will have 'wide eyes' that make contact with you – and they will probably smile. When people are excited they move their arms and hands to signal this.

We can guess another person's feelings and thoughts by looking at their eyes, using eye-to-eye contact. Our eyes get wider when we are excited, attracted to, or interested in someone else. A fixed stare may send the message that someone is angry. In European culture, looking away is often interpreted as being bored or not interested.

Most people can recognise emotions in the non-verbal behaviour of others. You will also need to understand how your own non-verbal behaviour may influence other people.

Touch

Touch is another way of communicating without words. Touching another person can send messages of care, affection, power over them or sexual interest. The social setting and a person's body language will usually help you to understand what their touch might mean. But touch can easily be misinterpreted. You might try to comfort someone by holding their hand but they may interpret this touch as an attempt to dominate. Sometimes it can be a good idea to ask if you may

Case study: Tonya

Tonya is 15 years old and attends meetings of a youth group. She often sits with her arms crossed and her head turned away, looking out of the window. She avoids making eye contact with people who are speaking to the group. When asked if she feels OK, she does make eye contact, changes her body posture and says she is happy to be in the group.

1 What messages would crossed arms and avoidance of eye contact normally send?

2 How many reasons can you think of to explain why someone might sit with their arms crossed, looking out of the window, while other people are speaking?

3 How can you find out what an individual's body language means?

All I can do is offer you a hug.

Fig 1.7: Gestures and words give a person the option of refusing touch

touch, or gesture in a way that allows another person to refuse your touch, before proceeding.

People may also look at, or feel, the degree of muscle tension that you show when you communicate with them. The tension in your feet, hands and fingers can tell others how relaxed or tense you are. If someone is very tense their shoulders might stiffen, their face muscles might tighten and they might sit or stand rigidly. A tense person may have a firmly closed mouth, with lips and jaws clenched tight, and they might breathe quickly.

Silence

One definition of friends is 'people who can sit together and feel comfortable in silence'. Sometimes a pause in conversation can make people feel embarrassed – it looks as if you weren't listening or you weren't interested. Sometimes a silent pause can mean 'let's think' or 'I need time to think'. Silent pauses can be OK, as long as non-verbal messages that show respect and interest are given. Silence doesn't always stop the conversation.

Voice tone

When you speak to other people, your tone of voice is important. If you talk quickly in a loud voice with a fixed tone, people may think you are angry. A calm, slow voice with a varying tone may send a message of being friendly.

Proximity

The space between people can sometimes show how friendly or 'intimate' the conversation is. Different cultures have different customs regarding the space between people when they are talking.

In Britain there are expectations or 'norms' as to how close you should be when you talk to others. When talking to strangers we usually keep 'an arm's length' apart. The ritual of shaking hands indicates that you have been introduced – you may come closer. When you are friendly with someone you may accept them being closer to you. Relatives and partners might not be restricted at all in how close they can come.

Proximity is a very important issue in health and care work. Many people have a sense of personal space. A care worker who assumes it is fine to enter the personal space of a person who uses services, without asking or explaining why, may be seen as dominating or aggressive.

Reflective listening

We can often understand other people's emotions just by watching their non-verbal communication. However, we can't always understand someone's thoughts without good listening skills.

Listening skills involve hearing another person's words, then thinking about what their words mean, then thinking about how to reply to the other person. Sometimes this process is called 'active listening' and sometimes 'reflective listening.' The word 'reflective' is used because the person's conversation is reflected back (like the reflection in a mirror) in order to check understanding. As well as remembering what a person says, good listeners will make sure that their non-verbal behaviour shows interest.

Skilled listening involves:

- looking interested and communicating that you are ready to listen

- hearing what is said to you

- remembering what was said to you, together with non-verbal messages

- checking your understanding with the person who was speaking to you.

We can learn about people who are different from us by checking our understanding of what we have heard. Checking understanding can involve listening to what the other person says and then asking questions. Reflection may also involve putting what a person has just said into our own words (paraphrasing) and saying it back to them, to check that we have understood what they were saying.

When we listen to complicated details of other people's lives, we often begin to form mental pictures based on what they tell us. The skill of listening involves checking these mental pictures. Good listening involves thinking about what we hear while we are listening and checking our understanding as the conversation goes along – we reflect on the other person's ideas.

Good listening can feel like really hard work. Instead of just being around when people speak, we have to build an understanding of the people we communicate with.

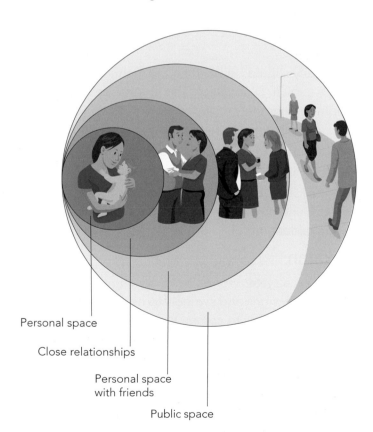

Personal space

Close relationships

Personal space with friends

Public space

Fig 1.8: There are different expectations about personal space

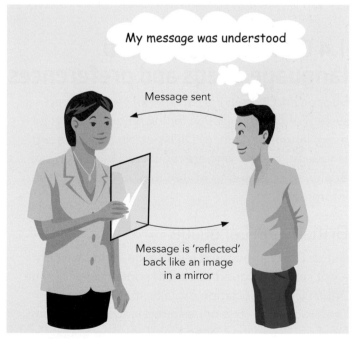

Fig 1.9: Why is it important to see our understanding reflected back to us?

Case study: Sarah

Sarah is unemployed and is looking for work in a specialised field. She looks worried and says *'I don't know what to do. I keep looking for work and going for interviews but I never get a job offer.'* Given that you know nothing about the kind of job she is looking for, how can you respond in a skilled way? Consider some of the possibilities below:

- Try to be reassuring, e.g. *'I'm sure you will get a job eventually.'*
  Unless you are an expert with detailed knowledge of the job market, reassurance is likely to sound false. You may come across as trying to avoid the topic or trick the person.

- Offer advice, e.g. *'Why don't you see a careers adviser?'*
  Receiving unwanted advice can sometimes be very irritating. The person may have already thought of seeing an adviser. You might come across as trying to sound clever and superior to Sarah. You might be seen as trying to avoid the issue, i.e. *'This is all I can think to say, please don't talk to me about this any more.'*

- Repeating what was said, e.g. *'You never get a job offer.'*
  Parroting some phrases back to a person may sound mechanical. The person might say: *'That's what I just said – didn't you hear me?'*

- Reflecting the other person's message, e.g. *'It must be worrying when you can't get a job.'*
  This shows that you have listened and it may be seen as an invitation to keep talking. Being able to talk to someone who is actively involved may make the other person feel that they are being taken seriously.

1 What is the difference between saying things such as 'Why don't you see an adviser' or 'I'm sure you will get a job eventually' and just saying 'I don't want to talk to you about it'?

2 Can you explain the difference between just repeating or parroting the words you have heard and the idea of reflective listening?

3 Why might another person feel that you care about them because you can reflect back what they have said?

1.4 Communication and language needs and preferences

Spoken and written English are not the preferred system of communication for everyone. The first (or main) language of many Deaf people may be a signed language. People who are registered blind may use Braille, as opposed to written text, in order to read information.

British Sign Language

British Sign Language is a language in its own right – not simply a signed version of spoken English. The British Deaf Association explains that British Sign Language is the first or preferred language of many Deaf people in the United Kingdom. The British Deaf Association also explains that BSL was recognised as an official British language in 2003 and the Association campaigns for the right of Deaf people to be educated in BSL and to access information and services through BSL. Many Deaf people argue that the Deaf community should be identified as 'culturally Deaf' by using a capital 'D' for Deaf. This emphasises that 'Deaf' people use another language system, as opposed to 'Deaf' people who are perceived to be impaired.

Further details of BSL can be found at www.bda.org.uk

Details of signs and a finger spelling alphabet can be found at www.british-sign.co.uk and at www.royaldeaf.org.uk

Makaton

Makaton is a system for developing language that uses speech, signs and symbols to help people with learning difficulties to communicate and to develop their language skills. People who communicate using Makaton may speak a word and perform a sign using hands and body language. There is a large range of symbols to help people with learning difficulties to recognise an idea or to communicate with others. Further information on Makaton can be found at www.makaton.org

Activity 4: Research people's understanding of BSL

Do people understand what British Sign Language is? Plan a short series of questions and ask people who are not studying this course if they have ever heard of British Sign Language and what kind of language it might be? You may find that the majority of people think that BSL is a way of signing English words – in other words that to sign in BSL you would first have to know English. Only a few people might understand that BSL is a separate language developed within the Deaf community. Discuss what consequences your research might have for both Deaf and hearing people.

PLTS

Independent enquirer: This activity will help you demonstrate that you can plan and carry out research and appreciate its consequences.

Braille

Braille (a system of raised marks that can be felt with the fingers) provides a means of written communication, based on the sense of touch, for people who have limited vision. The communication system known as Braille was first published by Louis Braille, a blind 20-year-old, in 1829. This system is now widely used, for reading and writing, by people who cannot see written script.

Modern computer software can translate written material into Braille, which can be printed out using special printers. Further details on Braille can be found at www.brailleplus.net

Use of signs and symbols

Gestures made with hands or arms, written symbols or diagrams (such as traffic signs) all communicate messages to people.

Fig 1.10: What meanings do these signs communicate?

Written communication

There is a Chinese saying that 'the faintest ink is stronger than the strongest memory'! Written records are essential for communicating formal information that needs to be reviewed at a future date. When people remember conversations they have had, they will probably miss out or change some details. Written statements are much more permanent and, if they are accurate when they are written, they may be useful later on.

Pictures and objects of reference

Paintings, photographs, sculptures, architecture, ornaments and other household objects can communicate messages and emotions to people. People often take photographs or buy souvenirs to remind them of happy experiences and emotions. Sometimes an object – such as a cuddly toy – can symbolise important personal issues and provide a source of meaning and comfort for an individual.

Key term

Object of reference – An object of reference is a physical object or picture that has become associated with an activity, person or other special meaning.

Objects can sometimes be used to communicate with people who do not use much signed or spoken language. A child or adult with a learning disability might understand that a cup stands for 'would you like a drink'. An object like a spoon tied to a card might communicate that it is time for dinner when the spoon is presented. A person without language might use a patch of cloth to communicate that they wish to sit in a favourite chair covered in that type of cloth. Sometimes a person might learn a symbol, perhaps a symbol like a horseshoe that can be used to label possessions or identify his or her room.

Finger spelling

People who use a signed language, such as British Sign Language, also use finger spelling. Finger spelling enables signers to spell out words that do not have a general sign, or words that may be misunderstood such as the names of people and places.

Communication passports

Communication passports are usually small personalised books containing straightforward practical information about a person and their style of communication. The passport may help health and care workers to understand the needs of a person with communication difficulties. Communication passports often include photographs or drawings that may help care workers to gain a better understanding of the person who owns the passport. They are put together by working with the person with communication difficulties and his or her carers; the person tells their own story of their likes, dislikes and communication styles.

Technological aids to communication

Information technology offers a wide range of facilities to help with communication. It is possible to provide enlarged visual displays or voice description for people with visual impairment. Electronic aids – such as the minicom for people with a hearing disability or voice typing for people with dyslexia – can turn

speech into writing. Some electronic communication systems can be activated by air pressure, so that a person can communicate via an oral tube connected to computerised equipment. At a simpler level, aids such as flash cards or picture books can also improve communication with people who do not use a spoken or signed language. Text messaging, using a mobile phone, provides an effective way of staying in touch for many people. For people with a hearing disability, text messaging may provide a major form of communication.

When you send text messages to friends, do you use symbols and shortened words that would not be acceptable in more formal academic work? If you send emails, do you use abbreviations, symbols and special terms or do you only use formal English? Do you think it should be acceptable to use 'texting' symbols and abbreviations for academic work? How formal should English be?

Human aids to communication

Many people have specific communication needs. It may be important to employ an interpreter if a person uses a different language such as BSL. Some carers learn to use communication systems, such as Makaton, in order to help them communicate with people.

If you are communicating with a person with a hearing impairment you should make sure that the person can see your face clearly so that they can see your expressions and the way your lips move. Sometimes people use clues from facial expression and lip movement to interpret what you might be saying. It is also important to speak in a clear, normal voice. If you raise your voice, your face and lips will become distorted. A person with a hearing impairment may realise that you are shouting and may assume that you

Think about the way children communicate through play using objects

are angry! It is also important to try and speak in an environment with little background noise.

If people have limited vision, it may be important to use language to describe issues that a sighted person might take for granted, such as non-verbal communication or the context of certain comments. Touch may be an important aspect of communication. For instance, some registered blind people can work out what you look like if they can touch your face in order to build an understanding of your features.

It is always important to choose the right style of language in order to communicate with people from different language communities.

Variation between cultures

Skilled carers use a range of conversational techniques when working with others. These include being sensitive to variations in culture.

Culture means the history, customs and ways of behaving that people learn as they grow up. People from different regions of Britain use different expressions. Non-verbal signs vary from culture to culture. White middle-class people often expect people to 'look them in the eye' while talking. If a person looks down or away a lot, they think it is a sign that the person may be dishonest, or perhaps sad or depressed. In some other cultures – for example, among some black communities – looking down or away when talking is a sign of respect.

No one can learn every possible system of **cultural variation** in non-verbal behaviour but it is possible to learn about the ones that are used by the people you are with! You can do this by first noticing and remembering what others do – in other words, what non-verbal messages they are sending. The next step is to make a guess as to what messages the person is trying to give you. Finally, check your understanding (your guesses) with the person. This involves reflective listening and thinking carefully about the person's responses.

Key term

Cultural variation – Communication is always influenced by cultural systems of meaning. Different cultures interpret verbal and non-verbal communication behaviours as having different meanings.

Care workers must be careful not to assume that statements and signs always have the same meaning. Cultural differences and different settings can alter what things mean. A vast range of meanings can be given to any type of eye contact, facial expression, posture or gesture. Every culture, and even small groups of people, can develop their own system of meanings. Care workers have to respect differences but it is impossible to learn all the possible meanings that phrases, words and signs may have.

Assessment activity 1.1

Explain, using examples you have observed, the role of communication and interpersonal interactions in health and social care.

Grading tip

 Maintain a logbook to record notes of interactions you have observed in class role plays, informally with your peers, with others at work and in school/college or in public spaces and particularly in health and social care settings when visiting or in placements. Note behaviours, non-verbal communication skills and how the communication cycle is/is not demonstrated. Remember that your notes should maintain the anonymity of individuals and any details that might enable individuals or settings to be identified.

Consider what is meant by 'effective' when discussing communication and interpersonal interactions in health and social care.

Consider formal and informal communication, differences between different language communities and cultures and the role of verbal and non-verbal communication in interpersonal interactions.

Include examples of different language needs and preferences in your explanation.

2 Understand factors that influence communication and interpersonal interaction in health and social care environments

2.1 Theories of communication

The communication cycle

Effective communication involves a two-way process in which each person tries to understand the viewpoint of the other person. Communication is a cycle because when two people communicate they need to check that their ideas have been understood. Good communication involves the process of checking understanding, using reflective or active listening.

Michael Argyle (1972) argued that interpersonal communication was a skill that could be learned and developed in much the same way as learning to drive a car. Argyle emphasised the importance of feedback in skilled activities. When you drive a car you have to change your behaviour depending on what is happening on the road. Driving involves a constant cycle of watching what is happening, working out how to respond, making responses and then repeating this cycle until you reach your destination.

According to Argyle, skilled interpersonal interaction (social skills) involves a cycle in which you have to translate or 'decode' what other people are communicating and constantly adapt your own behaviour in order to communicate effectively. Verbal and non-verbal communication is not always straightforward. The **communication cycle** involves a kind of code that has to be translated. You have to work out what another person's behaviour really means.

> ### Key term
>
> **Communication cycle** – Most important communication in care work involves a cycle of building understanding using an active process of reflecting on, and checking out, what the other person is trying to communicate.

One way of looking at this cycle might be:

1 **An idea occurs**: You have an idea that you want to communicate.

2 **Message coded**: You think through how you are going to say what you are thinking. You put your thoughts into language or into some other code such as sign language.

3 **Message sent**: You speak, or perhaps you sign or write, or send your message in some other way.

4 **Message received**: The other person has to sense your message – they hear your words or see your symbols.

5 **Message decoded**: The other person has to interpret or 'decode' your message (i.e. what you have said). This is not always easy, as the other person will make assumptions about your words and body language.

6 **Message understood**: If all goes well then your ideas will be understood but this does not always happen first time!

2. Message coded

1. Ideas occur

3. Message sent

4. Message perceived

5. Message decoded

6. Feedback – what was understood

Fig 1.11: What are the stages in the communication cycle?

Case study: Karen

Karen is talking to Jasmin, whose partner has died.

Jasmin: I can't believe it. I don't know how I'm going to cope on my own, I can't sleep or eat.

Karen: You must feel awful, it must have been a terrible shock.

Jasmin: I'll say it was – I just feel so anxious. I know I won't be able to cope.

Karen: Can you tell me a little about your life together?

In this brief example, there is no helpful advice or information that Karen can offer. Karen is careful to reflect back what Jasmin has said. This results in a communication cycle in which Jasmin can begin to share her feelings.

1 Can you explain why it is so important for care workers to say back what they understand?

2 What might have happened if Karen had responded with 'Don't worry, you'll feel better as time goes by'?

3 How can understanding the communication cycle help care professionals to develop skilled communication?

Activity 5: Observe the communication cycle

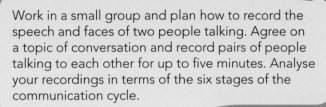

Work in a small group and plan how to record the speech and faces of two people talking. Agree on a topic of conversation and record pairs of people talking to each other for up to five minutes. Analyse your recordings in terms of the six stages of the communication cycle.

PLTS

Independent enquirer: This activity may help you demonstrate that you can analyse and evaluate information.

Functional skills

ICT: Discussing this activity may help you demonstrate that you can evaluate the selection and use of ICT tools and facilities used to present information.

Tuckman's stages of group interaction

Communication in groups can also be influenced by the degree to which people feel they belong together. When people first meet in a group they often go through a process of group formation. Many groups may experience some sort of struggle before people unite and communicate effectively. One of the best-known theorists to explain group formation stages is Tuckman (1965). Tuckman suggested that most groups go through a process involving four stages. These are:

1 forming

2 storming

3 norming

4 performing.

The first stage (forming) refers to people meeting for the first time and sharing information. The second stage (storming) involves tension, struggle and sometimes arguments about the way the group might function. The third stage (norming) sees the group coming together and consciously or unconsciously agreeing on their **group values**. Once they have established common expectations and values, the group will reach the fourth stage of being an effectively performing group.

Key term

Group values – Group members need to share a common system of beliefs or values in order for the group to communicate and perform effectively. You may be able to identify these values when you watch a group at work.

Jenna Black
Day centre team leader

Pinewoods is a day centre for adult people with learning disabilities. Jenna is the team leader for a new group of care workers who have only been working together for the past two weeks. They have regular team meetings and this is an extract from their third meeting in which they are discussing the activities that they lead with day centre members.

Jenna: Let's talk about the cookery sessions. I think that members are really enjoying learning to cook.

Carly: Maybe, but I worry about what we're doing. We don't watch people carefully enough. For example, Drew nearly burned himself last Tuesday because nobody was watching what he was doing.

André: Yes, but he didn't burn himself and he is learning to become independent. I think it's important to let people take risks. I could never have become independent if my parents hadn't let me take risks!

Deja: So it's all right for Drew to burn himself, is it? Is that what you're saying?

Shanice: I can't believe you just said that! André is talking about the importance of independence and you turn that round to saying he doesn't care about people burning themselves. That's not what he said – you didn't listen!

Deja: Now *you* listen to *me*! What I am saying is that we don't take safety seriously enough. These people are vulnerable, they can hurt themselves if we don't take proper care.

Jenna: OK, we all know that both safety and independence are central to our work here. So why are we talking as if we can't have both?

Deja: Well, I agree that both are important, but safety comes first as far as I'm concerned.

Shanice: Well I don't think things are that simple. It is possible to concentrate too much on safety and then we might stop people from reaching their potential of independence. It's a matter of getting the balance right.

Think about it!

1 Using Tuckman's theory, can you identify which stage of group formation this group is at?

2 Can you identify different norms that are being argued about in the group?

3 Can you identify the different 'sides' being taken in the discussion and how Jenna is starting to use her group leader role to get the team to focus on common values?

4 If this group is to succeed in working they will have to share common 'norms'. Can you guess on what norms the group might eventually agree?

5 If you were in Jenna's position, how would you lead the conversation on from Shanice's last comment in order to reach the 'norming stage' of team working?

Assessment activity 1.2

Using examples from your experience, discuss theories of communication. This assessment could be integrated with Assessment Activity 1.1.

For M1, you should also include an assessment of the role of effective communication and interpersonal interaction in health and social care.

Grading tips

P2 Consider how communication theory helps to explain effective communication in health and social care contexts.

Consider one-to-one and group interactions, formal and informal communication, different types of communication and different forms of interpersonal interaction in your discussion.

Reviews of filmed class role-plays in which you and your peers have participated would be helpful to gain understanding of the communication cycle.

Participation in a series of group tasks with the same group of individuals over a period of several weeks and an analysis of how your work with each other changes over time could provide useful understanding of Tuckman's theory. This could involve group work in class with your peers or how you settle into working with a group of individuals in a work experience placement or any employment.

M1 Integrate your assessment by using the examples explained for P1 and discussed in P2.

The assessment should consider strengths and weaknesses of communication and interpersonal interactions you have observed in relation to theories relating to the communication cycle and group formation

Remember to consider a range of health and social care contexts, different forms of communication and different types of interpersonal interaction in your assessment.

2.2 Environmental factors that influence communication

It is very hard to hear what someone is saying if there is a lot of background noise. It is also very difficult to make sense of other people's facial expressions if you can't see their faces properly due to poor lighting. Rooms with awkward seating positions might mean that a group of people cannot see each other comfortably. People sometimes feel uncomfortable if they are trying to communicate with a person who is too close or at a distance. A room that is too hot, stuffy or cold may inhibit communication if it makes people feel tired or stressed.

The environment also plays an important role in the effectiveness of communication aids. For instance, hearing aids will amplify background noise as well as the voice of the speaker. A noisy environment may therefore be difficult and unpleasant for someone who is using a hearing aid. Good lighting will be critical for someone who supports their understanding of speech with lip reading. Time limits on how long you can use a room can also interfere with communication.

Activity 6: Plan a good environment for group communication

Get together with a group of colleagues and make a list of what an ideal environment for videoing a group discussion would involve. Work out what practical changes you may be able to introduce into your own working environment.

PLTS

Creative thinker: This activity will help you demonstrate that you can generate ideas and explore possibilities and perhaps try out alternatives.

2.3 Barriers to communication

A barrier blocks things and stops them 'getting through'. There are different types of **communication barrier** that stop communication from being effective. Three types are shown in Table 1.2 on page 22.

Where the first and second types of barriers exist, it will usually be obvious that communication has failed. However, distorted understanding is not always easy to identify. Skilled use of the communication cycle may help you to check what has been understood or what communication barriers may exist.

21

Table 1.2: Communication barriers

Type of barrier	Examples
1 Communication is not received	Not responding to language needs or preferences. Not understanding sensory impairment or disability. Examples: Speaking to a Deaf person who uses a signed language. The sounds are not received. Environmental barriers: Background noise can stop you from hearing a message. You can't receive full non-verbal communication if you can't see a person's face or body.
2 Communication is received but not understood	A person using slang, jargon or complex technical terminology can be heard, but their message may not be understood.
3 Understanding is distorted	A wide range of emotional and psychological factors can act as barriers, resulting in distorted understanding of communication.

Key term

Communication barrier – Anything that stops the development of understanding when people interact.

Fig 1.12: Consider why barriers can mean that no information is communicated

Fig 1.13: How can psychological factors create communication barriers by distorting perception of a message?

Case study: Karen

Interviewer: Some people who need care have problems with understanding and memory. How do you know if a person has understood what you are talking about?

Karen: It's not easy but sometimes you can tell from a person's face. When a person looks puzzled, or if they don't respond, then you know you've got to try and explain something in a different way.

But some people will nod and smile although they haven't really understood you. So I try to keep the conversation going and find a way to check understanding. For example, I had to explain I would come on a different day. Now, I couldn't ask the person a direct question like 'Can you remember what I told you?' If I did that, the person might feel I was treating them like a child. So instead I asked them about what they would be doing on the day that I had changed from. They said that I would be coming to see them – and that was wrong – and so I was able to remind them of the change. One way of preventing misunderstanding is to just keep somebody talking.

1 Can you explain why Karen does not like to ask direct questions such as 'What did I just tell you?' or 'When am I coming next then?'

2 Can you think of some reasons why people might nod and smile as if they understand, even if they don't understand what you have tried to communicate?

3 In the example above, how is Karen using the communication cycle?

Types of communication: difficult, complex or sensitive

Some communication between people is simply about sharing or 'transmitting' information. For example, someone might want to know what number bus to catch, or they might ask for a drink of water. Sometimes communication will be complex. For example, a relative may want to know about funding arrangements for care. A communication about funding might involve a great deal of complex information. In this situation it would be important to check what the relative already knew, and whether or not the individual understood the information you were providing.

A great deal of communication in care work involves building an understanding of another person and providing emotional support. Burnard and Morrison (1997) argue that caring and communicating are inseparably linked. Communication that involves emotional issues is often experienced as being difficult or sensitive.

There is no advice or information that is likely to be very useful to a person who is overwhelmed by grief, but many people *do* want someone to be with them. Communication in this difficult or sensitive situation

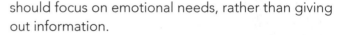

Reflect

What can you say to a person who is upset and crying because they can't cope, following the death of their partner?

should focus on emotional needs, rather than giving out information.

Engebretson (2003) uses the idea of a **caring presence** to explain what is needed in these situations. Creating a caring presence is about sharing an understanding of the feelings that other people may be experiencing. Sometimes simply being with a person who is lonely, anxious or depressed can provide comfort. If you believe that your carer understands your needs and is concerned about you, then just knowing that they are near you can help you to feel supported. Non-verbal communication may sometimes communicate emotions and feelings more effectively than words.

Key term

Caring presence – Being open to the experience of another person through a 'two-way' encounter with that person.

If you can support people just by the way you are 'present with them' this may be because you are developing empathy with them.

Empathy

Empathy involves a caring attitude where someone can see beyond his or her own assumptions about the world and can imagine the thoughts and feelings of someone else. A professional care worker who can empathise will be able to imagine the emotions associated with the pain and grief that another person is experiencing.

Did you know?

Empathy is often regarded as a skill that can be developed through training but Carl Rogers, a famous counsellor, argued that empathy was a state of being. This means that you have to experience your self and other people in a special empathetic way. In Rogers' view you couldn't simply use empathy as a communication tool or technique – you had to 'live' empathy.

Language needs/preferences

Most people will have a preferred first language. And this preferred language will sometimes be obvious to you. But language needs go beyond the choice of a preferred language. Different communities use a given language in different ways. People use different degrees of formality and informality, depending on the context. For example, people may use jargon, dialect or slang to communicate effectively with people in their own speech community. These differences can create barriers to understanding.

Sensory impairment and disability

A **sensory impairment** means that a person's senses do not work effectively. Impairments create the first kind of communication barrier, where information is not fully received.

Disability is not the same as impairment. Some people experiencing barriers because of their difference may have a **communication disability**. For example, a 'Deaf' person, whose preferred language is BSL, experiences no problems communicating with another person who is good at signing with BSL. This person may not be able to communicate with people who use spoken English without the aid of an interpreter.

Key terms

Empathy – The ability to develop a deep level of understanding of another person's experience.

Communication disability – Difference that may create barriers between people with different systems of communication.

Sensory impairment – Damage to sense organs such as eyes and ears.

However, in this case, the disability is a social issue (to do with needing an interpreter), rather than a sensory impairment issue.

Barriers associated with personality, self-esteem, anxiety and depression

Sometimes care workers can create their own barriers because they feel stressed by the emotional needs of the people they work with. Listening to others can involve hearing about frightening and depressing situations. Carers sometimes stop listening in order to avoid painful emotions. Tiredness, lack of time or a desire to avoid emotional stress can create a barrier to providing caring communication.

Building an understanding of another person and establishing a 'caring presence' can be very difficult when their personality or self-esteem needs create a barrier. Many people who are depressed or anxious experience negative thoughts that 'just come to them'. Attempting to understand these thoughts and feelings can feel like trying to find a way through a brick wall. It may feel as if there is an emotional barrier preventing the person from experiencing any positive emotions. The case study on the next page illustrates this type of situation.

The carer in the case study opposite is not 'just talking' – she is trying to steer the conversation round to positive memories. The worker is using her understanding of Liam's past to try and lead the conversation around the barrier of negative and depressed thoughts. If the worker is successful, the conversation might lead to Liam having positive thoughts and feelings and increasing his level of self-esteem.

Asking questions

Talking through difficult, complex or sensitive issues will involve the verbal skills of asking open questions and using probes and prompts within the conversation.

Case study: Liam

Liam: You can't possibly understand what it feels like to be me. Absolutely everything is wrong with my life, I've got no reason to be alive and you can't help me – what's the point of talking?

Carer: But perhaps I could be useful if I knew more about your life?

Liam: What do you want to know? I've got no money, no job, no future, no one cares about me – there's no point in going on.

Carer: Right, so it feels really terrible, really bad, but was there a time before things went wrong – a time when you were happy?

Liam: Yes, a few years back everything was good – but now I feel even more miserable because you are reminding me of how much I've lost!

There is no simple way of removing this emotional barrier but some skilled workers might try to keep the conversation going so that they could continue to learn about the person. It might be possible to positively influence the person's self-esteem as the conversation continues.

Carer: So when you ran your own taxi business you were on top of everything – nothing could get you down?

Liam: Yeah – but I've got health problems now, I'm finished, that time is all gone.

Carer: Yes, I know it feels terrible, but tell me about the good times. You dealt with problems then. I'd like to understand how you made it all work back then.

Read the information on probes and prompts below and answer the following questions.

1 Can you identify how the carer has used questions, probes and prompts in order to keep the conversation going?

2 Can you explain how the carer may have used reflective listening in order to build an understanding of Liam's situation?

3 Can you explain the importance of building an understanding of another person during a difficult and sensitive interaction?

- **Open questions:** These cannot be answered with a yes or no response – they require a person to think about their answer. Open questions are likely to involve a complex communication cycle in order to discuss issues. They include questions such as 'How would you describe your quality of life?'

- **Probes:** These are very short questions such as 'Can you tell me more?' Probes are used to dig deeper into the person's answer – they probe or investigate what the other person has just said.

- **Prompts:** These are short questions, which you offer to the other person in order to prompt them to answer. Prompts are questions such as 'Would you do it again?'

Barriers associated with aggression and submissiveness

When a person experiences strong emotions or their self-esteem is threatened, that person may become aggressive or withdrawn, creating barriers to communication.

See pages 30–33 for further information on aggression and submissiveness.

Barriers associated with assumptions

Building an understanding of other people's needs takes time and effort. Jumping to conclusions and making **assumptions** can save mental effort and time, but assumptions may cause us to misinterpret what another person is trying to communicate. For example, you might believe that you don't need to listen to a person because you already know what their needs are. But care workers who use the communication cycle are less likely to make assumptions because they check their understanding. Assumptions can create a barrier because people stop listening and checking their understanding of other people's communication.

Some people make assumptions that people who have a disability are damaged 'normal' people. When disabled people are seen in this way, they might be pitied or ignored. People with communication

Key term

Assumption – An idea that people think is true or correct without bothering to check.

differences are sometimes assumed to be mentally impaired. Older people are sometimes seen as demented or confused if they do not answer questions quickly, correctly and clearly. If care workers do not bother to check their assumptions about people, these assumptions can turn into prejudices. And a prejudice or pre-judgement can result in discrimination.

Barriers associated with values and belief systems

People have different **belief systems** – about what is important in life and how people should live their lives. **Values** are the principles that we think of as being important or valuable, in terms of how we live our lives.

Key terms

Belief systems – The assumptions we use to make sense of our lives. Our belief systems often include our values.

Values – What we think of as being important or valuable in terms of how we live our lives.

When people have different belief systems and values it is easy for them to misinterpret one another's intentions when attempting to communicate. Like assumptions, belief systems and values can therefore create barriers to understanding. It is important to try to learn about other people's beliefs and values in order to make sense of what they are trying to communicate.

Barriers associated with cultural variation

Culture refers to the different customs and assumptions that communities of people adopt. Different ethnic and religious groups may have different cultures, but different age, occupational and geographical groups also make different cultural assumptions.

Words and non-verbal communication can be interpreted differently depending on the context and on the culture of the person using them. For example, the word 'hot' can have different meanings depending on the context in which it is used and the culture of the person using it. In a formal context, 'hot' refers to having a high temperature. But in other speech communities an object might be 'hot' if it has been 'stolen' or if it is perceived as 'very desirable'. A hot person might be very good at something, or be someone who is overcome with sexual desire! If communication is interpreted only from a fixed cultural standpoint, serious misunderstandings can arise. To make sense of spoken and non-verbal language, you need to understand the context of the interaction and the intentions of the person communicating.

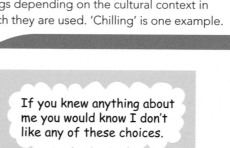

Reflect

Think of some words that can mean different things depending on the cultural context in which they are used. 'Chilling' is one example.

Fig 1.14: Why does learning about other people's beliefs help to avoid barriers to communication?

An example of a non-verbal cultural variation might be the hand gesture in which the palm is held up and facing forward. In Britain this means 'Stop, don't do that', whereas in Greece it can mean 'You are dirt' and is considered a very offensive gesture. Why do the same physical movements have different meanings? One explanation could be that the British version of the palm-and-fingers gesture means, 'I arrest you, you must not do it', whereas the Greek interpretation goes back to medieval times when criminals had dirt rubbed in their faces to show how much people despised them.

It is important not to make assumptions about non-verbal messages – they should always be checked. Non-verbal messages can mean different things depending on the circumstances of the people who are sending them.

Case study: Gerard

Gerard is a tall, muscular, middle-aged man who regularly talks to staff about his son's care. He prefers to stand squarely face-to-face and speaks quickly, using a loud voice. Staff say that they feel uncomfortable talking to Gerard because he sometimes 'stares at you' with a fixed gaze. Staff say 'He is in your face' because they feel that he stands too close to them. Some staff think that Gerard is aggressive and demanding because of the way he acts.

1 Can you identify how 'cultural variation' might be important when trying to understand this situation?

2 Can you think of possibilities, other than being demanding and aggressive, that might explain the non-verbal behaviours described above?

3 How could you check what certain non-verbal behaviours might mean during a conversation?

Use and abuse of power

The General Social Care Council (GSCC) Code of Practice for Social Care Workers (2002) requires all workers to respect individuality and support people who use services to control their own lives. However, there is always a danger that, if a care worker is short of time, they will seek to control people who use services. It is an abuse of **power** if care workers deliberately control and manipulate others.

If you cannot control and make decisions about your own life you may fail to develop, or you might lose your sense of being a worthwhile person. If care workers control and manipulate you, your self-esteem may be damaged.

Care workers should seek to empower people who use services. **Empowerment** means giving power to others. People who use services should be empowered to believe that they can make their own choices and take control of their lives.

Key terms

Empowerment – This enables a person who uses services to make choices and take control of their own life.

Power – In the context of interpersonal behaviour, 'power' means the ability to influence and control what other people do.

In order to empower others, care workers need to understand and value each person's unique story. Care workers must support the people they work with, in taking control of important decisions. Care workers must also carry out their work on the basis that everyone is of equal status. The care worker does not have higher status than people who use services.

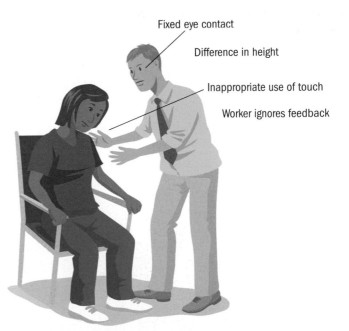

Fixed eye contact

Difference in height

Inappropriate use of touch

Worker ignores feedback

Fig 1.15: How do these non-verbal messages express power and domination?

Barriers associated with the effects of alcohol/drugs

Alcohol and drugs can influence a person's ability to send clear verbal and non-verbal messages. Drugs that affect the functioning of the central nervous system can easily result in messages not being received or understood and also in distorted interpretations of the message. Alcohol and drug abuse can therefore create all the barriers to communication shown in Figure 1.16 on page 29. People with a distorted perception of other people's communication may be more likely to become frustrated or aggressive.

Case study: Karen

Interviewer: Why do a lot of people worry about having care services?

Karen: Some people are afraid that you will come in and take control of their lives, boss them about, and make them feel stupid.

Interviewer: But care work is all about giving power to people who use services, making sure people are in control of their own lives – so why do people worry?

Karen: Well, I am always short of time and it is tempting to just take over and do everything my way to get it done quickly. It's easy to think you know best – but if you make that assumption, you upset people and make them feel powerless.

Interviewer: Don't some people like to sit back and let you be in control?

Karen: Some people say, 'You do what you like, buy me whatever you think I need – I don't care.' But that is a problem too. Sometimes people lose control of their lives and give up – they become 'helpless'. They want you to make all the decisions – have all the power. I still try to encourage them to make choices.

Interviewer: There is so much to think about when you are working with people. How do you manage?

Karen: You have to have the right attitude – it's a sort of feeling. If you've got the right attitude you tend to say and do the right things anyway. I enjoy meeting people and getting to know them. I value everyone I work with; I think of them as important. I am interested in their lives and I listen to what they tell me. I think values – what you believe in – are at the heart of how you work with people.

Interviewer: So do you really need theories like reflective listening and the communication cycle to be a good carer?

Karen: These ideas can help you to be more sensitive and to understand what might be going on. But care work is really about values, attitudes and feelings. Technical knowledge on its own, without the right values, isn't enough if you want to enjoy caring for others and if they are going to enjoy working with you.

1 Why should care workers not aim to control the lives of the people they work with?

2 Why does Karen try to encourage people to make choices, even if they appear not to want to?

3 Can you explain what is meant by power in the context of interpersonal behaviour?

4 Can you identify what values Karen uses when she talks to people who use care services?

5 What does Karen mean when she says 'If you've got the right attitude then you tend to say and do the right things anyway'?

6 Explain why Karen thinks technical knowledge, without the right values, isn't enough?

Assessment activity 1.3

 P3 **BTEC**

Again, use the examples used in the previous assessment activities to explain the factors that influence communication and interpersonal interactions.

Grading tip

P3 Integrate the evidence for this task with that for assessment Activities 1.1 and 1.2.

Consider both positive and negative influences.
Consider one-to-one and group interactions, different forms of communication and different types of interpersonal interaction.

3   Understand ways to overcome barriers in a health and social care environment

3.1 Communication and interpersonal interaction

Staff training

Many skills, such as communicating effectively with anxious, depressed or aggressive people, cannot be developed simply by obtaining information. Instead, people often develop their skills by reflecting on their own practice experience and discussing thoughts and experiences with colleagues. Formal training courses usually provide opportunities to practise important skills as well as theories about how to overcome communication barriers.

Assessment of need and using preferred methods of communication

It is important to build an understanding of the needs of people you work with in health and social care. Very often, people will make their preferred method of communication obvious. Sometimes a professional social work or medical assessment may be needed in order to clarify the person's needs and their preferred method of communication.

Promoting rights

As well as general human rights, people who use services have a range of rights that are established in national standards, codes of practice and legislation. People who use services may be seen as having the following rights.

Confidentiality

Confidentiality is an important right for all people who use services because:

- People may feel confident about sharing information if they know that their care worker won't pass things on. They may not trust a carer if the carer does not keep information to themselves.

- Keeping information confidential demonstrates respect for people who use services. A lack of confidentiality may threaten people's self-esteem.

- A professional service, which maintains respect for individuals, must keep private information confidential – in the same way that medical practitioners and lawyers have always maintained confidentiality.

- There are legal requirements (data protection) to keep personal records confidential.

- A person's safety may be put at risk if details of their property and habits are shared publicly. For example, if your home was empty and other people knew where you kept your money, someone might be tempted to break in.

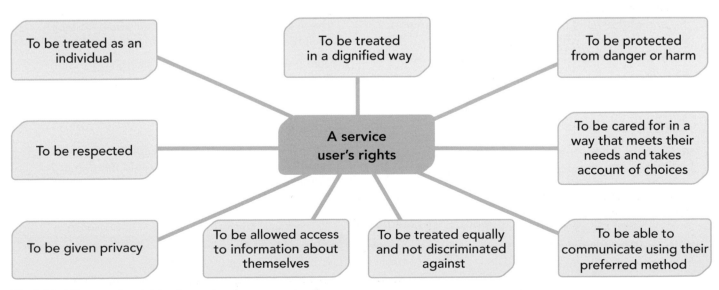

To be treated as an individual

To be treated in a dignified way

To be protected from danger or harm

To be respected

A service user's rights

To be cared for in a way that meets their needs and takes account of choices

To be given privacy

To be allowed access to information about themselves

To be treated equally and not discriminated against

To be able to communicate using their preferred method

Fig 1.16: What are the rights of people who use services?

Assertiveness

Fear and aggression are two basic emotions that we all experience. When we feel stressed, it is easy to give in to our basic emotions and be either submissive or aggressive. **Assertion** is an advanced skill, which involves controlling the basic emotions that usually prompt you to run away or fight. It involves a mental attitude whereby you try to *negotiate*, and try to solve problems rather than give in to emotional impulses.

During an argument, an aggressive person might insist that they are right and other people are wrong. They will want to win, while others lose. The opposite of aggression is submission. A submissive person accepts that they will lose, get told off, or be put down emotionally. Assertive behaviour is different from both these responses. In an argument, an assertive person will try to find an answer that means no one has to lose or be 'put down'. Assertion is a skill that helps create 'win-win' situations.

Key term

Assertion – Assertion is different from both submission and aggression. It involves being able to negotiate a solution to a problem.

To be assertive, a person usually has to:

- understand the situation they are in (including facts, details and other people's perceptions)
- be able to control personal emotions and stay calm
- be able to act assertively, using the right non-verbal behaviour
- be able to communicate assertively, using the right words and statements.

Some of the emotions, attitudes and behaviours involved in assertion are summarised in Table 1.3 on page 31.

Staying calm and in control of your emotions, displaying respect for others, using reflective listening and building an understanding of another person's viewpoint are all part of being assertive. Assertion is the skill of being able to understand another person's viewpoint, while being able to help them to understand your viewpoint. Assertion skills create a situation where negotiation is possible.

Assertion does involve a special kind of attitude. You are going to stick up for yourself – but you are not trying to dominate or get power over other people. You are trying to reach the best outcome for everyone. It is very easy to be aggressive – it is in our 'animal nature' to attack people who cause us problems.

Case study: Justin and Tyler

The manager of a care centre has asked that either Justin or Tyler should stay for an extra half-hour at the end of their shift to complete some paper work. Neither Justin nor Tyler want to do this work, so Justin could argue, using:

Aggression: Don't think I'm going to do it. I need to get away early and you're not going to stand in my way. I don't care what you say – either you do it or nobody does.

Assertion: Look – neither of us wants to stay late, but one of us has to stay. Let's work out a fair way to decide which of us stays.

Submission: I didn't really want to stay late, but if you don't want to stay, then I suppose I'll have to.

1 With a submissive response, Tyler will get what he wants and Justin will lose. But what are the likely consequences for their ability to work together in the future?

2 Justin will not necessarily win using aggression. Both people could become trapped in a cycle of aggressive responses. If one person does force the other to give in, will they be able to trust each other later?

3 Assertion is the most skilful response. Can you identify the skills that Justin would need in order to make this approach work?

Table 1.3: Differences between aggressive, assertive and submissive behaviours

	Aggressive behaviour	Assertive behaviour	Submissive behaviour
Main emotions	Anger	Control of own behaviour	Fear – wanting to please
Attitudes	Trying to win Wanting your own way Making demands	Trying to create a situation in which everyone wins Negotiating with others Trying to solve problems	Accepting that you will lose Letting others dominate Agreeing with others
Behaviours	Not listening to other people Putting other people down Shouting or talking very loudly	Listening to other points of view Showing respect for others Keeping a clear, calm voice	Not putting your own views across Withdrawing or showing fear Speaking quietly or not speaking at all
Body language	Fixed eye contact, tense muscles, waving of hands and arms, looking angry	Varied eye contact, relaxed face muscles, looking 'in control', keeping hands and arms at your side	Looking down, not looking at others, looking frightened, tense muscles

Case study: Karen

Interviewer: You must have to deal with some rude and aggressive people?

Karen: Yes, the first thing I do is to think to myself 'stay calm – don't feel threatened'. Very often people are rude or aggressive because they feel threatened. They are upset that you are in their home – they want to control you, to make themselves feel safe. For many people the only way they know to defend themselves is to get angry. Thinking this way helps me to stay calm.

Interviewer: That's a wonderful attitude – but don't people take advantage of you if you think like that?

Karen: No, you have to have the right attitude, you have to be patient, stay calm and try to get

people to talk to you. You have to show that you're not going to try and dominate or threaten them. But you can't let yourself be pushed around either. When people cross the line, I will talk firmly about how they make me feel, and what the consequences might be for them. Services can be withdrawn from really offensive people. Usually I think you get respect if you can put yourself in other people's shoes, but if you also stick up for yourself.

1 Do you think Karen has good assertiveness skills?

2 If Karen did behave aggressively towards people who use services, what would be the risks for her and the people she works with?

3 Why does Karen believe it is important to 'put herself in other people's shoes'?

Defusing aggression and staying confident

People do not always plan or choose to be aggressive. In health and social care contexts, a great deal of aggression is caused by stress, often because people feel powerless and out of control. Aggression sometimes results from frustration; aggression can be a last-ditch emotional response when a person feels that he or she is losing control.

Reflect

Have you ever seen a person shouting or swearing at a computer, or hitting the keyboard because the machine was not doing what they wanted? Do they really think the computer will be impressed?

People can become frustrated when they cannot control events, and aggressive behaviour is a natural emotional response.

Activity 7: Discussing sources of stress

Get together with a small group of colleagues and make a list of some of the stresses that people who receive care services might experience. Think about situations in which people may feel that they are out of control. Think about ways in which illness or pain might create stress. Think about barriers to understanding and how these might create stress.

Work out ways in which care workers could prevent the stresses from resulting in aggression.

PLTS

Independent enquirer: This activity will help you demonstrate that you can identify questions to answer, and consider the influence of circumstances on events.

When people feel stressed, emotions and tension often build up. Just one little misunderstanding can be enough to cause this tension to explode into an aggressive outburst. When a person becomes angry they may decide that it is someone else's fault that they have been made to be aggressive. Sometimes a person will have multiple aggressive outbursts as they struggle with their emotions.

When people become aggressive, care workers are likely to feel threatened. We all have a natural, animal response to run away or fight when we feel threatened. An unskilled response is to fight aggression with your own aggression – to 'get your own back' on someone who is threatening you. Within health and social care, this is wrong because it can increase the level of aggression or violence in someone who is stressed. A care worker could be injured in a violent outburst. Alternatively, your aggression could punish a person so that he or she gives up and withdraws from contact with you or your services. Being aggressive towards a person who is vulnerable will increase his or her problems and could result in **helplessness** and depression.

Key term

Helplessness – People can give up and become helpless when they learn that they cannot control or influence important personal events. Helpless people can become withdrawn and depressed.

Table 1.4: Skills for defusing aggression

1 Stay calm	Show that you are not going to become aggressive. Avoid a tense body posture, a tense face or clenched fists. Avoid fixed, staring eye contact. Breathe normally.
2 Communicate respect	Use your listening skills to show that you are taking the other person seriously. Use non-verbal skills to communicate respect.
3 Create trust	Try to meet the other person's self-esteem needs. Try to make the other person feel valued and important, without agreeing to everything they say.
4 Try to solve problems	You can only discuss issues or problems in detail after the other person responds to your listening and calming behaviour. You will note that the other person's non-verbal behaviour shows less tension.

Care workers are likely to break professional codes of conduct if they allow themselves to become aggressive. Instead it is vital that care workers learn the skills needed to defuse aggression.

It is not easy to stay calm if someone is threatening you. You will need to feel confident that you know how to work with the other person. If you have already established a sense of trust, it may be easier to cope with their aggression than with aggressive behaviour from a stranger. You will need to be sensitive about possible misunderstandings and barriers to understanding when you start to work with an angry person. You must avoid any spark that could light the fuse leading to an angry explosion.

All the skills of recognising and overcoming barriers to communication will be useful in helping you to avoid triggering aggression. Reflective listening skills are vital in order to make the other person feel valued.

Building relationships and appropriate verbal and non-verbal communication

Building relationships with people who use care services involves skilled listening, together with appropriate verbal and non-verbal communication. It may be important to use warm, friendly non-verbal behaviour that expresses interest in another person such as:

- making effective eye contact (varied and appropriate contact with another person's eyes)
- adopting a relaxed and calm body posture
- smiling – looking friendly rather than 'cold' or frozen in expression
- using hand movements and gestures that show interest
- nodding your head slightly while talking to communicate messages such as 'I see,' or 'I understand,' or 'I agree'
- using an appropriate gentle tone of voice.

Case study: Bill and Tony

Bill is a resident in a care home, who has been diagnosed with dementia. Tony is a care worker who knows Bill well. Bill will sit for long periods of time and then become agitated. While sitting in his chair he has started to shout angrily at other residents.

Bill (very angry):   You lot can get out of here, I don't want you round here anymore.

Tony (calm and gentle tone of voice):   Hello Bill, I am going to bring some coffee around in a minute. Would you like a cup?

Bill (raising his fist):   You can get out of here too. Go on, get off or I'll have you!

Tony (stepping back and lowering his head in a non-threatening way):   Bill, you remember me. You told me about your time in the Merchant Navy back in the fifties.

Bill (still angry):   Don't remember you – you weren't there!

Tony (calm, gentle, serious):   No – but you told me all about your time on the *Sea Princess*. How you went to South America, how you met your first wife.

Bill (less angry but accusing tone):   How do you know all that about me? Have you been spying on me?

Tony (serious, sincere but calm):   No Bill, honest, I would never spy on you. We had a long talk yesterday and I really enjoyed hearing about all the things you used to get up to. I was really interested – you've lived an exciting life. I was wondering whether you might have time to tell me a few more stories?

Bill (calmer tone of voice):   Well, what about all these people in here?

Tony (expressing genuine interest):   We could leave them for the moment – tell me more about your time in South America.

Bill (calm):   Not sure I can remember, what were we talking about?

1   What might have happened if Tony had confronted Bill and told him to stop shouting at the other residents?

2   Can you explain how Tony showed respect and created trust?

3   Why did Tony avoid talking about the other residents?

4   How did Tony use his personal knowledge of Bill to help defuse aggression?

Appropriate environment

The following ideas can help to reduce communication barriers in the environment:

- Improve the lighting.
- Reduce any noise.
- Move to a quieter or better-lit room.
- Work with smaller groups to see and hear more easily.
- Organise any seating so that people can see and hear each other.

Meeting self-esteem needs and maintaining an appropriate attitude

People who use services are often vulnerable. Many vulnerable people do not have the emotional security that comes from a high level of **self-esteem**. If a person feels dominated or threatened he or she may develop low self-esteem. If children don't feel valued, they may not develop self-esteem. Adults who do not feel valued may have difficulty in maintaining a high level of self-esteem.

Your communication with people in care settings should involve understanding and responding to their emotional needs.

Table 1.5: Aspects of communication that increase self-esteem

Appropriate non-verbal behaviour	• Smiling • Relaxed body posture • Looking interested • Being calm
Appropriate communication	• Using correct level of formality • Using language appropriate to speech community • Using appropriate preferred language • Using technological aids
Listening skills	• Using reflective listening • Having an appropriate attitude and valuing other people • Being willing to build an understanding of another person's views

Key term

Self-esteem – This is how you value or feel about yourself.

Case study: Karen

Interviewer: You talk about having the right attitude and 'putting yourself in other people's shoes' but doesn't that often make you feel sad and depressed?

Karen: No, you can understand how someone might feel without becoming overwhelmed. I always try to leave feeling happy or at least a little bit happier than when I arrived.

Interviewer: So how do you do that?

Karen: Well, keep people talking – most people have some happy memories. I try to get them to talk about some of the good things. I try to get a positive feeling going. Sometimes, if it feels right, I mention happy things in my life or else talk about some of the good things in the news – soaps and things like that! I try to create a happy atmosphere because that can sometimes make a person feel included and valued and increase their self-esteem.

Interviewer: So just talking through positive things in your life might make life seem more worthwhile – you value yourself more.

Karen: Yes, thinking over the good things is often a way to increase self-esteem.

1 What is self-esteem?

2 Why would talking about positive past life experiences help some people to increase their self-esteem?

3 How is Karen likely to know if she has been successful in making an individual feel happier after working with them?

Whether you work with children, older people or people with health needs, or physical or learning disabilities, it is always possible to think of ways to help increase another person's self-esteem.

Case study: Karen

Interviewer: You talked about creating 'positive feelings' – is there any more to this, other than just talking about positive past experiences?

Karen: Well, sometimes it's little things that make people feel good. First, you have to make the right relationship. I think it's important to be cheerful. I always think this is 'their time'. I have to be cheerful for them – and very often when I come out from a visit being cheerful with that person has made me feel better too. Then I always try to remember the little details from a previous visit. I think people often feel valued if you remember things about them. It always helps to give people a choice about how they want work done, what products they want and so on. I think people need to feel in control of their lives in order to maintain a sense of self-esteem. Then I think it's important to listen to people. If people listen to you then you matter, don't you? If people cut you short – well, then, perhaps you're not worth much.

1 What verbal and non-verbal behaviours might help to create a cheerful atmosphere?

2 Why does choice have anything to do with self-esteem?

3 Why is listening to people linked to self-esteem?

3.2 Aids to communication
Human aids

There are several services that may assist people to communicate or help to remove the barriers to effective communication.

Advocates

Sometimes, when people have a very serious learning disability or illness (such as dementia) it is not possible to communicate with them. In such situations, care services will often employ an **advocate**. An advocate is someone who speaks for someone else. A lawyer speaking for a 'client' in a courtroom is working as an advocate for that person. In care work, a volunteer might try to get to know someone who has dementia or a learning disability. The volunteer tries to understand and then communicate the person's needs and wants. Advocates should be independent of the staff team and therefore able to argue for people's rights without being influenced by what is the easiest or cheapest thing to do.

Key term

Advocate – Someone who speaks for someone else.

Advocacy is not straightforward; volunteers may not always understand the feelings and needs of the people for whom they are advocating. Some people argue that it would be better if people who use services could be trained and supported to argue their own case. Helping people to argue their own case is called self-advocacy.

Interpreters, translators and signers

Interpreters are people who communicate meaning from one language to another. This includes interpreting between spoken and signed languages such as English and British Sign Language. When an interpreter works with people, they become part of a communication cycle with that person.

Translators are people who change recorded material from one language to another. Translating and interpreting involve communicating meaning between different languages. Translating and interpreting are not just technical acts of changing the words from one system to another. Many languages do not have simple equivalence between words. Interpreters and translators have to grasp the meaning of a message (decode the message) and find a way of expressing it in a different language system. This is rarely easy, even for professional translators.

Activity 8: Exploring ICT translations

Use an automatic language translation system to translate a website that is written in a language other than English. You may find examples of confusing or even funny mistakes that the system makes. Compare your results with your colleagues' research and discuss the problems that can arise when words are simply changed to another language without any input from a human translator.

Functional skills

ICT: This activity may help you demonstrate ICT skills associated with presenting information and **English:** skills associated with reading and understanding text.

Interpreters may be professional people who are employed by social services or health authorities in order to communicate with people who use different spoken or signed languages. They may also be friends or family members who have sufficient language ability to be able to explain messages in different circumstances.

When people do not use English as their first language, they may experience difficulty accessing health or care services, unless they are supported by translators and interpreters. People who use signed languages may also need assistance from interpreters and translators – see page 14 for further details of signed languages.

Mentors

Mentors are usually people who are highly experienced in a particular job or activity; they advise others who are new to the activity or less experienced. Mentors need effective communication skills, coupled with some ability to explain issues and provide guidance. If a person is referred to as a mentor, it might be assumed that they will provide guidance based on their experience and knowledge of an issue.

Table 1.6: Important issues in interpretation

Knowledge of the subject matter	A professional interpreter may be able to explain details of legislation or procedures for claiming benefit because they understand the issues. If a relative or friend is acting as an interpreter, they will have to make sense of the technical details before they can communicate clearly.
Trust	People must have confidence in their interpreter. Some people may find it hard to trust a member from a different community. Many women may not feel safe and confident discussing personal issues using a male interpreter. The issue may not be about the interpreter's language competence, but about the interpreter's ability to understand and correctly convey what a person wants to say.
Social and cultural values	The choice of an interpreter must support the self-esteem needs of people who need to access interpretation services. Many people may feel that it is inappropriate to discuss personal details using an interpreter of the opposite sex. Some Deaf people do not feel confident using interpreters who have not experienced deafness themselves.
Confidentiality	Confidentiality is a right. Professional interpreters are likely to offer guarantees of confidentiality. Using a relative or volunteer may not necessarily provide people with the same guarantee of confidentiality.
Appropriate attitude	A professional interpreter is likely to offer advanced interpersonal skills, which include the ability not to judge what is being said. Volunteers, relatives and friends may have language competence, but these people may not be able to interpret without involving their own values, attitudes and beliefs.

Case study: Jasu

Jasu is 10 years old. Her father does not speak English although Jasu has grown up to be multilingual. Jasu's father is in poor health and needs to explain his problems to a health worker.

If Jasu had to interpret her father's problems in English:

1   How might she be affected emotionally while explaining her father's illness to someone she does not know?

2   Would Jasu be likely to find the right terminology to explain complex health issues to a professional?

3   Why might the services of a professional interpreter be more appropriate in this situation?

Befrienders

Befrienders seek to create a supportive relationship with others. A befriender will have good communication skills that enable them to listen to, and build an understanding of, another person's views and feelings. A befriender will work 'as if' he or she was a friend. Befrienders will not be assumed to have any particular professional knowledge.

Technological aids

Hearing aids

Hearing aids are battery-powered electronic devices with small microphones to pick up and increase the volume of sound received by a person. Hearing aids will often amplify background sounds as well as the voice or other signal that the person wants to hear. For this reason, a hearing aid will not always work effectively in a noisy environment.

Text phones, relay systems and minicoms

Text phones and minicoms have a small screen and a keyboard to enable messages to be typed. The reply can then be seen on the screen. The Royal National Institute for Deaf People (RNID) operates a text relay service, whereby an operator can enable conversations between speech phones used by hearing people and text phones used by people who may be Deaf or hard of hearing. A person can text their message to the operator, who will read it to the hearing person. The operator hears the reply and types what is said so that the Deaf person can read the typed message.

Loop systems

A loop system enables people who use hearing aids to hear sounds more clearly. A cable surrounds a given area such as a public area, room or even a car. Sound from a TV, microphone or music system can then be amplified into the loop. People with appropriate hearing aids can switch their aid to a special setting, enabling them to hear the amplified signal from the loop.

Voice-activated software

Voice-activated software enables a person to use speech commands to get their computer to perform a

What qualities do you think a befriender should have?

variety of tasks. Some people use speech recognition software to type messages without using a computer keyboard and this facility is particularly useful for people with dyslexia, who may find it harder to communicate using typing or writing.

PLTS

Independent enquirer: This discussion and thinking activity may help you demonstrate that you can support conclusions, using reasoned arguments and evidence.

Activity 9: Discussing barriers to communication

Think of particular examples of barriers to communication (perhaps taken from the table opposite) and discuss the strengths and weaknesses of different strategies to overcome them. Your discussion activities may help you to work out some reasoned arguments for using particular strategies within your work placement.

Case study: Gloria

Gloria grew up in the Caribbean and came to the UK 60 years ago. She now lives in a residential care home because she has developed some memory loss and disorientation associated with Alzheimer's disease. Gloria also has some hearing loss and uses a hearing aid. Gloria's first language is English but care workers sometimes have difficulty understanding her speech.

Sometimes Gloria will talk about places and events from the past that care staff have difficulty identifying with. Some care staff think that Gloria is 'confused'

and that trying to communicate with her is a waste of time. Gloria sometimes becomes distressed because she is lonely and there is no one to talk to.

1 Can you list the barriers to communication that Gloria is experiencing?

2 Can you list ideas for overcoming these barriers?

3 How could you use communication skills in order to increase Gloria's self-esteem?

Table 1.7: Ideas for reducing barriers to communication where people have a disability

Visual disability	• Use language to describe things. • Assist people to touch things (e.g. they might want to touch your face to recognise you). • Explain details that sighted people might take for granted. • Check what people can see (many registered blind people can see shapes, or tell light from dark). • Check glasses, other aids and equipment.
Hearing disability	• Don't shout. Use normal clear speech and make sure your face is visible for people who can lip-read. • Show pictures or write messages. • Learn to sign (for people who use signed languages). • Ask for help from, or employ, a communicator or interpreter for signed languages. • Check that hearing aids and equipment are working.
Physical and intellectual disabilities	• Increase your knowledge of disabilities. • Use pictures and signs as well as clear, simple speech. • Be calm and patient. • Set up group meetings where people can share interests. • Check that people do not become isolated. • Use advocates – independent people who can spend time building an understanding of the needs of specific individuals to assist with communication work.

Table 1.8: Strategies for overcoming communication barriers

Type of barrier	Possible strategies
Communication that involves difficult, complex or sensitive issues	Use listening skills/skilled use of the communication cycle. Develop a 'caring presence'. Professional workers may develop empathy.
Unmet language needs or preferences	Assessment of needs. Staff training to enable assessment of need. Use of preferred language. Training to learn to communicate using different languages or systems.
Sensory impairment	Use human or technological aids to compensate for impairment.
Disabilities	See Table 1.7 on page 38 for strategies.
Communication involving personality or self-esteem needs, or anxiety or depression	Use listening skills/skilled use of the communication cycle. Try to make the other person feel valued. Develop a 'caring presence'. Use open questions, keep the conversation going. Avoid focusing on/discussing emotionally negative issues.
Aggression/submissiveness	Stay calm, show respect. Use skills associated with assertion and defusing aggression (see pages 30–33).
Assumptions, values or beliefs	Use listening skills/skilled use of the communication cycle to detect barriers. Use reflective learning skills to question own values, beliefs or assumptions. Staff training to develop reflective learning skills.
Jargon	Use listening skills/skilled use of the communication cycle to detect barriers. Use appropriate language for other people.
Cultural variations	Use listening skills/skilled use of the communication cycle to detect barriers and check your understanding. Learn about the cultural variations among people you work with. Staff training to learn about cultural variations. Avoid making assumptions about people who are different. Consider involving advocates who will represent the best interests of others.
Abuse of power	Try to empower others. Reflect on and question own assumptions. Avoid behaviours aimed at controlling or manipulating other people.
Alcohol or drugs	Stay calm, show respect. Use appropriate non-verbal behaviour, avoid making demands. Assess risk of assault.

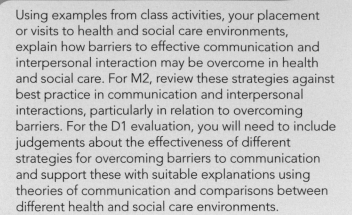

Assessment activity 1.4

Using examples from class activities, your placement or visits to health and social care environments, explain how barriers to effective communication and interpersonal interaction may be overcome in health and social care. For M2, review these strategies against best practice in communication and interpersonal interactions, particularly in relation to overcoming barriers. For the D1 evaluation, you will need to include judgements about the effectiveness of different strategies for overcoming barriers to communication and support these with suitable explanations using theories of communication and comparisons between different health and social care environments.

Grading tips

P4 Use examples already explained and discussed in the previous three assessment activities, plus others as appropriate, to explain the strategies used.

Continue to use the notes in your logbook as a source of examples to illustrate points you make.

A strategy is a plan of how things are intended to be done but actual practice may not be the same. Comparison of what is intended and what actually happens could be helpful.

M2 Consider strengths and weaknesses of observed interactions and communication practice and compare these with theories.

In preparation for the assessment, take part in role-plays designed to simulate possible barriers to communication and discuss in class the effectiveness of how they were overcome.

D1 An evaluation requires both a judgement to be made eg whether something is or is not effective in overcoming barriers and a justification or explanation of how this judgement has been reached.

Your evaluations should include references to relevant published sources in addition to your log book evidence or understanding gained from this book.

4 Be able to communicate and interact effectively in a health or care environment

4.1 Contexts

You will practise interactions and discuss their effectiveness before you present evidence of your own practical work. To begin with, you might watch videos or film clips of interpersonal interactions. You should practise identifying and describing different behaviours that you have seen and/or heard in recorded material. As you become more confident, you can role-play or simulate communicating in various contexts including: formal; one-to-one; group; with people using services; with professionals/colleagues.

This section of the unit is about your own skills in communicating in interpersonal interactions. It is your opportunity to demonstrate your ability to apply what you have learned from the unit.

4.2 Communication skills and effectiveness

To begin with, you might demonstrate your communication skills using role-play or simulation. In role-play you have to behave in such a way that other people can – at least temporarily – believe in the character you are portraying. Simulation does not require you to use acting skills or portray a character. If you simulate a conversation, you simply say (or sign) the appropriate responses. You do not expect people observing your behaviour to perceive you as anyone but yourself. Both simulation and role-play involve thinking through appropriate responses but role-play involves a greater level of acting skill.

To demonstrate your communication skills, you will need to cover verbal and non-verbal skills such as listening and responding, tone, pace, language, appropriate environment, proximity, clarifying or repeating, questioning, responding to difficult situations and defusing anger.

Resources and further reading

Argyle, M. (1972) *The Psychology of Interpersonal Behaviour*, second ed. Harmondsworth: Pelican

Burnard, P. (1996) *Acquiring Interpersonal Skills*, second ed. London: Chapman & Hall

Burnard, P., Morrison, P. (1997) *Caring and Communicating* Basingstoke and London: Macmillan Press Ltd

Engebretson, J. (2003) 'Caring presence: a case study' in *Communication, Relationships and Care* Robb, M., Barrett, S., Komaromy, C., Rogers, A. (eds) London & New York: OU & Routledge

Pinker, S. (1994) *The Language Instinct* Harmondsworth: Penguin

Tuckman, B. (1965) 'Development Sequence in Small Groups', *Psychological Bulletin*, Vol. 63, No. 6

Useful

Braille www.br

British Sign La

Makaton www.

Signs and fing

www.british-si

and at www.rc

Table 1.9: Checklist for analysing communication and interpersonal interaction

One-to-one interaction	• How did you start and finish your interaction? Did you try to meet the person's emotional needs? • Could you identify a communication cycle involving feedback on your understanding of the other person's ideas?
Group interaction	• Were you able to take effective turns in speaking? • Could you identify group values and/or purposes within the group? • Was there a group leader? How was the interaction managed?
Context	• Who was involved in the interaction? People who use services? Professionals? Colleagues? What role did you play?
Verbal listening and responding skills	• How effective was your use of language, pace of speech and level of formality? Was there any use of specialist language? How far did you encourage others to talk?
Non-verbal listening and responding skills	• How appropriate was your voice tone, posture, facial expression, eye contact and proximity?
Reflective listening skills	• How did you use reflective listening and the communication cycle? Can you identify examples of clarifying your understanding or repeating important ideas?
Questioning skills	• Did you keep the conversation going using open questions? Can you identify probes and prompts that you used?
Environment	• Did the environment create any barriers? Could everybody see and hear each other clearly?
Barriers	• What barriers did you detect? Were there any barriers to interpreting communication, such as language differences? • Were there any barriers to understanding, such as cultural differences, assumptions values or beliefs?
Difficult situations	• Did you act in a calm and respectful way? What skills did you use to interact with people with strong emotions?
Defusing anger	• Were you able to act in an appropriate, calm and respectful way? Were you able to avoid triggering aggression? Were you able to use assertive skills appropriately?

4.3 Effectiveness

You should demonstrate effective communication in both group and one-to-one situations including an awareness of the needs and preferences of others, interpersonal skills, attitudes, overcoming barriers, adjusting interactions, and your own assertiveness.

The checklist in the table below may be useful as a starting point for assessing role-plays and recordings of real interactions.

PLTS

Self-manager:
demonstrate y
and resources.

Reflective lea
demonstrate t
progress. You
learning and c
different ways.

Assessment activity 1.5

For P5 take part in a one-to-one interaction. For P6 take part in an interaction with a small group of individuals in a health and social care environment. At least one of the interactions should be with individuals using services although one could involve a specific interaction with a professional in the environment relating to an important aspect of care.

For both interactions produce evidence to demonstrate your role in each interaction. This should include a witness testimony from a professional in the environment who has been present whilst you have carried out the interactions. You should also provide your own account of each interaction.

For M3 you will need to include a detailed description of the skills you used in the interactions and how these related to the context of each interaction and the responses made by the individuals involved. For both interactions, you should explain how and why you applied theory, took account of influences on the interactions and minimised or overcame any barriers.

For D2 the account of the interactions should also include an evaluation of each and of the skills you used.

are not in p
environme
the contex
take these
interaction
a specific a
care task a
appropriat
the commu

Your contri
necessarily
evidence s
influences
and you sh
rights and
involved in
interaction

M3 To achieve
your own c
skills and p
including y
each intera
both one-t
could discu
one-to-one
supervisor
ability to a

D2 At this leve
evaluate th
and interpe
group inter
a more in-d
have influe
interaction
also those
need to pr

Grading tips

P5 P6 Gain written consent to carry out the interactions from a suitable professional in the health and social care environment and include this in your assignment.

Both interactions need to be specific planned activities for the purpose of the assessment and you should obtain confirmation from your tutor that the plans are appropriate before carrying out the interactions. It is not possible to achieve these criteria from casual, ongoing day-to-day interactions in a placement. If you

Just checking

1 Why is tone of voice categorised as a non-verbal rather than a verbal issue?
2 Is it true that effective, caring, communication can be defined as 'clear, concise transmission of information between people'?
3 What is reflective listening and why is it important?
4 Rachel says, 'I never let anyone else win an argument with me – I always get my own way!' Is it correct to describe Rachel's attitude as being assertive?
5 If you met a person who said, 'I can't hear you, I need to put my glasses on' what sense could you make of this communication?
6 Is it possible for a person who has no knowledge of the English language to be able to sign using British Sign Language?
7 What problems might arise if a relative (with the necessary language skills) acts in place of a professional translator?

edexcel ⠿

Assignment tips

1 Before you start to make logbook records you might like to state how you will record details of conversations and other interactions. You could include a statement about how you will respect confidentiality, respect the rights of others, and show respect for other people. You must also be sure that if you take notes about people who use services your note-taking will not create any misunderstandings or cause any stress to these people.

2 Use video recording of role-plays or simulations to help you identify how theories of communication work before attempting to analyse workplace interactions.

3 A range of potential barriers and misunderstandings can influence communication in care settings. Very often there will be a number of issues that are relevant to any particular observation you have noted.

4 Use role-play and simulation followed by discussion to help you develop skills for reviewing and evaluating strategies to overcome barriers.

5 It may be a good idea to record a practice one-to-one and group interaction and discuss your performance with colleagues, supervisors and/or tutors before undertaking the observation that you use for your assignment. If you practise taking notes and discussing the quality of your interaction you may pick up some good ideas that you can incorporate in your final assignment.

6 When you make notes about a one-to-one or group interaction you should make your notes immediately after the conversation or meeting. These notes will help you describe your interactions at a later date. You will not be able to remember everything that you said or did, or that other people did. You should aim to recall some of the key things you said and to remember the responses others made. You should also make notes about some of the non-verbal behaviours you saw in others as well as your own non-verbal behaviour.

2 Equality, diversity and rights in health and social care

This unit introduces you to equality, diversity and rights in the health and social care sector. You need to be aware of these issues because you will be faced with them on a daily basis. This is one of the most important units on the course and it is essential that you understand the regulations regarding equality, diversity and rights.

You need to know how to help a person who is being victimised and how to help the person inflicting such discrimination so they do not do it again. By doing this, you will ensure that you and others deliver a respectful and dignified service to everybody using and working in health and social care.

You have a huge responsibility to yourself and others to ensure that this happens. It is also very important to be aware of your own thoughts and prejudices. (Yes, everybody has them!) This will enable you to understand your own thought processes in a mature way, and not let them get in the way of your day-to-day tasks. It will also make you aware of your own rights and help to ensure that no one discriminates against you, which is also extremely important.

Learning outcomes

After completing this unit you should:

1 understand concepts of equality, diversity and rights in relation to health and social care
2 know discriminatory practices in health and social care
3 understand how national initiatives promote anti-discriminatory practice
4 know how anti-discriminatory practice is promoted in health and social care settings.

Assessment and grading criteria

This table shows you what you must do in order to achieve a **pass**, **merit** or **distinction** grade, and where you can find activities in this book to help you.

To achieve a **pass** grade, the evidence must show that you are able to:	To achieve a **merit** grade, the evidence must show that, in addition to the pass criteria, you are able to:	To achieve a **distinction** grade, the evidence must show that, in addition to the pass and merit criteria, you are able to:
P1 Explain the concepts of equality, diversity and rights in relation to health and social care **See Assessment activity 2.1, page 70** *achieved*		
P2 Describe discriminatory practice in health and social care **See Assessment activity 2.1, page 70** *achieved*	**M1** Assess the effects on those using the service of three different discriminatory practices in health and social care settings **See Assessment activity 2.1, page 70** *achieved.*	
P3 Describe the potential effects of discriminatory practice on those who use health or social care services **See Assessment activity 2.1, page 70** *achieved*		
P4 Explain how national initiatives promote anti-discriminatory practice **See Assessment activity 2.2, page 82** *achieved*	**M2** Assess the influence of a recent national policy initiative promoting anti-discriminatory practice **See Assessment activity 2.2, page 82** *achieved*	**D1** Evaluate the success of a recent initiative to promote anti-discriminatory practice **See Assessment activity 2.2, page 82** *achieved*
P5 Describe how anti-discriminatory practice is promoted in health and social care settings **See Assessment activity 2.2, page 82** *achieved*	**M3** Discuss difficulties that may arise when implementing anti-discriminatory practice in health and social care settings **See Assessment activity 2.2, page 82** *achieved*	**D2** Justify ways of overcoming difficulties that may arise when implementing anti-discriminatory practices in health and social care settings **See Assessment activity 2.2, page 82** *achieved*

Distinction

How you will be assessed

You will need to produce written evidence of examples of the effects of discrimination within health and social care. You will also have to explain recent national initiatives to promote anti-discriminatory practices. You will need to demonstrate your own skills both in one-to-one and group interaction situations. Varied assessment tasks are included throughout this unit to help you prepare your work.

Lola, 18 years old

For me this was one of the most interesting and useful units on the course. I realised soon after starting how important this was going to be for my future in health and social care. I have been aware of discrimination for a long time, as I studied it before and also witnessed it personally, as well as hearing my family talking about it.

After a class discussion about discrimination with myself and other students getting really involved in the subject, we carried out research with different groups researching a topic. My group found the equality and human rights website a great source of information, and with guidance from our tutor we were able to give an interesting presentation. The other groups also presented good topics and this gave us a good starting point for the unit.

We then had to look at different health and social care settings and see what effect discrimination had on people using them, and how this could negatively affect their health. The research and findings were quite shocking and I remember talking to my family about it, and it made it clear to me how important it is to get this right. My research also included the law and what I needed to know about it, especially before I started my work experience. Overall, this unit was intense but interesting and I really enjoyed researching it. This was reflected in my mark – I'm glad to say I got a distinction.

Over to you!

1   Why do you think this unit is so important?

2   What topic do you think you will find the most difficult and why?

3   Do you think discrimination happens in health and social care and why?

1 Understand concepts of equality, diversity and rights in relation to health and social care

Get started

Diversity – a personal view

A very good starting point is to look at yourself, your family or friends.

First answer the questions below on your own:

- What are the nationalities of your family or friends?
- What music do you like?
- What is your favourite food?
- What languages can you or your family/friends speak?
- What and how do you celebrate in your culture?

Now get together in a group selected by your tutor to discuss the range of different responses to these questions, then report back to the other groups.

Discuss as a whole class how you can each benefit from knowing about the differences raised in the last exercise.

Finally, consider the question: what does your culture mean to you?

Working in the health and social care sector, **equality**, **diversity** and **rights** are at the core of everything you will be doing. These terms embrace all individuals using the health and care sectors and every person working within them. It is essential that people working within health and social care recognise the need to treat every individual equally no matter what their gender, race, beliefs, sexuality, age, disability, ethnicity, sexual orientation, education, language, background or skin colour.

You also need to recognise when individuals are being treated unfairly, to challenge such mistreatment, and help those being mistreated and those causing the mistreatment. This not only applies to people in your care but also if you witness someone being treated unfairly at any time.

Diversity should be recognised and celebrated and it is important to support individuals' diversity when working out health and care plans, as well as recognising any particular needs they may have as individuals. By doing this, the people in your care will feel valued and respected and will feel that they are being treated with dignity. All these things will help them feel more positive about their time in your care.

Key terms

Equality – Being equal, especially in rights, status or opportunities. All individuals should be treated equally, and there are laws in place to ensure that this happens. In accordance with the law, organisations have equality policies to ensure that everyone is treated equally.

Diversity – Diversity means accepting and respecting differences. This means that everyone is recognised as being different and their difference is valued and respected.

Rights – Rights are legal entitlements. For example, an individual has a right to live in society without being abused or intimidated because of their gender, sexuality, race, skin colour, beliefs or culture.

Reflect

Look at the words 'equality', 'diversity' and 'rights' again and think about how they will impact on your career in health and social care.

1.1 The benefits of diversity

Britain is a truly multicultural society with a huge variety of people from different backgrounds who live and work all over the country. The table below gives some indication of Britain's diversity and an idea of when the main groups of immigrants came to Britain.

The largest immigrant groups live in and around London, with other groups concentrated in industrial centres in Yorkshire, the Midlands and the rest of the South-East.

In total, 6.5 per cent of the British population consists of ethnic minorities. The British population is made up of the following ethnic groups:

- White – 53,074,000 (includes Irish, Polish, Italian, etc)
- Black Caribbean – 490,000

Table 2.1: Waves of immigration to Britain in the nineteenth and twentieth centuries

Time	Main groups of immigrants
1800s	Jewish arrivals from Russia/Poland; people from rural Ireland
1948–50s	Caribbean people (invited to help rebuild post-war Britain)
1950s–60s	Asians from India, Pakistan and Bangladesh
1970s	East African Asians and Vietnamese
1980s	Eastern European refugees from former Yugoslavia and other war torn states

Source: www.britishcouncil.org/languageassistant/

What do you think are the benefits of diversity?

- Black African – 376,000
- Black other – 308,000
- Indian – 930,000
- Pakistani – 663,000
- Bangladeshi – 268,000
- Chinese – 137,000
- Other Asian – 209,000 (includes Vietnamese, Malaysian, Thai)
- Other – 424,000 (people who did not think they fitted the above categories)

Source: British Council, 2009

Therefore people working within health and social care and the people who use the services provided will come from diverse backgrounds and bring with them a wide range of behaviours and beliefs. Everyone is an individual and expects to be valued for who they are and what they bring with them to a diverse country such as Britain.

Diversity should benefit all of us, with people valuing each other and experiencing a strong bond with others from different backgrounds. Unfortunately this is sometimes not the case. Some people may fear something they know nothing about and discriminate against those from different backgrounds. These people may use health and social care services themselves at some times in their lives and you need to be aware of any unfair and unwarranted discrimination from them. They usually act out of ignorance and may cause upset and offence. However, they still need to be treated fairly and this will undoubtedly test you. Fortunately this problem only seems to arise with a small number of people. Some, however, may be in a vulnerable mental state and again these individuals will need care and support, just as other individuals do.

Britain has passed laws to help bring together the many diverse groups in our country so that we, as a nation, can celebrate our multicultural society.

Social and cultural benefits of diversity

The benefits of diversity affect our whole lives as well as the health and social care sector, as Fig 2.1 shows.

The arts

The arts provide a valuable way of bringing diversity to a wide audience. For example, films made in other countries can demonstrate culture from around the world in a form that is easy to understand and

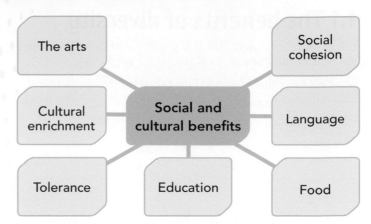

Fig 2.1: The social and cultural benefits of diversity

may intrigue as well as educate people about other cultures. Museums and exhibitions also give an understanding of cultures from around the world, past and present. Plays and other theatrical performances can bring an experience of contemporary world culture. All these things can help us understand and appreciate 'difference'. With knowledge from the arts, a person working in health and social care can develop a deeper understanding of diversity.

Reflect

Discuss in a group how the arts have enriched your life.

Diet

Another good reason to enjoy a multicultural society is its food. In a recent survey in Britain the Chinese dish Chow Mein was voted the favourite food, with Indian food being the other main choice. In fact these two foods accounted for 70 per cent of food choices according to the market leader in consumer survey analysis Mintel. Mexican food was extremely popular and stir-fries were considered a very healthy option. Only 6 per cent of the 1000 people questioned admitted to never eating ethnic food.

Did you know?

It is also interesting to know that diet is linked to social class. A British Heart Foundation food survey in 2006 found that 50 per cent more people in the highest income bracket ate five portions of fruit and vegetables a day more than people in the lowest income bracket.

Source: www.heartstats.org

This information is very important for the health and social care profession, as individual tastes have to be taken into account when planning a person's diet. More and more people are enjoying a diet with herbs and spices. This is partly due to our multicultural society and also because more people are travelling to other countries and tasting different types of food and drink. A person's diet also needs to be tailored to their health requirements. For example, diabetics and some older people may need to exclude certain foods. Likewise, a person's religious beliefs may mean that **halal** meat is a requirement. Asking people about their food likes and dislikes, and what they can and cannot eat, is all part of considering and respecting their diversity.

Reflect

Think about the food you like and what sort of meals you would like if you were in a health and social care environment.

Education

Education has seen big developments over recent years with diverse cultures being explored and valued within the curriculum. Schools and colleges now include studies in a wide range of cultures and languages. The education system has also benefited from people from different backgrounds reaching management positions and making positive changes in relation to diversity.

The inclusion of equality, diversity and rights training in the health and social care profession has increased and has become an important part of the professional training programme. The Royal College of General Practitioners, for instance, places great importance on the promotion of equality and diversity in GP training.

All organisations are required by law to train their staff in equality, diversity and rights, usually under the equal opportunities framework. This is usually done in the induction programme. In-service training is also regularly given on equality, diversity and rights for all Britain's workforce. Education is an important tool in helping to get rid of ignorance about diversity.

Language

Learning another language can be very beneficial for health professionals. It can give them the chance to work abroad as well as learn something new. With the development of online services, there is a wealth of information in most spoken languages. Information is also available in sign language, and the visually impaired can use specialised software, which speaks to the viewer. Most websites now have an 'accessibility' option for people who cannot read the text.

People who can speak languages other than English are highly sought after in health and social care because many of those using the services may not speak English. Interpretation is seen as a new career in the health service, so speaking another language is clearly beneficial for health and social care professionals.

Reflect

If you know of someone who cannot speak English and has used health and social care services, ask them how they managed to communicate.

PLTS

Independent enquirer: By exploring communication from a different perspective, you can show independent enquiry skills.

Tolerance

Tolerance is a very important quality to have when working in health and social care. You may come across people you do not get on with or who have different views from you. This is life and has to be accepted; after all, we are all individuals. You have to be mature and professional when working with colleagues and helping people, even though you may sometimes not feel you want to be. Difference has to be accepted – even more in health and social care than in other occupations.

Social cohesion

This could be better described as community cohesion, where a community (social group) sticks

Key terms

Tolerance – The ability or willingness to tolerate the existence of opinions or behaviour that you dislike or disagree with.

Halal – Religiously acceptable according to Muslim law. Food prepared in a way prescribed by Muslim law.

together (cohesion). You may know of a close community and may live in one. This may be formed for a number of reasons, such as ethnicity. Belonging to a community is very important to human behaviour, as it provides a safe and understanding environment, and a group that sticks together.

In times of crisis (such as the 'big freeze' in December 2009, when people said on the news that strangers were helping each other cope with the icy conditions), strong bonds are formed between individuals. Social cohesion can be strengthened under such circumstances; if you experience a difficult situation with other people, you feel a common bond because you are the only ones who have experienced it at first hand.

Health and social care team members need to form this type of bond. Working in diverse teams requires each member to respect all the others in the team and to value each person as an individual. Without this, the team will operate ineffectively and eventually fall apart, causing major difficulties for the people using the service.

Activity 1: Supporting a member of staff

Discuss in a small group how you would support a member of your team who has been racially abused by a person using your service.

Cultural enrichment

All the social and cultural benefits described above will bring about cultural enrichment through diversity, which will improve life for everyone, both those who work in health and social care and those who use the services provided.

The economic benefits of diversity

The economic benefits of diversity to Britain can be seen everywhere, from the clothes we wear and the foods we eat to the people who work here. The many diverse shops (ranging from big names on the high street to small independent manufacturers and those who sell their products on the Internet) all add up to a richly varied community. Imports and exports now make this a global community. All of these aspects underline the importance of diversity to the economic well-being of Britain and the world. In relation to the

health and social care profession, new techniques, equipment and software developments are being shared all round the world. This all means that people are benefiting from diversity.

Employment and expertise

Many organisations, including the health and social care services, have come to realise that their customers are from a wide range of diverse backgrounds and it is therefore important that their workforce also reflects this.

Organisations have also realised that by positively encouraging potential employees to apply for jobs they increase the chance of getting the right person, which they may not have done otherwise.

The Race Relations (Amendment) Act 2000 promoted race equality, equality of opportunity and good race relations in public bodies including the health and care service. This has helped to build an appropriate diverse workforce.

1.2 Terminology

When working in the health and social care profession you must know and understand how to use appropriate terminology with regard to equality and diversity. Words like empowerment, diversity, stereotyping must be used in the right context. Without this knowledge you will find it difficult to communicate in a diverse workforce and you may find yourself in an embarrassing situation if you use the words incorrectly.

On the following pages are key words and terms that you will need to understand for this unit.

Activity 2: Developing your own glossary

You may wish to develop your own glossary of terms used within the health and social care professions. Get a small notebook or keep a file on your computer and keep adding new terms as you come across them.

PLTS

Self-manager: Organising your time to develop health and social care resources, such as a glossary of terms, will help you demonstrate self-management skills.

Lamiley Frank
Care home assistant

Lamiley studied the BTEC Health and Social Care course and found work as a care home assistant at a local care home. The home didn't have a great reputation but it was nearby, which was convenient for Lamiley, so she was pleased to get the job.

The residents in the care home were all in their seventies and eighties, and Lamiley noticed that there were a few who were Indian or Pakistani, a couple of them were black, one was Chinese, and the other fifteen were white.

Lamiley: When I started work, I soon found out why the home didn't have a great reputation. During the day there was no stimulus for the people in the home. They were washed in the morning and then just plonked in front of the television. They were then pushed in their chairs or walked to the main eating room and given lunch, which consisted of a white bread sandwich with lettuce, cheese and pickle and a cup of tea. They were then taken back to the television lounge again for the rest of the afternoon.

At teatime they were given a meal of what I was told was breaded turkey escalopes, mashed potato, cabbage and gravy, followed by rhubarb and custard. When I asked one of the carers about the food they said it was nutritious and typical of the meals that were served. The carers hardly talked to the residents while they fed them. After the meal the residents had another cup of tea before being returned to their bedrooms for the night at about 5.30 pm.

Think about it!

1 Identify the diversity issues here.
2 What do you think of the food that was given to all the residents, and how would you go about making changes?
3 What other changes would you make to their day and why?

poorer diet. This can lead to less paid work and keep families trapped in poverty. These factors will have an impact on the local health services, which may be under more pressure than those in more affluent areas. The government has a duty to improve conditions but poorer areas do exist and you can see the differences when walking around these areas and comparing them with 'richer' areas. The important point is that in health and social care everyone has a right to the same treatment and care as everyone else, no matter what their background.

Beliefs

Beliefs can be religious, or they can be beliefs about ourselves or what is happening around us. Beliefs can be very powerful and can influence our thoughts about the world and about people we meet. This may impact on the way people are treated in health and social care. For instance, you may come across people who believe that something harmful will not happen to them. For example, they may believe that smoking will not give them lung cancer. ('It happens to other people but it won't happen to me.') Or you may be supporting and respecting a family of Jehovah's Witnesses who do not believe in blood transfusions but have a son who could live if he received a blood transfusion. (In this case, there will be legal implications concerning the child's right to life, meaning that the decision may be taken away from the parents – see Section 2.4: Loss of rights.) Or perhaps you could be treating someone who is in denial concerning their medical condition (for example a diabetic, who doesn't control their diet, as they do not believe they have diabetes). These situations can all be very trying in the health and social care profession, but respect always has to be shown.

Values

People's values are usually developed as they grow and are influenced by the adults that they are in contact with. This socialisation process impacts on how we see ourselves in the world. It can be positive or negative or a mixture of both. For example, someone may decide to be a vegan because they think animal welfare is very important. In health and social care you will come across the psychological values that impact on people. For example, some individuals don't value their health enough and so they become unwell and may require a lot of help from health and social care services.

Vulnerability

People may be vulnerable because of their mental state or age. Someone who is frail is vulnerable to the cold in winter and perhaps also to high temperatures in the summer. Vulnerable groups (e.g. older people and people with diabetes) are offered free flu vaccines in the winter months. Some people cannot protect themselves and are easily abused because of their mental state. Your role is to help and support them, ensure their health and safety while in your care, and make sure that there is a support network in place when they leave your care.

Abuse

Abuse refers to a range of negative behaviours that can have the potential to harm or damage individuals in various ways.

Verbal abuse

This occurs when one person uses words and body language to criticise another person inappropriately.

Psychological abuse

Also known as mental abuse or emotional abuse, this occurs when one person controls information that is available to another person so as to manipulate or distort that person's sense of reality.

Physical abuse

This occurs when one person uses physical pain or the threat of physical force to intimidate another person.

Sexual abuse

This includes any sort of unwanted sexual contact perpetrated on a victim (child or adult) by an abuser.

Neglect (fail to care for properly)

This occurs when a person fails to provide for the basic needs (e.g. food, warmth and shelter) of one or more dependants that he or she is responsible for.

Hate crimes

Hate crimes include verbal, physical, emotional or sexual abuse aimed at an individual or a group of people. The abuses may be based on various characteristics of the people it is aimed at – religion, sexuality or the colour of their skin.

In the health and social care profession you will come across abuse on a regular basis. Whether you are dealing with the abused or the abuser, you have to remember that both will need support.

Empowerment

This means that someone has control of certain tasks they have been asked to do or over their own lives. Working in health and social care, you will have to ensure that people take control of their health and well-being by empowering them to do so. This will be done by giving them support and encouragement and in some cases it will require a lot of patience. Some vulnerable people may not feel able to take control of their health and this is why your supportive role is so important. Some people may think the health and social care services are too controlling and you will need to work with colleagues to find strategies that work in these cases too. Doing this course is empowering you to work in the health and social care profession.

Independence

Working with people to ensure they have an independent life, without others telling them what to do, is vital. It's empowering people. As a health professional, you work *with* an individual; you do not work *for* them. Helping clients to become independent in their health and social care is particularly important.

Ethnic minorities in the UK, on average, earn less than white people. How might racism contribute to this?

Interdependence

Interdependence means working within a team, where each person's role is as important as everyone else's. When working in a multi-disciplined team each person will rely on another, thus ensuring that everyone carries out their job properly. In this sense, all the team members depend on each other's expertise.

Racism

Racism is the abuse of people of a certain race. This could be at organisational level where promotion benefits one particular race over another, or outright hatred against a person or a group of people of another race.

According to recent research, black and Asian ethnic minority workers have lower pay than their white counterparts, are more likely to be unemployed and are less likely to be found in the higher ranks of management.

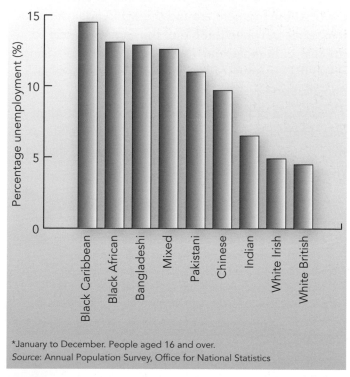

Unemployment rates of men: by ethnic group, 2004*

*January to December. People aged 16 and over.
Source: Annual Population Survey, Office for National Statistics

Fig 2.2: Ethnic minority disadvantage

Sexism

This covers a wide range of negative behaviours, including prejudice and discrimination towards other people based on their gender.

Women are usually the ones who are discriminated against, although sometimes it can be men. This can relate to unequal pay between men and women doing the same job, working conditions being different and unequal chances of promotion. It can also relate to an unequal level of health care based on a person's gender.

Did you know?

In Britain, one-third of the families headed by women live below the poverty line.

Homophobia

Homophobia is the fear or hatred of homosexuals and homosexuality. Individuals who are homophobic fear or hate the fact that others are sexually attracted to members of their own sex. This fear can lead to behaviour that discriminates against homosexuals and consequently advantages heterosexuals. There are drives at the moment around the world against lawful marriages between people of the same sex, due to the fear of homosexuals (gays and lesbians) breaking down the structure of society and the heterosexual constitution.

An example of this was when a gay college student was told by his parents that if he had a gay relationship they would refuse to help him financially and that he would have to move out of their home.

Reflect

Reflect on your thoughts on homophobia and be honest! Then reflect on how your thoughts may influence you when you are working with and supporting people in health and social care. This is personal to you, unless you want to discuss it openly.

PLTS

Creative thinker: Be really honest about questioning your own assumptions, and think before you write anything down. This will help you to be more creative in your responses.

1.3 Health and social care settings

In this unit you are asked to explore equality, diversity and rights in relation to four key types of health and social care setting:

- residential care
- day care
- nursing care
- domiciliary care (home care).

Residential care

Residential care is where a person leaves their home to be cared for in a safe and secure home environment. People who use this type of care may not be able to live on their own and maintain their health but they do not necessarily need nursing care. The residential care setting caters for the person's social care needs, which may include:

- personal care
- ensuring they take their medicine at the required time
- arranging health visits when needed
- encouraging independence.

Some residential care settings care for people with the same type of attention needs, such as Alzheimer's or physical frailty.

Activity 4: Residential care

Visit a residential care home and interview two residents to find out what they think about being there (both benefits and disadvantages), and how their independence is encouraged. You should also interview a carer to see what type of work they do on a day-to-day basis. Analyse your findings.

PLTS

Independent enquirer: For this activity, you need to think of a range of questions that will lead to broader responses and give you more in-depth information. This will demonstrate independent enquiry skills.

Day care

This type of care is for people who need care on a daily basis but not in a residential home. They still live in their own home but can access the day care they require to maintain their health. This may involve:

- physiotherapy and occupational therapy services
- visiting a local community day care centre for social reasons
- visits to see health care professionals at hospitals.

The person may also have carers during the day to help with personal care, if they cannot bathe themselves, for example. Each person is assessed, and his or her needs are met on an individual basis.

Nursing care

This is where a person needs more nursing care because they are ill and/or need specialist health care. For example, one person may have had a heart attack and be seriously ill, whereas another may be going to hospital to have a baby. Nursing care covers a wide range of treatment for people of all ages, from Great Ormond Street Hospital where they treat sick children to mental health nurses based in hospitals, GP practices or within community centres, who may need to treat some very elderly patients. Specialist nursing staff include:

- practice nurses
- health visitors
- ward nurses
- occupational health nurses
- midwives
- school nurses
- mental health nurses
- paediatric nurses.

Each of the above nurses work in different settings, with different groups of patients.

Activity 5: Research nursing jobs

Research two different nursing jobs in a hospital setting, and find out about the qualifications they require. Look at how these types of nurses work with their patients and the main job criteria. If you wish, you can research other nursing jobs apart from those listed above. Prepare a Powerpoint presentation to share your information with the class.

Functional skills

ICT: You can demonstrate your ability to develop, present and communicate information by putting together a clear, interesting Powerpoint presentation.

Domiciliary care

The word domiciliary means 'at home' so this is health and social care carried out at home. This may be the person's choice – for example, if they want to give birth at home, or a health visitor is calling to check on a person just released from hospital, or a meal service is being provided for people who cannot cook at home, or a terminally ill person wants to die at home. Again, there is a wide range of nursing services available to suit individual needs.

Activity 6: Research the specific role of a Macmillan nurse

Research the role and responsibilities of a Macmillan nurse in a domiciliary setting.

PLTS

Independent enquirer: You can demonstrate your independent enquiry skills by evaluating the information gathered and analysing its relevance and value.

1.4 Active promotion of equality and individual rights

A good understanding of the key concepts used in health and social care is central to all roles within the sector. Health and social care professionals need to actively promote equality and the rights of individuals, whether they are working in or using services. The word 'Active' emphasises the need to ensure that action is taken on these issues.

The principles of the care value base

These seven principles put the individual at the heart of health and social care provision. These principles form a value base. They are all of equal importance and should form the basis of all your relationships with clients and colleagues.

The seven principles are:

1 the promotion of anti-discriminatory practice

2 the promotion and support of dignity, independence and safety

3 respect for, and acknowledgement of, personal beliefs and an individual's identity

4 the maintenance of confidentiality

5 protection from abuse and harm

6 the promotion of effective communication and relationships

7 the provision of personalised (individual) care.

Together, these principles can be broken down into the following key concepts:

- inclusivity
- participation
- access
- honesty and openness
- trust
- respect
- confidentiality
- safety
- choice.

Promoting the rights, choices and well-being of individuals

If you follow the seven principles of the care values in your everyday work you will automatically be promoting individuals' rights and choices. This has been shown to have a positive impact on people's feelings of well-being and their sense of control over their lives when they may be at a vulnerable stage.

Activity 7: Promoting the individual's rights, choices and well-being

Work together in a group to discuss how you can promote the rights, choices and well-being of people in a health and social care setting. You should look at:

- how to demonstrate equality
- how to show respect
- how to take appropriate action to increase awareness
- how to challenge stereotypes
- how to ensure access to services for all
- how to improve overall quality of service.

Using your findings, arrange a display for an open evening, explaining how you will ensure rights, choices and well-being for all those using the setting. You need to think of questions that will lead to a broad range of responses. You need to think about situations where things don't go according to plan – use 'what if…' questions. Use different sources of information, not just one website or book. Think of unusual circumstances, such as different responses because of religious beliefs, etc.

PLTS

Independent enquirer: This activity may help you demonstrate that you can analyse and evaluate information.

Functional skills

ICT: You can use your ICT skills to find and select information, and research and investigate national initiatives to reduce discriminatory practice.

Anti-discriminatory practice – empowering individuals

By remaining true to the underpinning principles and values of care practice at all times, you will automatically demonstrate anti-discriminatory practice.

However, actively promoting anti-discriminatory practice is another thing entirely. You may need to challenge others who, perhaps inadvertently, discriminate. This can mean challenging colleagues and people using the service about their discriminatory behaviour. This may be a hard thing to do but you need to be prepared to hold on to your care value base and challenge people if necessary. If you do not, you may be drawn into the discrimination yourself. You may need to seek the support of a line manager or other person that you trust straight away if you feel that you cannot challenge the discrimination yourself. Reporting it is in itself challenging the anti-discriminatory practice.

The health and social care profession can empower its staff by encouraging them to promote individual rights, choices and well-being at all times. You can promote empowerment in the people using the service by helping them maintain, regain, or gain independence as far as they are able.

Dealing with tensions and contradictions

In your career in health and social care there will be many tensions and contradictions. There is really only one way for you to cope with this and that is to use your team of colleagues to support you. By asking for help in this way situations are dealt with in a professional manner, you will feel supported and good about yourself and it will encourage the team to work together. If you make use of your colleagues' skills and guidance and follow high-quality professional standards, you will find it easier to make decisions and deal with any tensions that arise.

Did you know?

Many employees feel that poor interpersonal relations are a source of stress at work.

Staff development and training

Health and social care workers, like all professionals, need to keep their training and skills updated so that they can keep up with new ideas and new technology and procedures. In terms of the underpinning values of care practice, health and social care workers need to be familiar with the new legislation and new terms that should be used when working with individuals. Training can be gained from a variety of sources, as shown in Fig 2.3.

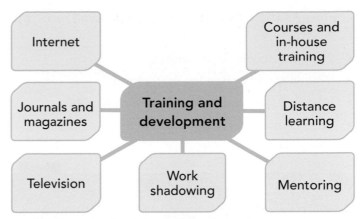

Fig 2.3: Sources of training and development

Practical implications of confidentiality, e.g. recording, reporting, storing and sharing of information

The law and the underpinning values of care practice demand that all health and social care professionals maintain people's confidentiality at all times. Confidentiality refers to all information relating to those using health and social care services and the records associated with them, no matter what format those records are in.

Whenever you are handling information you must:

- respect people's wishes and their privacy
- follow the guidance and procedures of your organisation
- comply with the requirements of the law.

When gathering confidential information you must ensure that:

- only information that is needed is collected
- the data is only used for the purpose for which it was intended
- all records are kept safe and secure
- each workplace has a policy or guidelines for staff to follow.

All this places a huge burden on people concerned with the management of these records. For example:

- Where can paper-based records be stored?
- Who should have access to them?
- How can they be kept secure?
- How long should they be kept?
- What kind of information should be recorded?
- How often do they need to be updated or reviewed?

There are extra concerns for computer-based records such as:

- Who has access to passwords?
- What happens when the system fails?
- Who will carry out the necessary training?
- Who carries out repairs and can they see the information?

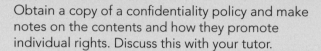

Activity 8: Confidentiality policy

Obtain a copy of a confidentiality policy and make notes on the contents and how they promote individual rights. Discuss this with your tutor.

PLTS

Independent enquirer: You can use your independent enquiry skills to analyse the confidentiality policy, evaluate the information and judge its relevance. What is its value to anti-discrimination and rights?

1.5 Individual rights

Reflect

Re-read the section on 'Rights' (page 54) and keep this in mind as you work through this section.

In health and social care, rights refer to the underpinning principles of care practice. Examples of an individual's rights are to:

- be respected
- be treated equally and not discriminated against
- be treated as an individual
- be treated in a dignified way
- be allowed privacy
- be protected from danger and harm
- be allowed access to information about themselves
- be able to communicate using their preferred method of communication and language
- be cared for in a way that meets their needs

- have their choices taken into account and be protected.

You have covered the above in the 'Terminology' section (pages 52–58). In this section, we will use further activities and case studies to gain a deeper understanding of individual rights.

The right to be respected

All individuals have the basic human right to be respected. Demonstrating respect for the individual is at the core of the health worker's responsibility. Respect is about preserving a person's dignity, core beliefs, choice and privacy, even if someone's choice of treatment does not match your own. A previous example concerned a person with diabetes not accepting their condition and not taking their medicine or controlling their diet. These situations can be very frustrating, as you may feel that it has nothing to do with you if the person is severely ill due to them not accepting their illness but you still have to respect individual choices.

To be able to demonstrate respect you should have:

- good listening and communication skills with the individual
- patience
- acceptance of choices.
- and be non-judgemental

Case study: Women's refuge

Sarah is a support worker in a women's refuge where women come to get away from their abusive partners. Mrs Gee has been in the refuge for a month after being physically abused for almost three years by her partner. One day she tells Sarah that she wants to return to her partner.

1 What do you think Sarah should say to her?
2 How do you think Mrs Gee is likely to react?

The right to be treated equally and not discriminated against

Health and social care professionals work with a wide range of individuals and must take great care that they do not discriminate against anyone.

Case study: Language barrier?

Yasmin is a nurse at a busy hospital. When passing by reception she heard the receptionist, who was obviously annoyed, talking on the phone. She was saying, 'Tell your mother that she needs to clearly understand English before she sets foot in here. Otherwise she will not understand what she is told, unless you fly over from Argentina and help her.'

1 How should Yasmin challenge the receptionist in a professional manner?

2 If Yasmin doesn't feel able to challenge the receptionist herself, what should she do?

The right to be treated as an individual

This is central to the underpinning values of care practice. By recognising and valuing difference, you can treat all people as individuals.

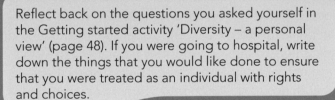

Activity 9: Reflect on your own rights and choices

Reflect back on the questions you asked yourself in the Getting started activity 'Diversity – a personal view' (page 48). If you were going to hospital, write down the things that you would like done to ensure that you were treated as an individual with rights and choices.

The right to be treated in a dignified way

All individuals deserve to be treated in a manner that preserves their dignity and sense of self-worth.

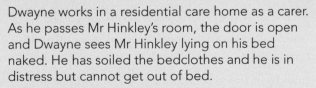

Case study: Distressed person

Dwayne works in a residential care home as a carer. As he passes Mr Hinkley's room, the door is open and Dwayne sees Mr Hinkley lying on his bed naked. He has soiled the bedclothes and he is in distress but cannot get out of bed.

1 What should Dwayne do?

2 How could this type of situation be avoided in future?

The right to be allowed privacy

Privacy is another human right, as long as people are not going to hurt themselves or others. All of us have the right to expect that:

- our treatment and care will be kept private
- no information will be passed to people who have no right to access it (this confirms the right of confidentiality)
- our dignity will be maintained throughout any procedures necessary.

Privacy may not be easy to arrange, especially working in a busy hospital or care centre, but with thought and care it can be achieved.

Why is it important to treat people with respect and allow them privacy?

Have you finished, Mark?

Case study: Patients' privacy

Jennifer works in a hospital as a rheumatologist. As she passed the rheumatology reception desk today, she saw patients' notes laid out on top of the desk with people waiting and no staff present.

1 What should Jennifer do?
2 What steps should she take to make sure this doesn't happen again?

The right to be protected from danger and harm

Everyone working in or using the health and social care sector has the right to be kept safe from danger and harm. To ensure this happens, all settings should have a health and safety policy that sets out the actions, rules and regulations that must be followed to keep staff and those using the service safe and healthy.

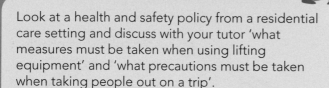

Activity 10: Looking at a health and safety policy

Look at a health and safety policy from a residential care setting and discuss with your tutor 'what measures must be taken when using lifting equipment' and 'what precautions must be taken when taking people out on a trip'.

The right to be allowed access to information about themselves

In accordance with the Freedom of Information Act, and the Data Protection Act, all individuals have the right to see their health records and any information written about them. This means that if you are responsible for a person's health records you must be responsible for:

- keeping their records up to date and in order
- being able to find the information quickly and easily
- enabling colleagues to find information quickly and easily if you are absent
- keeping that person safe and secure.

The right to able to communicate using their preferred methods of communication and language

Every individual has a language they prefer to communicate in. If you went to hospital for treatment, what language would you want to talk in to describe your concerns and ask about what happens next? Is English your first language? If it is, think how you would feel if you went to hospital in another country where the main language was different from yours. How would you feel if the staff didn't speak your language when you got there? How would you feel if they were telling you something serious (you could tell it was serious by their body language, tone and facial expression) but you didn't understand what they were saying? Reflect on this for a while.

Clearly, it is extremely important to ensure that the right language is used in order to ensure that there is good communication between people. However, this can be a strain on health and social care resources. For example, a health authority may find it hard to justify payment for interpreters or translators when there are other things to do which may seem more important. Under the Discrimination Act, there is a rule entitled 'making reasonable adjustments'. This is where an adjustment has to be made to help someone, as long as it is reasonable, and in this case providing a means of communication would be seen as reasonable. This means that if the hospital did not provide a means of communication the person could take them to court and sue them.

Health and social care settings can support communication in other languages by:

- employing staff with different language skills.
- employing staff who speaks the local common language
- buying in the skills of interpreters and translators
- communicating in a variety of formats (e.g. pictures, Braille, leaflets in different languages)
- finding out if the person has a family member who can act as an interpreter.

The right to be cared for in a way that meets their needs

This right includes all those that have been previously discussed.

The right to have their choices taken into account and be protected

The care value base (page 60) refers to choice. Whether it is selecting a certain hospital, care facility or form of treatment, people should have choices that are taken into account by health and social care staff while still ensuring that they are protected.

2 Know discriminatory practices in health and social care

The cause of any discrimination is termed the 'basis of discrimination'. For example, a person may be discriminated against on the basis of their diversity. In this section you will be exploring the different bases on which discrimination can occur.

2.1 Bases of discrimination

As you have already learned, the bases of discrimination are:

- culture
- disability
- age
- social class
- gender
- sexuality
- health status
- family status
- cognitive ability.

You may find it hard to believe that anyone working in health and social care would discriminate against another person on any of these grounds. Unfortunately it does happen, but you also need to be aware of the possibility of discrimination from everyone you encounter when working in health and social care, including those using the services.

As a health and social care professional, it is part of your role to understand the bases of discrimination and to champion diversity and the rights of individuals so that no one suffers because of discrimination.

Culture

A person's culture is important to them and identifies who they are in the world. It is developed within the social group they are raised in, and can change when they are mature enough to decide for themselves what culture best suits them.

In the health and social care profession, respecting a person's culture is important for all concerned. It is important for the individual because it creates a sense of support and understanding, promotes their well-being and can help their health. It is also important to health and social care professionals because they see the benefits of their care value base and this underlines the importance of respecting an individual's culture.

Disabilities

In health and social care, you will work with and support people with various disabilities.

The Disability Discrimination Act (DDA) makes it unlawful to discriminate against someone who has a disability. The act covers employment, access to goods, facilities and services of organisations,

Just checking

1 What are the benefits of diversity in society and the workplace?
2 Describe three discriminatory practices in health and social care.
3 Explain the consequences of the three discriminatory practices described above.
4 Name four national initiatives that promote anti-discriminatory practices in a health and social care setting.
5 What would you do if you heard or saw someone being discriminatory against:
   a another member of staff?
   b someone using the service?
6 How are anti-discriminatory practices promoted in a health and social care setting?
7 How successful have new initiatives been in tackling anti-discriminatory practices?
8 What are your responsibilities when working in a health and social care setting with regard to discrimination?

Assignment tips

1 Ask your tutor for a copy of the unit content sheet, so you can see what you need to include.

2 'Describe' involves saying how and 'explain' involves saying why something happens. If you keep using the word 'because' this will lead you towards achieving the higher grades.

3 Talk to the staff at your placement to gain an understanding of how anti-discriminatory practices are applied in the way care is delivered so you can really see the relevance of what you are learning.

4 Go to the school/college learning centre or to your local library and read journals such as the *British Journal of Nursing*, *Community Care* and *Child Care*.

5 Visit the Equality and Human Rights Commission website (www.equalityhumanrights.com). It is full of useful information and case studies on discrimination. Other good sources of information include the following websites:
- www.direct.gov.uk
- www.dh.gov.uk
- www.nhs.uk

6 Read newspapers and watch the news on television, looking out for any cases of discrimination in health and social care, then research the case further. This will help you explore the issues more deeply, using live stories.

7 Talk to friends and family and ask about their personal experiences of discrimination. If they are willing to share their feelings, you can get a real insight into how it feels to be discriminated against in health and social care.

3 Health, safety and security in health and social care

This unit introduces you to health, safety and security issues in health and social care settings. In the UK health and safety is taken extremely seriously, and we take it for granted that our workplaces will be safe. However, as a practitioner you will have to consider what risks exist, and be able to plan a safe environment. You will need to know what the law requires you to do, and how to carry it out. If you become a manager of a setting, you must make sure that everything possible has been done to keep your staff and the people you care for safe, and that you can prove you have done so.

To be good at health and safety, you need to be creative and innovative, and be able to think ahead and remain calm in an emergency. You will gain a thorough understanding of potential hazards. You will also learn how legislation, policies and procedures work to reduce risk, and the consequences of not following them, both for your safety and your career! You will learn about the health, safety and security responsibilities of employees and employers, and their relevance to you as a student. Finally you will learn how to deal with all sorts of incidents and emergencies that could occur in health and social care settings.

Learning outcomes

After completing this unit you should:

1 understand potential hazards in health and social care
2 know how legislation, policies and procedures promote health, safety and security in health and social care settings
3 be able to implement a risk assessment
4 understand priorities and responses in dealing with incidents and emergencies.

Assessment and grading criteria

This table shows you what you must do in order to achieve a **pass**, **merit** or **distinction** grade, and where you can find activities in this book to help you.

To achieve a **pass** grade, the evidence must show that you are able to:	To achieve a **merit** grade, the evidence must show that, in addition to the pass criteria, you are able to:	To achieve a **distinction** grade, the evidence must show that, in addition to the pass and merit criteria, you are able to:
P1 Explain potential hazards and the harm that may arise from each in a health or social care setting. **See Assessment activity 3.1, page 97** *achieved*		
P2 Outline how legislation, policies and procedures relating to health, safety and security influence health and social care settings. **See Assessment activity 3.2, page 112** *achieved*	**M1** Describe how health and safety legislation, policies and procedures promote the safety of individuals in a health or social care setting. **See Assessment activity 3.2, page 112** *achieved*	
P3 Carry out a risk assessment in a health or social care setting. **See Assessment activity 3.3, page 118** *achieved*	**M2** Assess the hazards identified in the health or social care setting. **See Assessment activity 3.3, page 118** *achieved*	**D1** Make recommendations in relation to identified hazards to minimise the risks to the service user group. **See Assessment activity 3.3, page 118** *achieved*
P4 Explain possible priorities and responses when dealing with two particular incidents or emergencies in a health or social care setting. **See Assessment activity 3.4, page 126** *achieved*	**M3** Discuss health, safety or security concerns arising from a specific incident or emergency in a health or social care setting. **See Assessment activity 3.4, page 126** *achie*	**D2** Justify responses to a particular incident or emergency in a health or social care setting. **See Assessment activity 3.4, page 126** *achieve*

How you will be assessed

This unit will be internally assessed by your tutor. Varied exercises and activities are included to help you understand all aspects of health and safety in health and social care environments, and prepare for the assessment. You will also have the opportunity to work on some case studies to further your understanding.

Jodie, 17 years old

I knew this was an important unit before I started the course. My gran nearly died last year. She was in hospital following a car accident. She had been taking antibiotics for a chest infection and caught *Clostridium difficile*. She was so ill and dehydrated. There were three other people on her ward with the same infection, so it must have been spread by poor hygiene.

My tutor went through lots of potential hazards in all different care settings, so when I came to write my report I had loads of ideas.

She really made me realise how health and safety legislation can be used to maintain standards, and what can happen to care providers who cut corners in health and safety. It really made me think, if I don't practise good health and safety it could be my career on the line!

Carrying out the risk assessment helped me to realise that you can reduce the chance of mishaps by thinking ahead.

I loved the last task, as we did a first-aid course and discussed all sorts of other crisis situations. Then we did a role-play, which we videoed.

I got a distinction overall, which made me really proud!

Over to you!

1 Why do you think health and safety is so important in health and social care?

2 How are you going to get to grips with understanding and implementing legisation?

3 What do you think is the most effective way of approaching the risk assessment?

Ben Jago
Health and social care student

I am in my second year of the BTEC National Diploma in Health and Social Care. I have been attending my final placement at Little Acorns Day Nursery and they asked me to plan an activity afternoon for the six children aged 4 to 5 years on the theme of 'Summer Holidays'. They will all be leaving for primary school at the end of the summer term.

The nursery is across the road from the beach and I had loads of ideas buzzing round my head, thinking of picnics, sand, sea, and sun. I wanted to do something out of the ordinary. My main concern was how to achieve this without putting any of the children in danger.

Fran, my supervisor, sat down with me to do the risk assessment. She let me do it and then gave suggestions to improve it, which I found a great learning experience.

I wanted to take them onto the beach looking at rock pools.

I wrote a letter to all the parents to get their permission. The day arrived, and we had some very excited children. Fran let me take charge, but of course she was there in case I forgot anything, or anything went wrong.

The children really enjoyed themselves. They were so fascinated by the creatures hidden under the rocks none of them even thought about wandering off. But I was glad I had thought of all the possible dangers beforehand, as it made it less stressful.

Think about it!

1 Identify all the hazards that would exist in a trip of this nature.

2 What is the potential severity of each of the hazards you have identified? Could they potentially lead to death or serious injury, or are they only likely to lead to cuts and bruises? Score them according to a scale where 5 is serious and 1 is minor.

3 How likely is it that these hazards will lead to injury, illness or an incident? Score the likelihood according to a scale where 5 is very likely and 1 is very unlikely.

4 Make a list of precautions you would take to reduce the risk of the hazards causing harm.

Assessment activity 3.1

In this activity, you need to explain potential hazards and the harm that may arise from each in a health or social care setting.

Ideally you should base this on a real care setting, gathering information through a visit or when on a placement. If this is not feasible, you could base your answer on the following scenario.

Riverglade House is a small residential care home for ten older people, all of whom have some impairment. Some have dementia, meaning that they are confused and forgetful. Some have arthritis, making it difficult for them to move around independently. Some have had a stroke, meaning they have poor sensation in the affected side of their body.

Riverglade House is a converted Victorian house in large grounds on a main road.

Taking into consideration the building, situation and

residents, identify as many hazards as you can for residents, staff and visitors to the home. Include health hazards, safety hazards and security hazards. Explain the harm that could result from each hazard you have identified.

Grading tip

P1 'Explain' means state what the hazards are, the harm that might occur and how or why the hazards might cause harm.

To achieve P1, you must provide evidence for at least six hazards, relating the hazards to the abilities and limitations of the group you are basing your answer on.

You will find it helpful to read the section following this activity.

PLTS

Independent enquirer: Visit a care setting and investigate actual hazards for the individuals. This will give you a much better understanding of the topic.

Creative thinker: Discuss the hazards with someone at the setting and incorporate their thoughts and your own.

Self-manager: Take the initiative to contact a care setting yourself to arrange a visit.

Effective participator: Make suggestions to minimise the risk of harm.

Community settings

Community settings are potentially among the most hazardous of all care environments, as it is almost impossible to have much control over health and safety.

The health and safety of community care workers is given a high priority. For example, moving and handling equipment can be provided for use in private houses. Staff have the right to be safe, so they can refuse to carry out tasks if the necessary equipment, such as a hoist, is not provided.

People receiving care in their own home may be offered advice on health and safety (including removing mats, which can be a trip hazard, and having

safety equipment fitted, such as a raised toilet seat) but you can't force people to make changes.

Community care workers also need to consider how to manage security for people who are unable to get to the door. Years ago it was not uncommon to leave front doors unlocked all day, and sometimes all night, or to leave a key hanging on a string inside the letterbox. Obviously neither of these would be acceptable today. Finding the right balance between security and safety requires careful thought.

Another risk to lone workers (such as home care assistants, social workers, community nurses, GPs and health visitors) is their vulnerability to attack by aggressive clients or by members of the public when out working in the community. Staff are often required to work unsocial hours, including evenings and nights. Social workers may have to take children into foster care, and this is often a highly distressing experience for parents, children and social workers. Home care staff sometimes visit on foot and may have regular patterns of visits, making them vulnerable targets for attack. Workers have to consider their own safety when travelling between assignments, particularly at night. In May 2009 it was announced that community healthcare workers would be issued with security alarms that link directly to a call centre, which can pinpoint each worker's location.

Just checking

1 What is the difference between 'hazard' and 'risk'?
2 Who is responsible for health and safety in a care setting?
3 What might the consequences for a care provider be if health and safety law is breached?
4 Which organisations can provide advice on health and safety topics?
5 How can care workers reduce the risk of harm to themselves and the people they care for?
6 How can employers make sure that employees work to high standards of health and safety?
7 What is the Independent Safeguarding Authority's Vetting and Barring Scheme?
8 Why has the introduction of legislation, policies and procedures improved health and safety standards over the years?
9 What is meant by personal protective equipment and how does this reduce harm?
10 Give an example of unintentional abuse.

edexcel :::

Assigment tips

1 Ask your tutor for a copy of the unit content sheet, so you can see what you need to include.

2 Take note of the verbs in each task. 'Describe' involves saying how, and 'explain' involves saying why something happens. If you keep using the word 'because' this will help you achieve the higher grades.

3 Make use of the staff at your placement to gain an understanding of how health and safety applies to the way care is delivered so you can really see the relevance of the theory.

4 Show your placement supervisor the assignment brief so s/he is aware of the tasks you need to complete, particularly the risk assessment.

5 Remember to bring learning gained at the beginning of the unit into the answers to the later tasks. For example, you need to ensure that recommendations in the risk assessment reflect legal and organisational requirements, especially if you are aiming for the distinction grade.

6 Your justification for your responses to incidents/emergencies for LO4 must explain how your response would result in a successful outcome.

4 Development through the life stages

This unit is about understanding the way we change over time. It explores the course of human development and the range of genetic, biological and social factors that influence how your life turns out. You will investigate the major events which affect people throughout their lifetimes and look at the effects of ageing, and theories about it.

You will need to think creatively about some very deep questions. Will you have a fixed life course where you can predict much of what will happen to you? How can people with genetic conditions be helped? And how far is your life fixed for you, by your genetic inheritance, or by the social and economic environment you grow up in?

You will also need to consider the ageing process. How and why do we age? What does it take to ensure a long and happy old age? And how can health and social care provision provide opportunities for older people to remain as active as they wish?

Learning outcomes

After completing this unit, you should:

1 know the stages of growth and development throughout the human lifespan

2 understand the potential effects of life factors and events on the development of the individual

3 understand physical and psychological changes of ageing.

Assessment and grading criteria

This table shows you what you must do in order to achieve a **pass**, **merit** or **distinction** grade, and where you can find activities in this book to help you.

To achieve a **pass** grade the evidence must show that you are able to:	To achieve a **merit** grade the evidence must show that, in addition to the pass criteria, you are able to:	To achieve a **distinction** grade the evidence must show that, in addition to the pass and merit criteria, you are able to:
P1 Describe physical, intellectual, emotional and social development for each of the life stages of an individual **See Assessment activity 4.1, page 145** *achieved*	**M1** Discuss the nature-nurture debate in relation to the development of an individual **See Assessment activity 4.1, page 145** *achve*	**D1** Evaluate how nature and nurture may affect the physical, intellectual, emotional and social development for two stages of the development of an individual **See Assessment activity 4.1, page 145** *achvee*
P2 Explain the potential effects of five different life factors, on the development of an individual **See Assessment activity 4.2, page 162** *achieved*		
P3 Explain the influences of two predictable and two unpredictable major life events on the development of the individual **See Assessment activity 4.2, page 162** *achieved*		
P4 Explain two theories of ageing **See Assessment activity 4.3, page 171** *achieved*	**M2** Discuss two major theories of ageing in relation to the development of the individual **See Assessment activity 4.3, page 171** *achieved*	**D2** Evaluate the influence of two major theories of ageing on health and social care provision **See Assessment activity 4.3, page 171** *achieved*
P5 Explain the physical and psychological changes which may be associated with ageing **See Assessment activity 4.3, page 171** *achved*	**M3** Discuss the effects on self esteem and self confidence, of the physical changes associated with ageing **See Assessment activity 4.3, page 171** *achved*	

1.1 Life stages

The human lifespan has been described in terms of life stages for centuries. The life stages are listed in Table 4.1. The age ranges of some life stages are defined by social criteria. However, the age ranges for certain stages can vary depending on the expert who is describing it.

Table 4.1: Life stages

Life stage	Age	Key features
Conception	9 months before birth	Egg and sperm fuse after sexual intercourse and create a new living being
Pregnancy (gestation)	9 months to birth	Physical development of embryo and foetus
Birth and infancy	0–3 years	Attachment to carers
Childhood	4–9 years	First experience of education
Adolescence	10–18 years	Identification with peer group – puberty takes place during this period
Adulthood	18–65 years	The right to vote, and manage one's own financial affairs, happens at 18
Older adulthood	65 years onwards	65 is the current age when men (and women born after 6 April 1955) receive a state pension
Final stages of life	Variable	Physical 'decline'

Life expectancy

Social Trends (2009) states that boys born in 2006 can expect to live to 77 while girls born in 2006 can expect to live to 82 years of age. So **life expectancy** at birth is 77 for males and 82 for females. Life expectancy at birth is an average, not some kind of limit. As you grow older there is more chance that you might live longer than the average expected life at birth. A man who has already reached the age of 65 is expected, on average, to live until the age of 82 while a woman who has lived to be 65 is expected to live until the age of 85. So the life expectancy of a man who is already 65 is a further 17 years and the life expectancy of a woman of 65 is a further 20 years.

Can you map your 'life course

A life course describes the path of the Stages such as infancy, childhood and can be described alongside the socia expectations associated with different life course.

In the past many experts assumed tha **life course** would be controlled by bi and development progress until adul reproduce. As people get older a pro decline sets in and continues until the This view of the life course can be de 'springboard theory'.

In the past people often assumed tha have similar experiences of the life co at the beginning of this unit provides people's expectations.

Reflect

Do you think that there is a 'best age to every period of life be the best time in

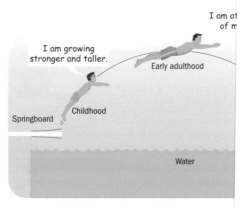

I am growing stronger and taller.

I am at of m

Early adulthood

Childhood

Springboard

Water

Fig. 4.2: The 'springboard' model of the

How you will be assessed

In this unit you will be assessed through written work. You will be given an assignment which will require you to develop a fact file. Your fact file will contain a wide range of material about the human lifespan, life factors and the effects of ageing. Your file may focus on imagining the development of an individual person. Guidance is included throughout this unit to help you prepare your work.

Kiara, 17 years old

At first I thought – 'oh there's so much to learn for this unit', but my tutor helped me to see how stages of development work. To begin with I set up a fact file to contain information on life stages. Then I chose to study the biography of a famous tennis player. This gave me lots of information about a real person's life experiences. I focused on adolescence and adulthood and explored the nature–nurture debate in order to write my own conclusions about intellectual, emotional and social development.

For the second assignment I had to work out how five life factors may have influenced the famous person's adolescence and adulthood. I also had to explain the influence of two predictable and unpredictable life events. At first this seemed complicated but it all clicked into place for me when we discussed the idea of holistic development. I realised that you have to step back and see the big picture and not get tripped up with all the detail.

For the third assignment I explained disengagement and activity theory and went on to discuss how my celebrity would keep an interest in tennis after he was unable to carry on playing. I looked at ways in which care workers could help to support someone like my celebrity. I also had to imagine the effects of physical and psychological changes on the person as they became older. I was careful not to think that later life is always unpleasant and has to involve withdrawing from life. The person I studied had faced great challenges in order to become successful and I realised that they might find ways of coping with the problems of later life. I said it was possible that my person would maintain a high level of self-esteem and confidence because of their previous life.

Over to you!

1   What do you think it takes to become famous? Can anyone become anything that they want to be – what are the limitations?

2   Do things always get worse for people as they grow old?

3   Which sections of this unit do you think will help you to answer these questions?

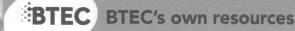

1 Know the stages of growth and developm... throughout the human lifespan

Get started

Life stories

What do you think? Can someone become successful and famous just ... they want to? Do you believe that people become important and succe... because they are born to do well? How far does success and fame dep... upbringing and your opportunities? What does later life hold for peop... will help you to explore and make sense of individual people's life stori...

Case study: An interview with John

Talking to John now:

John: It makes me laugh looking back at my old school work. When you're only 10 you don't have much idea of life. I got some of it right. I did start delivering milk and I did get married in my twenties, but I ended up having loads of different jobs and have been divorced twice.

Interviewer: So you would say you can't predict your life course?

John: Well, life throws you lots of challenges – things don't always work out like you want them to. I worked for lots of companies but they went out of business and I had to retrain to do different jobs. Nowadays I work in IT – in 1960 there wasn't any information technology. As the world changes you have to change too.

Interviewer: Would you say that there is no such thing as a life course?

John: No, you do change as you get older, and some things you can predict. I mean, I'm just not fit enough to play football any more – too many aches and pains – your body does let you down as you get older. But I think if you've got a dream, something you really want to do – well you just might achieve your dream eventually. For instance I'm really happy now – good job, happy family – everything is going great, but I had a lot of setbacks along the way.

John had a clear idea of his life course w... he was 10, but his life experiences did n... a straightforward pattern.

Fig. 4.1: John's school book from 1960

My life in the future

I will finish with school w...
When I get out of school ...
the milk rounds like my ...
am 17 I will meet a girl ...
will get married. Then I w...
I will play football at the ...
When I am 50 I can st...
watch TV all day. By then ...
too go on holiday to the moon ...
be so old to go on holiday
any more.

1. Do you think John is unusual in no... a straightforward life story?

2. Why is it difficult to predict what ... in your life?

3. How far can you choose how your ... out?

Intellectual development

We do not simply learn more as we grow older – we also develop more useful ways of thinking. Piaget (1896–1980) was a famous theorist who studied how our ability to think and reason develops. Piaget believed that there were four stages of intellectual development which mature or 'unfold'. In his theory, infants and children learn from experience, but the ability to think logically depends on an underlying process. A 4-year-old cannot use abstract logic because they are not mature enough to think this way (no matter how well they are taught).

Nowadays, research suggests that infants are more able to understand their world than Piaget thought. It also appears that most people take a lot longer than 11 years to become skilled at **abstract logical thinking**. Your ability to use formal logical thought may depend on how much encouragement you have received to think logically. The ability to use formal

Key terms

Concrete logical thinking – the ability to solve problems providing you can see or physically handle the issues involved.

Abstract logical thinking – the ability to solve problems using imagination, without having to be involved practically; an advanced form of thinking that does not always need a practical context in order to take place.

logic may not be part of a process of maturation – it might depend on your education.

Piaget's theory stops in adolescence but many theorists believe that adults continue to improve their thinking ability. Some psychologists suggest that there is a 'post-formal operations' stage of thinking where adults become more skilled in their ability to make flexible judgements. It may be that many adults develop an ability that could be called 'wisdom' as they grow older.

Table 4.3: Piaget's stages of development

The sensorimotor stage: birth to 1½ or 2 years   Learning to use senses and muscles – thinking without language
• Babies are born with the ability to sense objects.
• Babies are also born with a range of reflexes such as the sucking reflex to enable them to feed. These reflexes lead to 'motor actions' controlling body muscles.
• The sensorimotor stage is a stage when thinking is limited to sensing objects and performing motor actions.
• Piaget believed that a baby would not have a working system for remembering and thinking about the world until they were about 18 months old.

The pre-operational stage: 2–7 years   Pre-logical thinking – thinking in language but without understanding logic
• Pre-operational means pre-logical; during this stage Piaget believed that children could not think in a logical way. Children can use words to communicate but they do not understand the logical implications involved in language.
• Piaget explained that pre-operational children cannot properly understand how ideas like number, mass and volume really work. A child might be able to count to 10 but might not understand what the number 10 really means. For example, in the case of 10 buttons stretched out in a line and the same number of buttons in a pile, a young child might agree that there are 10 buttons in the line and 10 buttons in the pile, but then they might say that there are more buttons in the line because it is longer!

The concrete operational stage: 7–11 years   A stage where logical thinking is limited to practical situations
• Children in the concrete operations stage can think logically provided the issues are 'down to earth' or concrete. In the concrete operational stage children may be able to understand simple logical puzzles.
• For example, if you ask a question such as 'Samira is taller than Corrine, but Samira is smaller than Leslie so who is the tallest?' you might find that the 7- or 8-year-old has difficulty in mentally imagining the information in a way that will enable them to answer the question. But if the child can see a picture of Samira, Corrine and Leslie they might quickly point out who is the tallest.

The formal operational stage: from 11+ years   Thinking using logic and abstract thought processes – adult thinking
• With formal logical reasoning, an adult can solve complex problems in their head.
• Formal logical operations enable adolescents and adults to use abstract concepts and theories in order to be able to gain an understanding of the world beyond their own experiences.
• Adults with formal operations can think scientifically. For example, an adult can use formal logic to reason why a car won't start. They can work out that perhaps the car won't start because the fuel is not getting to the engine or because there is insufficient air or an electrical fault; each theory can be tested in turn until the problem is solved.
• Abstract thinking enables us to think through complicated ideas in our head without having to see the concrete pictures.

Language development

Both Noam Chomsky (1959) and Steven Pinker (1994) believe that the ability to develop a signed or spoken language is genetically programmed into us. Chomsky states that we are born with a 'language acquisition device' that enables us to recognise and develop languages that we experience. Children do develop language extremely rapidly and it is likely that the ability to use language is genetically programmed in the same way as our ability to stand and walk. The ability to use language develops because of maturation – it is an unfolding of our biological potential. We need to experience other people using language but we do not need to be trained in order to speak.

Some children will develop speech much more rapidly than others. Just because language development involves a maturation process, it does not mean that every child will develop at the same rate. Language development is outlined in Table 4.4.

Activity 3: 'Learning languages' discussion

Get together with other course members and discuss how quickly you learned to speak when you were young. Compare this with your experience of trying to learn a second language in school. Reflect on how far personal experiences can be explained in terms of a genetic basis for first language.

PLTS

Independent enquirer: This activity may help you to evidence independent enquirer skills by exploring issues from different perspectives. It may also contribute towards team worker and effective participator skills.

Table 4.4: The development of language

Age	The development of language
Around 3 months	Infants begin to make babbling noises as they learn to control the muscles associated with speech.
Around 12 months	Infants begin to imitate sounds made by carers such as 'da-da'; this develops into the use of single words.
Around 2 years	Infants begin to make two-word statements such as 'cat goed' (meaning the cat has gone away). The infant begins to build their vocabulary (knowledge of words).
Around 3 years	Children begin to make simple sentences such as 'I want drink'. This develops into the ability to ask questions, 'When we go?' Knowledge of words (vocabulary) grows very rapidly.
Around 4 years	Children begin to use clear sentences that can be understood by strangers. Children can be expected to make some mistakes with grammar 'We met lots of peoples at the shops today'.
5 years onwards	Children can speak using full adult grammar. Although vocabulary will continue to grow, and formal grammar will continue to improve, most children can be expected to use language effectively by age 5.

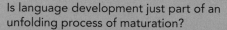

Is language development just part of an unfolding process of maturation?

Activity 4: Observing speech

Visit a playgroup, nursery or household where you can observe some young children. Listen to the way that they speak and make notes of some examples of one or two word utterances or phrases that you hear. Later, get together and discuss your examples with other course members. Can you identify a general pattern in the way children develop language? Can you identify ways in which individual children develop differently?

Social development

There are great differences and cultural variations in the way individuals will experience social relationships during the course of their life. Some generalisations are listed in Table 4.5.

PLTS

Independent enquirer: This activity will enable you to demonstrate independent enquiry skills by carrying out research and analysing information.

Table 4.5: Key aspects of social development

Life stage	Social development
Infancy 0–3 years	**Interacting with carers** Infants appear to have an in-built tendency to interact with carers. By 2 months they may start to smile at human faces. At 3 months they will respond when adults talk. At 5 months infants can distinguish between familiar and unfamiliar people. Infants make their first relationships as they form an emotional attachment to carers. In the later stages of infancy, infants will play alongside other children (parallel play).
Childhood 4–9 years	**First social learning** Young children are emotionally attached and dependent on the adults that care for them. Children begin to learn social roles and behaviour within their family context. This is called first or primary socialisation. A family environment might provide a 'safe base' from which to explore social relationships with other children through play. Children will learn to co-operate with other children (co-operative play). As children grow older they will become increasingly independent and begin to form friendships based on a sense of mutual trust. Friendships become increasingly important as children grow towards adolescence. Children may begin to form social networks or 'circles' of friends who like and agree with each other.
Adolescence 10–18 years	**Secondary social learning** During adolescence a person's sense of self-worth may be more influenced by other adolescents than by the family. Adolescents will copy the styles of dress, beliefs, cultural values and behaviours of their own network of friends. Historically, adolescence was seen as a time of 'storm and stress'. Adolescents have to cope with the development of their own sexuality (the impact of sex hormones at puberty) and the social transition to full independence from the family. Recent research suggests that many adolescents experience a smooth transition to adult roles without serious conflict with parents.
Adulthood 19–65 years	During early adulthood, friendship networks continue to be very important. For most people, early adulthood is dominated by the formation of adult sexual partnerships and by the need to find employment/establish a career. For many people marriage and parenthood represent major social developments in their life. Many adults in their forties and fifties experience time pressures that may limit their social activity. Mature adults may have to split their time between work, care of parents, other family commitments and wider social activities. Some mature adults report a reduction in the amount of social activity due to these pressures.
Older adulthood 65+ years	Following retirement, older adults have more free time. However, many older adults may choose to increase their involvement with close friends and family rather than extend their network of social contacts. See page 170 for further details.

Activity 5: Discussing adolescence

Fifty years ago adolescence was often seen as a time of 'storm and stress' where young people would automatically find themselves in conflict with (or rebel against) their parents and older people. Organise a discussion with other course members to decide how far this idea is still true today and what may have changed since the 1960s. Record your conclusions for incorporation into information sheets on lifespan development.

Functional skills

English: In discussing the changes in social development, you will develop your speaking and listening skills and skills of presenting arguments and listening to others. Recording your conclusions will develop your writing skills.

Emotional development

The way we understand and feel about ourselves and other people develops as we grow older. Some key features of emotional development associated with life stages are set out in Table 4.6.

Table 4.6: Key features of emotional development

Life stage	Emotional development
Infancy 0–3 years	**Attachment** Bowlby (1953) argued that infants have an in-built need to form an attachment with a carer. The quality of this attachment may affect emotional development for the rest of the child's life. Ainsworth et al (1978) and Marris (1996) argue that the quality of our early attachment influences the assumptions we make about our self and others. Infants who are securely attached will grow up with the emotional resources needed to cope with uncertainty in life. Infants who are insecurely attached may have a reduced ability to cope with stress and major life events.
Childhood 4–9 years	**Understanding self and others** Children use their imagination to begin to understand the social roles that other people play. Children begin to imagine a 'me' – an idea of self. Relationships with other family members may influence how a child feels valued – a sense of self-worth. The way a child gets on with teachers and friends may influence their self-confidence. The child might develop a permanent sense of confidence or a sense of failure and inferiority.
Adolescence 10–18 years	**Identity** During adolescence this sense of self continues to develop. An adolescent needs to develop a secure sense of identity. Identity theory was first proposed by Erikson (1963). A person needs a clear understanding of identity in order to feel secure when working with other people or in order to make a loving sexual attachment. This may be a stressful time as self-esteem may depend on the development of identity.
Adulthood 19–65 years	**Intimacy** Erikson argued that the key task of early adulthood was learning to cope with emotional attachment to a sexual partner. This may involve not being too self-centred or defensive and not becoming emotionally isolated. **Staying involved** Later on adults may face a risk of emotional 'stagnation' when they lose interest in social issues. According to Erikson, the developmental task is to stay emotionally involved with social life.
Older adulthood 65+ years	**Making sense of your life** Erikson argued that older people need to develop a secure sense of self that enables them to cope with the physical changes associated with ageing and death. People who fail to make sense of their life might experience emotional despair.

actively involved with social activities as they become older. You might like to consider the role of continuity (how important it will be for your celebrity to keep their interests) when you discuss disengagement and activity theory.

M3 To achieve M3 you will need to discuss how these changes could affect your celebrity's self-esteem and self-confidence.

D2 To achieve D2 you should evaluate how theories of ageing influence health and social care provision. If your celebrity was being supported at home or in care would they be supported to maintain continuity with their past? Would they be expected to withdraw, or would they be encouraged to remain active in order to prevent excessive disengagement?

Resources and further reading

Atchley, R.C (1989) 'A continuity theory of normal aging', *The Gerontologist, 29*,183–190

Ainsworth, M.D.S., Blehar, M. C., Walter, E., Wall, S. (1978) *Patterns of Attachment: A Psychological Study of the Strange Situation* New Jersey: Lawrence Erlbaum Associates Inc.

Berryman, J.C., Hargreaves, D., Herbert, M., Taylor, A. (1991) *Developmental Psychology and You* London: Routledge

Bowlby, J. (1953) *Childcare and the Growth of Love* Harmondsworth: Pelican

Bromley, D.B. (1966) *The Psychology of Human Ageing* Harmondsworth: Penguin

Bromley, D.B. (1974) *The Psychology of Human Ageing,* second ed. Harmondsworth: Penguin

Chomsky, N. (1959) Review of Skinner's *Verbal Behaviour, Language,* 35, 26–58.

Coleman, P. (1994) 'Reminiscence within the study of ageing: the social significance of story', in Bornat, J. (1994) *Reminiscence Reviewed* Buckingham: OUP

Cumming, E. (1975) 'Engagement with an old theory' *International Journal of Ageing and Human Development*, 6, 187–191

Cumming, E., Henry, W.E. (1961) *Growing Old* New York: Basic Books

Erikson, E.H. (1963) *Childhood and Society,* second ed. New York: Norton.

Havighurst, R.J. (1972) *Developmental Tasks and Education,* third ed. New York: David McKay

Heim, A. (1990) *Where Did I Put my Spectacles?* Cambridge: Allborough Press

Levinson, D.J., Darrow, D.N., Klein, E.B., Levinson, M.H., McKee, B. (1978) *The Seasons of a Man's Life* New York: A. A. Knopf

Marris, P. (1996) *The Politics of Uncertainty* London: Routledge.

Paxton, W., Dixon, M. (2004) *The State of the Nation – an Audit of Injustice in the UK* London: Institute for Policy Research

Pinker, S. (1994) *The Language Instinct* London: Penguin

Sugarman, L. (1986) *Life-Span Development* London & New York: Methuen

Sugarman, L. (2001) *Life-Span Development* 2nd Edition Hove & New York: Psychology Press

Social Trends, Vol. 34 (2004) London: HMSO

Social Trends, Vol. 39 (2009) London: HMSO

Unleashing Aspiration (July 2009) Report of the Panel on fair Access to the Professions Cabinet Office: London www.cabinetoffice.gov.uk/accessprofessions

Walters, R. (2009) *Crime is in the air: air pollution and regulation in the UK* Centre for Crime and Justice Studies Kings College London. www.crimeandjustice.org.uk.

Zimbardo, P.G. (1992) *Psychology and Life* London: HarperCollins

Useful websites

Institute for Public Policy Research www.ippr.org

National Statistics www.statistics.gov.uk

The Food Standards Agency www.eatwell.gov.uk

The Poverty site www.poverty.org.uk

Kayla works at a day centre for older people. About 20 people attend the day centre each day, although most members only come twice a week. The centre offers a range of activities including artwork on Thursdays, keep fit exercises, music and discussion groups. Many members enjoy taking part in reminiscence sessions where a volunteer will bring in old photographs from 40 or 50 years ago and ask members to talk about their memories of that time.

Kayla is talking with the centre manager at the end of the day after the members have gone home. She is concerned about Mary who refused to join in discussion with other day centre members.

Kayla: I enjoyed that reminiscence session. Some of the members had so much to say, you could tell they were really enjoying it too, but I can't understand why Mary wouldn't join the discussion. I invited her to but she refused. She said: 'Wait till you're my age my girl, then you'll know how it feels to be old. I don't want to do the things younger people do, I just want peace and quiet'. The other members enjoyed talking, so why is Mary so difficult?

Manager: Mary isn't being difficult. It's her choice to join in or not. It would be against our code of practice to try and make her.

Kayla: I understand that we must respect people's choices but wouldn't Mary be happier in the long run if we could find a way to help her to be more active?

Manager: Perhaps not. You have to try and imagine Mary's point of view. She's not used to taking part in group discussions. She does like doing art on Thursdays though, so perhaps individual art work is more right for her?

Think about it!

1 Can you identify the theory of ageing that describes the way Kayla thinks?
2 Why might Mary think that discussion groups are not appropriate for her?
3 How would disengagement theory explain Mary's behaviour?
4 Can you describe how continuity theory explains Mary's behaviour differently?
5 How could Kayla have talked with Mary in order to find out what Mary would enjoy doing at the day centre?

Just checking

1 It can be argued that children develop language through a process of maturation. What does this statement mean?
2 Are people biologically programmed to grow to be a certain height, no matter what?
3 If you have a genetically inherited disease, does that mean that nothing can be done to help you?
4 If you knew everything about a new born baby's genetic inheritance and her current environment, would it be possible to accurately predict her life course?
5 Some older people have difficulty with walking and moving around the home. Can you describe two possible reasons for these difficulties?
6 Do the physical changes associated with ageing force all older people to lose confidence and self-esteem?
7 Should older people be made to be more active in order to prevent excessive disengagement?

edexcel

Assignment tips

1 When you choose a famous person to study remember to 'keep it real'. You will need to find somebody who has made details of their life story public. You can use your imagination about general issues: for example you could speculate about the way in which nature and nurture might affect people, but you should not choose your favourite star and then make up a story about them. You must be careful not to write things that could be seen as unfair, judgemental or offensive about real people. Celebrities have human rights too!

2 You could construct a grid or chart listing the main issues associated with the five life factors. You can then think about the information you have collected about your celebrity while looking at your grid. It may help you think creatively about ways in which life factors interact within a real person's story.

3 Within your fact file you could emphasise that different people experience different problems as they grow older. It could be interesting to plan an article which starts with the question 'Does physical ageing always make life unpleasant for older people?' You could identify the problems that your celebrity may face as an older person, and also ways in which older people can adapt successfully to the changes age brings. No one knows what will happen to your celebrity in the future, so you could leave your fact file with an open ending.

5 Anatomy and physiology for health and social care

If you are studying for a career in health and social care, you need to have a basic knowledge of where organs are in the body and how they do their jobs. You must have this knowledge to ensure the safety of those you are caring for, and also to maintain your own health and well-being – because you cannot give good care to others if you cannot look after yourself!

This unit explains the basic anatomy and physiology of the human body before moving on to look at selected body systems. The body is made of billions of cells and, after looking at the structure and functioning of cells, you will discover how these work together, managing the energy we use. You will also learn how other body systems are controlled – for example, how your body temperature remains the same, whether you are sunning yourself in summer or shivering in a winter snowstorm.

This unit provides a basic understanding of human physiology that underpins the specialist physiology units. It also provides an overview of body functioning that is valuable for anyone working in health and social care.

Learning outcomes

After completing this unit, you should:

1   know the organisation of the human body
2   understand the functioning of the body systems associated with energy metabolism
3   understand how homeostatic mechanisms operate in the maintenance of an internal environment
4   be able to interpret data obtained from monitoring routine activities with reference to the functioning of healthy body systems.

Assessment and grading criteria

This table shows you what you must do in order to achieve a **pass**, **merit** or **distinction** grade, and where you can find activities in this book to help you.

To achieve a pass grade, the evidence must show that you are able to:	To achieve a merit grade, the evidence must show that, in addition to the pass criteria, you are able to:	To achieve a distinction grade, the evidence must show that, in addition to the pass and merit criteria, you are able to:
P1 Outline the functions of the main cell components **See Assessment activity 5.1, page 183** *achieved*		
P2 Outline the structure of the main tissues of the body **See Assessment activity 5.2, page 191** *achieved*		
P3 Outline the gross structure of all the main body systems **See Assessment activity 5.3, page 197** *achieved*		
P4 Explain the physiology of two named body systems in relation to energy metabolism in the body **See Assessment activity 5.4, page 216** *achieved*	**M1** Discuss the role of energy in the body. **See Assessment activity 5.4, page 216** *achieved*	**D1** Analyse how two body systems interrelate with each other to perform a named function/functions. **See Assessment activity 5.4, page 216** *achieved*
P5 Explain the concept of homeostasis with reference to the control of heart rate, breathing rate, body temperature and blood glucose levels **See Assessment activity 5.5, page 235** *achieved*	**M2** Discuss the probable homeostatic responses to changes in the internal environment during exercise. **See Assessment activity 5.5, page 235** *achieved*	**D2** Evaluate the importance of homeostasis in maintaining the healthy functioning of the body. **See Assessment activity 5.5, page 235** *achieved*
P6 Follow guidelines to interpret collected data for heart rate, breathing rate and temperature before and after a standard period of exercise. **See Assessment activity 5.5, page 235** *achieved*	**M3** Present data collected before and after a standard period of exercise with reference to validity. **See Assessment activity 5.5, page 235** *achieved*	

Distinction

How you will be assessed

This unit is internally assessed by your tutor. Various activities, exercises and scenarios have been included to assist you with studying different aspects of anatomy and physiology and in preparation for assessment.

Mia, 17 years old

At school, I wasn't really into science although I did know it was important to pass my GCSE because of all the nagging from my parents. There seemed to be so many bits to it, and it was really difficult to see how it fitted together. Uncle Pete hadn't been well that year. He was losing a lot of weight and his skin turned a yellowy-brown and the whites of his eyes went yellow. I was really worried about him and went to see him a lot. My Mum told me that he had jaundice and was very ill. He died later, only 44 years old – I really miss him, he always made me smile.

After the funeral, I wanted to know what exactly had been the matter with Pete. My mum showed me the death certificate, which said that Pete had died from cancer of the pancreas – I had only a vague memory of the pancreas and had no idea what it did. The family expected me to know more just because I am now studying Health and Social Care. I realise that it is important to have an understanding of the human body, even for everyday life. After doing this unit, I know more about the pancreas but am still not sure about the skin. It is more interesting to focus on one branch of science now. I think I will write about Uncle Pete in Physiological Disorders next year and I *will* find out about yellow skin.

Over to you!

1   How good is your understanding of the human body?

2   Which parts of this unit do you think you will enjoy the most?

3   How does the unit relate to your life and what you would like to do in the future?

1 Know the organisation of the human body

Get started

Build on what you know!

In small groups, make a list of the human body systems that you already know about (on a large sheet of paper), and the organs associated with each system. Using your list, write down all the functions of each system that you can think of. If you bounce ideas off other members of your group, you will be surprised at how much knowledge you can collect.

Each group can then share their list with the rest of the class.

1.1 Organisation of the body

Every individual is composed of billions of microscopic units called **cells**. The cells carry out vast numbers of chemical reactions and processes that make up the essence of life itself.

Cells rarely exist in isolation; they are usually grouped together with other similar cells carrying out particular tasks. Groups of cells are known as tissues.

Different types of tissues are commonly grouped together to form an organ, which carries out a particular function.

Finally, groups of organs that are responsible for major tasks or functions in the body are called organ systems or sometimes body systems.

Activity 1: Sorting out

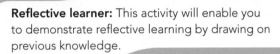

Get into groups. Each group should write on four large pieces of paper: 'cells', 'tissues', 'organs' and 'body systems'. Each group member should then write out the name of a type of cell, tissue, organ and body system on four smaller slips of paper. Mix them up and give four to every individual. Each member should place their slips under the correct label. The group can then discuss the accuracy of their decisions.

If you are working on your own, you can sort the following examples into cells, tissues, organs and body systems: heart, bone, blood, skeleton, red blood cell (or erythrocyte), cartilage, nervous system, kidney, brain, digestive system, skin, stomach, muscle cell, bladder, muscle, renal system.

PLTS

Reflective learner: This activity will enable you to demonstrate reflective learning by drawing on previous knowledge.

1.2 Cells

The largest cell in the human body is the female ovum, which can just be seen with the naked eye. Most cells are much smaller than this, and microscopes are required to view them. Ordinary light microscopes, such as those found in school or college laboratories, are quite good for viewing tissues and organs, but not very useful for looking inside individual human cells.

Electron microscopes are necessary to see the detail of cell contents. However, as these are highly expensive instruments requiring trained operators to prepare and interpret the specimens, we use diagrams and **photomicrographs** instead.

Details of the interior of a cell are often referred to as the ultrastructure of the cell ('ultra' means 'beyond what is considered normal'). This is because they can only be seen with immense magnification. Before the electron microscope was developed, the inside of a cell was considered to be a granular sort of 'soup' but

Key terms

Cell – The basic unit of living material.

Electron microscope – A very powerful type of microscope needed to see inside cells.

Photomicrograph – A photograph taken of an object magnified under a microscope.

we now know that the ultrastructure is highly organised and composed of many different bodies carrying out their own functions.

Do you remember the definition of an organ? The very tiny bodies inside a cell are known as **organelles** because they have different physical (and chemical) compositions and carry out their own functions.

Although you will learn about a typical human cell, there are actually lots of different types of cells each with their own characteristics. The 'typical cell' exists only for study purposes and has no specialisation. When studying actual cells in the body, you must therefore adapt your knowledge to the specific type of cell being considered. For example, a mature red blood cell does not have a **nucleus**, so any description of the ultrastructure of a red blood cell would not include the nucleus.

Living material making up a whole cell is called **protoplasm** and this is subdivided into the **cytoplasm** and nucleus.

Under the light microscope, cytoplasm appears granular with no distinct features. This is the site of most complex chemical reactions, mainly directed by the nucleus, which is also responsible for inherited characteristics. The nucleus is a dark body, usually centrally placed; a smaller, darker spot, the nucleolus, is often visible. Both the whole cell and the nucleus are surrounded by a membrane, which appears as a single line (see Figure 5.1).

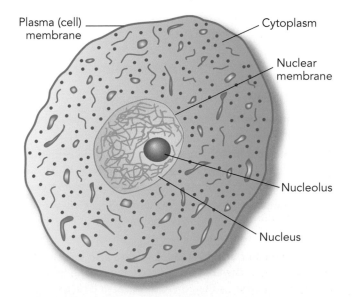

Plasma (cell) membrane
Cytoplasm
Nuclear membrane
Nucleolus
Nucleus

Fig 5.1: Diagram of a cell viewed under a light microscope (× 300)

Cell ultrastructure is so complex and highly organised that a separate branch of science has arisen – cytology, the study of cells. In this unit you will learn about the structure and functions of the cell membrane, the organelles in the cytoplasm, and the nucleus.

Cell (or plasma) membrane

The electron microscope shows the cell membrane to be a phospho-lipid-protein bi-layer. The lipids are small, fatty molecules in two layers (bi-layer), with larger protein molecules inserted at intervals partly or completely through the bi-layer. The lipid molecules are phospholipids; the phosphate head is water soluble and two lipid chains are insoluble in water. This is why the two layers align themselves, with the lipid chains facing one another. The fluid surrounding cells (called tissue fluid) and the cytoplasm are both watery environments next to the phosphate heads (see Figure 5.2, next page).

Protein molecules often form channels through the membrane for substances to pass to and from the cell. The protein molecules also act as identity markers or reception sites for other molecules such as hormones, which are important to those cells. This structure is often termed the 'fluid mosaic model' of the cell membrane.

Cytoplasm

Cytoplasm is a semi-fluid material likened to a gel and capable of flowing slowly. Many chemical reactions are carried out here. The collective term for these reactions is **metabolism** and you will find that this term is frequently used in physiological and biological texts. Complex storage sugars such as glycogen and melanin

Key terms

Organelle – A tiny body inside a cell, which carries out its own functions.

Nucleus – The central part of the cell, which is usually darker than the rest because it absorbs stain quickly.

Protoplasm – The word means 'first material'; the protoplasm refers to anything inside the cell boundary. Cell or plasma membrane surrounds the protoplasm.

Cytoplasm – The word means 'cell material'; the cytoplasm refers to anything inside the cell boundary and outside the nucleus.

Metabolism – The metabolism is the sum of all the chemical reactions occurring in human physiology and these involve using or releasing energy from chemical substances.

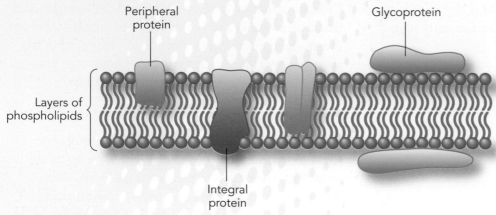

Fig 5.2: Model of the structure of the cell membrane magnified several thousand times

(the dark pigment responsible for skin and hair colour) are found in cytoplasm.

Nucleus

This is usually the largest structure inside the cell and, as it takes up dyes or stains very easily, it stands out as a dark shape. Most cells have a single, central, spherical nucleus but there are many variations. Some muscle cells have many nuclei and are therefore called 'multinucleate'; some red blood cells have lost their nucleus during development and are said to be 'anucleate'; and some white blood cells have distinct, lobed nuclei. Apart from red blood cells (which cannot reproduce and have a limited lifespan), most cells that are separated from their nuclei will die.

The nuclear membrane has a structure similar to that of the cell membrane but contains gaps or pores, through which proteins and nucleic acids pass. When a cell is not dividing (known as 'resting') the nuclear material appears like a thick, tangled mass and is called the **chromatin network**. A smaller, darker sphere is often visible, the nucleolus, and this is a source of **ribonucleic acid (RNA)**, one of the nucleic acids. There may be more than one nucleolus present in some cells. When a cell is in the process of dividing, the chromatin network separates into distinct black threads known as **chromosomes**. There are 23 pairs of chromosomes in a human cell, containing specific sequences of **deoxyribonucleic acid (DNA)**, another nucleic acid, which is responsible for all our inherited characteristics such as hair and eye colour. The sequences of DNA are our genes.

The nucleus controls nearly all the activities of the cell and has been likened to the architectural drawing or blueprint from which the cell operates.

Cell organelles

Organelles are various components of a cell with a distinct structure and their own functions and can be likened to miniature organs (hence the term 'organelles').

Organelles include:

* mitochondria
* the endoplasmic reticulum
* the Golgi apparatus
* lysosomes.

Before looking at the organelles in detail, you will see in Fig 5.3 a diagram of a typical cell that might be seen under the electron microscope; refer to the diagram as you learn about the organelles. Note that the magnification is still not sufficient to make out the full structure of the cell and nuclear membranes.

Key terms

Chromatin network – The dark tangled mass seen in the nucleus of a resting cell.

Ribonucleic acid (RNA) – A nucleic acid found in both the cell and the nucleus. RNA is responsible for the manufacture of cell proteins such as pigments, enzymes and hormones.

Chromosomes – Long threads of DNA and protein seen in a dividing cell. They contain the genetic material or genes responsible for transmitting inherited characteristics.

Deoxyribonucleic acid (DNA) – A nucleic acid found only in the chromatin network and chromosomes of the nucleus. DNA is responsible for the control and passing on of inherited characteristics and instructions to the cell.

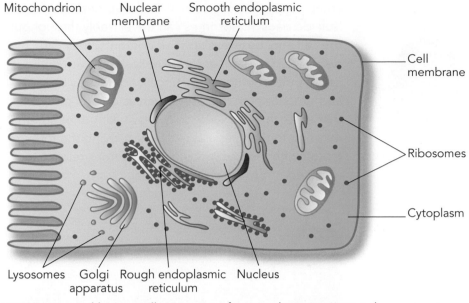

Fig 5.3: A typical human cell appearance from an electron micrograph

Labels: Mitochondrion, Nuclear membrane, Smooth endoplasmic reticulum, Cell membrane, Ribosomes, Cytoplasm, Lysosomes, Golgi apparatus, Rough endoplasmic reticulum, Nucleus

Activity 2: Organelle recall

You may be feeling somewhat bewildered by these difficult terms that are also hard to spell. Don't be disheartened! It really is surprising how quickly you can learn them if you keep repeating them over and over and pointing them out in electron micrographs. When you feel confident about recognising their shapes, try adding their functions too. Your tutor will be able to find different copies of electron micrographs and you can research your own for practice. One image is included on page 182. Try identifying each organelle on the image and list each one with its main function.

PLTS

Effective participator: You will demonstrate effective participation when planning and carrying out research on cell organelles.

Functional skills

ICT: You will use ICT skills to access, search for and use information on cell organelles in different types of cells.

Mitochondria

Every cell in the body has at least 1000 of these rod-shaped or spherical bodies, and very energy-active cells (like muscle and liver cells) will have many more. **Mitochondria** are concerned with energy release. Each mitochondrion (singular) has a double-layered membrane like the cell membrane but the inner layer is folded at intervals, producing a series of 'shelves' or ridges known as **cristae**. The enzymes responsible for the end stages of glucose oxidation (or cell respiration) are located on the cristae. The energy released from glucose is trapped and stored until required by a 'chemical battery' called **adenosine triphosphate (ATP)**. When energy is required for building complex molecules or doing work like contracting muscles, ATP breaks down to **adenosine diphosphate (ADP)**, releasing energy to build chemical bonds. The ADP is then recycled, to be built up once more into ATP, using the energy released from glucose. This occurs in the mitochondria.

Key terms

Mitochondria – Spherical or rod-shaped bodies scattered in the cytoplasm and concerned with energy release.

Cristae – Folds of the inner layer of mitochondrial membrane on which the enzymes responsible for the oxidation of glucose are situated.

Adenosine triphosphate (ATP) – A chemical in mitochondria that is capable of trapping lots of energy in the last chemical bond: for example, A-P-P~P, where P is a phosphate group (an ordinary chemical bond) and ~ is a high energy bond.

Adenosine diphosphate (ADP) – A chemical left after ATP has released its stored energy to do work.

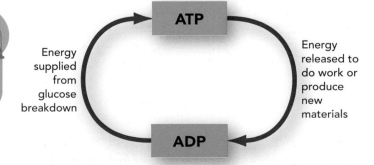

Fig 5.4: Flow chart of energy production in cells

Labels: ATP, ADP, Energy supplied from glucose breakdown, Energy released to do work or produce new materials

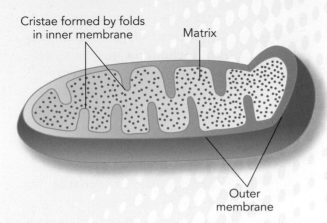

Cristae formed by folds in inner membrane
Matrix
Outer membrane

Fig 5.5: Structure of a single mitochondrion

Endoplasmic reticulum

This can be shortened to ER. There are two variations, called rough and smooth ER. 'Endo-' means 'within' and 'reticulum' is a technical term for 'a network'. ER is a branching network that fills the cell interior. The membrane of the channels is similar in structure to the cell membrane and continuous with the nuclear membrane. The channels form passageways for transporting materials to and from different parts of the cell.

- *Rough ER* is so-called because it is studded with tiny black bodies, known as ribosomes, and has the function of making cell proteins and acting as a temporary storage area. Sometimes sugars are added to the proteins to make glycoproteins, in secretions such as mucus.

- *Smooth ER* has no attached ribosomes and is involved in the metabolism of lipids or fats.

Golgi apparatus

This appears as a series of flattened, fluid-filled sacs stacked like pancakes. Many tiny fluid-filled globules or bags lie close to the main stack and these are often known as vesicles. Golgi was a famous Italian scientist who specialised in cells and tissues in the nineteenth and twentieth centuries and this organelle takes its name from him. It is believed that the Golgi apparatus packages proteins for delivery to other organelles or outwards from the cell in secretions. The Golgi apparatus is also responsible for producing lysosomes.

Lysosomes

Lysosomes can be found in all parts of the cell cytoplasm and are also small vesicles produced by part of the Golgi apparatus. Because they contain powerful enzymes capable of digesting all major chemical

components of living cells, they are sometimes called 'suicide bags'. Lysosomes can travel freely throughout the cell and, by releasing their contents, they can destroy old or damaged organelles and even entire cells. Another of their functions is to destroy bacteria and other foreign materials, such as carbon particles, that enter the cell. They do this by taking the foreign matter into their vesicles. After destroying the foreign matter with their enzymes, the lysosomes release the digested or broken-down material.

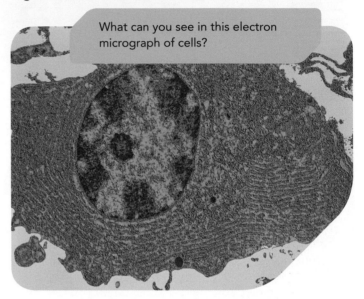

What can you see in this electron micrograph of cells?

Some types of white blood cells – phagocytes (literally 'eating cells') and monocytes – and tissue cells known as macrophages (meaning 'large eaters') are loaded with lysosomes because their function is to destroy bacteria, viruses and foreign material entering the body cells and tissues.

Many disease-causing agents are thought to be capable of damaging lysosome membranes, bringing about internal cell destruction.

Now try Activity 3 and, when you feel that your learning is complete, try the assessment activity which follows. You can improve your work if you are not satisfied with it.

Did you know?

The electron microscope enables you to see extremely small objects to identify their structure but it does not tell you what the structures do. Researchers with a range of expertise (such as chemists, physicists and biochemists) have to separate out the different structures and carry out many tests to identify the functions of the tiny objects they observe.

Activity 3: Interpreting photographs of cells

Using a copy of the electron micrograph on the previous page and/or similar material from your tutor and the labelled diagram in Figure 5.3 (on page 181), match the different parts of a cell and the organelles. You can download some electron micrographs from the Internet as well. As you carry out this exercise, describe the appearance and the function of each part. You will soon realise that interpreting photographs of real cells is more difficult than it

appears! Although you can carry out this activity on your own, you can learn more with a 'study buddy' because you can check each other's learning and interpretation of the cell parts. After each 'journey' through the cell parts, check your recall against this text and any class notes you may have. You and a small group of peers can carry out a 'thought shower' on the roles of cell organelles and carry out research on any you are not sure of.

Assessment activity 5.1

P1 **BTEC**

Using a large piece of paper, produce an annotated poster of a cell as it is seen under an electron microscope. You must include the following organelles: nucleus, cytoplasm, mitochondria, smooth and rough endoplasmic reticula, Golgi apparatus and lysosomes.

The notes accompanying the labels should include the main activities carried out by the organelles.

Grading tip

P1 To achieve P1, you need to outline the functions of the main cell components. This means giving an overview of the cell structure and

function without including any more detail than is covered in the text. Although you are not obliged to include a separate image of each organelle, your work will clearly be more comprehensive if you do. If you download material from the Internet you must show clearly how you have adapted it to show your learning, as well as providing a detailed reference and acknowledgement. It would be acceptable to obtain an image and label it carefully yourself to show the relevant parts. Make sure that you use colour and make the poster clear, attractive and interesting.

1.3 Tissues

Tissues are groups of similar cells carrying out specific functions. In this unit you will learn about the following tissues:

- epithelial
- connective
- muscle
- nervous.

Epithelial tissues

Epithelia are the linings of internal and external surfaces and body cavities, including ducts (tubes or channels) carrying secretions from glands. They may be composed of several layers of cells, called compound epithelia, or just a single layer known as simple epithelia. The lowest or bottom layer of cells

is attached to a basement membrane for support and connection. Part of the basement membrane is secreted by the epithelial cells. There are nerve supplies to epithelia but they are supplied with oxygen and nutrients from deeper tissues by **diffusion**. As they are surface tissues and exposed to friction, their capacity for growth and repair is greater than other tissues and usually occurs during sleep.

Simple epithelia

Simple epithelial cells may be squamous, cuboidal, columnar or ciliated. Squamous epithelial cells are

Key term

Diffusion – This is the passage of molecules from a high concentration to a low concentration.

very flat, with each nucleus forming a lump in the centre. The word 'squamous' means 'scaly', referring to the flatness of the cells. They fit together closely, rather like crazy paving. Clearly, such delicate thin cells cannot offer much protection and their chief function is to allow materials to pass through via diffusion and **osmosis**. Simple squamous epithelium is found in the walls of:

- lung alveoli
- blood capillaries
- Bowman's capsule of nephrons.

As their name suggests, cuboidal epithelial cells are cube-shaped, with spherical nuclei. They often line ducts and tubes and can allow materials to pass through in a similar way to squamous epithelia. They often occur in glandular tissues making secretions. They can be found in:

- kidney tubules
- sweat ducts
- glands like the thyroid gland and breast tissue.

Key term

Osmosis – The passage of water molecules from a region of high concentration (of water molecules) to one of low concentration through a partially permeable membrane such as the cell membranes of simple epithelial cells.

Columnar epithelial cells are much taller, with slightly oval nuclei. They can often be associated with microscopic filaments known as cilia and are then called ciliated epithelia. Cilia move in wave-like motions, beating towards the orifices, and are commonly found associated with goblet cells, which secrete mucus in the respiratory and alimentary tracts. The mucus traps unwanted particles like carbon, and the cilia transport the flow of 'dirty' mucus towards the exterior.

Columnar cells are found lining:

- the trachea and bronchi
- villi in the small intestine.

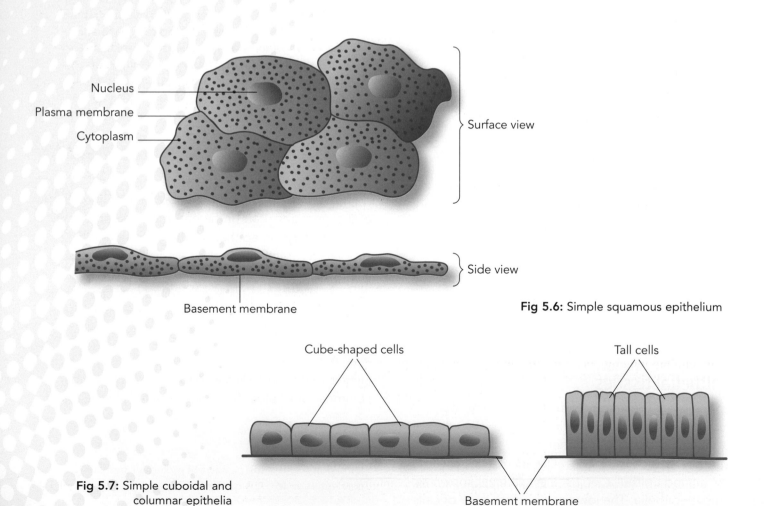

Nucleus

Plasma membrane

Cytoplasm

Surface view

Side view

Basement membrane

Fig 5.6: Simple squamous epithelium

Cube-shaped cells

Tall cells

Basement membrane

Fig 5.7: Simple cuboidal and columnar epithelia

Compound epithelia

The principal function of compound epithelia is to protect deeper structures, and multiple layers of cells hamper the passage of materials. The vagina, mouth, tongue and oesophagus are lined by stratified epithelia consisting of layers of squamous, cuboidal or columnar cells, which gradually become flattened by pressure from below as they reach the surface. The lowest layer of cells on the basement membrane actively divides and the older cells are pushed upwards. This type of epithelia is usually a pink colour and is often termed mucous membrane.

The skin has an outer layer of epithelium similar in structure to the stratified epithelium but with the important addition of a layer of flattened dead cells on the outside. This is known as the epidermis. As the cells advance from the basement membrane, they gradually become filled with a protein called keratin and are said to be keratinised or cornified. This layer is vital to prevent micro-organisms invading deeper structures, and it has a waterproofing effect on the skin. The skin can be variously coloured, with pigment produced by pigment cells in the lowest layer. The pigment melanin darkens under the influence of the sun. The numbers of pigment cells in the skin is genetically inherited, although they can divide during exposure to sunshine.

The structure of the skin epidermis can be seen in Figure 5.8 below.

Connective tissues

These tissues are the most widely distributed in the body and lie beneath the epithelial tissues, connecting different parts of the internal structure.

Various types of cells lie in a background material known as a **matrix**. The matrix may be liquid as in blood, jelly-like as in areolar tissue, firm as in cartilage, or hard as in bone. The matrix of a tissue is usually secreted by the connective tissue cells.

The functions of these tissues are to transport materials (as in blood), give support (as in areolar tissue and cartilage), and strengthen and protect (as in bone). Many tissues contain different fibres secreted by the cells to provide special characteristics.

In this unit you will learn about the connective tissues of:

- blood
- cartilage
- bone
- areolar tissue
- adipose tissue (fatty tissue).

Blood

Blood consists of straw-coloured plasma (the matrix), in which several types of blood cells are carried. Plasma is mainly water, in which various substances are carried, such as dissolved gases like oxygen and carbon dioxide, nutrients like glucose and amino acids, salts, enzymes and hormones. There is also a combination of important proteins, collectively known as the plasma proteins, which have roles in blood clotting, transport,

Key term

Matrix – Background material in which various types of cells lie.

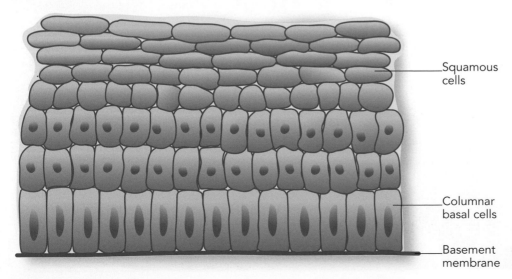

Squamous cells

Columnar basal cells

Basement membrane

Fig 5.8: Section through stratified epithelium

defence against invading organisms (part of the immune system) and osmotic regulation.

The most common cells by far in the plasma are red blood cells, also known as erythrocytes. These are very small cells with an elastic membrane, which is important because the membrane often has to distort to travel through the smallest capillaries. Erythrocytes have no nucleus in their mature state (the loss produces a depression in the top and bottom of the cell, hence their bi-concave shape), which provides a larger surface area to be exposed to oxygen. They are packed with haemoglobin, which gives them a red colour. (This is why blood is red.) In oxygenated blood (**arterial blood**), the oxyhaemoglobin is bright red but, in deoxygenated blood (**venous blood**), after the dissolved oxygen is delivered to body cells, the reduced haemoglobin is dark red in colour.

Due to the absence of nuclei, erythrocytes cannot divide and have a limited lifespan of around 120 days.

White blood cells (or leucocytes) are larger, nucleated and less numerous. There are several types but the most numerous are the granulocytes (also known as

polymorphs, neutrophils and phagocytes). They are called granulocytes because they contain granules in their cytoplasm as well as lobed nuclei. They are capable of changing their shape and engulfing foreign material such as bacteria and carbon particles. This process is known as phagocytosis. A granulocyte acts rather like an amoeba and is sometimes said to be amoeboid. Granulocytes, because of their ability to engulf microbes and foreign material, are very important in defending the body against infection.

Key terms

Arterial blood – Blood flowing through arteries that are coming from the heart, usually carrying oxygenated blood to the tissues.

Venous blood – Blood flowing through veins that are returning blood to the heart from the tissues; the blood has left considerable amounts of oxygen behind to supply the cells and is known as deoxygenated blood.

Can you identify the cells shown in this photograph of human blood?

Did you know?

The number of granulocytes rises significantly in infections, so a blood count can often be a valuable indicator of infection when diagnosing illness.

Lymphocytes are smaller white blood cells with round nuclei and clear cytoplasm – they assist in the production of antibodies. Antigens are found on the surface coats of disease-causing microbes or pathogens and act as identity markers for different types of pathogens (rather like name tags on a school uniform). Antibodies neutralise antigens and prevent the microbes from multiplying. They can then be phagocytosed by granulocytes and monocytes. Antibodies are chemically globulins (types of protein carried in the plasma).

In a completely different way from granulocytes, lymphocytes also contribute to the defence of the body because of their role in the production of antibodies. They form an important part of the immune system.

Monocytes are another type of white blood cell, larger than lymphocytes. They also have large, round nuclei and clear cytoplasm. They are very efficient at phagocytosis of foreign material and, like granulocytes, can leave the circulatory blood vessels to travel to the site of an infection and begin phagocytosing pathogens very rapidly.

Thrombocytes are not true cells but are usually classed with the white blood cells. They are more commonly called platelets. They are products of much larger cells that have broken up and they have an important role in blood clotting.

Did you know?

Granulocytes, monocytes, platelets and red blood cells are made in bone marrow but lymphocytes are produced in lymphoid tissues.

Cartilage

This is the smooth, translucent, firm substance that protects bone ends from friction during movement, and forms the major part of the nose and the external ear flaps, called pinnae. The matrix is secreted by cartilage cells called chondrocytes and is a firm but flexible glass-like material of chondrin (a protein). ('Chondro-' is a prefix associated with cartilage.) The cells become trapped in the matrix and sometimes divide into two or four cells, giving a very characteristic appearance. It does not contain blood vessels and is nourished by diffusion from underlying bone.

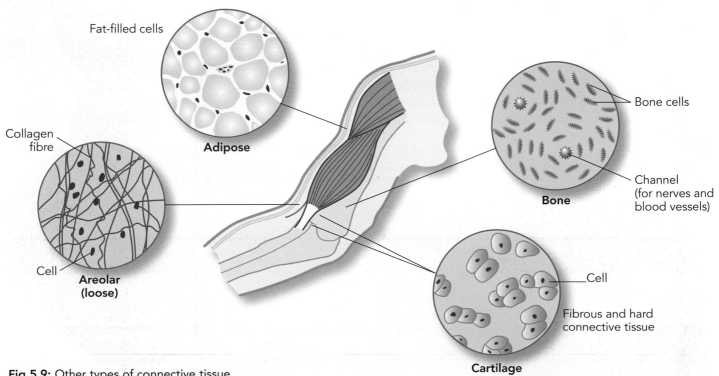

Fat-filled cells
Adipose

Collagen fibre
Cell
Areolar (loose)

Bone cells
Channel (for nerves and blood vessels)
Bone

Cell
Fibrous and hard connective tissue
Cartilage

Fig 5.9: Other types of connective tissue

Bone

Bone is a much harder substance than cartilage but it can be worn away by friction. The rigid matrix has two major components:

- calcium salts, which form around **collagen** fibres and give bone its hardness
- collagen fibres, which offer some ability to bend under strain and prevent bone from being too brittle and therefore likely to fracture.

Osteocytes (or bone cells) are trapped in the hard matrix on concentric rings called lamellae. A system of these rings is known as a Haversian system or osteone. ('Osteo- ' is a prefix associated with bone.) Blood vessels and nerves pass through the hollow centre of each osteone.

Bone is designed to bear weight and the limb bones are hollow, like girders (the strongest mechanical structures). Bone is also used to protect vital weaker tissues such as the brain, lungs and heart. Bones contain marrow in their central hollow and in some bones, marrow makes vital blood cells.

Areolar tissue

This is the most common tissue in the body and you have probably never heard of it before! If you eat meat, you will have seen it many, many times. It is the sticky, white material that binds muscle groups, blood vessels and nerves together. The matrix is semi-fluid and it contains collagen fibres and elastic fibres secreted by the cells found in this loose connective tissue. Elastic fibres give flexibility to the tissue, which is located around more mobile structures. The deeper skin layer known as the dermis is a denser type of areolar tissue, with extra fibres and cells. Areolar tissue offers a degree of support to the tissues it surrounds.

Adipose tissue

Adipose is a technical term for fatty tissue and it is a variation of areolar tissue, in which the adipose (or fat)

cells have multiplied to obscure other cells and fibres. When mature, an adipose cell becomes so loaded with fat that the nucleus is pushed to one side and, as fat is translucent, the cell takes on a distinctive 'signet ring' appearance. Adipose tissue is common under the skin and around organs such as the heart, kidneys and parts of the digestive tract. It helps to insulate the body against changes of external temperature, acts as a 'hydraulic shock absorber' to protect against injury, and is also a 'high-energy storage depot'.

Muscle tissue

Muscle is an excitable tissue because it is capable of responding to stimuli. There are three different types of muscle in the human body:

- striated
- non-striated
- cardiac.

Each is composed of muscle fibres that are capable of shortening (or contracting) and returning to their original state (known as relaxation). Contraction causes movement of the skeleton, soft tissue, blood or specific material such as urine, food and faeces. Muscle has both blood and nerve supplies.

Did you know?

Muscle activity generates heat and contributes to maintaining the body temperature.

Striated muscle

Most striated muscle (also called voluntary, skeletal or striped muscle) is attached to the bones of the

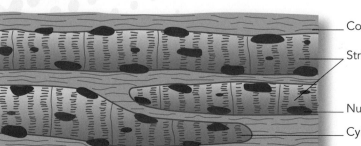

Connecting tissue covering

Stripes or striations

Nuclei

Cylindrical muscle fibre

Fig 5.10: Microscopic appearance of striated muscle

skeleton, although some facial muscles are attached to skin. Striated muscle makes up the familiar animal meat seen in the butcher's. This type of muscle will contract when it receives nerve impulses controlled by conscious thought from the **central nervous system** – hence its alternative name of voluntary muscle. The name striated means 'striped'; each individual fibre shows alternate dark and light banding from the muscle protein filaments from which it is made.

Each fibre is cylindrical and multinucleate, lying parallel to its neighbours. There may be hundreds or thousands of fibres in a muscle, depending on its size. Some fibres are 30 centimetres long and one-hundredth of a millimetre wide. Muscle fibres contain many thousands of mitochondria to supply ATP for the energy used in muscular contraction.

Non-striated muscle

Although this type of muscle tissue (also called involuntary, smooth or plain muscle) still contains protein filaments, they do not lie in an ordered pattern and therefore do not produce the banding that is characteristic of striated muscle. The muscle fibres are spindle- or cigar-shaped, with single central nuclei, and dovetail with each other. This type of muscle tends to form sheets and, although still requiring nervous stimulation to effect contraction, this is not under conscious thought, but supplied by the **autonomic nervous system** (which is why it is called involuntary muscle). This type of muscle is found around hollow internal organs such as the stomach, intestines, iris of the eye, bladder and uterus; it is not attached to bones.

Non-striated muscle frequently occurs in two sheets running in different directions, known as **antagonistic muscles**. In the digestive tract, one sheet runs in a circular fashion around the intestines, while another outer sheet runs down the length. The two sheets are said to work antagonistically (against each other) to propel the food contents down the tract. This type of movement is known as peristalsis (see page 213).

In the iris of the eye, one set of muscle runs radially outward from the centre, like the spokes of a wheel, while the other set runs in a circular fashion around the central pupil. This arrangement allows for the control of light entering the eye and the pupil is said to be dilated (open) or constricted (narrowed).

Cardiac muscle

This type of muscle is found only in the four chambers (atria and ventricles) of the heart. It is said to be myogenic because it can rhythmically contract without receiving any nervous stimuli, and in this it differs from other muscle. The muscle cells branch repeatedly to form a network, through which contraction spreads rapidly. Each cell has a central nucleus and is both horizontally and vertically striped. The divisions between cells are known as intercalated discs and are specially adapted for transmission of impulses.

Under normal healthy circumstances, cardiac muscle is not allowed to contract myogenically because the atrial or upper chamber muscle has a different contraction rate to that of the lower ventricular muscle and this would lead to inefficient and uncoordinated heart action. The autonomic nervous system controls the rate of contraction via the nerves in order to adapt the flow of blood to specific circumstances such as rest and exercise.

Key terms

Central nervous system – The brain and spinal cord.

Autonomic nervous system – Part of the nervous system responsible for controlling the internal organs.

Antagonistic muscles – One muscle or sheet of muscle contracts while an opposite muscle or sheet relaxes.

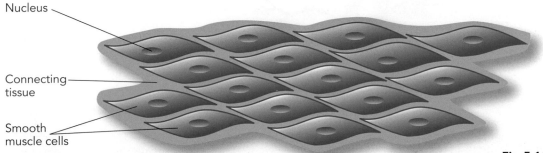

Nucleus

Connecting tissue

Smooth muscle cells

Fig 5.11: Non-striated muscle tissue

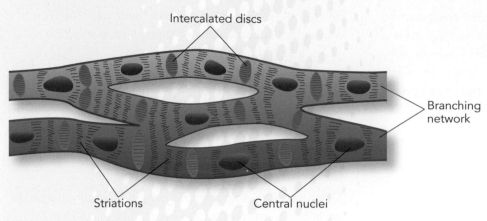

Fig 5.12: Cardiac muscle tissue

Intercalated discs

Branching network

Striations

Central nuclei

Nervous tissue

Nervous tissue is only found in the nervous system and consists of the brain, spinal cord and nerves. Receiving stimuli from both external and internal sources, it serves to create consistency (particularly regarding **homeostasis**), co-ordination, and communication between different parts of the body. The nervous system interprets stimuli from the sense organs so that vision, hearing, smell and the other senses become apparent.

Activity 4: Placing tissues within organs

Working in pairs, use the Internet, bioviewers or reference books to research the different tissues found in four organs of the body (take two each). Write a description of each tissue and outline the role it plays within the named organ.

PLTS

Independent enquirer: This activity will enable you to demonstrate independent enquiry skills when you plan and carry out research on the tissues of the body, and analyse and evaluate information on tissue types.

Functional skills

ICT: You will use ICT skills to access, search for and use information on different types of tissues in organs.

Key term

Homeostasis – The process of maintaining a constant internal environment despite changing circumstances. For example, the pH, temperature, concentrations of certain chemicals and the water content in the fluid surrounding body cells (the internal environment) must be kept within a narrow range even when you are consuming acids (vinegar, lemon juice), are in a freezing climate, or are doing vigorous exercise.

Nervous tissue is composed of:

- neurones – highly specialised nerve cells that transmit nervous impulses. They are present only in the brain and spinal cord, but their long processes (nerve fibres) form the nerves
- neuroglia – connective tissue cells, intermingled with neurones in the brain and spinal cord, that offer support and protection.

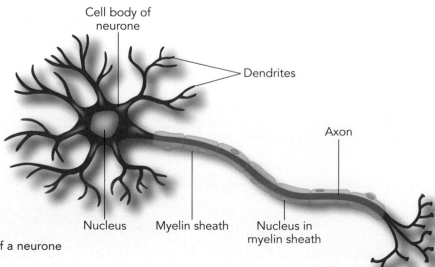

Cell body of neurone

Dendrites

Axon

Nucleus

Myelin sheath

Nucleus in myelin sheath

Fig 5.13: General features of a neurone

Assessment activity 5.2

Produce a written assignment that shows an understanding of the main tissue types and the roles they play in two named organs.

Two organs you could choose might be the stomach and skin. Here are some examples of tissue types that occur in these two organs:

1 The stomach has three layers of non-striated muscle in its wall and an inner lining of columnar epithelium with goblet cells. The tissue connecting the lining with the muscular coat is areolar tissue. Describe these three tissues and their roles in the functioning of the stomach.

2 Skin has an outer layer of keratinised stratified epithelium and a deeper layer of areolar tissue overlying adipose tissue and skeletal muscle. Describe keratinised stratified epithelium, adipose tissue and striated muscle and their roles in the functioning of the skin.

Grading tip

P2 To achieve P2, you need to outline the structure of the main tissues of the body. You could supplement your written description with large annotated diagrams of the named organs to provide illustrated accounts. Ensure that the functions you describe are specific to the named organs and not general.

PLTS

Independent enquirer: Planning and carrying out research on the tissues of the body will help you demonstrate your enquiry skills; this activity will also help you show that you can analyse and evaluate information on tissue types.

Table 5.1: The major organs and where they can be found

Body organ	Associated body system	Location description
Heart	Cardiovascular	Middle of the chest, between the lungs, with apex lying to the left.
Lungs (2)	Respiratory	Each lung lies to one side of the heart, filling the chest or thorax.
Brain	Nervous	Within the skull of the head.
Stomach	Digestive	Abdominal organ lying just beneath the diaphragm on the left side.
Liver		Beneath the diaphragm, mainly on the right side but also overlapping part of the stomach.
Pancreas		Lies just below the stomach, in a curve of the duodenum.
Duodenum		C-shaped part of the small intestine immediately beyond the stomach.
Ileum		Long coiled tube, which follows the duodenum in the abdomen.
Colon		Begins after the ileum in the right pelvic area, runs up the right side to the liver, then sweeps across under the stomach and down the left side of the abdomen to end at the rectum in the lower central pelvic area.
Kidneys (2)	Renal	One on each side of the posterior wall of the abdomen. The upper poles of the kidneys lie just inside the ribs. The left kidney is slightly higher than the right due to the bulk of the liver.
Bladder		Lies centrally in the lower pelvis at the front.
Ovaries (2)	Reproductive	One on each side of the posterior wall of the pelvis, below the kidneys.
Testes (2)		Below the pelvis, between the upper legs, one each side of the penis in a skin bag called the scrotum.

1.4 Body organs

You need to know the locations of major body **organs**; most of these will be illustrated in detail later in the unit. A quick reference list can be found in Table 5.1 (page 191).

The structure and functions of the skin will be described on pages 221–222.

1.5 Body systems

You are required to learn the gross structure of ten **body systems**. Some systems will be considered in much greater detail later in the chapter. You will find the gross structure of the cardiovascular system included on pages 199–206. The gross structure of the respiratory system is included on pages 206–209 and that of the digestive system on pages 210–212. Remember, gross structure is only what the eye can see.

The renal system

The renal system consists of two kidneys with emerging tubes (called the ureters) running down the posterior abdominal wall to a single pelvic collecting organ, the bladder. The passage from the bladder to the exterior is via the urethra, and the flow of urine is controlled by a sphincter muscle located just below the bladder. The kidneys are supplied by short renal **arteries** coming off the main artery of the body, the aorta. Renal **veins** take the blood from the kidneys straight into the vena cava, the main vein of the body.

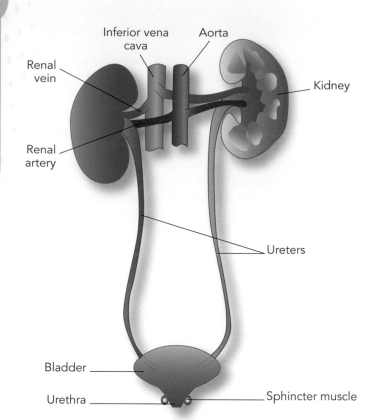

Fig 5.14: Gross structure of the renal system

Key terms

Organ – A collection of different tissues, such as the heart or the brain, working together to carry out specific functions.

Body systems – A collection of organs with specific functions in the body.

Artery – A blood vessel coming from the heart, usually carrying oxygenated blood to the tissues.

Vein – A blood vessel returning blood to the heart from the tissues; the blood has left considerable amounts of oxygen behind to supply the cells and is known as deoxygenated blood.

The nervous system

The nervous system comprises the central nervous system (the brain and spinal cord) and the peripheral nervous system, the nerves running to and from the brain (cranial nerves) and spinal cord (spinal nerves). A chain of ganglia runs close to the spinal cord and is associated with the autonomic nervous system, which controls internal organs. Autonomic nerve fibres are also contained within the peripheral nerves.

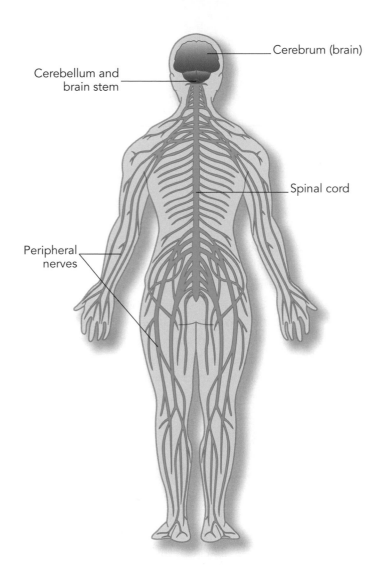

Fig 5.15: Gross structure of the nervous system

The endocrine system

This is a collection of ductless glands scattered throughout the body. Endocrine glands pass their secretions (known as hormones) directly into the bloodstream so they are always adjacent to blood vessels.

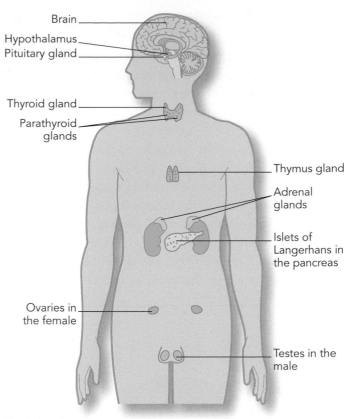

Fig 5.16: Gross structure of the endocrine system

The reproductive system

Males and females have different reproductive organs, as these serve different purposes.

Female reproductive system

This system comprises two ovaries, each with an emerging oviduct (or fallopian tube) connecting to the thick-walled uterus (or womb). The neck of the uterus protrudes into the muscular vagina and this opens to the exterior at the vulva. Two fleshy folds, known as the labia, conceal the vaginal orifice.

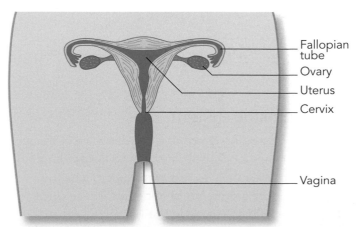

Fig 5.17: Gross structure of the female reproductive system

Male reproductive system

Two testes hang in a skin sac called the scrotum, just outside the abdomen, and are connected by long tubes (each known as the vas deferens) to the urethra. The urethra is much longer than that of the female and enclosed in an organ called the penis. Two columns of erectile tissue lie alongside the urethra in the penis. Two pairs of glands, the seminal vesicles and Cowper's glands, pour their secretions into the vasa deferentia (plural), close to the bladder. A single ring-shaped gland, called the prostate gland, also adds secretions and is located around the upper part of the urethra, just below the bladder. The urethra and vasa deferentia unite within the prostate gland.

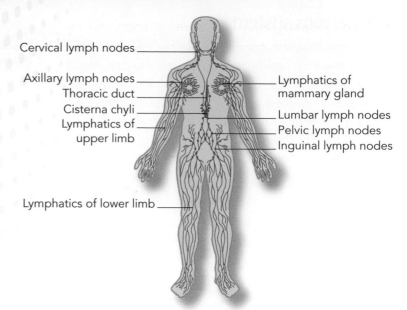

Fig 5.19: The lymphatic system

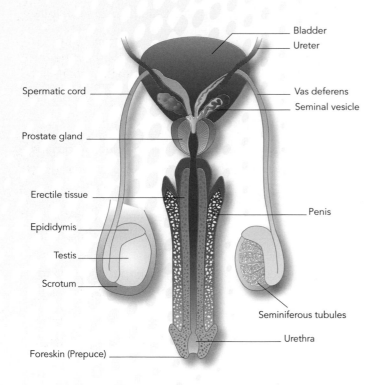

Fig 5.18: Gross structure of the male reproductive system

The lymphatic system

Minute blind-ending lymphatic capillaries lie in tissue spaces between body cells and join to larger lymphatic vessels and eventually to two lymphatic ducts, the thoracic duct and right lymphatic duct. These ducts transfer the fluid collected in the lymphatic vessels back into the blood circulation close to the heart. Each lymph vessel passes through at least one lymph node (sometimes mistakenly called 'glands') and usually more than one. There are hundreds of lymph nodes all over the body, often associated in groups. Lymphoid tissue also occurs in specialised areas more associated with potential sources of infection, such as the tonsils, adenoids, small intestine, spleen and thymus gland. Tiny lymphatic vessels, called lacteals, are present in the villi of the small intestine (see Figure 5.34, on page 211) and are associated with the absorption of lipids from the digestive tract.

The musculo-skeletal system

The bones of the skeleton and their attached striated muscles form this system. You are not required to learn the names of the muscles or the individual bones, although you will probably know some of these already.

The skeleton forms the framework of the body and is composed of the:

- axial skeleton, in the midline of the body – the skull and vertebral column or spine
- appendicular skeleton, comprising the limb bones and their girdles, which attach them to the trunk.

The meeting place of two or more bones is known as a joint and joints may be:

- fixed by fibrous tissue and therefore immoveable; this type occurs between several bones of the skull
- slightly moveable because the bones are joined by a pad of cartilage; this type is found in between the vertebrae and joining the two halves of the pelvic girdle together
- freely moveable with a more complex structure known as synovial joints; examples of synovial joints are found at the shoulder, elbow, knee, hip, fingers and toes.

Striated muscle fibres are bound together to form muscles that pull bones into different positions by contracting. Muscles never push so an 'opposite' muscle is required to return the bones to their original positions. As well as individual names (such as biceps and triceps), muscles are often given names like **flexors** and **extensors**, which describe their action.

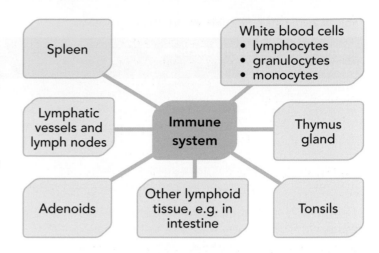

Fig 5.20: The major components of the immune system

Key terms

Flexors – These carry out flexion, which decreases the angle between two bones; for example, the biceps (a flexor) raises the forearm.

Extensors – These carry out extension, which increases the angle between two bones; for example, the triceps (an extensor) straightens the forearm after flexion.

Activity 6: Researching systems

In small groups, share out the body systems and research their structure and how they work. Share your findings with each other and provide useful references.

PLTS

Self-manager: Sharing out the work and organising your own research in this activity may help you to demonstrate your self-manager skills.

Activity 5: Finding your own muscles

Try bending and straightening your forearm and feel the muscles that increase in firmness as you carry out this action. Identify the biceps and triceps muscles. Repeat the action but this time raising and straightening your leg. Identify where the flexors and extensors are located.

1.6 Main functions of body systems

Interactions of different structures within each system

You will find this information in each section detailing the different systems.

The immune system

The immune system is more scattered than most other systems and is often not included as a major system in textbooks. It is a collection of cells, tissues and proteins that protects the body from invasion by harmful micro-organisms. Figure 5.20 (above) illustrates the main components of the immune system.

Activity 7: How systems interact

Working in small groups of three or four, research how two or more systems work together, making posters for records and then feed back to the rest of the class in a plenary session.

Table 5.2: The main functions of the 10 body systems

Name of system	Main functions
Cardiovascular system	• Major transport of materials to and from cells • Distributes heat around the body and assists in temperature regulation • Defence of the body • Water regulation
Respiratory system	• Maintains oxygen supply to cells • Removes carbon dioxide and water from the body
Digestive system	• Reduces complex food molecules to simple substances capable of being absorbed and delivered to cells • Removes undigested waste at intervals • The liver is the main producer of important chemicals
Renal system	• Removes excess water and salts • Eliminates nitrogen-containing waste in the form of urea • Assists in the production of new red blood cells • Involved in the maintenance of blood pressure
Nervous system	• Receives and interprets information from the environment • Controls and co-ordinates the internal organs • Associated with the endocrine system • Reflex actions protect the body from injury
Endocrine system	• Controls and co-ordinates organs • Maintains blood glucose, water and salt levels • Assists in reproduction and growth
Reproductive system	• Produces gametes that can create new life when united with a gamete from the opposite sex • Assists in growth • Responsible for secondary sexual characteristics
Lymphatic system	• Removes excess tissue fluid and proteins from spaces between cells • Defence of the body • Transports fatty acids from the digestive system
Musculo-skeletal system	• Effects movement (with the nervous system) • Stores calcium • Protects vital organs • Supports organs • Manufactures many blood cells
Immune system	• Defends against invasion by micro-organisms • Has an anti-cancer role • Rejects material perceived as 'foreign'

Assessment activity 5.3

Imagine that you wish to explain to individuals using a local health centre how the body works, and produce a series of annotated diagrams to provide an overview of each body system.

1 On large sheets of paper, draw your own version of the gross structure of each body system listed below, labelling each part with its name and adding a short description of the function of the part.

Body systems to be included are:

- cardiovascular
- respiratory
- digestive
- renal
- nervous
- endocrine
- reproductive – male and female
- lymphatic
- musculo-skeletal
- immune.

2 Download images of the more complicated systems from the Internet. Delete any prepared text and make the images your own by inserting labels and functions as in question 1 above.

Grading tip

P3 To achieve P3, you have to outline the gross structure of all the main body systems. You need not include any details of microscopic structures (such as alveoli or nephrons), as these are not part of the gross structure.

Make sure each image you download is of good quality and clear enough to label.

The renal, female reproductive and endocrine systems are particularly suitable for your own diagrams, as they are less complex than others.

PLTS

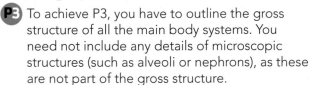

Creative thinker: You can demonstrate creative thinking by generating ideas and exploring possibilities when providing information about body systems.

Self-manager: By using initiative and perseverance when preparing posters of body systems and submitting the posters to a deadline around other commitments, you will show self-management skills.

Reflective learner: You will show you are a reflective learner when preparing the diagrams of the body systems to display in a health centre.

Functional skills

ICT: Presenting posters that are fit for purpose and audience demonstrates ICT skills.

2 Understand the functioning of body systems associated with energy metabolism

The role of energy within the cell, respiratory, cardiovascular and digestive systems has already been briefly discussed. This section will investigate the concept of energy in more detail.

2.1 Energy laws

Energy can be defined easily as the capacity to do work – but energy doesn't just appear, it must come from somewhere!

The first law of thermodynamics, sometimes known as the conservation of energy, states that:

Energy can be transformed (changed from one form to another), but cannot be created or destroyed.

The first part of this law refers to the transformation of energy from one form into another. The second form may not be of use or be capable of being measured.

2.2 Forms of energy

Energy can exist in several forms and chemical energy is the most common. The energy is in the chemical bond that unites atoms or molecules with each other. When a new bond is made between two atoms, energy is required for its formation and this is usually in the form of heat, although light and electrical energy can be used. When a bond is broken and atoms are

released, the energy in the bond is released as well. Heat, light, sound, electrical and nuclear are other forms of energy.

> ### Did you know?
>
> Placing a lump of coal or wood on a fire illustrates the energy laws. As the coal burns, the chemical energy contained within it is released and transformed into heat, light and sometimes sound (crackling). The chemical energy in the wood or coal has come from the sun, and the tree has converted this into stored glucose by means of photosynthesis.

2.3 Energy metabolism
The role of energy in the body

At this stage, you may be wondering why there is so much emphasis on energy and be thinking that it is only concerned with muscular activity and movement. However, energy is also needed to circulate blood, lymph and tissue fluid throughout the body; it is necessary for breathing and taking in oxygen; it is necessary for making new cells for carrying out growth and repair; it is used to transmit nerve impulses so that we can respond to changes in the environment; and it is needed to build different complex molecules such as enzymes and hormones from the simple molecules produced after digestion of food.

Anabolism and catabolism

You have already learned about metabolism and how some chemical reactions involve breaking down

> ### PLTS
>
> **Creative thinker:** You can show creative thinking ability when considering different types of energy.

> ## Case study: An illustration of energy forms
>
> Ian slid down a climbing rope in the gym wearing only a vest and shorts. Later that day the skin on his hands and inner legs became red, swollen and painful. Ian had friction burns from the slide. The kinetic (motion) energy had been partly converted into heat energy, which had caused the burn. Friction is the resistance to motion when two bodies are in contact. This was neither useful nor measurable!
>
> 1 Which two items were in contact to cause the friction burn?
>
> 2 Name the two forms of energy in the slide and the relationship between them.
>
> 3 What is the name given to the law associated with this example?
>
> 4 What type of energy had Ian used to climb the rope?

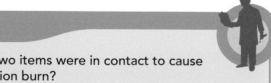

molecules and releasing energy – these are catabolic reactions. The oxidation of glucose inside cells is a catabolic reaction and there are many more. The opposite process is building complex molecules from simple substances and using energy – these are anabolic reactions.

Reflect

Athletes are regularly tested for banned substances that might make them perform better than other competitors. Many of these tests look for anabolic steroids which build up muscle tissue.

Metabolism = catabolism and anabolism

Activities involved in supplying energy to the cells

The activities involved in energy supply include the roles of the cardiovascular, respiratory and digestive systems.

You will learn about these systems in more detail in the sections that follow but we will start with a brief overall view of how they interact:

- The digestive system is responsible for taking in food and water and, using enzymes, breaking up complex molecules into simple soluble materials that are capable of passing into the adjacent capillaries of the cardiovascular system.
- The cardiovascular system transports these simple materials to the liver and body cells via the bloodstream, driven by the pumping action of the heart.
- At the same time, the respiratory system constantly refreshes lung oxygen and disposes of waste products (such as carbon dioxide and water) through the process of breathing. Dissolved oxygen passes through the thin alveolar walls into the bloodstream and is transported to cells. Body cells thus have a constant delivery of raw materials, such as glucose and other nutrients and dissolved oxygen, so that the breakdown (catabolic) process of glucose oxidation can take place and release energy to do work. This takes place initially in the cytoplasm and is completed in the mitochondria.

The released energy is trapped as chemical energy in ATP (see 'Mitochondria' on page 181).

Did you know?

Very large numbers of mitochondria are found in tissues that use a lot of energy such as muscle tissues.

2.4 The cardiovascular system

The heart is a muscular pump that forces blood around the body through a system of blood vessels – namely arteries, veins and capillaries. Blood carries dissolved oxygen to the body cells and at the same time removes the waste products of respiration (carbon dioxide and water). However, blood is also important in distributing heat around the body, along with hormones, nutrients, salts, enzymes and urea.

The structure of the heart

The adult heart is the size of a closed fist, located in the thoracic cavity between the lungs and protected by the rib cage. It is surrounded by a tough membrane, the pericardium, which contains a thin film of fluid to prevent friction (remember Ian and the rope!)

The heart is a double pump, each side consisting of a muscular upper chamber (the atrium) and a lower chamber (the ventricle). The right side of the heart pumps deoxygenated blood from the veins to the lungs for oxygenation. The left side pumps oxygenated blood from the lungs to the body, and the two sides are completely separated by a septum. The blood passes twice through the heart in any one cycle and this is often termed a 'double circulation'.

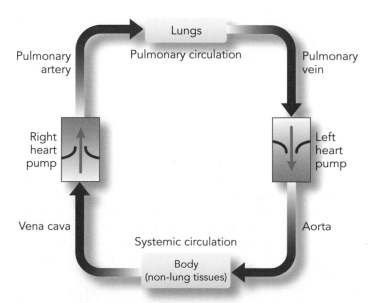

Fig 5.21: The double circulation of the heart

A schematic diagram showing the double circulation, with the heart artificially separated, is shown in Figure 5.21 (page 199). Each of the four heart chambers has a major blood vessel entering or leaving it. Veins enter the atria, and arteries leave the ventricles.

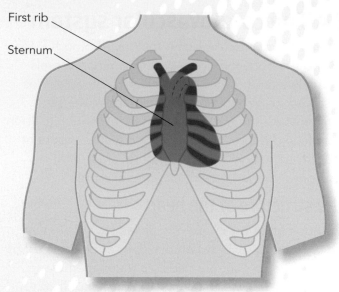

First rib

Sternum

Fig 5.22: The location of the heart

Did you know?

Atria have veins entering and ventricles have arteries leaving. A and V for each chamber – NEVER two As or two Vs.

The circulation to and from the lungs is known as the pulmonary circulation and that around the body is the systemic circulation. Arteries are blood vessels that leave the heart, while veins take blood towards the heart.

In the pulmonary circulation, the pulmonary artery carrying deoxygenated blood leaves the right ventricle to go to the lungs. You will realise that it must divide fairly soon after leaving the heart because there are two lungs to be supplied – hence the right and left pulmonary arteries. The pulmonary veins (there are four of them), now carrying oxygenated blood, must enter the left atrium.

The main artery to the body leaving the left ventricle is the aorta and the main vein bringing blood back to the heart from the body enters the right atrium and is the vena cava. The vena cava has two branches: the superior vena cava returning blood from the head and neck, and the inferior vena cava returning blood from

the rest of the body. In many diagrams of the heart, these are treated as one vessel.

It is important that the blood flows in only one direction through the heart so it has special valves to ensure that this happens. There are two sets of valves between the atria and the ventricles, one on each side. Sometimes these are called the right and left atrio-ventricular valves but the older names are also used – the bicuspid, or mitral (left side), and tricuspid (right side) valves. These names refer to the number of 'flaps', known as cusps, that make up the valve; the bicuspid has two cusps and the tricuspid has three cusps. Each cusp is fairly thin so, to prevent them turning inside out with the force of the blood flowing by, they have tendinous cords attached to their free ends and these are tethered to the heart muscles of the ventricles by small papillary muscles. The papillary muscles tense just before the full force of the muscle in the ventricles contracts, so the tendinous cords act like guy ropes holding the valves in place.

The two large arteries, the pulmonary and the aorta, also have exits guarded by valves called semi-lunar valves (so-called because the three cusps forming each valve are half-moon shaped). These valves are needed because when the blood has been forced into the arteries by the ventricular muscle contractions, it must not be allowed to fall back into the ventricles when they relax. These valves are also called the pulmonary and aortic valves.

Did you know?

It is easy to recall which side each valve is on if you think that the TRIcuspid is on the RIghT side, a rearrangement of the letters TRI, so the bicuspid must be on the left!

How to work out the left and right sides of the heart

Sometimes learners are confused about the correct labels for the heart chambers. When you look at an image in front of you, it is like a mirror image so the left side of the image is opposite your right hand and vice versa. A paper-based image can be placed facing outwards on the front of your chest to make the sides the same as your left and right hands. You do need to know which is your right and left hand though!

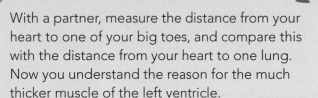

Activity 8: Hearing heartbeats

Using a stethoscope over the heart area, either on your own or with a partner, listen for the heartbeat. Try to count the number of beats you hear in one minute. What does each beat sound like?

A heartbeat makes a 'lubb-dup' sound, with a very short interval between each beat. Valves, like hands clapping, make sounds when closing not opening. 'Lubb' represents the atrio-ventricular valves closing while 'dup' is the sound made by the semi-lunar valves closing. In some people, swishing sounds can be heard between heart sounds and these are called heart murmurs. All murmurs should be investigated but most are not related to disease. Murmurs are the result of disturbed blood flow.

Heart muscle, as you learned on page 189, is cardiac muscle, composed of partially striped interlocking, branched cells. It is myogenic, which means that it is capable of rhythmic contractions without a nerve supply. However, the atrial muscle beats at a different pace from the ventricular muscle so it needs a nerve

supply to organise and co-ordinate the contractions to ensure that the heart is an efficient pump. The heart muscle has its own blood supply, provided by the coronary arteries and veins.

The muscular walls of the atria are much thinner than the ventricular walls, as the flow of blood is aided by gravity and the distance travelled is merely from the atria to the ventricles. The ventricles are much thicker than the atria but they also differ from each other. The right ventricle is about one-third the thickness of the left ventricle because this has to drive oxygenated blood around the whole of the body including the head and neck, which is against the force of gravity. The right ventricle only has to deliver blood a short distance – to the lungs on either side of the heart.

Activity 9: Comparison of distances travelled

With a partner, measure the distance from your heart to one of your big toes, and compare this with the distance from your heart to one lung. Now you understand the reason for the much thicker muscle of the left ventricle.

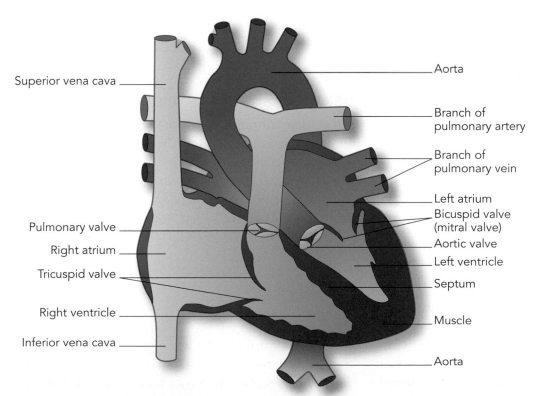

Superior vena cava

Aorta

Branch of pulmonary artery

Branch of pulmonary vein

Left atrium
Bicuspid valve (mitral valve)

Pulmonary valve

Right atrium

Aortic valve

Tricuspid valve

Left ventricle

Septum

Right ventricle

Muscle

Inferior vena cava

Aorta

Fig 5.23: A section through the heart

The cardiac cycle

The cardiac cycle comprises the events taking place in the heart during one heartbeat. Taking the average number of beats in a minute (or 60 seconds) at rest to be 70, then the time for one beat or one cardiac cycle is 60 divided by 70 seconds, which works out at 0.8 seconds. You must remember that this is based on an average resting heart rate. When the heart rate rises to say 120 beats during moderate activity, the cardiac cycle will reduce to 0.5 seconds. As you can see, the higher the heart rate, the shorter the cardiac cycle, until a limit is reached when the heart would not have time to fill between successive cycles.

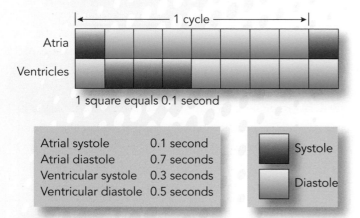

1 square equals 0.1 second

Atrial systole	0.1 second
Atrial diastole	0.7 seconds
Ventricular systole	0.3 seconds
Ventricular diastole	0.5 seconds

Systole

Diastole

Fig 5.24: The timing of events in the cardiac cycle

The cardiac cycle appears in Figure 5.24 as a series of boxes, each one representing 0.1 seconds, to show the events occurring in the heart; red boxes signify when contraction is occurring and green boxes signify relaxation time. The technical term for contraction is systole and the term for relaxation is diastole. The activity of the atria is shown on the top line and the ventricles at the bottom.

The events in the cardiac cycle can be described in stages as follows:

1 Both atria contract, forcing blood under pressure into the ventricles.

2 Ventricles are bulging with blood and the increased pressure forces the atrio-ventricular valves shut (giving rise to the first heart sound – lubb).

3 Muscle in the ventricular walls begins to contract, pressure on blood inside rises and forces open the semi-lunar valves in the aorta and pulmonary artery.

4 Ventricular systole forces blood into the aorta (left side) and pulmonary artery (right side). These arteries have elastic walls and begin to expand.

5 As the blood leaves the ventricles, the muscle starts to relax. For a fraction of a second blood falls backwards, catching the pockets of the semi-lunar valves and making them close (the second heart sound – dup).

6 With the ventricles in diastole, the atrio-ventricular valves are pushed open with the blood that has been filling the atria. When the ventricles are about 70 per cent full, the atria contract to push the remaining blood in rapidly and the next cycle has begun.

You can see that when the chambers are in diastole and relaxed, they are still filling. The heart is never empty of blood. The cycle is continuous. With a high heart rate, it is the filling time that has shortened.

Activity 10: Changes during exercise

Run on the spot for a few steps and listen to the heartbeat again. What do you notice? Count the heart rate again in one minute.

Copy the set of boxes similar to those in Figure 5.24 and discover how much time the atria and ventricles have to fill when the heart rate is at the new level. Work out the new value for the length of the cardiac cycle and shade in the boxes for atrial and ventricular systole. On your chart, mark clearly the places where the heart sounds will be heard.

Heart rate and stroke volume

The **cardiac output** is the quantity of blood expelled from the heart in one minute. To calculate this, you need to know the quantity of blood expelled from the left ventricle in one beat (known as the **stroke volume**) and the number of beats in one minute (or the **heart rate**). The average individual has a stroke volume of 70 cm³ and a heart rate between 60 and 80 beats per

Key terms

Cardiac output – The volume of blood forced out of the heart in one minute.

Stroke volume – The volume of blood forced out of the heart in one beat.

Heart rate – The number of beats counted in one minute.

minute. An individual who trains regularly might have a lower heart rate but a higher stroke volume.

Control of the cardiac cycle

The heart is controlled by the autonomic nervous system, which has two branches – the sympathetic nervous system and the parasympathetic nervous system. These two systems act rather like an accelerator and a brake on the heart. The sympathetic nervous system (NS) is active during muscular work, fear and stress, causing each heartbeat to be stronger and the heart rate to be increased. The parasympathetic NS calms the heart output and is active during peace and contentment.

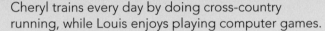

Case study: Individual differences in matters of the heart

Cheryl trains every day by doing cross-country running, while Louis enjoys playing computer games.

1 Complete the table below.

2 Explain the figures in the table in the light of their different lifestyles.

3 Explain how exercise benefits the cardiovascular system.

Heart features	Cheryl	Louis
Stroke volume (cm³)	95	72
Resting heart rate (beats/minute)	62	72
Cardiac output (cm³/min)		

PLTS

Reflective learner: This activity will show that you can communicate learning in relevant ways when considering the effect of exercise on the cardiovascular system.

The sympathetic NS is boosted by the hormone adrenaline during periods of fright, flight and fight!

Blood pressure

The force blood exerts on the walls of the blood vessels it is passing through is known as the blood pressure (BP). It can be measured using a special piece of equipment called a sphygmomanometer, often abbreviated to 'sphygmo' (pronounced *sfigmo*). Systolic blood pressure corresponds to the pressure of the blood when the ventricles are contracting. Diastolic BP represents blood pressure when the ventricles are relaxed and filling. BP is usually written as systolic/diastolic (for example, 120/80) and the units are still mm Hg or millimetres of mercury. Newer SI (International System of Units) units are kPa or kiloPascals but few establishments have converted.

The standard BP for a young healthy adult is taken as 120/80 mm Hg (or 15.79/10.53 kPa).

BP is highest in blood vessels nearer the heart, like the aorta and the large arteries. BP drops rapidly as blood is forced through the medium-sized arteries and the arterioles, as these muscular vessels present considerable resistance. BP in the capillaries is very low and blood in the veins has to be assisted back to the heart by a so-called 'muscle pump'. Veins in the limbs are located between muscle groups and, as they have thinner walls than arteries and possess valves at intervals, muscle action 'squeezes' the blood upwards in columns, and the valves prevent backflow. The slightly negative pressure in the chest during breathing also tends to 'suck' blood back towards the heart.

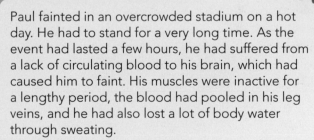

Case study: Why did Paul faint?

Paul fainted in an overcrowded stadium on a hot day. He had to stand for a very long time. As the event had lasted a few hours, he had suffered from a lack of circulating blood to his brain, which had caused him to faint. His muscles were inactive for a lengthy period, the blood had pooled in his leg veins, and he had also lost a lot of body water through sweating.

1 Can you suggest a way of avoiding fainting in these circumstances?

2 Describe the effect on Paul's legs.

3 Why is fainting an effective way of managing a lack of circulating blood to the brain?

PLTS

Creative thinker: Generating ideas and exploring possibilities when producing information on venous return to the heart will allow you to demonstrate your creative thinking skills.

Blood vessels

Arteries and arterioles

Arteries leave the heart and supply smaller vessels (known as arterioles), which in turn supply the smallest blood vessels, the capillaries. Arteries usually carry oxygenated blood. The exceptions are the pulmonary and umbilical arteries, which carry, respectively, blood to the lungs and placenta in pregnancy for oxygenation. The arterioles provide an extensive network to supply the capillaries and, in overcoming the resistance of these muscular vessels, BP drops significantly at this stage. Arteries and arterioles are lined by endothelium (see simple squamous epithelium on pages 183–184) and have a thick muscular coat. The lumen (or central hole) is round.

Capillaries

These single-cell walled vessels are supplied with blood by the arterioles (see simple squamous epithelium on pages 183–184). Body cells are never very far from capillaries, on which they rely for nutrients and oxygen. A protein-free plasma filtrate is driven out of the arterial ends of capillaries to supply the cells with oxygen and nutrients. This is called tissue (or interstitial) fluid. Tissue fluid re-enters the venous ends of the capillaries, bringing the waste products of the metabolic activities of the body cells (such as dissolved carbon dioxide and water).

Venules and veins

Venules are small veins, which are supplied by capillaries and feed into veins. The largest vein is the vena cava, which enters the right atrium of the heart. Limb veins contain valves to assist the flow of blood back to the heart because of the low BP in the veins. Veins have a much thinner muscular coat than arteries, more fibrous tissue and an oval lumen. BP is low in veins and venules. Generally, veins carry deoxygenated blood, with the exceptions of the pulmonary and umbilical arteries, which bring blood back from the lungs and placenta respectively.

Did you know?

A first-aider learns that arterial bleeding is bright red and spurts out in time with the heartbeat; capillary bleeding oozes from a wound and is most common, while venous bleeding is dark red (less oxygen) and flows at a low pressure.

Each type of blood vessel has structural and functional differences outlined in the table on the next page.

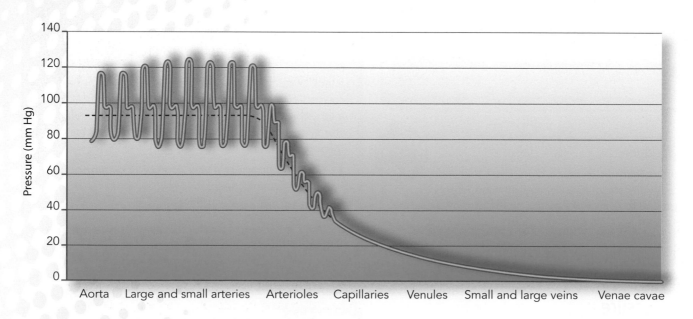

Fig 5.25: Graph showing the fall in blood pressure as blood moves through the circulation

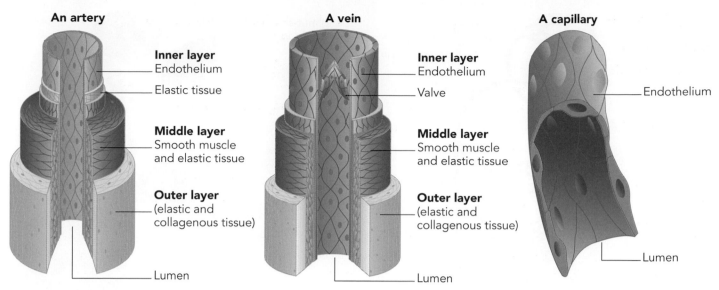

Fig 5.26: Arteries, veins and capillaries

Table 5.3: The roles of different blood vessels

Arteries	Veins	Capillaries
Carry blood away from heart to organs	Carry blood to heart from the organs	Connect arteries to veins
Carry blood under high pressure	Carry blood under low pressure	Arterioles and capillaries cause greatest drop in pressure due to overcoming the friction of blood passing through small vessels
Have thick, muscular walls, round lumen	Have thin, muscular walls, oval lumen	
Usually contain blood high in oxygen, and low in carbon dioxide and water	Usually contain blood low in oxygen, and high in carbon dioxide and water	Deliver protein-free plasma filtrate high in oxygen to cells and collect respiratory waste products (carbon dioxide and water)
Large elastic arteries close to the heart help the intermittent flow from the ventricles become a continuous flow through the circulation	Veins in limbs contain valves at regular intervals and are sandwiched between muscle groups to help blood travel against gravity	Walls are formed from a single layer of epithelium cells

Pulmonary and systemic circulations

The pulmonary circulation comprises the pulmonary arteries (which supply the lungs with deoxygenated blood from the right ventricle) and the pulmonary veins (which carry oxygenated blood back to the left atrium of the heart).

Each organ has an arterial and venous supply that brings blood to the organ tissues and drains blood away respectively. The link vessels supplying the cells of the organ tissues are the capillaries.

The systemic circulation comprises all the blood vessels not involved in the pulmonary circulation.

Structure and functions of blood

You have already learned about blood in the section on tissues on pages 185–187. You might like to read this section again before reading about haemoglobin below.

Erythrocytes contain haemoglobin, an important respiratory pigment that is essential for human life.

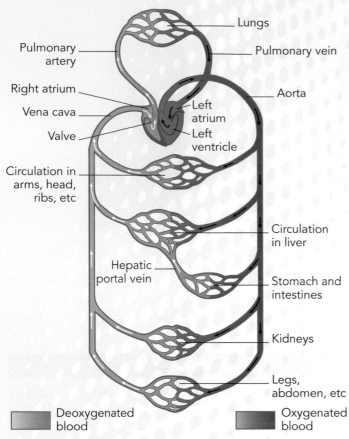

Fig 5.27: A simplified diagram showing human circulation

Haemoglobin is a very special iron-containing protein because:

- in an environment containing a high concentration of oxygen, the *haem* part of the molecule forms a strong chemical bond with oxygen, becoming oxyhaemoglobin. Oxyhaemoglobin is formed in the blood of the lung capillaries and carries oxygen to tissue cells

- in an environment containing a low concentration of oxygen, the oxygen is released to pass down a concentration gradient to body cells. Haemoglobin is now said to be reduced haemoglobin.

2.5 The respiratory system

Respiration can be artificially subdivided into four sections to facilitate study, three of which are grouped under 'External respiration'. These are:

A External respiration, comprising:
- Breathing
- Gaseous exchange
- Blood transport.

B Internal or tissue respiration carried out *inside* body cells.

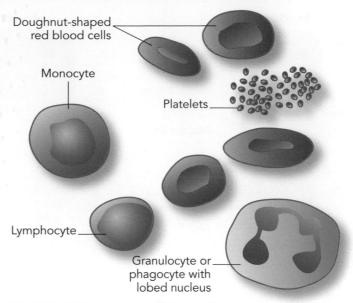

Fig 5.28: Different types of blood cell

Breathing

The thorax, better known as the chest, is an airtight box containing the lungs and their associated tubes, the bronchi and the heart. Air can enter the thorax via the nose or the mouth; the nose is specially adapted for the entry of air in breathing and is the recommended route.

Role of the air passages in the nose

The nose contains fine bones on its side walls, which are curled like scrolls and covered with moist ciliated mucous membrane, rich in blood capillaries. This arrangement produces a large surface area over which incoming air flows. During the passage through the nose, the air is warmed and moistened by the close contact with the mucous membrane and filtered by the ciliated cells. By the time the air reaches the throat, it is warmed to almost body temperature, moistened to almost saturation point and most foreign materials (such as dust, carbon particles and many pathogens) have been filtered out.

The structure and function of the trachea and bronchi

The trachea starts at the back of the throat, or pharynx, and divides into two main bronchi, each serving one lung on each side of the heart. The first part of the trachea is specially adapted to produce sound and is called the larynx, or voice box. It is protected by a moveable cartilage flap, the epiglottis, which prevents food entering during swallowing.

When any material, such as a crumb, manages to pass the epiglottis it provokes an intense bout of coughing by reflex action, to expel the foreign body.

The trachea (or windpipe) and the bronchi have rings of cartilage to prevent them collapsing; those in the trachea are C-shaped, with the gap at the back against the main food tube, the oesophagus. This is because, when food is chewed in the mouth, it is made into a ball shape (called a bolus) before swallowing. The bolus stretches the oesophagus as it passes down to the stomach, and whole rings of cartilage in the trachea would hamper its progress. The gap is filled with soft muscle that stretches easily, allowing the bolus to pass down the oesophagus.

Reflect

It is not possible to breathe and swallow at the same time so, when helping someone to eat, you must allow time for breathing between mouthfuls of food.

Each bronchus divides and sub-divides repeatedly, spreading to each part of the lung. The tiniest sub-divisions, supplying oxygen to air sacs in the lung, are called bronchioles, and even these are held open by minute areas of cartilage. This branching arrangement is often called the bronchial tree.

The inner lining of the trachea and bronchi is composed of mucus-secreting and ciliated, columnar epithelial cells. Mucus is the sticky white gel which traps dust particles that may cause infection.

The structure and function of the lungs

Each lung is a pale pink, smooth structure that closely mimics the interior of half the chest in shape. Each is divided into a few lobes and has a hilum, or root, that marks the entry of the bronchus, blood vessels and nerves on the inner side.

The lungs themselves have a spongy feel to them, and are lined on the outside by a thin, moist membrane known as the pleura. The pleura continues around the inner thoracic cavity so that the two pleural layers slide over one another with ease and without friction. The **surface tension** of the thin film of moisture does not allow the two layers to pull apart but does allow them to slide. This means that when the chest wall moves when breathing, the lungs move with it.

Key term

Surface tension – The pull of water molecules so that the surface of the liquid occupies the smallest possible area.

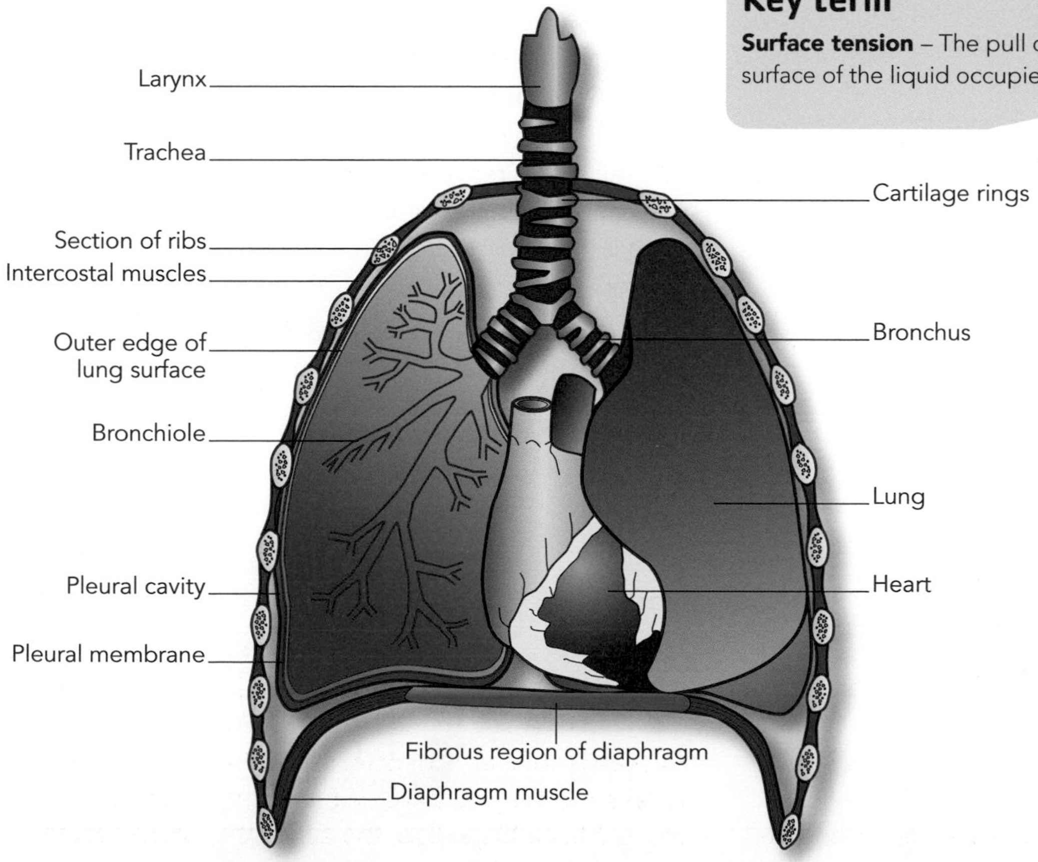

Larynx

Trachea

Section of ribs

Intercostal muscles

Outer edge of lung surface

Bronchiole

Pleural cavity

Pleural membrane

Cartilage rings

Bronchus

Lung

Heart

Fibrous region of diaphragm

Diaphragm muscle

Fig 5.29: A section through the thorax showing the respiratory organs

Each bronchus, after repeatedly dividing, ends in a group of single-layered globe-shaped structures called alveoli, which look rather like a bunch of grapes on a stem. The walls of the alveoli consist of very thin, flat, simple squamous epithelium, and each alveolus is surrounded by the smallest blood vessels known as capillaries. The walls of the capillaries are also composed of simple squamous epithelium, in a single layer. This means that the air entering the alveoli during breathing is separated from the blood by only two single-layered, very thin walls. There are elastic fibres round the alveoli, enabling them to expand and recoil with inspiration and expiration respectively. A film of moisture lines the inside of each alveolus to enable the air gases to pass into solution. As the two layers of epithelium are very thin and semi-permeable, the dissolved gases can easily and rapidly pass through, in a process called gaseous exchange.

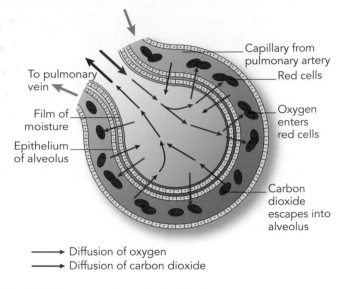

Fig 5.30: Gaseous exchange in the alveolus

Ventilation, or breathing, and the respiratory muscles

Ventilation is the movement of air in and out of the thorax to replenish the oxygen supply and remove surplus waste products (carbon dioxide and water). Ventilation has two phases, namely inspiration (or inhalation) and expiration (or exhalation). The movements in these phases are effected by respiratory muscles attached to the skeleton. Two sets of intercostal muscles run obliquely at right angles to each other between the ribs, and the diaphragm is a dome-shaped muscle attached to the lower ribs and separating the thorax from the abdomen.

Inspiration

When the intercostal muscles contract, the ribs move upwards and outwards and at the same time the contraction of the diaphragm causes it to flatten. All these movements increase the volume of the thorax and the lungs and thus reduce the pressure inside the lungs, causing air to rush in from the environment. This is known as inspired, or inhaled, air.

Expiration

The main force in expiration during quiet breathing is the elastic recoil of the fibres around the alveoli, and the relaxation of the diaphragm. However, during exertion, more forcible expiration can occur with the assistance of the other set of intercostal muscles contracting to move the ribs downwards and inwards. The volume of the thorax decreases, the pressure increases above that of the environmental air, and air rushes out.

Normal ventilation rate is 16 to 20 breaths per minute but this rises significantly during exertion.

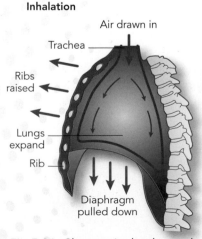

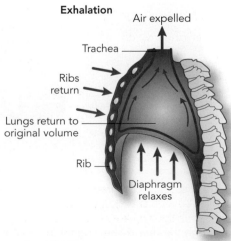

Fig 5.31: Changes in the thorax during inspiration and expiration

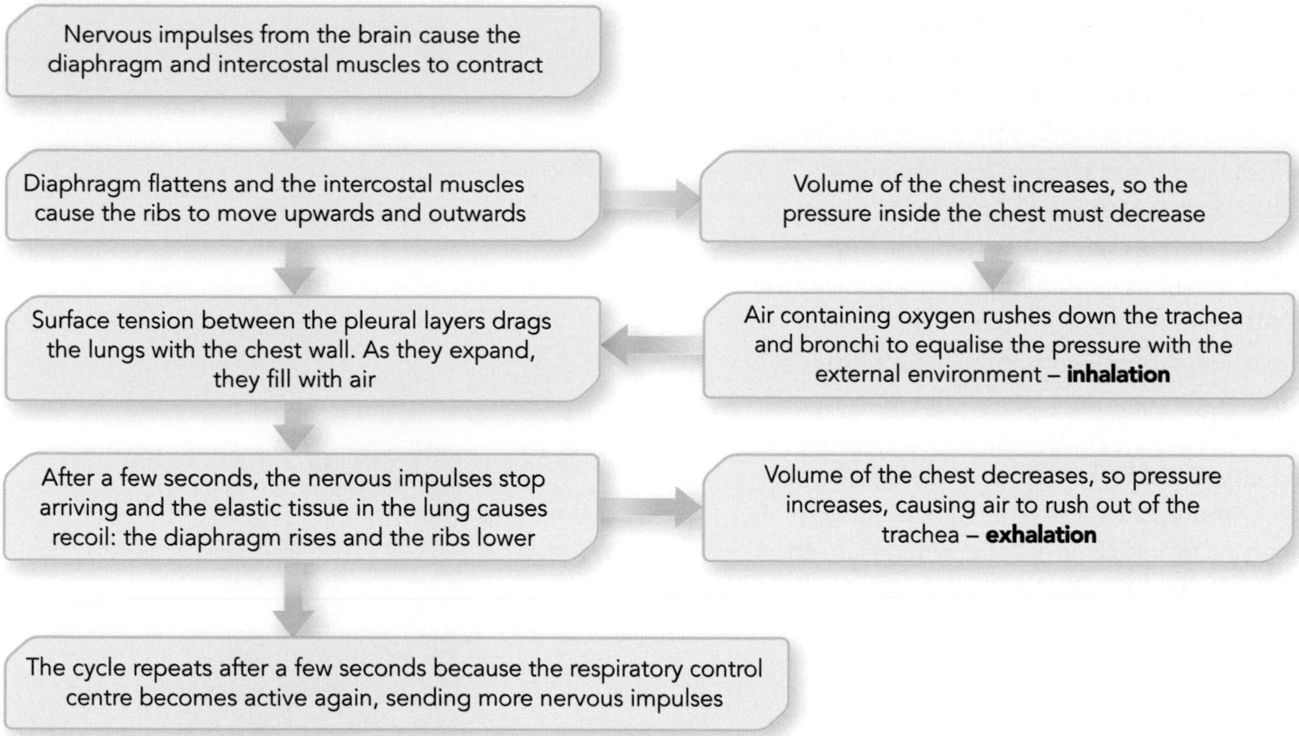

Nervous impulses from the brain cause the diaphragm and intercostal muscles to contract

Diaphragm flattens and the intercostal muscles cause the ribs to move upwards and outwards

Volume of the chest increases, so the pressure inside the chest must decrease

Surface tension between the pleural layers drags the lungs with the chest wall. As they expand, they fill with air

Air containing oxygen rushes down the trachea and bronchi to equalise the pressure with the external environment – **inhalation**

After a few seconds, the nervous impulses stop arriving and the elastic tissue in the lung causes recoil: the diaphragm rises and the ribs lower

Volume of the chest decreases, so pressure increases, causing air to rush out of the trachea – **exhalation**

The cycle repeats after a few seconds because the respiratory control centre becomes active again, sending more nervous impulses

Fig 5.32: The process of breathing

Gaseous exchange

The composition of inspired air (which is the air around us) and that of expired air is shown in the table below:

Table 5.4: The composition of inspired and expired air

Component	Inspired air	Expired air
Oxygen	20 per cent	16 per cent
Nitrogen	80 per cent	80 per cent
Carbon dioxide	Virtually 0 (0.04 per cent)	4 per cent
Water vapour	Depends on climate	Saturated

Although the largest component of air is nitrogen and this too passes into solution, it takes no part in the process of respiration. Breathing in fresh air replenishes the high concentration of dissolved oxygen molecules in the lung alveoli, and the removal of diffused oxygen by the bloodstream maintains the low concentration. With carbon dioxide, the situation is reversed – the high concentration is in the blood and the low concentration is in the refreshed air, so diffusion (see below) moves dissolved carbon dioxide from the blood into the expired air from the lungs. Carbon dioxide and water are waste products from internal respiration in cells.

Diffusion

Diffusion occurs in liquids or gases because the molecules are in constant random motion, and diffusion is an overall 'equalling up' of a situation where you have a lot of molecules meeting a few molecules. Diffusion will stop in time, as the numbers of molecules become more evenly distributed. This is

Activity 11: Air changes

Write down the differences between inspired and expired air that you can see in Table 5.4. Why have these changes happened?

PLTS

Creative thinker: When generating ideas and exploring possibilities about air changes, you can demonstrate your creative thinking abilities.

Key term

Diffusion – The movement of molecules of a gas or a liquid from a region of high concentration to a region of low concentration.

said to be equilibrium. (Note that this does not mean the molecules stop moving, only that there are now equal numbers of molecules passing in all directions.)

In the human body, where diffusion is a common method of transport, the state of equilibrium is not desirable, as it means overall transport ceases. To prevent equilibrium being attained, the high concentration must be continually kept high, and the low concentration must also be maintained.

Diffusion can only occur where there is no barrier at all to the molecules or where the barrier (in gaseous exchange, this is cell membranes) is thin. The rate of diffusion is enhanced by having an increased surface area (usually created by folds or similar structures to alveoli) and a raised temperature, since warmth increases the random motion of molecules.

2.6 The digestive system
The alimentary canal

The alimentary canal is a tube that extends from the mouth to the anus. It is dilated, folded and puckered in various places along its length. You will need to know the names of the various regions, their main purpose and the outcomes of their activities. Many glands are associated with the alimentary canal, and have important roles to play in digestion.

When food is taken into the mouth it is mixed with saliva, chewed or masticated by the action of the tongue and teeth, rolled into a small ball known as a bolus, and swallowed. This process is called mechanical digestion and it is an important part of physically breaking the food down at an early stage.

The salivary glands

Three pairs of salivary glands pour their secretions known as saliva into the mouth. Saliva, a digestive juice, contains an **enzyme** known as salivary amylase, which begins the digestion of carbohydrates as well as lubricating the mouth and helping bolus formation.

The oesophagus

The oesophagus (or gullet) transports the food bolus from the back of the mouth (the pharynx) to the stomach in the abdomen. The swallowed bolus is in the oesophagus for a few seconds only and no enzymes are secreted here, although salivary amylase will continue to act during this brief journey. The oesophagus is mainly a transit for food boluses which it moves by muscular contractions known as peristalsis (see page 213).

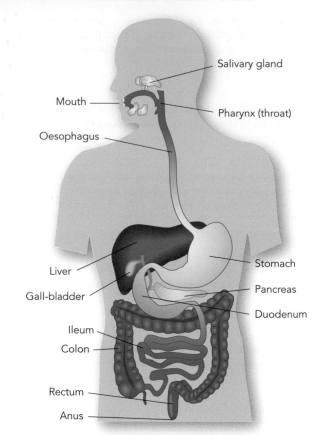

Labels: Mouth, Salivary gland, Pharynx (throat), Oesophagus, Liver, Gall-bladder, Ileum, Colon, Rectum, Anus, Stomach, Pancreas, Duodenum

Fig 5.33: The alimentary canal

The stomach

The stomach is the widest part of the alimentary canal, tucked mainly behind the rib cage under the diaphragm on the left side and receiving food from the mouth by way of the oesophagus. Food can stay in the stomach for up to three hours, with a protein meal remaining the longest and food not containing protein passing through relatively quickly. During this time, the strong stomach walls roll and churn the food around and pour on secretions from the gastric glands. The resulting paste-like material is called chyme.

Gastric glands produce gastric juice that contains gastric protease and hydrochloric acid. The gastric juice works on proteins. In babies, another enzyme, rennin, solidifies and digests milk protein. The pH of the stomach is 1–2; this is strongly acidic. The epithelial lining of the stomach contains goblet cells, which produce thick mucus to protect the lining from acid erosion.

Key term

Enzymes – These are biological catalysts that alter the rates of chemical reaction (usually speeding them up) but which are themselves unchanged at the end of the reactions. You can read more about enzymes on pages 213–214.

The stomach empties the chyme in spurts into the duodenum through the pyloric sphincter, a thick ring of muscle that alternately contracts and relaxes.

The duodenum

The next part of the alimentary canal is the small intestine, so-called because of its small diameter – certainly not its length, for it is around 6 metres long! The first C-shaped part, and the shortest, is called the duodenum; it is mainly concerned with digestion and is helped by two large glands, the liver and the pancreas, that pour their secretions or juices into this area. The duodenal wall also contains glands which secrete enzyme-rich juices (called succus entericus) that continue the digestive process on proteins, carbohydrates and lipids, or fats. These work either on the surface or inside the epithelial lining cells.

The ileum

The remainder of the small intestine, known as the ileum, is mainly concerned with the absorption of the now fully digested food. It is specially adapted for this by its:

- long length
- folded interior
- lining covered in many thousands of tiny projections called villi

- epithelial cells of villi covered in microvilli, projections so small that they can only be detected using an electron microscope.

These adaptations enormously increase the surface area for absorption of nutrients from digested food.

Each villus is lined by columnar cells and goblet cells only one-cell thick, with an extensive internal capillary network and a blind-ended branch of the lymphatic system called a lacteal.

The chief products of protein and carbohydrate digestion pass into the capillary network, which drains to the liver via the hepatic portal vein. Products of fat digestion pass into the lacteal and eventually they pass, via the lymphatic system, into the general circulation.

The colon

In the right-hand lower corner of the abdomen, the small intestine meets the large intestine; there are two biological remnants at this point, the caecum and the appendix. In grass-eating animals the caecum is a large structure with the worm-like appendix at the end. They are known as biological or evolutionary remnants because, in the human species, neither the caecum nor the appendix has any function. The appendix can become inflamed or pustulous and threaten life

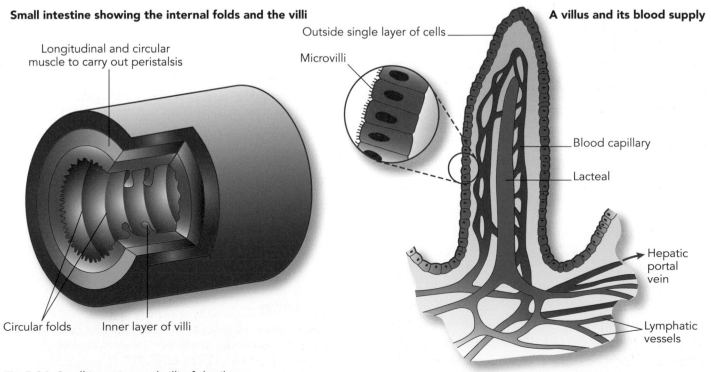

Small intestine showing the internal folds and the villi

Longitudinal and circular muscle to carry out peristalsis

Circular folds   Inner layer of villi

A villus and its blood supply

Outside single layer of cells

Microvilli

Blood capillary

Lacteal

Hepatic portal vein

Lymphatic vessels

Fig 5.34: Small intestine and villi of the ileum

– a condition known as appendicitis. As well as the caecum and appendix, the large intestine consists of the colon and rectum, ending in the sphincter (the anus) for the elimination of faeces.

The colon runs up the right side of the abdomen and turns to travel across to the left side before ending at the anus. There are no enzymic juices in the large intestine.

The colon has a puckered appearance because the outer longitudinal muscle coat splits into three bands and the circular muscle bulges out between the bands. During the journey down the alimentary canal, many glands have poured watery juices onto the chyme. The body cannot afford to lose so much water and the purpose of the large intestine is to slow down the passage of food waste. (Food waste is all that is left at this stage because all the absorption of nutrients occurred in the small intestine.) This means that water can be reabsorbed and the motion, or faeces, becomes semi-solid. It can then be eliminated by muscular action of the rectum and relaxation of the anus at a convenient time.

Faeces contain:

- cellulose (fibre or roughage) from plant cell walls from fruit and vegetables
- dead bacteria, including the usually harmless bacteria living in the large intestine that have died a natural death, and other bacteria, which are often killed by the hydrochloric acid in the stomach
- scraped-off cells from the gut lining.

The brown colour of faeces is due to bile pigments.

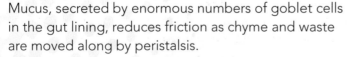

Reflect

When faeces become pale yellow and skin becomes dark yellow/brown, what may have happened? See Student Voice on page 177.

Mucus, secreted by enormous numbers of goblet cells in the gut lining, reduces friction as chyme and waste are moved along by peristalsis.

The liver

The liver is a large, dark-red organ occupying the top right half of the abdomen and partly overlapping the stomach. It has many vital functions in the body, one of which is to produce bile. Bile flows down the bile duct into the duodenum, after temporary storage in the gall bladder on the undersurface of the liver. Bile contains no enzymes at all, but it provides important bile salts that cause the **emulsification** of fats (lipids) in the duodenum. You will recall that protein and carbohydrate have already experienced enzymic action. Lipids, like all fats, do not readily mix with water, so the enzymes have only a small water/lipid surface on which to work.

The emulsification results in the fats forming millions of tiny globules, each with a water/lipid surface so that enzymes can work efficiently over a massively enlarged surface area. Bile also contains bile pigments – bilirubin and biliverdin. These are the waste products of degraded haemoglobin from old, broken, red blood cells. They give the brown colour to faeces. Bile is secreted continuously by the liver and temporarily stored in a sac called the gall bladder. When a lipid-rich meal arrives, the gall bladder releases bile into the small intestine.

The liver also removes glucose and other sugars from the blood coming from the small intestine and converts them into glycogen for storage. Surplus amino acids not required for manufacturing cell proteins are broken down in the liver to form glycogen and urea – a nitrogenous waste product transported by the bloodstream to the kidneys for elimination in urine.

The pancreas

The pancreas is a slim, leaf-shaped gland, located between the intestines and the stomach, close to the duodenum. It secretes enzyme-rich pancreatic juice as well as alkaline salts needed to neutralise the acidic secretions from the stomach. Pancreatic enzymes go to work on all three macronutrients (protein, fat and carbohydrate) and are important agents for the complete breakdown of complex food molecules into amino acids, glucose and similar simple sugars, fatty acids and glycerol.

Breakdown and absorption of food materials

It is vital to understand that, without the organs and glands of the digestive system, we would be unable

Key term

Emulsification – This occurs when an emulsifier causes oil or lipids to be suspended as a large number of tiny globules in water.

to use the substances collectively called food by means of **digestion**. Taking food in through the mouth (what we would call 'eating') is known technically as **ingestion**. Food is generally composed of large complex molecules of protein, carbohydrate and lipids (or fats) that would be unable to pass through the lining of the alimentary canal. Converting these complex molecules into simple soluble molecules enables their **absorption** into the bloodstream and onward transit for metabolic processes. Waste material that has not been capable of absorption is passed out through the anus periodically: the technical term for this is **egestion**.

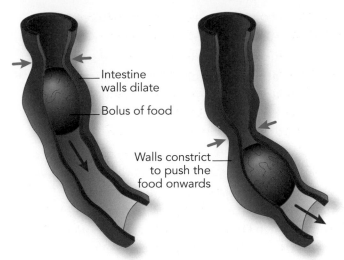

Fig 5.35: Muscular coats involved in peristalsis

Intestine walls dilate

Bolus of food

Walls constrict to push the food onwards

Key terms

Digestion – The conversion of food into simple, soluble chemicals capable of being absorbed through the intestinal lining into the blood and being utilised by body cells.

Ingestion – The taking in of food, drink and drugs by the mouth.

Absorption – The taking up of substances to be used by the body cells and tissues.

Egestion – The process involved in eliminating waste material from the body as faeces.

Peristalsis

Food and chyme move down the alimentary canal by a process known as peristalsis. Note that in Figure 5.35 there are two sheets of muscle surrounding the tube – one sheet runs in a circular fashion around the tube while the other runs down the tube. Behind the bolus or chyme, the inner circular muscle contracts (and the longitudinal muscle relaxes), pushing material in front of it. This is rather like your fingers pushing toothpaste up the tube. In front of the material, the circular muscle relaxes and the longitudinal muscle contracts, to hold the tube open to receive the food. Two sets of muscles acting in this way are said to be antagonistic.

Did you know?

Even if you stand on your head, peristalsis will still push your food down your alimentary canal!

Strong peristaltic waves will cause abdominal pain (usually called colic) and the food will be hurried down the intestines.

2.7 The role of enzymes in digestion

To break down large complex molecules in the laboratory we would use heat (as in cooking) or add chemicals such as acids or alkalis. These processes are not possible in the human body, since cell and tissue structures would be destroyed or severely damaged.

Body cells are able to produce 'magical' substances called enzymes that can alter the rate of chemical reactions to build up or break down other molecules without using heat or harmful chemicals.

Enzymes are biological catalysts. This means that they are substances that can act within living organisms to enable the breakdown or building-up of other chemicals, but they remain unchanged themselves at the end of the reactions or tasks.

Enzymes are specific to the material on which they act (called a substrate). For example, a protease only acts on protein and a lipase only acts on lipids or fats. You may have noted that adding '–ase' at the end of the substrate name signifies that it is an enzyme. Not all enzymes are named in this way, but most are.

The main bulk of the human diet consists of protein, fat and carbohydrate so these are called macronutrients. They provide calories or joules of heat energy. Vitamins and mineral salts are only required in tiny amounts and are called micronutrients. They do not provide energy but are often important in energy release processes, oxygen carriage, metabolic rate, red blood cell formation and so on.

Enzyme reactions have some special features:

- Enzymes are sensitive to temperature. At low temperatures they work very slowly, or stop working; at high temperatures, they become distorted (denatured) and permanently stop working. Enzymes work best, or optimally, at body temperature.

- Enzymes are sensitive to the acidity or alkalinity of their surroundings, known as pH. Some digestive enzymes like pepsin (also known as gastric protease) work best in an acidic environment. The stomach lining secretes gastric protease and hydrochloric acid for maximum efficiency in breaking down proteins. Lipase prefers alkaline conditions and the pancreas secretes alkaline salts, such as sodium hydrogen carbonate, to provide optimal conditions. Salivary amylase prefers neutral or pH7 conditions. (Amylum is the Latin name for starch, so amylase works on starch.)

- Relatively few molecules of enzymes are required to break down lots of large food molecules because they are catalysts.

- Amylases work on cooked starch substrates (bread, rice, potatoes, etc.), converting the molecules to simple sugars like glucose.

- Proteases act on proteins, breaking them down into amino acids and peptides (two amino acids joined together chemically).

- Lipases convert lipids to fatty acids and glycerol.

Table 5.5, on page 215, summarises the sites of enzyme secretion and their role in digestion.

2.8 Major products of digestion

Roles in the body, storage and deamination

- Peptides and amino acids are nitrogenous compounds; they travel via the bloodstream to areas of need in body cells. They are important in making enzymes, some hormones, plasma proteins, new cells (growth) and in repair processes. Surplus amino acids are broken down in the liver, as they cannot be stored. Some parts of the molecules are used for energy but the nitrogen-containing part is converted into urea in the liver, by a process called deamination, and excreted by the kidneys in urine.

- Sugars, chiefly glucose, are transported to cells to be broken down in internal respiration to release energy; excess carbohydrate is stored in liver and muscles as glycogen or converted into fat to be stored around organs or under the skin. Glycogen is converted back to glucose when energy is required to top up the blood glucose supply to cells or for muscle contraction. The end products of internal respiration, carbon dioxide and water, are removed by the respiratory and renal systems.

- Glycerol and fatty acids: glycerol is used for energy or reconverting fatty acids into a form of fat that can be stored. Fatty acids travel from the lacteals, through the lymphatic system into the main veins of the neck; this circuitous route enables smaller quantities of potentially harmful lipids to enter the circulation gradually.

- Fatty acids are also used in internal respiration to release energy to drive metabolic processes. The end products of internal respiration, carbon dioxide and water, are removed by the respiratory and renal systems.

- Fat is stored under the skin and around organs, where it forms a long-term energy store to be used after glycogen stores are depleted.

2.9 Absorption of food

This topic is to be found under the heading 'The ileum' on page 211.

Table 5.5: The main digestive processes, locations and outcomes

Location	Gland and juice	Contents	Substrate	End product	Other comments
Mouth	Salivary glands/ saliva	Salivary amylase	Carbohydrate: starch	Disaccharides: 'double' sugar molecules	Salivary amylase is mixed with food during mechanical digestion. Requires a neutral pH to function efficiently.
Oesophagus	None	None	None	None	Salivary amylase still acting on short journey.
Stomach	Gastric glands/ gastric juice	• Gastric protease* • Hydrochloric acid • Rennin in babies	Protein	Amino acids and peptides (like double amino acids)	The pH of gastric juice must be acid for pepsin to work. Food is churned into chyme. Bacteria in raw food are killed by acid.
Small intestine a) Duodenum	Intestinal glands/ intestinal juice (succus entericus)	• Peptidase • Various carbohydrates	• Peptides • Disaccharides: 'double' sugar molecules	• Amino acids • Glucose and other simple soluble sugars	Alkaline medium (pH8).
b) Liver, an associated gland (not part of the alimentary canal)	Liver/bile	• No enzymes • Bile salts • Bile pigments	None	None	Bile salts are important in emulsifying lipids or fats. Convert small intestine contents from acid to alkaline.
c) Pancreas, an associated gland (not part of the alimentary canal)	Pancreas/ pancreatic juice	• Lipase • Pancreatic amylase • Pancreatic protease* (formerly called trypsin) • Alkaline salts	• Lipids or fats • Carbohydrates • Proteins and peptides	• Glycerol and fatty acids • Glucose • Amino acids	An important digestive gland. Salts convert acid stomach secretions to alkaline so that enzymes work optimally.
d) Ileum	None	None	None	None	Main area for absorption of the end products of digestion through millions of villi.
Large intestine a) Colon	None	None	None	None	Main area for reabsorption of water.
b) Rectum	None	None	None	None	Muscular walls expel semi-solid faeces through anus at periodic intervals.

*Gastric protease and pancreatic protease are secreted as inactive precursors; they become activated by other substances once they are mixed with chyme in the lumen (hole) of the tube.

Assessment activity 5.4

You are an adviser in your local sports centre and you have been asked to design and produce an information booklet to explain to clients how the body requires and utilises energy. This should include:

- an outline of the respiratory, cardiovascular and digestive systems
- an overview of how energy is utilised in the body
- and how two main body systems are linked to this utilisation.

Grading tips

P4 To achieve P4, you need to explain the physiology of two named body systems in relation to energy metabolism in the body. First you have to decide which two systems you will choose. The cardiovascular system should really be one of them, to help understanding and give coherence. Imagine the booklet is for an athlete or an individual on a restricted diet.

If digestion is one of your selected systems you need only consider the three major macronutrients present: protein, carbohydrate and lipids. Start with mechanical digestion in the mouth and explain what happens in each part of the alimentary canal. You need not go beyond the ileum but you do need to include absorption and the fate of the end products of

digestion, where this is associated with energy metabolism.

The focus for the respiratory system should be on breathing, gaseous exchange and cell respiration.

The cardiovascular system should include the role of the blood and transport of materials within plasma and haemoglobin.

M1 To gain M1, you have to discuss the role of energy in the body. You will need to explain that energy in the body comes from the diet and describe how it is transformed into energy used by the body as well as saying where the energy is used.

D1 For D1, you have to analyse how two body systems interrelate with each other to perform a named function or functions. Use examples to explain how these body systems interrelate with each other. As you explain your work, you will naturally make links – for instance the regulation of plasma glucose by the endocrine system, or the way in which the nervous system is involved in the regulation of the cardiac cycle. This will lead you towards a distinction. Try to make at least five substantial links of this nature. It might be advisable to draw attention to such links by the use of headings.

PLTS

Self-manager: This activity will allow you to illustrate self-management skills when working towards the goal of producing an information booklet by a specified date and dealing with competing pressures to meet deadlines.

Functional skills

ICT: By storing work on a password-protected storage device you are using ICT systems. Use ICT to present information in a booklet that is fit for purpose.

3 Understand how homeostatic mechanisms operate in the maintenance of an internal environment

You have learned how tissue fluid bathes body cells and is a protein-free plasma filtrate driven out of leaky capillaries by blood pressure, and how (digestive) enzymes are sensitive to pH and body temperature. You will not be surprised therefore to extend this by realising that blood and tissue fluid and consequently cell contents require stability in their chemical and physical make-up. All metabolic processes are governed by enzyme actions, which are subject to the same characteristics as digestive enzymes.

3.1 Homeostasis

Homeostasis is the technical term for the process of maintaining a constant internal environment despite external changes. The 'internal environment' comprises blood, tissue fluid, body cell contents and all the metabolic processes taking place.

It is important to realise that the use of the term 'constant' in this context is not absolute and fixed; it is more flexible and dynamic and refers to the physical and chemical composition being kept within a limited range of variables for maximum efficiency, well-being of the whole body and, indeed, the maintenance of life itself. This limited range of variables is said to be regulated.

Negative feedback as a form of regulation

Negative feedback occurs when an important variable, sometimes known as a key variable, such as the pH of blood and tissue fluid, deviates from the accepted range or limits, and triggers responses that return the variable to within the normal range. In other words, deviation produces a negative response to counteract or nullify the deviation. It is a 'feeding back' of the disturbance to the status quo. During your study of the liver as part of the digestive system, you learned that when blood glucose levels fall, the liver glycogen is converted into glucose in order to top up those crucial energy levels in cells. This is an example of a negative feedback system and we shall study this further in due course.

The brain and nervous system play a vital role in controlling homeostatic mechanisms and they also help us to anticipate when key variables might rise or fall beyond the accepted range. For example, if it is several hours since your last meal and you are beginning to feel tired and cold, you will try to eat a warm, energy-giving meal to counteract these feelings. This can be termed 'feedforward' (rather than feedback), as you are taking steps to avoid a low energy state before it has happened.

Negative feedback systems require:

- receptors to detect change
- a control centre to receive the information and process the response
- effectors to reverse the change and re-establish the original state.

Most control centres are located in the brain.

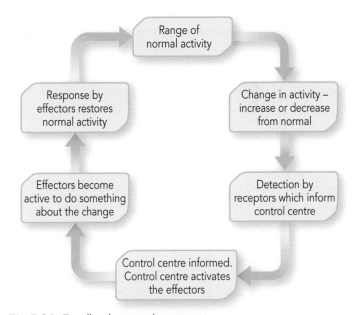

Fig 5.36: Feedback control systems

Range of normal activity → Change in activity – increase or decrease from normal → Detection by receptors which inform control centre → Control centre informed. Control centre activates the effectors → Effectors become active to do something about the change → Response by effectors restores normal activity

Activity 12: Prevention is better than cure

Can you think of other examples of times when your brain might be suggesting feedforward strategies? Try a thought shower with your peers and see how many examples you can suggest.

PLTS

Creative thinker: This activity will help you to demonstrate that you can question your own and others' assumptions when thinking of examples of feedforward strategies.

3.2 Homeostatic mechanisms for regulation of heart rate

First we will learn how the heartbeat is regulated. Let's begin by looking at the control of the cardiac cycle and the role of the autonomic, parasympathetic and sympathetic nervous systems.

The heart is controlled by the autonomic nervous system which has two branches, namely the sympathetic nervous system and the parasympathetic nervous system. These two systems act rather like an accelerator and a brake on the heart. The sympathetic nervous system is active when the body is undergoing muscular work, fear or stress. It causes each heartbeat to increase in strength as well as causing an increase in heart rate. The parasympathetic nervous system calms the heart output and is active during resting, peace and contentment. The main parasympathetic nerve is the vagus nerve and if this is severed the heart beats faster.

The sympathetic nervous system is boosted by the hormone adrenaline during periods of fright, flight and fight! Its nerves are the cardiac nerves.

The sympathetic and parasympathetic nervous systems supply a special cluster of excitable cells in the upper part of the right atrium. This is called the sino-atrial node (S-A node) or in general terms 'the pacemaker'. An interplay of impulses from the sympathetic and

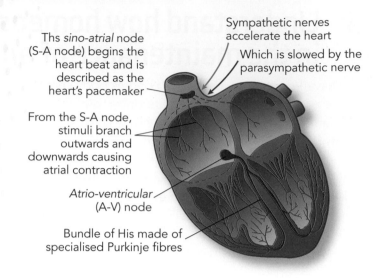

Ths *sino-atrial* node (S-A node) begins the heart beat and is described as the heart's pacemaker

Sympathetic nerves accelerate the heart

Which is slowed by the parasympathetic nerve

From the S-A node, stimuli branch outwards and downwards causing atrial contraction

Atrio-ventricular (A-V) node

Bundle of His made of specialised Purkinje fibres

Fig 5.38: Control of the cardiac cycle by the conduction system

parasympathetic nerves acting on the S-A node regulate the activity of the heart to suit circumstances from minute to minute, hour to hour and day to day.

Every few seconds, the S-A node sends out a cluster of nerve impulses across the branching network of atrial muscle fibres to cause contraction. The impulses are caught by another group of cells forming the atrio-ventricular node (A-V node) and relayed to a band of conducting tissue made of large, modified muscle cells called Purkinje fibres.

The transmission of impulses is delayed slightly in the A-V node to enable the atria to complete their contractions and the atrio-ventricular valves to start to close.

Heart valves are located on a fibrous figure-of-eight between the atrial and ventricular muscle masses, and the first part of the conducting tissue (the bundle of His) enables the excitatory impulses to cross to the ventricles. The bundle of His then splits into the right and left bundle branches, which run down either side of the ventricular septum, before spreading out into the ventricular muscle masses.

Impulses now pass very rapidly so that the two ventricles contract together, forcing blood around the body organs.

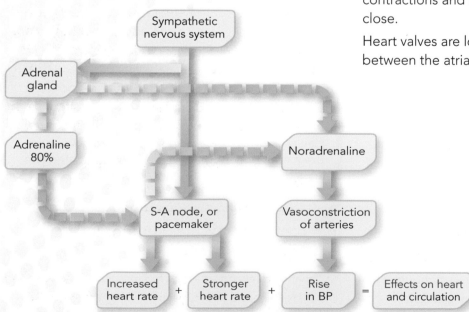

Fig 5.37: Sympathetic and parasympathetic control of the heart

Cardiac centres

The medulla of the brain is the lowest part, located just above the spinal cord and often known as the 'brain stem'. Two important centres for control of the heart rate are located here. The cardio-inhibitory centre is responsible for the origins of the parasympathetic fibres of the vagus nerve reaching the S-A node, while the sympathetic fibres descend through the spinal cord from the vasomotor centre.

Role of internal receptors

Baroreceptors detect changes in blood pressure and are found in the walls of the aorta and part of the carotid arteries delivering blood to the head and neck and called the aortic and carotid bodies. A small upward change in blood pressure (BP) in these arteries often indicates that extra blood has been pumped out by the ventricles as a result of extra blood entering the heart on the venous or right side. Baroreceptors detect the change and relay the information in nerve impulses to the cardiac centres. Activity in the vagus nerve slows the heart rate down and decreases BP back to normal.

Receptors sensitive to temperature are known as thermoreceptors and these are present in the skin and deep inside the body. They relay information via nerve impulses to a part of the brain called the hypothalamus, which activates appropriate feedback systems.

Effects of adrenaline on heart rate

Circulating adrenaline, a hormone from the adrenal gland released during fear, stress and exertion, stimulates the S-A node to work faster, thus boosting the effect of the sympathetic nervous system.

Effect of increased body temperature on heart rate

Thermoreceptors indicating a rise in body temperature to the brain cause the hypothalamus to activate the sympathetic nervous system. This in turn causes the heart rate to increase.

3.3 Homeostatic mechanisms for regulation of breathing rate

We are mainly on 'automatic pilot' for our rate of ventilation and do not notice minor variations that are the result of homeostatic regulations. Only when taking deep breaths, speaking or holding a breath are we voluntarily controlling our breathing. When metabolism produces extra carbon dioxide, for example, breathing rates will increase slightly until this surplus is 'blown off' in expiration. Similarly a period of forced ventilation, such as gasping, will lower the carbon dioxide levels in the body and homeostatic mechanisms will slow or stop breathing temporarily until levels return to normal.

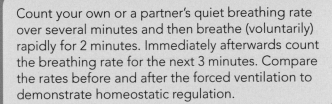

Activity 13: Voluntary or involuntary?

Count your own or a partner's quiet breathing rate over several minutes and then breathe (voluntarily) rapidly for 2 minutes. Immediately afterwards count the breathing rate for the next 3 minutes. Compare the rates before and after the forced ventilation to demonstrate homeostatic regulation.

Roles of internal receptors

Internal receptors can be stretch receptors in muscles and tissues that relay nervous impulses to the brain about the status of ventilation from the degree of stretch of muscles and other tissues. The intercostal muscles are the site of many stretch receptors.

Chemoreceptors detect changes in chemical stimuli (such as H^+ ions and oxygen levels) and supply the brain with this information. There are central and peripheral chemoreceptors. The central chemoreceptors monitoring H^+ ion concentration are located in the medulla of the brain; an increase in H^+ ion concentration results in increased ventilation rate. Peripheral receptors, monitoring changes in oxygen concentration, increase ventilation when oxygen levels decrease. Peripheral chemoreceptors are scattered around the aorta and carotid arteries in groups labelled the aortic and carotid sinuses (see Figure 5.39 on page 220).

Autonomic nervous system – parasympathetic and sympathetic branches

Most internal organs have a dual autonomic supply and the respiratory system is no exception. What can be different, however, is the way they act. It would be easy to say that the sympathetic always causes contraction

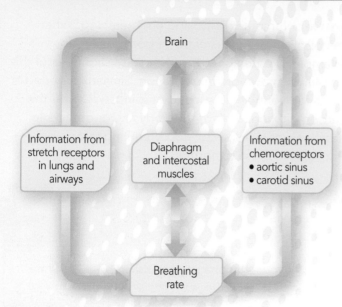

Fig 5.39: The role of internal receptors

and the parasympathetic causes relaxation of muscle coats – but unfortunately this is not so. In the case of bronchial muscle, the sympathetic causes it to relax and the parasympathetic causes contraction, resulting in narrowing of the bronchi. Most of these fibres run in the vagus nerve (which you have already met) in serving the heart. The vagus nerve is so-called because it wanders all over, supplying internal organs; vagus means 'a wanderer' – like a vagrant! Sympathetic nerves emerge from a chain of ganglia (places where nerves interconnect), to run to the bronchi.

Activity 14: Emergency action

The parasympathetic is active during rest, peace and contentment and the sympathetic during emergencies. A useful way to work out the actions is to imagine yourself in a life-threatening situation – such as being in the middle of a road when a car is suddenly closing fast. What would be likely to happen physiologically to your body? Try a thought shower with your peer group.

PLTS

Creative thinker: You can show your creative thinking skills by generating ideas and exploring possible actions associated with adrenaline release.

Respiratory centre, diaphragm and intercostal muscles

The brain area responsible for voluntary control of breathing is in the upper part of the brain known as the cerebral cortex. The involuntary centre, known as the respiratory centre, is in the medulla and the area just above, known as the pons. These are both at the base of the brain. Each centre gets information from internal receptors regarding the state of ventilation.

The respiratory centre is similar to a respiratory 'pacemaker'. There are two groups of nerve cells, known as the inspiratory and expiratory centres, and when one is active the other is inhibited. Clearly, the inspiratory centre is actively sending nerve impulses

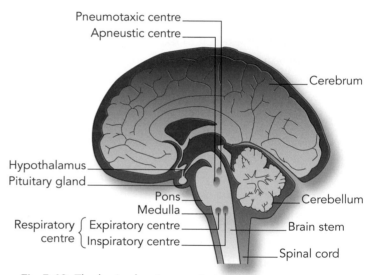

Fig 5.40: The brain showing respiratory centres

to the nerve to the diaphragm – the phrenic nerve – and the thoracic nerves are sending impulses to the intercostal muscles to cause contraction, resulting in inspiration. Inspiration ceases when the stretch receptors send bursts of impulses to the inspiratory centre, saying that the chest and lungs are fully expanded, and the flow of impulses subsides, releasing the expiratory centre from inhibition. This centre then sends nerve impulses to the respiratory muscles, causing relaxation and expiration. This cycle of activity is monitored and modified by the information coming from the other internal receptors, such as the chemoreceptors, effecting homeostatic regulation.

Before exercise starts, the body predicts the changes because the sympathetic nervous system is stimulated and adrenaline is released to increase cardiac output and stroke volume; BP rises because arterioles narrow,

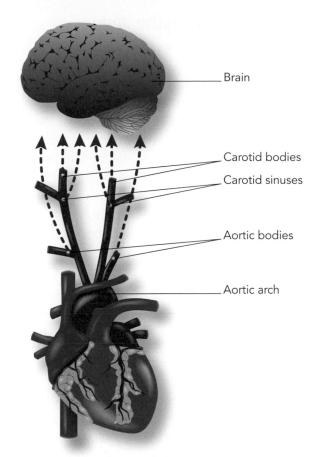

Fig 5.41: Location of internal chemoreceptors

except for those in muscle, which relax. The extra demands for oxygen and glucose are met by increased blood flow and ventilation rate (the latter caused by enhanced chemoreceptor activity on the medullary brain centres).

3.4 Homeostatic mechanism for regulation of body temperature

Human beings are the only animals that can survive in both tropical and polar regions of the earth. This is largely due to efficient thermo-regulatory homeostatic processes and the use of intelligence (for shelter and clothing), which mean that body temperature varies only minimally.

The fundamental precept is to keep the inner core of the body (containing the vital organs) at normal temperatures while allowing the periphery (skin, limbs, etc.) to adapt to changing conditions of external temperature.

At very low temperatures such as –30°C, the water component of the body would freeze and at high temperatures such as +50°C, enzymes and body proteins would be permanently altered or denatured. Life would not be possible under these conditions so homeostatic regulation of body temperature or thermo-regulation is vital. The skin plays an important role in this so we will start with an explanation of its structure and functions.

Structure and functions of skin

The skin covers the outer surface of the body and surprisingly forms the largest organ. New cells are continually forming to replace those shed from the surface layers. The skin is a significant part of our in-built or innate immunity and forms not only a waterproof layer but also a microbe-proof covering. It plays an important part in the homeostatic regulation of body temperature and is considered to be part of our nervous system because of its sensitivity.

The skin varies in thickness throughout the body, being thinnest over the eyelids and lips and thickest on the soles of the feet. For study purposes, it is divided into an outer thinner layer, the epidermis, and a deeper layer called the dermis. The dermis covers adipose, areolar, striated muscle, and some cartilage and bone. You have already learned about the structure of the epidermis as a tissue on page 185 and the keratinisation of its cells. Hair follicles are also extensions of the epidermis, which run down into the dermis and produce hairs made of keratin. Attached to these are the sebaceous (or oil) glands that coat the surface in hairy parts, assisting the water-proofing. Sweat ducts penetrate the epidermis as they emerge from the actual sweat gland in the dermis. In the basal layer, there are collections of pigment cells known as melanocytes that produce skin colour. The pigment melanin protects against damage to deeper structures from ultra-violet light radiation.

The dermis is connective tissue, mainly areolar, in which blood vessels, nerves, sweat glands, elastic and collagen fibres intermingle.

Nerve endings form specialised receptors for temperature changes, pain, touch and pressure.

Hair erector muscles have their origins low down on the hair follicles and their attachments to the basal layer of the epidermis. When hair erector muscles contract (usually from fear or the sensation of coldness) the hair becomes more erect, making the skin surface lumpy (known as 'goose bumps').

The major functions of skin are:

- to protect the underlying tissues against friction damage
- to waterproof the body
- to protect deeper structures from invasion by micro-organisms
- to protect against ultra-violet radiation
- for thermo-regulation (control of body temperature)
- to relay nerve impulses generated from the specialised skin sensory receptors for heat, cold, touch, pain and pressure, thus informing the brain of changes in the environment
- to synthesise vitamin D from sunlight acting on the adipose layers.

Production of heat by the body

Heat is generated by the metabolic processes taking place in the body. Although energy released during chemical reactions is used to drive processes such as muscle contraction (heart pump, breathing, movement, nerve impulses, etc.) some of it is always released as heat. Hundreds of chemical reactions take place in the liver, for example, every day and the liver is a massive generator of body heat. It doesn't feel hot because the blood distributes this heat around the body, particularly the extremities. Some heat is also gained from hot food and drinks and, under some circumstances, from the sun's rays.

Loss of heat from the body

Skin capillaries form networks just below the outer layer or epidermis. When you are hot, you need to lose heat from the skin surface to cool yourself down. There are four ways of losing heat from the skin:

- Conduction – warming up anything that you are in contact with (like clothes and seats); even a pen becomes warm from your hand when you are writing!
- Convection – this is when you warm up the layer of air next to your skin and it moves upwards (because hot air is less dense and rises), to be replaced by colder air from the ground.

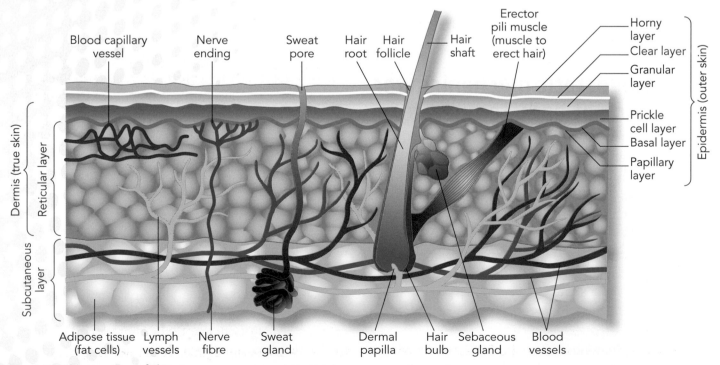

Fig 5.42: The structure of skin

- Radiation – you can think of this as being rather like diffusion but of heat temperature. In other words, heat will pass from your skin to warm up any colder objects around you; and, conversely, you will warm up by radiation from any object hotter than yourself, like a fire or the sun.

- Evaporation of sweat – when liquid water is converted into water vapour (the technical term is evaporation), it requires heat energy to do so. When you are hot, sweating will only cool the skin if it can take heat energy from the skin surface to convert to water vapour and evaporate.

organs. These are specially adapted cells with nerve fibres that run up the spinal cord to the temperature control centre in the hypothalamus of the brain (see Figure 5.44 below). The hypothalamus sends nerve impulses to muscles, sweat glands and skin blood

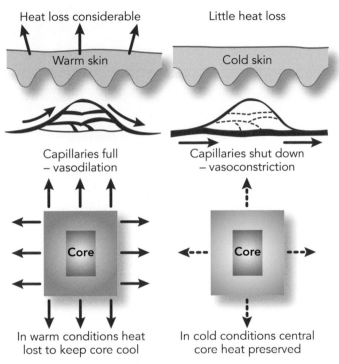

Fig 5.43: Changes in skin radiation

Did you know?

Parents fuss about drying children properly with towels after getting wet because if water evaporates from the skin naturally it chills the body. This is because the process of evaporation uses heat energy from the body.

Although conduction and convection take place, they cannot be changed significantly to alter body temperature. The main methods of regulating temperature are by changing radiation and sweat-evaporation processes.

Role of the hypothalamus

The receptors for temperature, both heat and cold, are located in the peripheral skin and around the internal

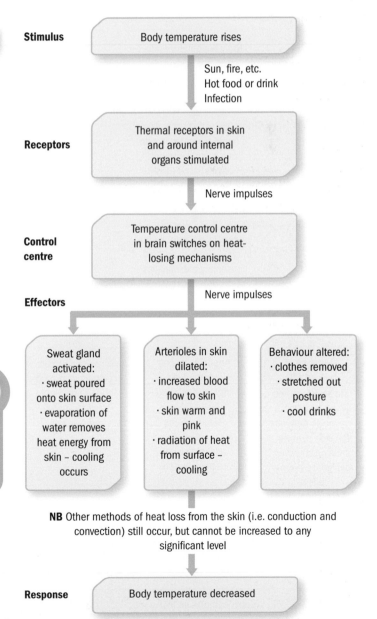

Fig 5.44: Homeostatic regulation of an increasing body temperature

vessels to cause changes that counteract the external changes. You can see the precise effects of a rising and falling external temperature in the flow charts in Figures 5.44 and 5.45.

Roles of the parasympathetic and sympathetic nerves

The parasympathetic nervous system has no significant role in thermo-regulation (although it helps the unstriated muscle coats of the skin arterioles to relax), but the sympathetic nervous system controls both sweat glands and the calibre of the arterioles.

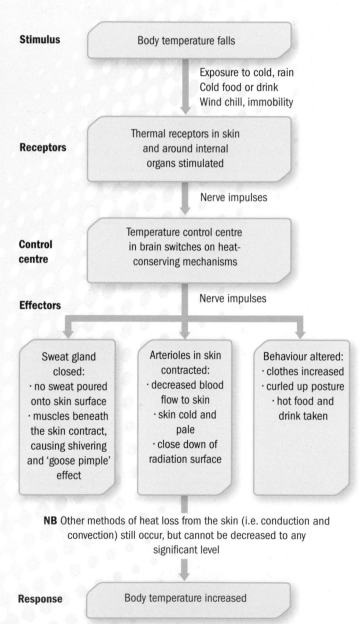

Stimulus
> Body temperature falls

Exposure to cold, rain
Cold food or drink
Wind chill, immobility

Receptors
> Thermal receptors in skin and around internal organs stimulated

Nerve impulses

Control centre
> Temperature control centre in brain switches on heat-conserving mechanisms

Nerve impulses

Effectors

> Sweat gland closed:
> · no sweat poured onto skin surface
> · muscles beneath the skin contract, causing shivering and 'goose pimple' effect

> Arterioles in skin contracted:
> · decreased blood flow to skin
> · skin cold and pale
> · close down of radiation surface

> Behaviour altered:
> · clothes increased
> · curled up posture
> · hot food and drink taken

NB Other methods of heat loss from the skin (i.e. conduction and convection) still occur, but cannot be decreased to any significant level

Response
> Body temperature increased

Fig 5.45: Homeostatic regulation of a falling body temperature

Role of arterioles and sweat glands

As thermoreceptors tell the hypothalamus in the brain that the temperature is rising, sweat glands are activated by the sympathetic nerves, and arterioles are dilated to let more heat reach the surface of the skin, thus increasing heat loss by radiation and evaporation of sweat. Conversely, if the core temperature is cooling, the sympathetic is active in causing constriction of the arterioles but sweating is 'turned off'. This reduces heat loss, makes the skin colder to touch, and thus preserves the core temperature.

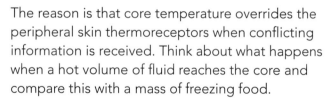

Activity 15: Seems all wrong!

It is a very hot day and you feel that a long iced drink is needed but your mother wants to make a warm drink because it is more cooling. Explain why she is correct.

PLTS

Creative thinker: Demonstrate that you can question your own and others' assumptions about ways of cooling by completing this activity.

The reason is that core temperature overrides the peripheral skin thermoreceptors when conflicting information is received. Think about what happens when a hot volume of fluid reaches the core and compare this with a mass of freezing food.

Effects of shivering

Rhythmic involuntary contractions of the skeletal muscles are known as shivering. Muscular activity generates heat so in a cold environment we may stamp our feet, swing our arms, rub our face, hands and feet and also shiver. This is a very effective way to generate heat, as it is all available to warm the body up.

Implications of surface area to volume ratio in the care of babies

Babies have a larger surface area to volume ratio than adults and cannot effect changes to gain or lose heat for themselves; this means that they are at risk of developing **hyperthermia** or **hypothermia**.

Case study: Seasonal behaviour

In winter I curl up in a ball in bed and add layers of clothing to keep warm. In summer, I wear one thin layer of clothing and stretch out in bed.

1 Explain why these different behaviours occur.
2 Explain the main way that heat is lost by increasing the surface area to volume ratio in hot weather.
3 Adolescents commonly go out in very cold weather wearing skimpy clothing and no coats without feeling cold. Explain why this might be dangerous for older people.
4 Explain why babies need to wear hats in colder weather.

PLTS

Creative thinker: Demonstrate that you can question your own and others' assumptions about methods of thermal control by completing this activity.

Babies do not sweat much and newborn babies do not shiver. Therefore, it is important in cold weather to wrap babies warmly, including the extremities and the head, and to guard against over-heating in hot weather.

Fever

Fever is one type of hyperthermia and is most usually caused by infection; other types are heat stroke and heat exhaustion – all can be life-threatening. Factors released as a result of disease act on thermoreceptors in the hypothalamus, raising the upper **set point**. Consequently the sufferer feels cold, curls up, pulls on covers, looks pale due to vasoconstriction (narrowing of the arterioles) and even experiences intense shivering

Key terms

Hyperthermia – Increased body temperature above the normal range of values

Hypothermia – Decreased body temperature below the normal range of values.

Set point – The temperature of the 'hypothalamic thermostat', when autonomic thermo-regulatory mechanisms start to act to reverse the rise or fall and restore normal temperature.

known as rigors. It is not until the new set point has been reached (often called 'the crisis') that sweating and other heat loss mechanisms begin. When the infection has subsided the set point is reset at a lower level.

Did you know?

To reduce temperature during a fever, the usual practice is to bathe with tepid water, blow cold air from a fan over exposed skin and/or use appropriate medication.

3.5 Homeostatic mechanisms for regulation of blood glucose levels

Role of the pancreas, liver, insulin and glucagon

You have learned how carbohydrates are broken down by digestive enzymes to produce simple soluble sugars, mainly glucose. After a meal rich in carbohydrates (such as rice, bread, pasta and certain vegetables), blood glucose will start to rise. This increased level of glucose stimulates the production of the hormone insulin from the beta cells in the islets of Langerhans in the pancreas. Insulin has two main functions:

*   to regulate the concentration of glucose in the blood
*   to increase the passage of glucose into actively respiring body cells by active absorption.

In the absence of insulin, very little glucose is able to pass through cell membranes (with the exception of liver cells) and so the plasma level of glucose rises. Individuals with untreated diabetes mellitus (caused by a lack of insulin secretion) have high plasma glucose levels and this leads to other biochemical disturbances. In healthy people, the plasma glucose hardly varies at all because liver cells, under the control of insulin, convert glucose into liver (and muscle) glycogen for storage. When blood glucose starts to fall as a result of fasting or being used up by respiring cells, another hormone, glucagon, from the alpha cells in the islets of Langerhans, is secreted and this converts liver glycogen back into glucose for release into the bloodstream. These two hormones regulate the amount of glucose in the blood plasma by negative feedback mechanisms. Both have receptors attached to their islet cells to identify rising and falling plasma glucose levels.

Insulin also promotes the conversion of glucose into fat (once again removing surplus glucose from the circulation) and delays the conversion of amino acids into energy (see 'Roles in the body, storage and deanimation' on page 214).

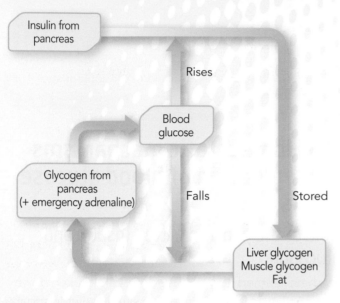

Fig 5.46: Negative feedback mechanism to maintain plasma glucose concentration in blood

Did you know?

Normally, there is no glucose in urine because it has been completely reabsorbed in the first part of the renal tubule and is transported back into the bloodstream. However, when the blood glucose is abnormally high, as in Diabetes mellitus, this part of the tubule is simply not long enough for complete reabsorption and a large amount of glucose is left behind to flow onwards into the urine. This can be tested for chemically. Blood glucose is high because it is not able to enter cells due to lack of active insulin.

glucose. This outpouring of glucose provides energy for muscles to become active under emergency conditions. In addition, adrenaline converts fats to fatty acids for muscle contraction. When the emergency is over, insulin will once more become active and store any surplus as before.

Case study: Jonathan

Jonathan goes jogging before breakfast and eats nothing but a slimming type of cereal bar (low sugar, low fat) until lunch. Describe the homeostatic mechanism for restoring his plasma glucose levels to normal.

Remember that:
- muscular activity requires energy
- energy stores are in the liver and in fat deposits
- hormonal action is necessary to release stored energy.

PLTS

Creative thinker: Generating ideas and exploring possibilities about homeostatic control of glucose may enable you to demonstrate creative thinking skills.

It is also necessary to identify the role of another hormone, adrenaline, in the homeostasis of glucose. Adrenaline, released by the adrenal glands when the sympathetic nervous system is active under stressful conditions, acts antagonistically to insulin and overrides it, to convert glycogen in the liver to

Case study: Mia's mother

Mia noticed that her mother seemed to get tired very quickly and she disliked going upstairs as she became breathless quite rapidly. Her father was becoming quite concerned about his wife's health and asked Mia to help out a lot more around the house. Mia's mother was having heavy monthly bleeds as a result of starting the menopause. She also looked very pale and complained of having no energy.

Eventually they persuaded her to visit her GP, who sent her to the local hospital to get blood checks.

On receiving the results from the hospital, the GP diagnosed iron-deficiency anaemia and prescribed some 'iron' tablets.

1 Discuss the reasons for Mia's mother's signs and symptoms.
2 Why do you think the anaemia occurred?
3 What role does iron play in the blood?
4 Examine the relationship between 'having no energy' and anaemia.
5 How do you think the anaemia might impact on heart rate and breathing rate?
6 Justify your answer to question 5.

4 Be able to interpret data obtained from monitoring routine variations with reference to the functioning of healthy body systems

In this section you will collect data by measuring the temperature, pulse and breathing rates of a healthy individual at rest and at intervals during recovery from a standard exercise test. You will need to know:

- how to take the measurements using safe practice
- the range of normal values
- the factors that affect the reliability of the data you obtain.

You will have to interpret and analyse your data and demonstrate how homeostatic mechanisms respond to exercise.

4.1 Measurements

You will now learn best practice in taking routine measurements.

Pulse rate measurements – normal values and range

A pulse can be detected when an artery is close to the surface of the body and runs over a firm structure such as bone. The pulse is the elastic expansion and recoil of an artery caused by the left ventricle of the heart contracting to drive blood around the body. You are feeling the 'shock' wave of the contraction as it travels rapidly down the arteries.

Factors affecting reliability of pulse rate measurements

As well as the pulse rate, professional health care workers will also monitor the rhythm of the pulse, noting any irregularities and the quality of the pulse. Terms used are: full, bounding, normal, weak or thready. They will also take note of the character of the blood vessel: in a young person it feels straight, flexible and elastic; but in an elderly person it might feel much firmer, even hard, and take a winding course due to arteriosclerosis. This condition might mean that the pulse is harder to count.

Key term

Mean pulse – The mean of a set of numbers is calculated by adding the numbers and dividing by the number of numbers. If an individual's pulse rates were 70, 68 and 64 beats per minute, then the mean would be 70 + 68 + 64 ÷ 3 = 67 (to the nearest whole number). As this calculation has considered three readings, it is more accurate than taking the first reading only.

Activity 16: Practising practical work 1

You will need a watch with a second hand or a stop clock that can measure in seconds.

1 Wash your hands to prevent cross-infection.

2 Explain what you are going to do to the person on whom you are carrying out the measurement and obtain their consent.

3 Make sure that the person is comfortable and relaxed, as this will help you to achieve an accurate measurement. Observe the individual while taking the measurement (this takes practice) so that you can stop if there are any signs of distress or anxiety.

4 Find the radial artery, preferably on the arm that is free from any restrictions such as a watch strap. You will find the artery on the wrist, just below the base of the thumb.

5 Place the first and second fingers lightly on the artery – get used to the feel of the pulse before you start counting for 60 seconds. Record the measurement, with the date and the time. Wash your hands.

You may wish to repeat the measurement twice more, as this is a practical exercise and a **mean pulse** is more useful for recording, as either you or the individual might be a little apprehensive at first.

An average resting pulse in a healthy individual ranges from 60 to 80 beats per minute. Increases in pulse rates during vigorous exercise vary, depending on the fitness of the individual and the intensity of the exercise, but can rise to 190–200 beats per minute.

A pulse taken in babies or young children is much faster than in adults. Exercise, or even just moving about before or during the pulse-taking, will cause an increase in rate, as will an increased body temperature. Hypothermia will produce a slow pulse rate.

Many carers measure the pulse rate for 10- or 15-second periods and multiply by 6 or 4 respectively to gain the pulse rate per minute. Any error in counting will thus be magnified six- or four-fold. However, a single error is still unlikely to be **significant** in terms of results for monitoring purposes. Counting for the whole 60 seconds is not a long time and reduces these errors.

Irregular pulses, found in patients with heart disease or ectopic (extra) beats, and fast pulses (tachycardia or in babies and young children) can prove difficult to count. Arteriosclerotic arteries also make it more difficult to count heartbeats. Multiple counting errors are more likely to occur and, when multiplied, these could be significant.

Key term

Significant – A simple explanation of the term 'significant' in this context would be whether the error was meaningful and likely to distort any conclusions drawn. 'Not significant' means that the error can be ignored.

Many establishments use electronic digital recorders for measuring pulse rates, blood pressure, body temperature and other physiological features. You should be familiar with the manufacturer's instructions for safe practice, potential risks and levels of accuracy. In addition, you must be trained by an appropriately qualified person to use this type of equipment. Different pieces of equipment may operate in different ways.

All items of electrical equipment are potentially hazardous, both to the client and the carer operating the devices. The major hazards are burns and electric shock. You should be constantly on the look-out for:

- malfunction of the equipment
- frayed electric flexes and trapped wires
- loose connections, plugs and sockets.

Any fault must be reported immediately – verbally and in writing: most establishments have standard forms for reporting faults or damaged equipment. The device must be clearly labelled with a notice saying

'Faulty, Do Not Use' and taken out of use. No one should be asked to use faulty equipment in their job. Only suitably qualified personnel should investigate, modify, repair or scrap equipment belonging to the establishment.

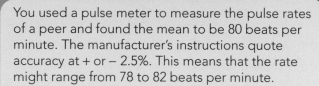

Case study: Calculating accuracy

You used a pulse meter to measure the pulse rates of a peer and found the mean to be 80 beats per minute. The manufacturer's instructions quote accuracy at + or − 2.5%. This means that the rate might range from 78 to 82 beats per minute.

Explanation: $(80 \times 5) \div 200$ (N.B. 2.5% = 5/200ths). This works out at 2 so the range is $80 - 2$ to $80 + 2$ (or 78–82).

Calculate the range of accuracy if the mean of the pulse rate is 65 beats per minute and the manufacturer's quote is + or − 1% accuracy.

Once you have familiarised yourself with taking pulse rate measurements at rest, practise taking them at different levels of activity on, for example, one of your peers.

Reflect

What different activities might you ask a peer to do? Try a thought shower, bearing in mind that it must be an appropriate safe activity for your subject. Once you have made your decision, take your practice measurements.

Take the pulse rate after light, medium or intense exercise of your own design or use the Harvard step test described on page 232.

Safe practice in taking pulse measurements

You must not compress the artery over the bone when taking measurements or you may stop the blood flow to part of the hand, causing pain and cramp. This is more likely to occur in babies and older people, in whom the pulse is more difficult to detect and count.

Ensure that the person being assessed is suitably healthy to undertake physical exercise. For example, you would not ask your grandmother to run up and down the stairs several times or do a 'step test', as this might trigger angina or a heart attack. The person must be used to participating in, and happy to carry out, the type of exercise you devise. There must be no risk to health in carrying out the activities.

Ensure that you wash your hands before and after the procedure to prevent cross-infection.

> ### Did you know?
>
> A baby's pulse rate is much faster than an adult's and the radial pulse is difficult to find. Health professionals usually take a baby's pulse over the larger brachial artery in the arm.

Breathing rate measurements – normal values and range

You will need to observe the rise and fall of the person's chest in order to count the respiratory rate. It is best to do this after pulse-taking. The problem you may find is that, as soon as the person is aware of the count, voluntary control takes over and the rate may alter. Many carers continue to keep their fingers on the pulse for an extra 60 seconds to distract the individual while counting the respirations. One rise and one fall counts as one respiration. You can then record both rates. Normal respiratory rate is said to be 12–20 breaths per minute – during exercise, breathing rate can rise to 30–40 breaths per minute.

Factors affecting reliability of breathing rate measurements

You should be alert for any changes in chest movement as the individual may have become aware of the measuring and alter their pattern of breathing. When you are taking a resting breathing rate measurement, ensure that the person is not disturbed or anxious and has been resting for at least 10 minutes or you might get a false reading. The individual should not have smoked recently, as this too will produce a false reading.

Sometimes the rise and fall of the chest is slight and it is easy to miss and to miscount when you are registering two movements as one count.

Safe practice in taking breathing rates

As you are observing a phenomenon rather than actually doing anything, the risks are low. However, clothing may need to be adjusted, and it is important to wash hands before and after the procedure to prevent cross-infection.

Body temperature measurements – normal values and range

Body temperature must be kept within a narrow range so that the physiological processes of the body can function at their maximum efficiency.

However, body temperature varies between individuals even when they are in the same environment. They can vary in the same person, at different times of the day, during different activity levels and depending on whether or not food and drink has been consumed. In women, body temperature is affected by the stages of the menstrual cycle, being highest at ovulation and lowest during actual menstruation. Most people experience their lowest temperature around 3 a.m. and their highest around 6 p.m.

> ### Did you know?
>
> The range of temperature compatible with life is not known accurately. Experts believe that the upper limit is around 44°C and the lower 27°C. An individual will be seriously ill long before these limits are reached, and will be likely to die.

In addition to all these influences, body temperature varies according to the location of the measurement, for example, mouth, axilla (armpit), ear canal and rectum. The latter is only used when the other sites are unavailable and in patients who are unconscious and/or very seriously ill, as the procedure causes raised anxiety and stress levels. Rectal temperatures are nearer to actual body core temperatures but are slower to change. Mouth or oral temperatures are about 0.5°C higher than axillary temperatures.

Normal body temperatures range from 36.5 to 37.2°C. Most people will quote 37°C as normal body temperature but, given the range of influencing factors, this is rather too precise.

Temperatures are often taken once or twice daily as a routine but the frequency can be varied according to need. A patient suffering from (or at risk of developing) an infection, or who is recovering from hypothermia or who is post-operative, may have their temperature taken hourly or every four hours.

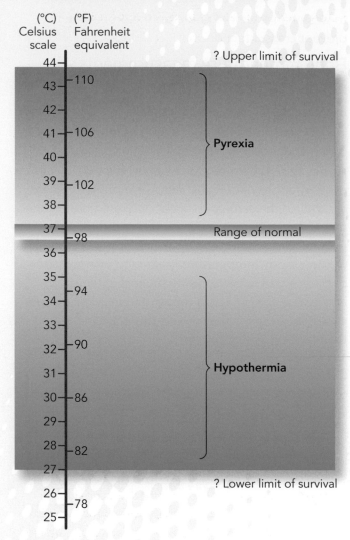

(°C) Celsius scale / (°F) Fahrenheit equivalent

? Upper limit of survival

Pyrexia

Range of normal

Hypothermia

? Lower limit of survival

Fig 5.47: Body temperature range

Since mercury-filled thermometers were banned in care establishments, several types of non-mercury thermometers have become available. These are:

- disposable thermometers
- calibrated electronic probes
- tympanic (ear canal) thermometers.

However, you must remember that in many private homes mercury-filled, clinical thermometers are still in use.

Temperatures were once measured in degrees Fahrenheit but now degrees Celsius are used. If you are using an old thermometer, you will need to look at it very closely to see the measuring scale.

The procedure outlined in Activity 16 below can be adapted to any type of axillary thermometer.

Disposable oral and oral probe thermometers should be placed under the tongue. There are right and left pouches on either side of the fold of membrane (the frenulum) on the underside of the tongue and either one is a suitable place for the thermometer. The individual should not bite or chew on the probe but should close their lips around it for the prescribed length of time. The rest of the procedure is the same as for axillary temperature-taking.

Rectal thermometry should not be carried out by unqualified individuals and so it will not be described here.

Activity 17: Practising practical work 2

You are most likely to take temperatures in the axilla (armpit).

1 Wash your hands first to prevent cross-infection.

2 Explain what you are going to do to the individual and obtain their consent and co-operation.

3 Make sure that the individual is sitting or lying comfortably and can hold that position for a few minutes.

4 Respect privacy, and help to remove clothing from one axilla.

5 Dry the axilla with a disposable tissue.

6 Place the temperature probe in the axilla so that it is surrounded by skin.

7 Observe the individual throughout the process to check for signs of distress.

8 Ask the individual to hold their arm across their chest to hold the probe in position.

9 Leave for the correct time (as per the manufacturer's instructions).

10 Stay with the individual to ensure the position is maintained.

11 After the appropriate time has elapsed, remove the thermometer, and read and record the temperature along with the date and time.

12 Safely dispose of, or clean and store, the thermometer as appropriate for the establishment. Wash your hands again.

13 Check that the individual is still comfortable and, if relevant, compare this reading with previous readings.

Tympanic thermometers measure the temperature of the ear drum (tympanic membrane) and this is very near to the body core temperature. A probe with a disposable cover is inserted into the ear canal while gently pulling the ear lobe downwards. When the ear drum can no longer be seen (because it is obscured by the probe), hold the thermometer still and take the recording. Remove the probe and dispose of the cover before storing the equipment safely. Otherwise, use the same procedure as for axillary recordings. This is the preferred method for taking temperatures in children, as it is fast and well-tolerated.

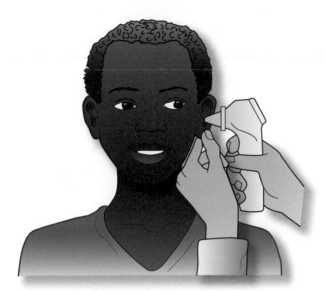

Fig 5.48: Taking a tympanic temperature

LCD (liquid crystal display) thermometers are cheap, disposable, safe and easy to use. They are also available in high street pharmacies, and parents of young children are encouraged to keep a supply at home. They are single-use only and the manufacturer's instructions must be followed to obtain correct results.

Activity 18: Comparing measuring devices

Using an LCD strip thermometer, take your temperature and then compare it with an oral temperature reading. Comment on the difference between skin and oral temperatures and refer back to the manufacturer's stated accuracy for a final conclusion.

Safe practice in taking body temperatures

See the information on dealing with electrical equipment on page 228.

Oral thermometers should only be used with attentive, co-operative adults to ensure that the probe is not bitten or chewed, with the accompanying risks to safety. All equipment should have disposable covers or sheaths or be thoroughly cleaned after use to prevent cross-infection.

Even with the use of disposable covers, tympanic thermometers have been found to transmit ear infections (often with drug-resistant bacteria) between individuals. Extra care should be taken with personal and equipment hygiene.

Mercury and glass thermometers are now considered obsolete and even domestic settings should be encouraged to replace them with LCD thermometers. The danger is from mercury poisoning and glass inhalation or ingestion.

Factors affecting reliability of body temperature measurements

Several factors are discussed under normal values and range (page 229).

Ensure that you fully understand how to use the temperature measuring device and know both the correct location of the sensitive probe, strip or bulb and the length of time needed for measuring. Failure to comply with the manufacturer's instructions may lead to inaccurate readings and errors.

Did you know?

You should always allow an individual to rest before taking temperature measurements and ask whether they have had hot food or drink or taken exercise recently. Such activities may lead to inaccurate readings.

Prepare the equipment correctly and make sure that it is calibrated where this is appropriate.

The accuracy of a temperature reading depends on fully functioning equipment and your skill in carrying out the measurements. When taking oral temperatures do not ask the individual questions or allow them to talk, as the colder air flowing over the thermometer will cause inaccuracies.

There have been several studies relating to the accuracy of temperatures taken with tympanic thermometers but, over time, carers are becoming more experienced at using these devices.

LCD strips, while valuable in domestic and community settings, are not absolutely accurate but they do provide useful guidance when the temperature is raised.

Consult the manufacturer's instructions on accuracy levels.

4.2 Normal variations measured at rest and following exercise

In this section you have to obtain data by measuring the temperature, pulse and breathing rates of a healthy individual at rest and at intervals during recovery from a standard exercise test. You will need to know:

- how to take the measurements using safe practice
- the range of normal values
- the factors that affect the reliability of the data you obtain.

You will need to interpret and analyse your data and demonstrate how homeostatic mechanisms respond to exercise.

You can use a standard exercise test of your own choosing, subject to your tutor's approval, but a useful resource is the Harvard step test described here.

Activity 19: Practising practical work 3

You can practise assessments on yourself once you are competent with making routine measurements. The procedure that might be used is outlined below.

Harvard step test

You will need a safe step about 50 cm high and a stop-clock or stop-watch.

Procedure:

1 The subject being tested steps up and down (one foot, then both feet) at a rate of 30 steps per minute for 5 minutes.

   Note: if the stepping cannot be maintained for 15 seconds at any time, this is deemed to be

exhaustion and the test is stopped at that point and the precise time noted.

2 The individual sits down after the test and the measurements are taken as below. You will need to start the stop-watch again immediately after the subject has stopped the test.

Taking results:

3 Count the rate of pulse or breathing or take the temperature at 1–1.5, 2–2.5 and 3–3.5 minutes after the test.

   Note: it is a good idea to draw up relevant chart/s for the recording of results before you start. An example is provided in Table 5.6 below.

Table 5.6: Recording the results of a Harvard step test

Subject name or code for confidentiality: _____			
Date of test: _____		Tester's name: _____	
Measurement	**Rest**	**1–1.5 mins**	**2–2.5 mins**	**3–3.5 mins**
Pulse/heart rate beats/minute				
Breathing rate breaths/minute				
Temperature °C				
Duration of test if not 5 minutes		Test 1:	Test 2:	Test 3:

It is worth noting that taller individuals have a mechanical advantage in this type of test.

Note: you may need to repeat the test more than once, as it might be difficult for you to take more than one measurement accurately per test.

The Harvard step test is commonly used to assess cardiovascular fitness and a scoring system has been devised for this. You might wish to use this or leave the results in beats per minute.

Activity 20: Working out the Harvard step test results

To use the scoring system for cardiovascular fitness with the Harvard step test, use the following method:

1 Calculate, in seconds, the duration of the test as it was carried out by the subject. If the subject did not become exhausted and finished the test before the due time, this will be $5 \times 60 = 300$ seconds. This figure will be represented by T.

2 Add together the number of pulse beats recorded in the three time periods. This figure will be represented by B.

3 Substitute your data for T and B in the following equation: $100 \times T \div 2 \times B$

4 The product for this equation can be interpreted from the following table indicating cardiovascular fitness.

Excellent	>90
Good	80–89
High average	65–79
Low average	55–64
Poor	<55

Example: Chris completed only 4 minutes 35 seconds of the test before he was exhausted. His heart rates for the three time periods were: 108, 92 and 75. His assessment on this scoring was $100 \times 275 \div 2 \times 275 = 50$. Chris therefore has a poor cardiovascular rating.

4.3 Data presentation and interpretation

Graphs and charts

Ensure that the data you have obtained is clear and accurate by drawing up charts to record your results before you start the exercise tests. It is depressing and frustrating to find that you are unable to remember the details of the work afterwards because you just noted figures haphazardly during the tests. You are likely to be analysing and presenting your data on a different day to the one when you carried out the tests.

Charts should have each column headed with a title and the unit of measurement. There should be clear indications of the time the measurements are taken, their frequency and the date.

Graphs can be an effective way to display data and trends as they are generally easier to interpret than columns of figures.

Each graph should have:

- a title such as: 'Graph to show how pulse measurements vary with exercise'
- labels on both axes denoting what is being measured and the units of the measurement
- the vertical axis should be the unknown variable – in this case, it will be pulse rate, breathing rate or body temperature
- the horizontal axis should be the known variable – in this case it will be time
- clear marks and values on the axes denoting the scales being used
- a key, if more than one trend is shown
- points plotted as accurately and finely as possible
- fine lines linking the plotted points.

Your graph will also need the period of exercise to be defined and labelled after the resting period. You might wish to lightly shade or hatch this area.

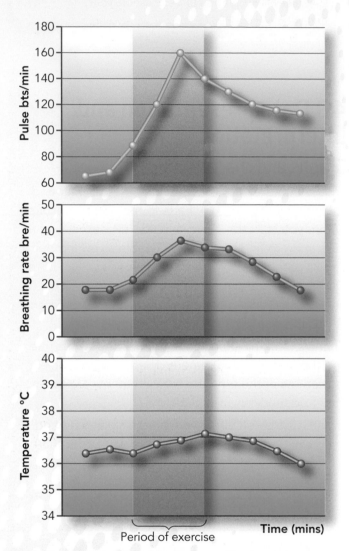

Fig 5.49: How pulse, breathing rates and body temperature vary with exercise

Supporting explanations of collated data

Presenting a chart of results and a graph is not sufficient for your practical assessment; you will need to describe details of the equipment you used and say how you used it – in other words, explain your method. Your account of the way you organised the resting and exercise periods in conjunction with the measurement of the data needs to be clear, accurate and complete.

The reader should understand exactly how you have conducted the assessment.

After displaying the results, chart and graphs, you will need to identify the trends shown by the figures and graphs and, from your knowledge of homeostatic mechanisms, attempt an explanation for each rise or fall.

For example:

The readings immediately after the exercise ceased showed a marked rise above resting levels in both pulse and breathing rates. This is because muscular activity demands a massive increase in oxygen and glucose. As the muscles use up oxygen and produce extra carbon dioxide, chemoreceptors are stimulated and these act on the cardiac and respiratory centres in the brain.

You can also comment on the **reliability** and **validity** of your data.

Key terms

Reliability – Relates to the extent to which a set of results can be replicated by repeating the test.

Validity – Relates to the quality of test results provided to tackle the study in question. 'Valid' means true, sound or well-grounded.

PLTS

Creative thinker: Questioning assumptions when carrying out and recording data from physical activity will require creative thinking.

Team worker: Reaching agreement and managing decisions to achieve results during practical work on physical activity, including collecting and recording data, will allow you to show team working ability.

Self-manager: Working towards goals of collecting and recording data to meet completion dates and dealing with competing pressures to meet deadlines will show self-management skills.

Assessment activity 5.5

P5 P6 M2 M3 D2 · BTEC

Produce a written report on the body's response to exercise. The report will be based on primary and secondary research. The report will include

1 An explanation of the concept of homeostasis and its role in exercise and healthy functioning of the body.

2 Measurements collected from practical work involving physical activity and your interpretation of them together with comments on the validity of the data collected.

Grading tips

P5 Using your knowledge of body systems, explain the concept of homeostasis. Using examples of the homeostatic mechanisms involved in regulating the heart rate, breathing rate and body temperature would be particularly relevant for this report.

P6 You should follow guidelines from your teacher to measure heart rate, breathing rate and body temperature before and after a standard period of exercise.

- Design a pattern of exercise for your individual, taking into account their state of health and general fitness.

- You are recommended to take measurements before the exercise, immediately after it stops and then two or three more readings in the first five minutes of recovery and at longer intervals until the individual's measurements have returned to their pre-exercise levels.

- Design your results chart.

- Carry out the practical work, recording the data collected on the results chart you have designed. You should obtain a witness testimony from your tutor to confirm you have collected measurements yourself and done so safely.

You must also interpret the data by stating what it tells you about the changes that are taking place inside the body during and in a period straight after the exercise period.

M2 This criterion requires you to discuss probable homeostatic responses to changes in the environment inside the body brought upon during exercise.

- When you start to run, your muscles need a lot more oxygen and glucose. How is this accomplished? What prevents the cardiovascular, respiratory and endocrine systems from over-compensating during exercise?

- Muscular activity generates heat. How does the body resist over-heating?

You will need to consider a falling glucose level as energy is being utilised for muscular activity, an increased demand for oxygen and the need to eliminate more carbon dioxide (cardiovascular and respiratory mechanisms), and an increased body temperature from working muscles. You could use the data you have collected to support your discussion as well as other sources of information.

D2 To gain D2, you have to evaluate the importance of homeostasis in maintaining the healthy functioning of the body.

- What might happen if body temperature and blood glucose fall below or rise above their normal ranges?

- What might be the consequences of having a very slow or very rapid heart and breathing rate?

You will need to show the importance of keeping to a narrow range of variables and what can happen if this is not done. Remember how cell enzymes are responsible for speeding up chemical reactions in processes like respiration and how sensitive enzymes are to some changes.

M3 You should present all the data you have collected before and after the exercise period with reference to validity. You should present the data recorded on your results chart as tables and charts and must make comments about the validity of your data. Validity refers to the soundness of your results or how true they are. Often, this will include how many readings you have taken or whether you have assumed certain trends which may not have been so had you taken more results. You could explain any perceived errors or times when the activity did not quite go to plan.

Body temperature may vary very little over the period of time of the exercise and a graph may not be useful.

Ayesha Smith
Nurse practitioner

Willow Grove is a health centre in the UK; there are five doctors, two practice nurses, a health visitor and a nurse practitioner working in the centre. Ayesha Smith is the nurse practitioner (NP) at Willow Grove and has been there for five years. Mia and her mother often see Ayesha instead of a GP.

Ayesha runs daily surgeries in a rota with the other GPs and this involves sensitive questioning and examining, as well as planning and providing appropriate treatment and support for individuals registered with Willow Grove.

Patient confidentiality and being non-judgemental are important features of her work.

Ayesha must collaborate with the GPs and sometimes she makes referrals to other health professionals. She provides counselling and health education and can prescribe certain medications.

NPs can diagnose, treat and monitor both acute and chronic diseases as well as carrying out immunisations and routine medical examinations.

Think about it!

1 Why does Ayesha need to have a detailed knowledge of anatomy and physiology?

2 When might an NP need to refer an individual to a specialist?

3 Name two other services that a modern health centre like Willow Grove might offer patients.

4 Explain why Ayesha still has to study anatomy and physiology to keep up to date with medical developments, even though she has an advanced nursing degree.

5 Outline two different medical situations relevant to this unit that Ayesha might meet in the surgery.

6 Discuss the importance of close and prompt liaison between Ayesha and the GPs at Willow Grove.

7 Ayesha often has to undertake routine medical examinations of individuals for a variety of reasons. Thinking about the body systems you have learned about in this unit, suggest how each might be tested when carrying out a time-constrained examination.

Resources and further reading

Baker, M. et al (2001) *Further Studies in Human Biology (AQA)* London: Hodder Murray

Boyle, M. et al (2002) *Human Biology* London: Collins Educational

Clancy, J. & McVicar, A. (2002) *Physiology and anatomy: A Homeostatic Approach* London: HodderArnold

Givens, P. & Reiss, M. (2002) *Human Biology and Health Studies* Cheltenham: Nelson Thornes

Indge, B. et al (2000) *A New Introduction to Human Biology (AQA)* London: Hodder Murray

Jenkins, M. (1996) *Human Physiology and Health* London: Hodder &Stoughton

Jones, M. & Jones, G. (2004) *Human Biology for AS Level* Cambridge: Cambridge University Press

Moonie, N. et al (2000) *Advanced Health and Social Care* Oxford: Heinemann

Pickering, W.R. (2001) *Advanced Human Biology through Diagrams* Oxford: Oxford University Press

Saffrey, J. et al (1997) *Maintaining the Whole* Milton Keynes: The Open University

Shaw, L. (2005) *Anatomy and Physiology* Cheltenham: Nelson Thornes

Stretch, B. et al (2007) *Core themes in Health and Social Care* Oxford: Heinemann

Vander, A.J. (2005) *Human Physiology: The Mechanisms of Body Function* London: McGraw Hill

Ward, J. et al (2005) *Physiology at a Glance* Oxford: Blackwell Publishing

Wright, D. (2000) *Human Physiology and Health for GCSE* Oxford: Heinemann

Journals

Biological Science Review

New Scientist

Nursing Times

Nursing Standard

Useful websites

BBC Science and Nature www.bbc.co.uk/science

Get Body Smart www.getbodysmart.com

Instant Anatomy www.instantanatomy.net

Biology Guide www.biologyguide.net

BBC Schools GCSE Bitesize Biology www.bbc.co.uk/schools/gcsebitesize/biology

British Heart Foundation www.bhf.org.uk

Net Doctor www.netdoctor.co.uk

NHS Direct www.nhsdirect.nhs.uk

Index of body systems illustrations www.webschoolsolutions.com/patts/systems

Just checking

1   Complete the table below to outline the functions of the named organelles:

Name of organelle	Main function
Lysosome	
	Energy release
	Contains DNA
Rough endoplasmic reticulum	
Cell membrane	

2   Explain one location of the type of tissues given below:
* simple squamous epithelium
* ciliated columnar epithelium
* keratinised epithelium.

3   Describe the characteristics of each matrix in blood, cartilage and bone.

4   State the law of conservation of energy.

5   How is tissue fluid formed? Why is tissue fluid important in the sphere of energy metabolism?

6   Define diffusion and explain how this process is important in energy metabolism.

7   Describe the characteristics of enzymes.

8   Explain the role of baroreceptors in the homeostatic mechanisms controlling heart rate.

9   Why is it difficult to stay cool in a tropical humid atmosphere?

10 Explain how plasma glucose is regulated by hormones.

edexcel

Assignment tips

1   This unit is internally assessed by your tutor on the evidence you present in your portfolio. The evidence must be entirely your own work. Due to the nature of this unit, you will probably use many images, which can be your own diagrams (or photographs), or professional images from reference texts, leaflets and websites.

2   Work that is not your original creation must be appropriately referenced to the source and adapted to demonstrate the scope of your knowledge and understanding. It is not acceptable to download or copy images that you have not referenced, explained, adapted or annotated in any way. As you collect samples, write on the back how you think you will use them and what adaptations you will make. It is very easy to collect pieces of paper and then forget how you intended to use them.

3   To obtain merit and distinction grades, you will need to be able discuss energy metabolism and homeostasis so reading around the topics is essential. Keep a notebook or file with all your text and Internet references and the research notes you have made. Read these through before you begin your reports and discussions.

4   Plan your practical work carefully and ensure that you have made out a results chart and practised taking measurements beforehand. You must take account of health and safety issues and include them in your written report.

6 Personal and professional development in health and social care

This unit is mainly about *you*: how you develop as an individual and as a learner while preparing for future work in health and social care. All those who work in health and social care need to have a good understanding of themselves and their skills and abilities in order to contribute positively to the care, health and well-being of others. In addition, once qualified, health and social care professionals are expected to continue keeping up to date with new developments in relevant knowledge, care practices and social policies.

Early on, you will identify your strengths and those areas where you require further development. Your initial self-assessment will help you draw up a plan for your development over the course and for progression to professional training either in the workplace or in higher education. The different units in the course and the understanding gained from the placements that are an essential part of this unit, will provide you with evidence of your personal and professional development, which you will regularly review against your initial development plan. You will also investigate a health or social care setting and assess how it contributes to the provision of services nationally.

Learning outcomes

After completing this unit you should:

1 understand the learning process
2 be able to plan for, and monitor own professional development
3 be able to reflect on own development over time
4 know service provision in the health or social care sectors.

Assessment and grading criteria

This table shows you what you must do in order to achieve a **pass**, **merit** or **distinction** grade, and where you can find activities in this book to help you.

To achieve a **pass** grade, the evidence must show that you are able to:	To achieve a **merit** grade, the evidence must show that, in addition to the pass criteria, you are able to:	To achieve a **distinction** grade, the evidence must show that, in addition to the pass and merit criteria, you are able to:
P1 Explain key influences on the personal learning processes of individuals. **See Assessment activity 6.1, page 254** *achieved*	**M1** Assess the impact of key influences on the personal learning processes of own learning. **See Assessment activity 6.1, page 254** *achieved*	**D1** Evaluate how personal learning and development may benefit others. **See Assessment activity 6.1, page 254** *achieved*
P2 Assess own knowledge, skills, practice, values, beliefs and career aspirations at start of programme. **See Assessment activity 6.2, page 267** *achieved*		
P3 Produce an action plan for self-development and achievement of own personal goals. **See Assessment activity 6.3, page 271** *achieved*		
P4 Produce evidence of own progress against action plan over the duration of the programme. **See Assessment activity 6.4, page 272** *achieved*	**M2** Assess how the action plan has helped support own development over the duration of the programme. **See Assessment activity 6.5, page 272** *achieved*	**D2** Evaluate own development over the duration of the programme. **See Assessment activity 6.7, page 282** *achieved*
P5 Reflect on own personal and professional development. **See Assessment activity 6.6, page 282** *achieved*	**M3** Use three examples to examine links between theory and practice. **See Assessment activity 6.6, page 282** *achieved*	
P6 Describe one local health or social care service provider and identify its place in national provision. **See Assessment activity 6.8, page 292** *achieved*		
P7 Describe the roles, responsibilities and career pathways of three health or social care workers. **See Assessment activity 6.9, page 299** *achieved*		

How you will be assessed

This unit will be assessed through assignment tasks that you will complete in stages over the duration of the unit.

Your assessments will include:

* written assignments
* a detailed action plan for your own research project
* a report on the findings from your project.

Jude, 17 years old

I was a bit daunted by Unit 6 at first, especially when I realised the unit wouldn't be finished until the end of the second year. Still, our tutor explained what we would be doing in the unit and we did lots of the activities each week. These were really helpful in making me think about myself and how much I had learned about caring from helping my mum look after my younger brother who has cerebral palsy.

At first, I wasn't sure about how to reflect in my journal but I got the hang of it once I'd been on placement. There was much more to think about, with something happening most days that I could relate to one or other of the units on the course. Unless they were really busy, most days the supervisors were good at telling me what I was doing well or suggesting how I could improve.

The school's placement officer visited me on each placement and gave me useful tips and after each block week, we spent time in class talking about our experiences. The question and answer sessions helped me make sense of what I had learned and made it much easier to keep my journal.

At the end of the course, it helped to go back and compare what I had written in my first placement with what I was doing in my last one. Also, some of the things that seemed really important at the time they happened, worried me much less when I came to look back on them much later. Maybe that is what is meant by learning from experience.

Over to you!

1   What are you looking forward to most about Unit 6?
2   What do you think you will find most difficult?
3   Why do you think Unit 6 is important?

1 Understand the learning process

How much do you know about health and social care?

How much have you learned about health and social care up to now? What health and social care services have you used? Which health or care professionals looked after you? What qualities do you think you need to work in health and social care? Which of these qualities do you think you already have? And how do you need to develop your abilities so that you can progress successfully in a career in health and social care?

An overview of learning

Learning is a process by which we acquire knowledge, skills and an understanding of abstract concepts. Learning starts with early experiences as an infant and continues through formal schooling and academic study or training. You will need to complete specialist training to acquire the knowledge and skills for work as a care assistant, nurse or social worker, for example. The process is summarised in Figure 6.1 (on the next page). Learning also continues informally throughout life, and most health and social care workers expect to support the learning of other staff as a routine aspect of their work. Workers may also need to support individuals to learn new information or skills.

Health and social care workers are expected to *take active steps* to develop their learning appropriately for the specific care they do. This unit will help you to:

- understand how *you* learn
- understand *what* you have learned from your formal study and life experiences to date
- *set goals* for your personal development during the course
- *plan* for your personal development and *implement* the plan
- *monitor* your progress against the plan, amending it as learning proceeds
- *reflect* on the progress of your learning and development on the national programme, especially with regard to your career aspirations.

Before you qualify as a professional, learning from experience is called **personal and professional development (PPD)** but learning *after* qualifying is called **continuing professional development (CPD)**. You will come across both terms in this unit.

Reflect

Workers in health and social care are required to undertake CPD. Why do you think this is necessary?

As an older adolescent or adult, you will learn from formal study but you will also learn from your experience of daily life (jobs you have had, your home life, etc.). You will have innate abilities that you are born with, such as having a good singing voice, or practical skills you have acquired, such as learning to play a musical instrument through practice. Often learning blends skills with theory – driving a car involves practical skills and knowledge of the Highway Code. Figure 6.1 shows how these three different areas overlap. As you go through the course, you will

Key terms

Personal and professional development (PPD) – Learning acquired from experience before qualifying as a professional.

Continuing professional development (CPD) – Learning acquired after qualifying as a professional.

develop your abilities in all three areas as preparation for qualifying to work in health or social care.

Reflect

How do the theories presented here compare with the theories of learning you explored in Unit 4 (Development Through the Life Stages)? Theories relating to how adults learn are different.

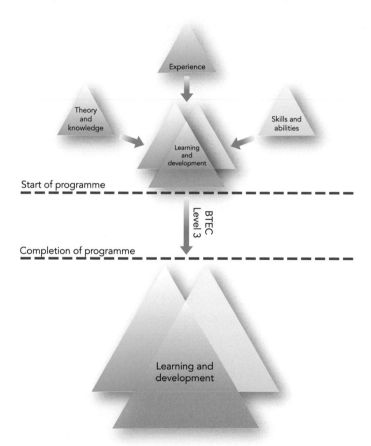

Fig 6.1: A model to show personal and professional development

1.1 Theories of learning

This section explores a limited selection of theories that help understanding of how older adolescents and adults learn. The aim is to enable you to recognise how you learn and then plan your own development while on the course.

The simplest way of looking at learning from experience is using the experience-reflection-action cycle, or the 'plan, do, reflect' cycle shown in Figure 6.2.

You may already know what sort of learner you are, i.e. whether you are:

- a visual (seeing)
- auditory (hearing)
- kinaesthetic (movement) or
- tactile (touching/feeling) type of learner.

Two of the best-known theories related to learning from experience are Kolb's experiential learning cycle (1984) and Honey and Mumford's learning styles theory (1982).

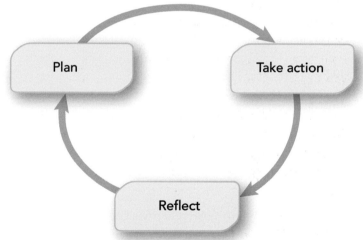

Fig 6.2: The plan, do, reflect cycle — a basic model of learning from practice

Activity 1: How do people learn? How do I learn?

What (and who) has influenced your learning throughout your life so far? Write each point on a separate sticky note. Write as many points as you can in five minutes.

Work with two or three others. Stick everyone's notes on a wall or table and sort them into groups by moving individual notes round until you have agreed the groups.

1   What categories/groups have you identified?
2   Why have you decided on these categories of influences?
3   Share your findings with other groups in the class.
4   Make notes on the influences on learning identified by the whole class.

Kolb's experiential learning cycle

Kolb helps us to understand how adults learn. The ways in which people learn are called their **cognitive abilities**. He suggested that during adolescence and early adulthood we begin to develop instinctive preferences as to the way in which we process information and use it to make sense of our experiences. Kolb identified two pairs of opposing factors that, combined together, show learning as a cyclic process with four stages (see Figure 6.3).

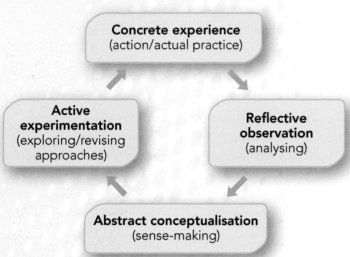

Fig 6.3: Kolb's experiential learning cycle

Key term

Cognitive abilities – Ways in which you think, using your knowledge and experience.

He claimed that, although it is possible to enter the cycle at any stage, for learning to be effective, each stage must be followed in the correct sequence.

Kolb described each stage as follows:

1 Concrete experience: the *doing* stage where you actually carry out or participate in an action or actions.

2 Reflective observation: the reviewing or *reflecting* stage where you think about what you did and what happened during the concrete experience.

3 Abstract conceptualisation: the *concluding* stage in relation to the concrete experience, sometimes called the *theorising* stage. In this stage you use all the information you have gained about the experience and organise your thoughts into some sort of order and so make sense of the experience.

4 Active experimentation: This is the *planning* or *trying out* stage. The next time you do the activity, you tackle an aspect of it *differently* from the first time, thus demonstrating that you have *learned* from the first concrete experience.

Case study: Zofia

Zofia speaks English as a second language. She is talking to residents at her placement. One of the residents, Gladys, who is very elderly and frail, corrects her English. Zofia apologises but Gladys explains very clearly where she had been going wrong in her phrasing and vocabulary. Later, Zofia thinks about what she had been taught in her ESOL evening class and realises that Gladys has enabled her to understand several rules of English that she had had difficulty understanding in class. After lunch in the care team meeting, Zofia feels more confident in how she expresses herself and her supervisor congratulates her on the improvement in her English.

How does Kolb's experiential learning cycle explain Zofia's learning?

The above example shows how Kolb's learning cycle theory can be applied to everyday practice. The following activity gives you a chance to try it for yourself.

Activity 2: Applying Kolb's learning cycle

Use Kolb's experiential learning cycle to review three recent tasks you have carried out for the first time in the last two or three days. For each task, note down:

- the aspects you judged to be successful and why
- the aspects you judged to be less successful and why
- what you would do differently for the 'active experimentation' stage before doing each of the activities again.

Kolb developed his theory further and described four learning styles. Research Kolb's learning styles theory and the definitions of each style. How well do the descriptions of each style match your preferred way of learning?

Although Kolb's learning cycle is useful in helping us recognise that thinking involves a series of stages, there are some criticisms of his theory:

1 The learning cycle does not take account of the role of feedback from others; it only considers what the individual is thinking.

2 Some argue that it is not necessary to follow the same order of the different parts of the cycle for learning to be effective.

Honey and Mumford's learning styles theory

Honey and Mumford (1982) also developed a learning styles theory. They reviewed the way in which different employees learned, and identified four *learning style preferences*: reflector, theorist, activist and pragmatist. The characteristics of each learning style help to identify preferred situations for learning, and situations that are less favourable (see Table 6.1).

Table 6.1: A summary of the characteristics of Honey and Mumford's learning styles and their impact on learning

Learning style	Characteristics	Preferred learning situations	Less favourable learning situations
Activists	• Like to be involved • Like new ideas • Lose interest quickly • 'Jump first/think later' mentality • Like to dominate	• New experiences • Working with others • Taking the lead • Taking on difficult tasks	• Listening (e.g. lectures) or when passive • Doing things on their own • 'Working to the rules'
Reflectors	• Like to observe from the edge of a group • Consider things from a range of different perspectives • Collect information before drawing conclusions • Let others contribute before they do	• Observing from the edge of a group • Having time to think before contributing • Analysing • Working without tight deadlines	• Taking a lead or performing in front of others • Having no time to prepare in advance • Facing the unexpected • Feeling rushed or pressurised by deadlines
Theorists	• Like to bring together different ideas to produce new ways of looking at things • Think logically • Like things to fit into an ordered scheme • Often detached and remote rather than emotional	• Having the opportunity to apply their knowledge and skills in complex situations • Working with abstract ideas • Having opportunities to question and probe for information and ideas • Having a clear structure and purpose	• Cannot identify with different approaches taken by others • Having a lack of structure or purpose • Working with emotions and feelings of others
Pragmatists	• Like to experiment/try things out • Seek feedback from others • Practical, like to get on with things rather than talk about them • Relate things to their own role	• Having a clear link between thinking and what has to be done • Having an opportunity to try things out • Like having new ideas that have clear benefits • Happy to copy from role models	• Being unable to identify the relevance of what has to be done • Not having guidance on how to do things • Benefits being unclear • Focus being only on theory and not including practical aspects

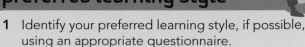

Case study: Katya

Four health and social care students have been asked to make a wall display for a health promotion assignment. Katya is already planning out her ideas on paper, referring back to the assignment task to check she has understood what is required. Sally is full of enthusiasm, talks eagerly, has lots of ideas and is trying to persuade the others to follow them. Lee is attentive but quiet and not contributing to the discussion. Surinder is picking up some of Katya's and Sally's ideas and is trying to form them into a sensible order. After a while, Katya starts chatting to her friend in the neighbouring group, Lee gets up to go to the library, and Surinder expresses exasperation at not having made any progress with the task.

1 What is the preferred learning style of each member of the group?

2 Why do you think the group has ceased to function?

3 What could you suggest to the group to help them achieve their task?

Activity 3: Using my preferred learning style

1 Identify your preferred learning style, if possible, using an appropriate questionnaire.

2 Identify a situation where your learning was particularly effective from your:

- course
- placement
- home life.

3 Repeat the exercise, choosing one example from each situation where your learning was less effective.

4 Compare the effective and less effective learning experiences and analyse the extent to which your preferred learning style helps to explain the differences in your learning.

5 What steps could you have taken to enhance your learning, from the situations you have identified?

6 Do further research on recent findings about the importance of learning styles.

Honey and Mumford devised a questionnaire for individuals to identify their preferred learning style. Most individuals tend to use a range of learning styles, depending on the situation, but we use our preferred learning style most easily, especially if we are tired or stressed. Being aware of your preferred learning style may help you work in a way that enhances your learning and avoid situations that are unhelpful.

1.2 Influences on learning

Learning style is only one influence on how people learn. Understanding how you learn is helpful for your progress on the course so that you can focus on the positive influences. However, you should remember that other people's learning may be influenced by factors outside your own experience.

Reflect

Compare Honey and Mumford's learning styles with those of Kolb. To what extent are they the same or different?

Being aware of your preferred learning style means that you can select an approach when planning your study activities and personal development that fits your style. However, in working life, being able to adopt a range of different learning styles according to the circumstances can make you more flexible and less dependent on a single learning style.

Some people now consider that learning styles have less effect on an individual's ability to learn than was previously thought.

Activity 4: How do others learn?

Observe one of your peers learning a new skill or routine. Note the factors that seem to help the individual's learning and those that hinder it.

1 How could the learning experience be altered to improve the individual's learning?

2 What would have affected your learning in a similar situation to your peer?

PLTS

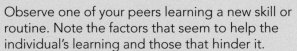

Independent enquirer: Processing observed information on complex subjects concisely and clearly will allow you to demonstrate your independent enquiry skills.

Reflect

How could you reduce the negative influences on your learning? Could you do things in a different way or avoid unfavourable situations, e.g. work in a library rather than among distractions from other members of the family at home?

Reflect

What factors affect your own learning? In what way does each factor affect your learning? What actions could you take to reduce the negative influences on your learning? How might the other factors identified in Figure 6.4 affect how others learn?

Those working in health and social care need to be aware of the factors influencing other people's learning. If an individual needs to learn new information and skills, such as taking new medication or using physical aids, they can be supported by taking advantages of factors that help their learning and reducing those that hinder their learning. Some of the factors that may influence how different individuals learn are shown in Figure 6.4.

Kolb recognised that socialisation (the way in which a person learns to fit into a group – see Unit 7) experiences affect that person's learning style. Personal habits and routines, beliefs, customs, values, motivation and career aspirations are all influences because they can affect attitudes to study and whether or not it takes priority over other demands on an individual, such as home life or work.

1.3 Skills for learning
Study skills

During this Level 3 BTEC course, you may find that what is expected of you, and what your tutor does in the classroom, differs from your previous experiences of learning – perhaps when you were doing your GCSEs, for example. Studying on a BTEC programme requires a different balance of skills from those often used in examination-based courses. Some of the differences arise because the course is aimed at more adult learners, who may have more experience of using functional and interpersonal skills.

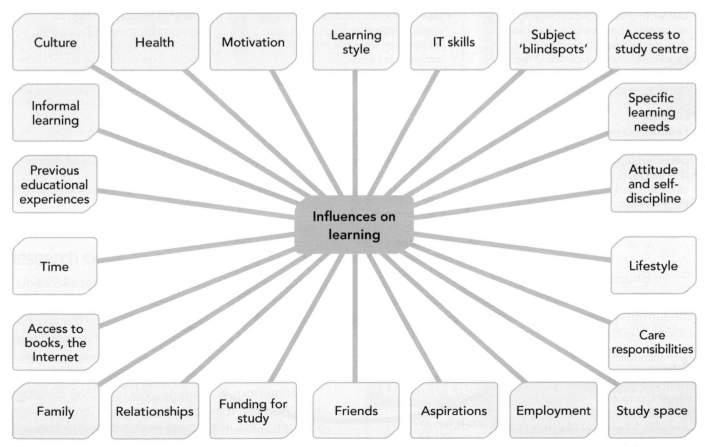

Fig 6.4: Examples of factors that may influence learning

1.5 Learning opportunities

Opportunities to apply the Kolb experiential learning cycle to learn something new, or to increase your understanding, can happen at any time. This might be during formal learning in the classroom, supported by a tutor, or on a placement, supported by a supervisor mentor. Everyday experience can also prompt reflection – for example, being a patient yourself or observing an incident in the street as a passer-by.

You might apply the Kolb theory soon after an active experience, perhaps after a classroom discussion or you might only apply it later. Your formal learning in college may enable you to reflect differently on an experience from your past so you might now have a better understanding of why you received the treatment you did when you were ill as a child. In this instance, the reflection forms part of the reflective observation and active conceptualisation part of the cycle. Opportunities for learning can also come from experiences in paid employment or voluntary work, where you might gain experience of using and developing your communication skills while working with customers in a shop or a restaurant.

Assessment activity 6.1

Produce a piece of writing that explains influences on the personal learning process of different individuals.

Include an assessment of how different influences in your life have affected your own learning. Consider influences on the development of your knowledge and understanding, skills and abilities. Present your assessment as a personal statement and include a curriculum vitae.

Evaluate how the personal learning and development of health and social care workers can benefit others.

Grading tips

P1 For P1, you should consider a wide range of influences that may affect people's learning and not just the factors that have influenced your own learning. Remember to explain the possible effects of the influences, applying the theories discussed in this section.

M1 Sketch a timeline to help collect your thoughts about the factors that have influenced your learning from your childhood, school, work and other life experiences. You could put the significant events and experiences (e.g. starting school, moving home) on top of the line and their effects below the line. Use the timeline as a tool to help you construct your personal statement. Research how to present a curriculum vitae.

D1 Before you prepare your evaluation for D1, you could carry out some research about PPD and its benefits in health and social care. You should talk to staff at your placement about how their learning and career backgrounds have helped them in their work. You could also consider how you have used your own learning throughout your life so far to help others.

Functional skills

English: Producing extended writing and communicating your ideas effectively and concisely will allow you to demonstrate your English skills.

ICT: Using word processing skills.

PLTS

Independent enquirer: Your exploration of the factors that influence your own learning and that of others will demonstrate your ability to explore issues and analyse and evaluate relevant information as an independent enquirer.

2   Be able to plan for and monitor your own development

Activity 8: What are my abilities?

Make a list of your abilities in a table, under three headings:

- knowledge
- skills and abilities
- experience.

Discuss your table with two or three of your peers, and add any abilities you may have overlooked.

While Section 1 introduced you to the concept of learning and development in general, this section focuses on your *actual* learning and development, both in the past up to the point at which you started the Level 3 BTEC course, and throughout the period on the course and for which you will be planning your development. This section has three themes:

- an assessment of your abilities at the start of the course
- an exploration of the skills and knowledge expected of those who work in health and social care
- a plan to help you develop new skills and knowledge and to enhance the skills and knowledge you already have.

These themes all need to be considered before the next assessment activity. In addition, while some of the assessment related to your development has to be completed at the start of the programme, other assessment activities require you to apply the material in this section throughout the programme. For this reason, these assessment activities cannot be completed until the end of the course.

2.1 Review at start of programme

In order to measure your development while you are on the course, you first need to know your starting point. You will therefore assess, or measure, your development in the first few weeks of the Level 3 BTEC programme by exploring this in relation to

the expectations of those who work in health and social care. This initial review will establish a personal **baseline** against which you can measure your progress.

Key term

Baseline – A starting point against which to make comparisons.

Case study: Surinder

Surinder has always wanted to be a nurse. She got a Merit grade for a Level 2 Diploma in Society, Health and Development at school but only just achieved the mathematics part of the functional skills. She got a D in GCSE Maths but managed to get C grades in English and Science. She has started the Level 3 BTEC in Health and Social Care at college because she wants to do as much work experience as she can. She really enjoyed her Year 10 work experience in a primary school. The class teacher said she was a 'natural' at teaching and should think about it as a career. In Year 11 she was the class representative on the school council and helped at the breakfast club for the Year 7s and 8s. Surinder helps at home, looking after her grandmother who has diabetes and uses a wheelchair, and she did her Diploma project on diabetes. Now, Surinder is not sure what she wants to do when she leaves college.

1   What are Surinder's strengths?

2   What is a priority for her development if she is to be able to progress to either teacher training or nurse training?

3   Who could help Surinder make her mind up about what career to choose?

4   What does Surinder need to do to ensure that she can put in a strong application for either of her career options?

- experience of using health or social care services
- specific experience of a health condition from personal experience or that of an individual close to you.

Reflect

Patients can find out very detailed information about their specific medical condition from the Internet. How would you feel, as a newly qualified nurse, caring for a patient who delights in telling you how things should be done or otherwise indicating that he knows much more than you do about his condition? What would your response be to this situation?

Understanding of theories, principles and concepts

These have similar meanings and tend to be used interchangeably in the context of study and learning. They involve more abstract thinking although they may be developed as a result of experience.

Activity 11: What's in a theory?

In a group, make a list of as many well-known theories as you can. Try to summarise each one for your peers.

Think of a concept or principle introduced at school, which you found hard to understand, e.g. fractions, politics or homeostasis. Work with a small group to improve your understanding of this concept.

Reflect

How could you use your learning from your previous study and experience to support your current study on the Level 3 BTEC Health and Social Care course?

How do you think the subjects that you are currently studying as part of your overall school or college programme will help you at placements?

Being aware of those aspects of your learning that you find more difficult helps you identify areas for development. Recognising your prior knowledge

and identifying where and/or when it might be useful can help you learn more quickly and effectively from experiences as they happen.

Understanding of potential careers

Your career aspirations at the start of your programme may be quite general – for example, to be a nurse or a social worker. Nurse training is divided into four different branches and you need to choose one branch before applying for training. Social work training tends to be generic at undergraduate level, with opportunities to specialise as a postgraduate. The university where you study is likely to deliver a degree programme that, while meeting the requirements of the relevant professional body, differs from the programme delivered at another university for the same qualification. You will need to research these details before applying for professional training, possibly in the second year of your course, so you can apply to the programmes that are right for you.

Different learning opportunities

The wider the range of your learning experiences, the more informed you become. Different placement experiences enable you to make comparisons and highlight contrasts between different health and social care options. Breadth of experience could include, for example:

- different types of settings, e.g. day centres, residential care, schools, nurseries, etc.
- different age groups, e.g. young children, older adults, older children or adults with learning disability
- different health and social care sectors, e.g. public sector, private sector or voluntary sector.

2.3 Skills

A skill is the ability to perform a practical activity appropriately, or with competence. If you are on the Level 3 BTEC course, you have reading and writing skills that are sufficient to achieve four GCSEs at grade C or above. You may have learned how to ride a bicycle during your childhood, or be able to draw, use a computer, or have football skills. On this course you will have to think about your skills in communicating, working with others, using equipment (technical skills), researching information and personal skills such as organising yourself.

Communicating

Being able to communicate effectively is an essential skill for all care workers and is addressed in detail in Unit 1 Developing effective communication in health and social care.

Activity 12: Using feedback

Use formal and informal feedback from others in order to judge how well you communicate:

- with text, e.g. when reading, in handwriting, sending emails or texts, understanding the written content of sources
- orally, e.g. your use of language and what you say, how you say it and how you convey your intended meaning
- non-verbally, e.g. how you listen, use gestures, facial expressions and posture
- using the communication cycle (see Unit 1).

You may get feedback as part of any unit in the course or informally from peers, friends and family. Reflecting on these points will help you assess your communication skills at the start of the course.

Functional skills

English: You can show your English skills by listening to complex information given in feedback and processing ideas.

Did you know?

Communicating all *relevant* information clearly, *sufficiently* and *accurately* and to the *right individuals* is essential in health and care so that the information is received and understood accurately by the recipient. Failure to do this could result in mistakes when providing care.

Working with others

Working in health or social care requires continual interaction with others, which is why communication skills are so important. Workers interact with individuals using services and often their relatives, and with

professionals, specialist care workers, supervisors, managers, support staff or people who work in different agencies or organisations. The skills and abilities required to contribute effectively to team work include:

- understanding your own skills, knowledge and experience so that you can contribute appropriately to the team task
- recognising how the skills, knowledge and experience of each of the other members of the team contribute to the team task
- supporting members of the team with their contributions to the team task
- respecting contributions from all members of the team
- evaluating the effectiveness of the team in carrying out its task
- evaluating your own contribution to the team effort.

Are you an effective team worker?

You will work with individuals with different care needs on your placements, under the supervision of placement staff. You will probably talk to them on a one-to-one basis and will work with small groups of individuals, helping them to meet their developmental, creative or recreational needs.

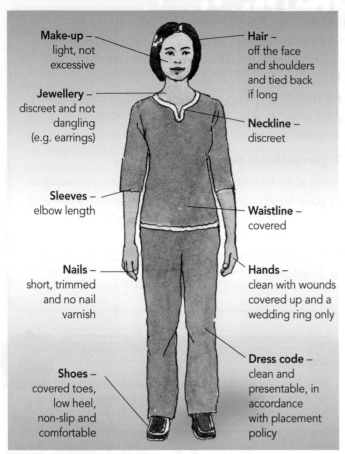

- Make-up – light, not excessive
- Hair – off the face and shoulders and tied back if long
- Jewellery – discreet and not dangling (e.g. earrings)
- Neckline – discreet
- Sleeves – elbow length
- Waistline – covered
- Nails – short, trimmed and no nail varnish
- Hands – clean with wounds covered up and a wedding ring only
- Shoes – covered toes, low heel, non-slip and comfortable
- Dress code – clean and presentable, in accordance with placement policy

Fig 6.7: Good practice in personal presentation for health and social care placements

Did you know?

Hospital-acquired infections are a major concern. According to the Health Protection Agency (HPA), thorough hand-washing is the single most effective way of controlling infection (HPA, 2009). There are lots of guides on the Internet to show you what is meant by thorough hand washing.

2.4 Practice

Working professionally

Everything that you do in your placements is your 'practice', although the detail of your work will vary according to the type of setting and the people using its services. You will be expected to demonstrate the skills and attributes that are expected of all those who work in health and social care. Even though, as a student, you are not yet working as a professional, you will still be expected to work professionally. What is expected of you as a professional is integrated

throughout this unit and highlighted by the headings in this unit. The requirements include:

- demonstrating the value base of care (care value base)
- recognising your own personal values and beliefs and developing these to support good practice
- interacting professionally with others
- contributing to team work
- demonstrating awareness of the impact of legislation, codes of practice and policies on your own practice
- accepting your responsibilities and recognising the limitations of your role as a student on placement.

Influence of personal values and beliefs

Your own values and beliefs influence how you interact with others. For the baseline self-assessment, you should consider what your values and beliefs are – because they may differ from the care value base, perhaps more in some aspects and less in others.

Influence of legislation, codes of practice and policies

Legislation

Before starting your placements, you will require an enhanced disclosure from the Criminal Records Bureau: this is a requirement under the Care Standards Act 2000 (CSA) for all those who work with children, young people and vulnerable adults. There are restrictions on some practical activities if you are under 18. For example, the CSA means you cannot assist with personal care (bathing, toileting and feeding). You should not be asked to assist with moving and handling individuals or equipment. You will also have personal responsibilities under the Health and Safety at Work Act 1974 (see Unit 3) and the Data Protection Act 1998 (see Unit 1).

Codes of practice

Codes of practice are statements about the behaviour expected of a group of individuals in carrying out their work. Each health and social care profession has its own code of practice that defines what is expected of all those who are on the professional register. Registration (usually following successful completion of the recognised training) is a requirement to gain employment as a professional. Members of the profession may be suspended or struck off

THE NURSING AND MIDWIFERY COUNCIL CODE OF PROFESSIONAL CONDUCT

Standards of conduct, performance and ethics for nurses and midwives

The people in your care must be able to trust you with their health and wellbeing.

To justify that trust, you must:

- make the care of people your first concern, treating them as individuals and respecting their dignity
- work with others to protect and promote the health and wellbeing of those in your care, their families and carers, and the wider community
- provide a high standard of practice and care at all times
- be open and honest, act with integrity and uphold the reputation of your profession.

As a professional, you are personally accountable for actions and omissions in your practice and must always be able to justify your decisions.

You must always act lawfully, whether those laws relate to your professional practice or personal life.

Fig 6.8: The NMC Professional Codes of Practice

the professional register if their behaviour does not conform to the code of practice of the professional body concerned.

Codes of conduct are internal codes used by individual organisations to set a standard of behaviour for those in the organisation. Health and social care settings may have a code of conduct, often for all staff, whatever their job role or professional status, and sometimes for the users of the service. For example, schools and colleges may have codes of conduct for their pupils and students. These are usually presented in a school or college handbook that all pupils or students receive. In recent years, some organisations have introduced codes of conduct to protect their staff from abuse by people using services.

Policies

Policies are the formal documents drawn up by each setting to state how their organisation will meet the requirements of legislation and relevant codes of practice. They are unique to each setting and written specifically to be appropriate for the services they are providing, the buildings and accommodation they are using, the staff who work there and the users of the

services. All settings must have a health and safety policy but the wording will not be identical in all your placements.

Reflect

Why do you think you always need an induction when you start work at a new placement setting?

Recognising personal responsibilities and limitations

Recognising your personal responsibilities and limitations is an important aspect of professionalism. The amount of responsibility you have taken for your life and affairs up to the start of the programme may be fairly limited if you have just completed your compulsory schooling at 16. If you are a bit older then you may be taking responsibility for many aspects of your day-to-day life such as your accommodation, meals, getting around in a car or on public transport, etc. You may have had responsibilities such as organising yourself with regard to GCSE coursework,

Table 6.4: Respecting an individual's rights

The rights of individuals	Examples of how you could respect this right
Diversity and respect for differences	• Attending to the needs of each person as an individual • Encouraging individuals to express their views, for example on a service they receive
Equality in care practice	• Showing respect and care for all individuals, including those who may be of a different culture or have different values from yourself
Anti-discriminatory practice	• Learning how to challenge appropriately the behaviour of a worker or individual who subjects another person to discrimination or abuse • Reporting discriminatory incidents to your supervisor or a manager
Confidentiality	• Never talking about any individuals to people outside the care team • When discussing placement learning in class, never identifying an individual or member of staff
Control (autonomy) over own life, choice, independence	• Allowing individuals to make choices about their day-to-day care and activities • Never presuming to carry out a task for an individual • Always asking whether a individual would like you to help
Dignity and privacy	• Not drawing attention to an individual in distress but helping them, without fuss, to a quiet area or to relieve their distress • Making sure an individual is dressed and covered, even if this is inconvenient for you
Effective communication	• Reporting events and observations accurately to staff • Explaining your actions to individuals when providing care
Safety and security	• Being observant of potential hazards for individuals and workers and reporting any hazards you see • Taking responsibility for your own safety • Being vigilant about your own safe practice • Reporting any abuse you witness • Following procedures to maintain the security of individuals

Activity 20: What are my career options?

Research the career options available to you at the end of the Level 3 BTEC. Make a shortlist of at least three options and investigate in detail the qualifications and experience you will need to gain for each. For each career option, what actions do you need to take:

• in the next few weeks?

• within six months/by the end of the first half of the programme?

• within eighteen months/by the end of the course?

Using your self-assessment, analyse the extent to which your experience and learning could enable you to follow the three career options chosen.

What further actions would you need to take to pursue any of these three options?

Functional skills

ICT: Retrieving relevant information about career options will enable you to demonstrate your ICT skills.

Reflect

To what extent have you made use of the support systems available to you in your school/college or locality to help you make an informed career choice?

Decisions about your career path do not need to be taken immediately but you do need to be aware of realistic options from which you can make choices later on in the course. However, you should find out about the entry requirements to training early on so that, if you need specific qualifications or experience to be eligible, you can plan to acquire these before applying. Entry to university also involves achieving qualifications at a sufficiently high level, and the Universities and

Colleges Application System (UCAS) awards points according to the grades you get. On a Level 3 BTEC programme, the grade for every unit contributes to the overall grade for the qualification. If the UCAS point score required is high, this could mean that most year 1 units may need to be achieved with a good grade as well as those studied in year 2. You should consider this when developing your PPD plan for this unit.

Assessment activity 6.2   BTEC

Write a report that assesses your own knowledge, skills, practice, values, beliefs and career aspirations at the start of the programme.

Grading tip

P2 Use each of the areas explored in this section to help you. You should consider in some detail how aspects of your experiences up to the

present that have contributed to your current knowledge and understanding. You should then consider the strengths and weaknesses of your experience thus far in your life in relation to your career goals. The recommendations you make in your report could then help you develop a suitable action plan for the next assessment activity.

Functional skills

English: You can show your English skills by writing using an essay format and conventions.

PLTS

Creative thinker: The discussion in your essay should enable you to demonstrate creative thinking through challenging your own assumptions, and those of others.

2.7 Plan for own development
Personal goals – short-term and long-term

Your initial self-assessment should now be complete. You have established your personal baseline and identified your strengths and areas for development against a benchmark standard appropriate for health and social care so you have some realistic career options. You can now start to plan your PPD as the third stage in the SAP approach. To do this, you will need to understand the principles of planning, which include:

- setting goals or targets
- drawing up an action plan to work towards achieving your personal goals
- implementing the actions in the plan.

Activity 21: A personal stock-take

Review your responses and what you have learned about yourself from all the activities completed so far in this unit.

List those aspects of your development where you think you could make improvements to your learning and personal skills.

Compare the assessment of your skills and abilities at the start of the programme with those you are likely to need to fulfil your career aspirations. Then identify any specific skills, quality and experience you could develop during the programme to support your application for the next stage of your career.

Assessment activity 6.4 P4

Formally review your progress against your plan on each of the review dates you specified in your plan. Keep a copy of your personal development action plan as it is at each of the review dates, and get your tutor to sign saying that they have seen your plan on each monitoring review date.

circumstances that have affected your progress against your personal goals and targets, including reasons for any changes you make to the goals themselves as you go through the programme.

Get your tutor to sign and date your working document in tutorials as evidence that you are monitoring your plan.

Present the starting version of your development plan and an updated final version that summarises the main outcomes of each monitoring review of your plan.

Grading tip

P4 Keep your plan in your day-to-day file so you can add changes easily, as and when necessary.

When you make a change to the plan, enter the date on which you make the change.

At each monitoring date, write a short personal statement summarising the challenges and

Functional skills

English: You can demonstrate your English skills by communicating progress on your plan concisely.

PLTS

Independent enquirer: Monitoring your plan and recording amendments will demonstrate that you are reviewing your progress as an independent enquirer.

At the end of the whole programme, when Unit 6 is completed, you will be able to assess to what extent your plan has helped you complete your Level 3 BTEC programme as well as Unit 6.

Assessment activity 6.5 M2

Write an informal report that assesses how well your action plan has supported your development over the duration of the programme.

Consider all aspects of the plan, e.g. your overall goals, the actions themselves, their sequencing and timescales, when assessing the usefulness of the plan in supporting your development from the start to the end of the programme.

Grading tip

M2 Review the original personal development plan you drew up at the start of the programme and all the records you have kept as part of the monitoring process.

3 Be able to reflect on own development over time

3.1 What is reflection?

You will be familiar with looking in the mirror and seeing a reflection of yourself to assess whether or not you look as you want to look. If, for example, you judge your hair to be out of place, you tidy it up and check again in the mirror until it is as you want it. In this scenario, you have

- reviewed your appearance – or 'performance'

- made a judgement about whether it is as required or not – the judgement is made against a personal standard you are aiming for

- taken an action to make an improvement – you may also have experimented with different ways of arranging your hair before you get to this point.

Reflection is a widely used term that describes the way in which we think about our experiences in order to understand them and, as explored in Section 1, this is an important aspect of the way adults learn.

We may still learn a few specific pieces of information by rote, e.g. 'ABC' as a mnemonic (memory aid) for remembering the order of priorities for resuscitating a casualty in first aid training (see Unit 3 Health, safety and security).

We use reflection to, for example:

- make positive, negative or qualified overall judgements about an experience

- make sense of a complex experience or situation by teasing out different aspects of it into individual components and dealing with each component separately

- assess our own performance either against an externally set standard (e.g. the correct technique for resuscitating a casualty) or against a personal standard (e.g. personal values, targets, etc.)

- consider alternative approaches to doing things

- seek explanations for feelings and emotions and the responses made as a result – these might be your personal feelings and responses or those observed in others

- find answers to questions and problems that confront us

- apply existing knowledge and understanding to a new situation to explain and understand it.

Reflection is important for all those who are faced with **complex**, **uncertain** or new situations as part of their day-to-day work activities. Health and social care professionals encounter complex, uncertain and variable situations continually because no two individuals are identical and their health condition or care needs are rarely exactly the same. The individuals may be users of health and social care services or people who work in the services.

Activity 23: Reflecting

Think of an incident that has happened in the last week but which you have found yourself thinking about again since. Jot down a few notes to remind you of the details of what happened.

- How did you feel at the time of the incident?

- Why did you return to thinking about it again later?

- How did you feel at that stage?

- In what way was your later thinking about the incident different from the time it actually happened?

- How do you feel about the incident now?

- What have you learned from the incident?

- Why do you think differently now than you did at the time?

In this unit, the emphasis is on demonstrating that you *can* reflect and that you have *learned* from the reflection, rather than *how far* you have actually developed over the duration of the Level 3 BTEC programme. At this stage of your professional

Key terms

Reflection – A conscious process of thinking about a problem in order to understand it.

Complex – Influenced by many inter-related factors.

Uncertain – Where there are many unknowns, where there are considerable gaps in the relevant information, or the strength of different influences could be variable.

development, learning through reflection should help you to:

- achieve as well as you can on each unit of the course
- understand work in health and care better so you know what to expect and what is expected of you in your placements
- understand yourself better so you can prepare yourself for future training or employment in health or care
- make an informed career choice for progression from the course
- be successful in progressing to the next stage of your career after you have completed the Level 3 BTEC programme.

Techniques to aid reflection

There are various techniques to help reflective thinking.

Questioning

Asking yourself lots of questions about an issue, topic, event or situation helps you explore different aspects of the issue so that you can consider each aspect in turn.

Talking to others

The process of having to express yourself orally to others helps you organise your thoughts. It can be particularly helpful when dealing with practice problems and is the basis of a supervisor or mentor role.

Writing about it

Again, committing your thinking to the page helps you organise your thoughts and make sense of experiences. Keeping notes about incidents, your feelings and your responses to them will be the basis of your practice journal or diary. For academic study, you may use abstracts or extracts from your journal in assignments and should make reference to academic theories.

Tools for thinking

These often use visual formats or mnemonics to structure your thinking. The SWOT analysis and 5Ws and H have been suggested already but you may have used other useful tools during your programme induction and tutorial activities. Examples are the Johari window, Venn diagrams, flow charts (see

Figure 6.2, page 243, and 6.3, page 244) and graphic organisers (most of the other diagrams in this unit).

Case study: Sara

On her first day on a placement in a care home, Sara was present when one of the residents collapsed in clear distress and died before an ambulance arrived. Sara had not been able to help, had never seen a person dying before, and has thought repeatedly about the incident ever since.

Compile a list of questions that Sara could ask herself to better understand why it worried her and to learn from the incident.

Did you know?

A simple model for reflecting on experiences is to ask three questions: What? So what? Now what?

3.2 Changes

Change happens continually and particularly in health and social care. It is also a feature of our personal lives and we have to adapt in order to cope with it. In this unit, you may experience change relating to:

- placements
- career aspirations
- changes of tutor
- changes in personal circumstances (e.g. moving home or getting a job)
- illness.

Reflecting on how well you have coped with change could help you identify for the future which coping strategies you have found helpful and which strategies to avoid. You also need to look at changes in relation to your ongoing development needs and goals.

3.3 Variety of contexts

You should have gained experience from at least three placements working with different users of services, different multidisciplinary teams, organisational structures and possibly in different health and social care sectors. Comparisons between these could form part of your reflection. You should demonstrate that

- inforr
  pract
- intera
- intera
  durin
  listen
  obser
- pract
  team
  imple
  servic

Also, list
on their
understa
settings

Routines
time on
benefici;
their dut
using th(

Aims ai
- How i
- Are th
  consic
- Is it ag

Health
- Equip
- Abiliti
  needs
- Numk
- Mana

you can apply theory learned in all the units of the programme to further your understanding of different experiences and observations made on placements, in employment or when volunteering and, if appropriate, in other aspects of your life.

3.4 Professional development portfolio

Evidence of PPD and CPD is usually placed in a portfolio, which includes a professional practice diary and indexed, authenticated records to demonstrate your personal progression. Your portfolio may be paper-based or it could be an e-portfolio in which all the relevant evidence is stored in an e-document. If you use a hard copy, the portfolio could be a ring binder or lever arch file but it should not be any bulkier than that.

Your Unit 6 portfolio should contain all the evidence that you submit for the Unit 6 assessments, systematically presented. (It should *not* contain all evidence relating to preparatory work and activities that help you generate that evidence but which are not themselves assessed. Examples of these items might be the notes you make when using 'tools' to help your reflection.) As part of this unit, you will store evidence of your development throughout the course in a PPD portfolio.

Structure of portfolio

The evidence in your assessment portfolio should be structured clearly so that you and your assessor both know what evidence it contains and where it is.

Index

A list of contents should be inserted at the front of your portfolio. You should identify (e.g. in a mapping table or in a short statement) how the evidence relates to the assessment criteria.

Authentication

You should obtain signatures from your tutors or placement supervisors as appropriate (e.g. for your plans or to verify your descriptive accounts).

Personal progression

This will be demonstrated partly by your records showing the monitoring of your developmental plan and partly by a reflective account of your overall development that you will need to complete at the end of the unit. Suggestions to help you reflect on your progress include:

- updating your self-assessment (i.e. strengths and areas still requiring development) and comparing it with your baseline assessment of your knowledge, skills, practice and values
- assessing the extent to which you have met the personal goals in your development plan
- consideration of unplanned or unexpected ways in which you have developed over the duration of the programme
- assessing the extent to which you feel prepared and ready for the next stage of your career
- discussion of how well you have made use of support and resources to aid your development.

3.5 Relevant evidence

Evidence is material that records your knowledge and abilities. Figure 6.9 (page 276) identifies several different forms of evidence that could be relevant for this unit.

Formal evidence

All assignments and reflective reports written for this unit are essential items of formal evidence as part of your professional development portfolio. Supporting formal evidence is that which enables others to judge your abilities objectively either by direct observation of you carrying out an activity or scrutinising materials you have produced (e.g. written evidence). Written assignments, forms (e.g. your individual learning plan or UCAS application) and certificates are formal evidence. A witness testimony form, signed and dated by a suitably qualified professional (e.g. your tutor or placement mentor/supervisor) is also formal evidence and necessary to capture practice skills in 'live' situations such as doing presentations and role plays or demonstrating awareness while on placement (e.g. working safely). DVDs can be used for classroom activities but are not acceptable for placement activities.

Did you know?

At this level, it is your responsibility to make arrangements for a witness to provide testimony as to your participation in an activity. You should make the request in advance for any planned activity and as soon as possible after the event for unplanned experiences (e.g. critical incidents). Always supply the form to be used promptly. A witness should not be a relative.

WorkSpace
Lesley James
Nurse

Lesley is an experienced nurse who qualified ten years ago. Until recently, all her experience had been working in a teaching hospital in theatre as a staff nurse and then as a sister on a surgical ward. The work was varied and interesting because one of the surgeons was a professor and gastrointestinal expert so difficult cases were referred to him. She enjoyed the work because she was responsible for managing the nursing care for patients before and after their operations. Some of the patients were seriously ill and needed specialist support and care.

Sometimes patients had to have central intravenous catheters inserted for their nutrition support and medication, and scrupulous standards of hygiene were required to prevent the catheters from getting infected, as this could be life-threatening.

After their surgery, many patients needed careful monitoring to ensure that they recovered from the effects of surgery, and because of the specialism, patients needed particular support to adjust to coping with stoma bags. Patients often found this very embarrassing but Lesley became expert at putting them and their families at their ease. Very careful attention to personal hygiene was needed and Lesley trained all junior nurses for the routines she expected on the ward.

Lesley had two small children and, after her maternity leave, chose to work shifts in the accident and emergency department of a district general hospital, as this was more convenient for childcare and her home. Throughout, she has taken various training courses to meet the relevant KSF specialist dimension requirements of these jobs.

However, now Lesley has moved to a rural area with her family and her choice of jobs in nursing is more limited than in the city. She has been appointed assistant manager of a local residential and nursing home and now finds she has to acquire skills for work in health and social care and as a manager. She has recently decided to enrol on a distance-learning Masters course to develop her management and leadership skills.

Think about it!

1 What has helped Lesley adapt her nursing skills to fit each of the jobs she has done?

2 What aspects of her past nursing experience might be useful for her new job?

3 How would you cope with changes in your career?

Professional codes of practice

Professional bodies regulate their profession by establishing codes of conduct for all registrants that define the minimum standards of behaviour that are expected. The codes of practice reflect the ethics and values of the profession, which are similar in all the health and care professions.

As already mentioned, all professional bodies have the power to remove an individual from the professional register after a formal process of enquiry, if the professional code of practice is breached. An individual who has been struck off their professional register is unable to work in any role requiring professional status. Employers usually suspend the individual concerned as soon as a claim of professional misconduct is made.

Other workers in health and social care services

Training for health and care work is statutory under the Care Standards Act 2000 and any untrained worker in health or social care must complete induction training.

Activity 36: The Induction Standards

Find out about the GSCC Induction Standards 2006 for those commencing work in health and social care for the first time.

Care assistants do not have to be registered with a professional body (in addition to the GSCC) but this situation may change in the future. Care employers must ensure that at least 50 per cent of their workers have a relevant qualification at least to Level 2 and

managers must be registered with the General Social Care Council (GSCC) and have an approved management qualification.

Reflect

Do you know where your GCSE certificates are, and those any from other similar qualifications? Have you stored them carefully so they will not get lost or damaged? Why do you think it is important to take care of all your certificates for qualifications gained from GCSEs onwards?

Multidisciplinary teams

Individuals using services are the most important people in any care setting and all work activity in a health or care organisation is either directly or indirectly associated with meeting the needs of its individuals. It is probable that for any one individual, the expertise of several different types of health and care worker will be required to meet their needs. Each worker will have a different job role but, by working together, they can meet the needs of the individual. This group of workers, each with different and specific roles, is known as a multidisciplinary team (MDT).

Case study: Khalid

Khalid is 7 years old. He has cerebral palsy, limited hearing and needs a laptop, as he has insufficient control over his arms and fingers to hold a pen. He is intelligent and he and his parents want him to remain in mainstream school.

What professionals would be involved in the MDT in supporting Khalid at school?

Activity 37: Work in practice

Investigate the qualifications and experience of three different types of worker in one of your placement settings.

1 What training have they completed and how did they obtain it, e.g. by full-time or part-time study?

2 How does the experience from training and previous employment help each of the workers in their current role? What has helped the staff to

adapt to new roles throughout their career?

3 What are the arrangements in the setting for staff to take part in PPD/CPD?

4 What opportunities are there in the setting for the staff to advance in their career by taking on new or additional responsibilities?

Career paths

In health and social care work, the pathways to reach a particular job role become more diverse as you proceed beyond your initial practitioner or professional qualification (see Fig 6.14). With an increasing amount of partnership working, health and care professionals find themselves working routinely in non-traditional settings within multidisciplinary teams.

Interaction with different professionals in different settings, and working with different individuals and groups using services and working at different levels of responsibility, provide diverse experiences that may be relevant for a wide range of job roles, sometimes only later in a career. Experience of health or care work is valued in a wide range of workplaces, not just those in health and social care – your career path may eventually take you into industry, work abroad, or the voluntary sector.

Broad pathway options after gaining practice qualifications may be in management, education and training, research or as an advanced practitioner in a specialist area. A higher-level qualification develops your abilities to use knowledge and understanding and to work with, and lead, others. With a licence to practise, you can work as a professional in an appropriate setting. Whatever career choices you make

Fig 6.15: Continuing professional development

in the future, ongoing reflection on your experience of working with individuals, other workers and different providers and agencies will continue to add to your knowledge and understanding. Gaining objective evidence of this CPD through formal qualifications and skill-set competencies will enhance your opportunity to progress your career in the direction you choose (see Fig 6.15).

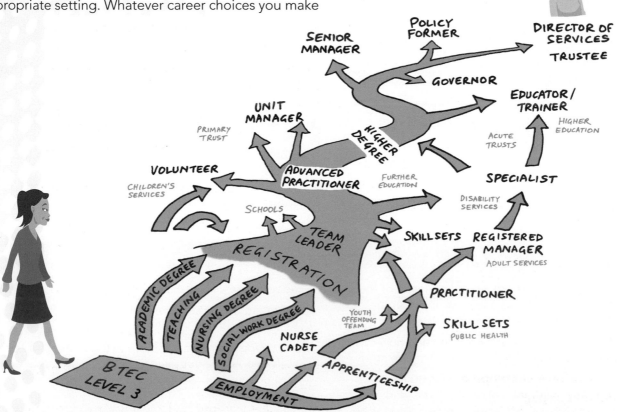

Fig 6.14: Where next? Career pathways in health and social care

Activity 38: Portfolio review

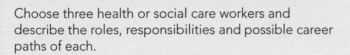

Review the evidence in your Unit 6 portfolio and diary.

1 What evidence do you have to demonstrate how you have worked with policies and procedures on your placements?

2 In what ways have funding and access issues affected the care that individuals have received in placement settings you have attended?

PLTS

Independent enquirer: Research carried out for this activity could demonstrate your skills as an independent enquirer.

Assessment activity 6.9

P7 BTEC

Choose three health or social care workers and describe the roles, responsibilities and possible career paths of each.

Grading tip

 The workers could work in the provider organisation described for P6.

Include description of the role of professional bodies, codes of practice and the training and development of staff in the work of each of the three workers.

Your description should include consideration of how each of the workers would work with other health or social care workers in a multidisciplinary team.

Your evidence could be presented as a reference card for display in your school or college.

References and further reading

Honey, P., Mumford, A. (1982) *The Manual of Learning Styles* Maidenhead: Peter Honey

HPA (2009) www.hpa.org.uk

Kolb, D.A. (1984) *Experiential Learning* Englewood Cliffs: Prentice Hall

Schön, D.A. (1983) *The Reflective Practitioner: How Professionals Think in Action* Basic Books

Useful websites

Care Council for Wales www.ccwales.org.uk

Care Quality Commission www.cqc.org.uk

Chartered Institute of Personnel and Development www.cipd.org.uk

Children's Workforce Development Council www.cwdcouncil.org.uk

Department of Health www.dh.gov.uk

Department of Children, Schools and Families www.dcsf.gov.uk

Department of Communities and Local Government www.communities.gov.uk

General Social Care Council www.gscc.org.uk

Health Professions Council www.hpc-uk.org

National Council for Voluntary Organisations www.ncvo-vol.org.uk

National Institute for Health and Clinical Excellence www.nice.org.uk

National Statistics Online www.statistics.gov.uk

NHS Careers www.nhscareers.nhs.uk

NHS www.nhs.uk

Northern Ireland Social Care Council www.niscc.info

Nursing and Midwifery Council www.nmc-uk.org

Sector Skills Council: Skills for Care and Development www.skillsforcare.org.uk

Sector Skills Council for Health: Skills for Health www.skillsforhealth.org.uk

Social Care Institute for Excellence www.scie.org.uk

Just checking

1   What are the three main components of learning and development?
2   What are the differences between learning styles, the learning cycle, support for learning and learning opportunities?
3   What are the three most influential factors that have affected your learning so far in your life?
4   What is the difference between primary and secondary sources?
5   Distinguish between qualitative and quantitative data.
6   What are SMART actions?
7   List four different sources of feedback obtained during the course that you could use when reflecting on your development on the course.
8   What is the difference between primary, secondary and tertiary care?
9   Identify three different types of support worker in health and social care.
10 What sort of work would each of the following workers do in health and social care:
   - occupational therapist
   - medical physicist
   - biochemistry laboratory technician
   - health service manager
   - community mental health nurse
   - health care assistant
   - manager of a day centre?

   What qualifications would be required for each of these occupations and what sort of experience would be expected?

edexcel

Assignment tips

1   Remember to be objective about your own performance on the course and on placements so that you neither understate nor exaggerate how well you have done something.

2   Always try to support your own views and judgments with an opinion from another source (e.g. feedback received from tutors, placement or work supervisors, peers in group activities and from books and diaries and so on).

3   Always date each entry in your diary, as this will enable you to see how you are developing over time. You might find it helpful to number the pages so you can easily refer back to a comment on a specific page in a later entry.

7 Sociological perspectives for health and social care

Why are UK teenage pregnancy rates the highest in western Europe? Why are recorded rates of anxiety and depression higher for women than for men? Why has there recently been a fall in the divorce rate in the UK? These are the kinds of questions that concern sociologists. This unit provides an introduction to sociology and explains how sociologists can help us to understand society and particularly disadvantaged groups within our society. In this unit you will study the different approaches that sociologists have used to explain health and social care issues.

The unit opens with an introduction to key sociological terms, and to the key sociological approaches. You will then relate these ideas to the study of health and social care issues. You will consider different definitions of health and illness and examine the impact of the family, occupation, social class and other aspects of our environment and culture on our health and well-being. There will be particular consideration of health differences among different social groups, particularly groups identified by social class, gender, ethnicity and age.

This unit also provides a very helpful foundation for those who, later in the course, go on to study Unit 19 Applied sociological perspectives.

Learning outcomes

After completing this unit, you should:

1 understand sociological approaches
2 understand sociological approaches to health and social care.

Assessment and grading criteria

This table shows you what you must do in order to achieve a **pass**, **merit** or **distinction** grade, and where you can find activities in this book to help you.

To achieve a **pass** grade, the evidence must show that you are able to:	To achieve a **merit** grade, the evidence must show that, in addition to the pass criteria, you are able to:	To achieve a **distinction** grade, the evidence must show that, in addition to the pass and merit criteria, you are able to:
P1 Explain the principal sociological perspectives. **See Assessment activity 7.1, page 319**	**M1** Assess the biomedical and socio medical models of health. **See Assessment activity 7.32, page 323**	
P2 Explain different sociological approaches to health and ill-health **See Assessment activity 7.2, page 323**		
P3 Explain patterns and trends in health and illness among different social groupings. **See Assessment activity 7.3, page 331**	**M2** Use different sociological perspectives to discuss patterns and trends of health and illness in **two** different social groups. **See Assessment activity 7.3, page 331**	**D1** Evaluate different sociological explanations for patterns and trends of health and illness in **two** different social groups. **See Assessment activity 7.3, page 331**

How you will be assessed

This unit will be assessed by internal assignments that will be marked by the staff at your centre. It may be subject to sampling by your centre's external verifier as part of Edexcel's on-going quality assurance procedures. The assignments will be designed to allow you to show your understanding of the unit learning outcomes. These directly relate to what you should know and be able to do after completing this unit.

Your assignments could be in the form of:

- presentations

- written assignments

- case studies

- essays.

Guidance is included throughout this unit to help you prepare and present your work.

Sam, 18 years old

I've been on placement at a hostel for homeless young people for six weeks so far. Many of the residents at the hostel have very sad life stories. Few of them have any family support. Some have been in care. They have come from poor areas, where unemployment and crime are high and drugs are easily available. They all seem to have had very deprived childhoods. Has this all led to the hostel being their home?

I think of Joe. He was brought up by his grandparents, who were retired and on a very low income. He never knew his dad, and his mum had a drug habit. When he left school he also left home. After that he lived with friends, sometimes in hostels and often on the streets. He has been in hospital at various times with chronic bronchitis, pneumonia and hypothermia. His diet has been very poor – sometimes eating from rubbish bins. He hasn't ever worked. He often seems very depressed. He doesn't seem to talk to anyone very much. His personal hygiene is poor and his self-esteem is low.

This unit helped me to see that guys like Joe are homeless partly because they haven't yet had much of a chance in life. Poverty, little family support, poor housing and poor health seem to have led them to this.

Over to you!

1   Which parts of this unit do you think you will find most interesting?

2   Which other units do you think are linked with the issues covered in this unit?

3   Which parts of this unit will help you better understand the homeless young people at the hostel?

1 Understand sociological approaches to study

Get started

Asking the big questions

Should the state support people who do not care for themselves? How far does family background influence health and well-being? Would reducing poverty lead to a healthier population? Are we all responsible for our own health? These are some of the questions that you will explore in this unit, using a sociological approach to consider the issues they raise. Discuss these questions now and then revisit them when you have completed this unit. It will be interesting to compare your views 'before' and 'after'.

1.1 Sociological terminology

Sociology is a word drawn from the Latin *socius* (meaning 'companion') and the Greek *ology* (meaning 'study of'). Sociologists are concerned with the study of human societies, but most specifically the groups within these societies and how these groups relate to each other and influence individual behaviour.

Social structures

Society can be viewed as the sum of its **social institutions** (its major building blocks). These may include the family, the education system, work and the economic system, the political system, religious groups and the health and social care services. Sociologists look at the way these institutions are structured, and how they relate to each other and influence the way we behave.

For example, sociologists describe the different forms of the family in our society, the changes that are taking place within the family, how the family structure influences our behaviour, and how the family relates to other social institutions. They examine how our family background may influence our values, attitudes, religious beliefs, educational achievements, employment prospects and our health and well-being.

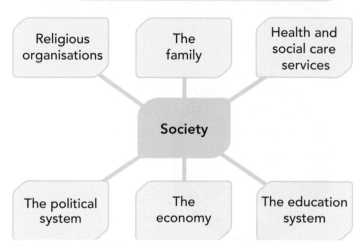

Fig 7.1: Key institutions in our society

Activity 1: Social institutions

Draw a personal spidergram identifying the social institutions to which you belong. Try to identify how two of these institutions have influenced your behaviour. In small groups discuss why you think these particular institutions have influenced you.

Key term

Social institution – A major building block of society, which functions according to widely accepted customs, rules or regulations. The family, the education system and the legal system are all social institutions.

PLTS

Independent enquirer: If you consider the impact of previous experiences on your attitudes and your behaviour, the above activity will help you demonstrate your ability to analyse and evaluate information.

Social diversity

Social stratification

Social stratification is a term used by sociologists and borrowed from geology. In geology, 'strata' refers to different layers of rock laid on top of each other. In sociology, the term is used to describe hierarchies in society, highlighting the fact that some groups of people are seen as having higher status than other groups. People identified as being of higher status are often wealthier and have easier access to the possessions and way of life most valued in that society. Almost all societies have some form of stratification.

In African countries following colonisation, and in America before the Civil War (1861–1865), groupings were based on race. Black communities had far less social status than white communities. Some people would argue that, despite legislation, such hierarchies and inequalities still exist.

In India, the Hindu caste system has five clearly defined social strata, into which people are born:

- Brahmins – the highest caste, priests
- Kshatriya – the military, rulers and administrators
- Vaisya – merchants and farmers
- Sudras – manual workers
- The Dalits, or social outcasts – the people who have almost no status (they have no caste at all).

There is no intermarriage and very little social contact between the castes. There is no **social mobility** (i.e. improving or changing your position in society). It is a closed system of stratification. Indian governments have passed laws attempting to remove the inequalities of the caste system but with limited success.

In feudal England the different strata were called 'estates' and were based on ownership of land. The monarchy and the knights, barons and earls formed the highest estate, the church and clergy were in the second estate, and the merchants, peasants and serfs were in the lowest estate.

Key terms

Social stratification – A term (borrowed from geology) describing the hierarchies in society, whereby some groups have more status and prestige than other groups.

Social mobility – The process of moving from one social stratum (level) to another. Social mobility can be upward or downward.

Social class

Social class is the form of stratification that describes the social hierarchies in most modern industrialised societies. Social class is largely based on economic factors (such as income, property ownership and other forms of wealth). Sociologists are particularly interested in the link between our social class position and other aspects of our lives such as educational achievement, lifestyle choices and health and well-being.

The official classification of social class used by British governments to measure and analyse changes in the population began in 1851. The broad classification of occupations into social 'grades' (later called social classes) was used for the analysis of death rates.

The five social classes identified by the Registrar General of 1921, based largely on perceived occupational skill, remained in place until 2001. Government statisticians and others used these categories to analyse population trends until very recently.

The Registrar General's Scale of Social Class included:

- Class 1: Professional class
- Class 2: Managerial and technical occupations
- Class 3: Skilled occupations:
  - Non-manual (3N)
  - Manual (3M)
- Class 4: Semi-skilled occupations
- Class 5: Unskilled occupations.

Since 2001, the National Statistics Socio-economic Classification (NS-SEC) has been used for official government statistics and surveys. It is still based on occupation but has been altered in line with employment changes and has categories to include the vast majority of the adult population:

- Class 1: Higher managerial and professional occupations
- Class 2: Lower managerial and professional occupations
- Class 3: Intermediate occupations
- Class 4: Small employers and own-account workers
- Class 5: Lower supervisory and technical occupations
- Class 6: Semi-routine occupations
- Class 7: Routine occupations
- Class 8: Never worked and long-term unemployed.

Social class differs from the more closed systems of the caste or feudal systems, or those based on race or gender, in that:

- the class differences are more difficult to define
- the class differences are not backed by law or regulation
- social class barriers are arguably far less rigid
- there is the possibility of social mobility
- people can rise, or indeed fall, in the class system.

We will be studying the links between social class and levels of health and sickness in our society.

Socialisation

Sociology is based on the idea that most of our behaviour is learned through the process of **socialisation** (and very little of our behaviour is instinctive). Socialisation is the process by which individuals learn the **culture** of their society – that is, the language, values and beliefs, customs and ways of behaving that are seen as acceptable. It may be argued that the most critical period of socialisation is in the early years of life.

Activity 2: Social class

Some people think that class differences in our society have disappeared. Write four short paragraphs, giving two arguments in favour of this view and two arguments against this point of view.

Functional skills

ICT: Using the information presented in this chapter, class discussion and your own view of the world, you will need to prepare and present clear points of view as they apply to social class. This may enable you to demonstrate your ability to find, select, present and communicate information.

Key terms

Egalitarian community – A community without hierarchies, where all members are regarded as equal.

Socialisation – The process of learning the usual ways of behaving in a society.

Culture – The values, beliefs, language, rituals, customs and rules associated with a particular society or social group.

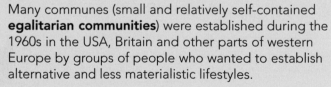

Activity 3: Communes and egalitarian communities

Many communes (small and relatively self-contained **egalitarian communities**) were established during the 1960s in the USA, Britain and other parts of western Europe by groups of people who wanted to establish alternative and less materialistic lifestyles.

Communes often try to develop an alternative type of household. Rather than separate family units, there is an emphasis on collective living. All adult members of these communities are seen as equal. Children are seen as the responsibility of the community, rather than of individual parents.

Many communes were short-lived but more longstanding religious communities and therapeutic communities still exist that support people with identified health and care needs.

In groups, carry out the following tasks.

1 Explain the difference between an egalitarian society and a hierarchical society.

2 Describe three differences between the experience of children living in a commune and the experience of children living in separate households with their parents or carers.

3 Discuss two advantages and two disadvantages of this type of community living.

Functional skills

English: In discussion, you will develop your speaking and listening skills and your skill at presenting arguments and listening to other people's arguments.

Reflect

Would you like to live in an egalitarian society, where all members are regarded as equal?

This period of **primary socialisation** takes place, for most of us, within a family – whether it is our birth family, a family of adoption or a foster family. **Secondary socialisation** is the process that carries on as our social life develops through playgroup, nursery, school, friendship or peer groups, religious groups, the mass media and employment.

Our socialisation affects our attitudes towards the care and support of vulnerable people, children and older people. For example, should we care for the very old at home, as part of the family? Or should we access residential care for them? In Islamic and Hindu cultures, care would normally be provided at home by grown-up children and grandchildren; whereas in white British families residential care and other support services would be far more usual. Sociologists would argue that this is largely because of a difference in the values and beliefs learned during primary and secondary socialisation.

The socialisation process affects our attitudes to education and our choice of career. Our home circumstances and the lifestyle of our friends and family can influence our attitudes and our behaviour at school and college. Consider Delton and Nadia in the case study below.

The **norms**, or expected way of behaving, of the society or group to which we belong are learned, it is argued, by absorbing and copying the behaviour of others in our social group. We adopt the main values and beliefs of the society to which we belong. Those who do not conform to expectations, i.e. those who disregard the norms of the society or group, are said to be **deviant**.

Key terms

Primary socialisation – The first socialisation of children that normally takes place within the family.

Secondary socialisation – The socialisation that takes place as we move into social settings beyond the family, such as nursery, school and friendship groups.

Norms – The guidelines or rules that govern how we behave in society, or in groups within society.

Deviant – Someone who does not conform to the norms of a particular society or group.

Reflect

The socialisation process varies from one culture to another. Health and social care workers need to be mindful of the contrasting socialisation of different people living in a multicultural society.

What happens when there is no socialisation? This question can be partly answered by reports on children who have been found living with animals in the wild – sometimes called 'feral children'. These children have no sense of personal hygiene and they are unable to interact with other human beings. They often 'walk on all fours', like the animals they have lived with.

Case study: Delton and Nadia

Imagine two 16-year-olds from very different social backgrounds.

Delton lives with his mother, who has no paid work. His father left them when he was a baby. None of his relatives or friends have been to college or university. Delton does not enjoy school and he and his friends often play truant. There is very little work about, and Delton has no idea what he will do when he leaves school.

Nadia's dad is a solicitor and her mother is a teacher. Nadia is at a very academic school, where most girls get good A levels and go on to university. She is very good at sport, plays the violin and is in the school orchestra. She hopes to go to university and study medicine.

1 Write down three factors that you think might influence Delton's achievements at school and plans for the future. Then write down three factors that might influence Nadia's achievements at school and future career plans.

2 In small groups share the factors that you thought were important and compare them with those identified by others in your group.

3 Discuss how these factors may influence other aspects of their lives, where they live, their range of leisure activities, their opportunities for travel, and so on.

Case study: Celebrating diversity

Karl is a senior member of staff in a residential care home for adults with disabilities. The residents have grown up in an ethnically mixed community and they are from diverse cultural and religious backgrounds.

Karl and the other care staff are committed to ensuring that all residents and their families feel welcome and that they celebrate and enjoy the customs and traditions of others who live at the setting.

1. Explain what is meant by 'celebrating diversity'.
2. In groups, identify two challenges that may face the care staff in promoting equality and diversity at the setting.
3. Discuss ways in which they could ensure that individual cultural needs are met and diversity is celebrated.

Activity 4: Social roles and expectations

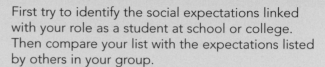

First try to identify the social expectations linked with your role as a student at school or college. Then compare your list with the expectations listed by others in your group.

Now describe your role at your placement or work. What expectations are associated with your role in the work setting? Present a summary of your ideas to your group.

PLTS

Creative thinker: This activity will help you develop your skills as a creative thinker. You will consider the social expectations linked with social roles in important areas of your life, as a student and as a future care worker.

Functional skills

English: The activity may also enable you to demonstrate your speaking, listening and presenting skills.

They have missed out on socialisation, the process by which the helpless infant gradually learns the norms (beliefs, customs and social expectations) of the society in which they have been born.

Our approach to health and social care issues may be influenced by our socialisation. For example, young people who smoke are more likely to live with carers who also smoke, and children are more likely to eat a wide range of foods at nursery (including a variety of fruit and vegetables) if they are introduced to these foods at home. In these kinds of ways, socialisation can influence our levels of health and well-being.

Social roles and expectations

You may have identified several social institutions or groups to which you belong. Membership of a group brings a range of expectations and obligations. In sociology, these expectations are called **social roles**. For example, there are expectations linked with the social position of being a parent, a son or daughter, or a student. The generally accepted social role (or social expectations) of parents in our society are that they will protect their children, ensure that they are kept safe and warm, provide a home, teach them acceptable ways of behaving, and ensure that they attend school ready to learn.

Of course the groups to which we belong will change throughout our lives and our position in those groups will change. For example, within our family, as the years pass, we may be the teenager, the married son or daughter, the parent and finally the grandparent.

Most of us occupy multiple roles, sometimes referred to as our 'role set', at any one time. You may be a son or daughter, a student, an employee, a carer and a member of a youth group. Sometimes the associated role expectations will have competing and conflicting demands. **Role conflict** is the term used to describe a situation where the demands of our various social roles clash or cause strain.

Key term

Social role – The social expectations associated with holding a particular position or social status in a society or group.

Role conflict – This exists when the demands of the social roles that we are expected to perform are not consistent with each other, making it difficult and sometimes impossible to meet all demands.

Reflect

Can you identify role conflict within your own role set, i.e. the range of social roles that you are expected to perform?

Case study: Multiple roles

John is a paramedic. His wife, Pat, is a community midwife and works full time. They have three children aged 10, 11 and 15. John's elderly mum has arthritis, lives on her own and needs considerable support with household jobs. She relies on John and Pat and they want to support her. The family are active members of their local church. John runs the youth club and Pat is the church secretary. The children all go to the youth club.

1 Identify the groups to which Pat and John belong and their positions within those groups.

2 Describe the social expectations or social roles associated with those positions.

3 Discuss how and when the various role expectations may cause role conflict.

Nature versus nurture

The **nature** versus **nurture** debate centres on the relative importance of environment and the socialisation process (nurture) in human development, compared to the impact of genetic inheritance (nature). This debate has been particularly important in:

- **education** – whether educational achievements are more influenced by inherited intelligence or by upbringing?

- **crime** – whether criminal tendencies are inherited or a product of environment?

- **gender** – whether observed differences between the behaviour and achievements of men and women are genetically determined or the result of different opportunities?

Sociologists tend to give more weight to environment and socialisation (nurture) when explaining individual differences. The nature/nurture debate is also considered in Unit 4.

Social control

Social control refers to the methods a society uses to ensure that its members conform to the expectations associated with their social roles. It is impossible to imagine a society without norms and rules to guide behaviour or ways of dealing with those who are deviant. Formal methods of social control in our society include the police and judicial system, as well as disciplinary systems in schools, colleges and in employment. There are also informal social control strategies, such as excluding people from group activities, embarrassing them, ridiculing them and gossiping about them. Methods of social control can be positive or negative. Positive methods include giving praise and other rewards for conformity; negative methods include punishment and other reactions to deviance.

Activity 5: Social control methods

In groups, identify and briefly explain two formal and two informal methods of social control used at your work placement. Present your ideas to the rest of your class. Be prepared to take questions at the end of your presentation.

Functional skills

English: In this activity, you can demonstrate your English skills by expressing your ideas clearly, listening carefully to each other and agreeing the key points to share with the rest of the group.

Key terms

Nature – Those human characteristics that are genetically determined.

Nurture – Those human characteristics that are learned through the process of socialisation.

Social control – The strategies used to ensure that people conform to the norms of their society or group.

1.2 Principal sociological perspectives

We are now going to look at the key sociological perspectives, or approaches, that have been used to describe and understand societies and the behaviour of individuals within societies. We will then consider how these approaches can help explain the impact of social life on health and well-being. The key terms introduced earlier will provide the main vocabulary for this discussion.

The first two perspectives that we will consider are structuralist approaches. Structuralists are interested in describing and understanding the main institutions of societies. In modern industrialised societies, these include the family, the education system, the health services, the economy, the political institutions, religious groups and the media. Structuralists are concerned with how these institutions relate to each other and how they influence and mould individual behaviour. The two structuralist approaches that we will discuss are known as **functionalism** (or the consensus model) and Marxism (the **conflict model**). Feminism, considered separately on pages 315–316, is normally regarded as an example of a conflict model that focuses on the continuing oppression of women in our society.

Functionalism

The functionalist approach to sociology can be best understood by likening society to the human body. Just as the body functions through the efficient interrelationship of major organs (such as the lungs, heart, liver and kidneys) and has mechanisms to deal with disease, so the different institutions in society each have particular contributions to make. They work together, and use methods of social control to deal with deviant members or groups, to ensure that society functions smoothly.

Key terms

Functionalism – A sociological approach that sees the institutions of society as working in harmony with each other, making specific and clear contributions to the smooth running of society.

Conflict model – A sociological approach first associated with Karl Marx, which sees the institutions of society as being organised to meet the interests of the ruling classes.

Talcott Parsons (1902–1979) played a vital role in the development of functionalism as a sociological approach. He saw society as a system made up of interrelated institutions, which contributed to its smooth running and continuity. He thought the main role of an institution was to socialise individuals and ensure that they understood the underlying values of their society and behaved in acceptable ways. This ensured that there was order in society.

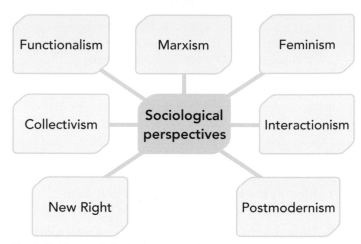

Fig 7.2: Key sociological perspectives

We can go on to consider the functions of the family and how it contributes to the order and stability of society, or the social system (a term that functionalists would often use). George Murdock (1897–1985), in his classic 1949 study of the family, examined over 250 societies, ranging from small hunter-gatherer communities to large industrialised societies, and found some form of the family in all of them.

Murdock claimed that in all societies the family had four functions:

- The sexual function allowed for the expression of sexuality in an approved context.
- The reproductive function provided stability for the rearing of children.
- Socialisation included the responsibility of teaching children the acceptable ways of behaving in society.
- The economic function meant that food, shelter and financial security had to be provided for family members.

Talcott Parsons (1951), writing about American society, argued that the family had two 'basic and irreducible functions':

- the primary socialisation of children

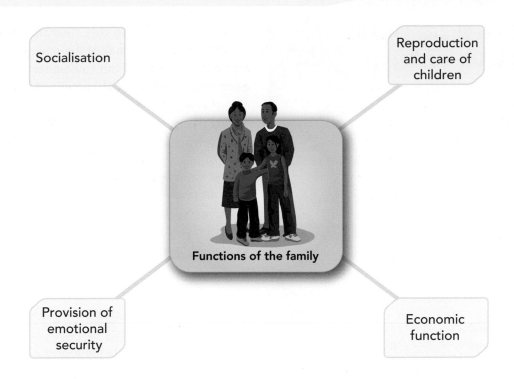

Fig 7.3: The functions of the family

- the stabilisation of adult personalities – in a complex, stressful and demanding world the family provides warmth and emotional security, especially, as Parsons saw it, for the male breadwinner.

Activity 6: The functionalist approach

In small groups, consider the social functions of one of the following social institutions:

- the family
- school or college
- work
- parliament.

1 Compare and discuss the range of answers.
2 Are you able to agree on the principal functions of these institutions?

Functional skills

English: This activity will enable you to demonstrate your listening skills and your ability to communicate clearly in group situations.

Criticisms of functionalism

Probably the most fundamental criticism of the functionalist approach is that it does not address areas of conflict, which certainly characterise modern societies and in principle could be found in all societies. Functionalists emphasise consensus and agreement and paint a rather rosy picture of institutions having clear, positive functions and co-operating effectively for the good of all. However, this does not seem to reflect many people's experience of the modern world, where there are often clear winners and losers and many non-conformists.

Functionalism is based on the idea that in all societies members share some basic values and beliefs – and that this **value consensus** underpins the socialisation process and the working of the main institutions. Researchers have not been able to find that common values are clearly shared in modern societies.

Key term

Value consensus – A general agreement as to the values and beliefs of a society.

Activity 7: Is there a common value system?

In groups, make a list of the values you think are most important for our society. Then compare your list with others in your group, and discuss the similarities and differences.

1 Can you agree a common value system to which most people would subscribe?

2 Do you think we have a common value system in our society?

PLTS

Independent enquirer: This activity may enable you to demonstrate independent enquiry skills by using previous learning and experience to evaluate information and judge its relevance and value.

Functionalists are also very clear that the way we behave is a direct result of the socialisation process and that very little of our behaviour is the result of our personal choices. They believe that we are largely 'programmed' to behave in particular ways. The interactionist model (see pages 316–317) provides an alternative to this view.

Reflect

Do you think we are 'programmed' by our socialisation or do we have some freedom of choice?

Finally, functionalists tend to present a picture of a socialisation process that never fails. They give no clear explanation of deviant behaviour and especially the extreme forms of deviance found in crime, delinquency and abuse, which are destabilising for society as a whole.

Activity 8: Key sociological approaches

Complete this table as you cover the key sociological approaches in your lessons. The first one has been completed for you, as an example.

Sociological approach	Key words	Key ideas	Identify two strengths	Identify two weaknesses
Functionalism	*Structuralism Function Common value system*	*All societies are made up of key institutions (e.g. the family) with functions to perform. These institutions ensure the smooth running of society.*	*Provides explanations for the smooth running of society. Analyses the role of key institutions.*	*Does not address areas of conflict in society. Does not allow for free will. We are socialised into our social roles.*
Marxism				
Feminism				
Interactionism				
Collectivism				
New Right				
Post-modernism				

Marxism

Marxism, as well as being a conflict model, is also a structuralist model. This approach was first developed by Karl Marx (1818–1883). He also thought that individual behaviour was shaped by society but he believed that the economic system defined society and people's place within it. Marx held the view that in the industrial society of his time there were two social classes:

- the **bourgeoisie**, or **capitalists** – the small powerful group who owned the factories and other places of employment

- the **proletariat** – a much larger, poorer group of 'workers' (the people or 'hands' that the bourgeoisie employed).

His view was that these two social class groups would always be in conflict: the owners of the factories, land and offices would want high profits; and the employees would want higher wages, which would eat into the profits. This is why Marxism is often called the conflict model. He thought that this conflict would lead to revolution. There was an unequal relationship between the bourgeoisie and the proletariat and conflict was inherent in the economic system.

Marxists argue that the ruling class (the bourgeoisie) also hold power in the other social institutions and they shape the society because they control the mass media and the legal system and it is their ideas that influence the curriculum in schools. Through the socialisation process, it is the values and attitudes of the ruling class that are passed on, rather than the common value system of the functionalists. This is so successfully achieved that the majority of the proletariat do not realise that they are being exploited or that they are serving the interests of the bourgeoisie rather than their own class. This lack of awareness by the proletariat is called **false consciousness** – and it is used to explain why the conflicting interests seldom erupt into actual conflict or revolution.

Key terms

Bourgeoisie – In Marxist theory, the bourgeoisie are the powerful social class, who own the factories, land and other capital and are able to organise the economy and other important social institutions to their own advantage.

Capitalist – Another word for a member of the bourgeoisie.

Proletariat – In Marxist theory the proletariat are the 'working class', who have only their labour to sell. They work for and are exploited by the bourgeoisie.

False consciousness – In Marxist theory, false consciousness is the taking on, by the proletariat, of the views and beliefs of their class enemy, the bourgeoisie. They do not realise that, by working hard, they are serving the interests of the capitalists much more than their own.

Like functionalists, Marxists have a structuralist perspective. They see the family as contributing to a stable social system and would regard the family as the servant of the capitalist system. They believe that it provides the context for the socialisation of children, preparing them for the disciplines and routines of work. Just as children have limited power in the family, so people are prepared to be obedient to their bosses at work as adults. In addition, Marxists see the family as providing a secure emotional base, a home, from which people will return to work rested and refreshed, ready to make large profits for their employer. As a servant of the capitalists, the ordered family is necessary for passing on inheritance. Children born within the nuclear family are the rightful inheritors of the family's wealth.

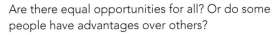

Reflect

Are there equal opportunities for all? Or do some people have advantages over others?

If you think there are inequalities in society, what could be done to reduce them?

Criticisms of Marxism

Like functionalists, Marxists believe that individual behaviour is the direct result of the socialisation process, with very little individual choice. In the case of Marxist theorists, however, it is a socialisation that meets the values and interests of the ruling classes.

Closely linked with this point is the view that Marxists put too much emphasis on different class interests and potential conflicts of interest. Although clear inequalities remain, the standard of living in industrialised societies has improved immensely over the last 100 years and arguably employers and employees share some common interests. All will potentially benefit from a successful company.

Some writers believe that the Marxist model, which sees the economy as the institution that drives all others, does not give sufficient emphasis to the power of other institutions – religion, race and family life – in moulding our behaviour.

Why do you think so many poor people lived in dreadful conditions in British cities in the nineteenth century?

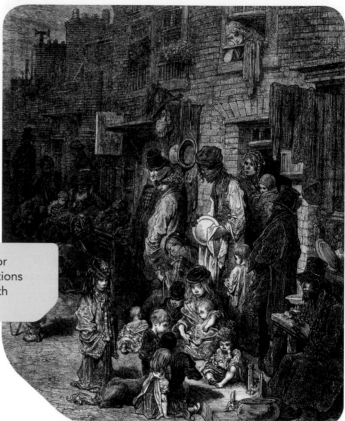

Case study: Child labour in the nineteenth century

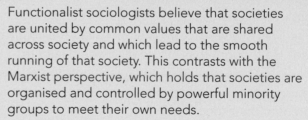

'Children of the poorer class worked from a very early age… Conditions in the factories were bad and the working day was at least 14 hours. Accidents were common and discipline very strict. Some factories operated the machines day and night, so that one shift of children used the beds vacated by the next shift… the work people were often responsible for recruiting and disciplining juvenile workers.'

Source: Clifford Lines (1990) *Companion to the Industrial Revolution* Facts on File Ltd (Oxford)

1 Which of the two social classes identified in the Marxist model are described in this passage?

2 Explain why Marx expected that working conditions such as these would lead to conflict and revolution.

3 Why might these conditions impact on the health and well-being of these children?

Activity 9: Structuralist approaches

Functionalist sociologists believe that societies are united by common values that are shared across society and which lead to the smooth running of that society. This contrasts with the Marxist perspective, which holds that societies are organised and controlled by powerful minority groups to meet their own needs.

In groups, consider whether the following groups or institutions work for the good of all in society or mainly for the successful and powerful groups:

- schools and colleges
- the economy
- health and social care services.

Feed back your ideas to the whole class.

Functional skills

English: This activity will enable you to demonstrate your listening skills and your ability to communicate clearly in group discussions and when preparing a group presentation.

Feminism in sociology

Feminism is normally seen as an example of a conflict model. There are three main types of feminist approach:

- Marxist feminism
- radical feminism
- liberal feminism.

Feminists have argued that sociology, as an academic discipline, was developed and dominated by men. Hence the term 'malestream' sociology was introduced. Pamela Abbott and Claire Wallace (1997) clearly summarised feminist concerns and criticisms of mainstream (or malestream) sociology. They argued that this male dominance has produced biased descriptions and analysis and that not enough attention has been paid to the issues of women and their unequal place in society.

Marxist feminism

Marxist feminists see women, especially working-class women, as oppressed both by capitalism and by men or the patriarchal society. Women produce the next generation of workers. They meet the physical, social and emotional needs of their children so that they are ready to work in the offices and factories of the future. They support their husbands and partners, cook meals, care for their children and clean their houses – for no pay! Thus they are dominated by their husbands and they are also subsidising industry. The family would not be ready for work if somebody did not take responsibility for domestic life and this, it is argued, remains the primary responsibility of women.

Radical feminism

For radical feminists, it is not capitalism that dominates women, but men. The family is seen as a patriarchal institution. They see the socialisation of women as housewives and mothers as a form of oppression and this oppression as a characteristic of nuclear family life.

Activity 10: Feminism in the home

Are these views dated? Who in your family would normally cook the meals, do the washing-up, vacuum, clean and tidy the house and/or mend electrical equipment? Are the traditional gender roles still in place?

Carry out a research activity in your group to test the hypothesis:

'Women take responsibility for most domestic tasks in the home.'

Each student in your group should identify two households with which they are familiar and identify who normally:

1 does the washing
2 does the ironing
3 mends electrical goods
4 does the household shopping
5 cooks the evening meal
6 tidies the living room
7 cleans the cooker
8 does the gardening
9 does the vacuuming.

Analyse your findings and write a brief report explaining whether your hypothesis is proven or not.

PLTS

Independent enquirer: This activity will enable you to demonstrate your ability to carry out individual research, to share your findings, collate your results and to present one group report.

Functional skills

English: Preparing the questionnaire, interviewing your respondents and discussing the results will develop your speaking and listening skills, and recording your conclusions will develop your writing skills.

Mathematics: Mathematical skills will be developed in analysing your results and justifying your conclusions with statistics.

ICT: You will have the opportunity to develop your ICT skills in presenting statistical information and your conclusions.

Liberal feminism

Liberal feminists would argue that changes have taken place. They believe that, through changing attitudes and legislation, such as the Equal Pay Act (1970) and the Sex Discrimination Act (1975), there is more equality. Liberal feminists believe that improvements will continue by means of legislation and policy.

How does this photo show that many women remain in traditional domestic roles?

Activity 11: Equal rights for men and women

1 Write a short report in which you identify and briefly describe the key legislation relating to sexual equality. Remember to include the introduction of civil partnerships through the Civil Partnership Act 2004.

2 Discuss in groups how far changes in the law can influence attitudes to the position of men and women in society, both at home and in the wider community.

3 Summarise your key points and report back to the rest of the class.

Functional skills

ICT: To complete this task, you will need to find and select relevant and up-to-date equality legislation.

English: In discussing how far changes in the law can influence individual attitudes, you will develop your speaking, listening and presentation skills.

Did you know?

Despite the Equal Pay Act of 1970, the 2009 Social Trends reported that the average wage for men in full-time employment was 12 per cent higher than the average wage for women in full-time work.

Interactionism

Interactionism, or the social action approach, contrasts with the structuralist perspectives in that the focus is not on the large institutions and how they function and link with each other. Instead, the focus is on small groups and how they influence individual behaviour and shape society. Interactionists may study

groups as diverse as teenage gangs, staff, patients and visitors on hospital wards or social interaction in school classrooms. They will study the dynamics within these groups. For example, they may ask:

• How do different members of the group see themselves?

• Do some have more power than others?

Key term

Interactionism – A sociological approach that focuses on the influence of small groups on our behaviour, rather than the power of large institutions. Interactionists believe that our behaviour is driven by the way we interpret situations in smaller groups, how we see ourselves in relation to other people in the group, how we see other members and how they see us.

- Who are the formal leaders?
- Are there some informal leaders who actually have power in the group?

Social action or interactionist theorists do not believe that we are 'programmed' by the socialisation process. They see individuals as being *influenced* by the socialisation process but having the power to choose how they will actually behave and create their own roles. These theorists have very little interest in social structure as a whole. They see our behaviour as driven by the way we interpret situations, how we see ourselves and other people and how they see us.

In the family, a mother may understand what is expected of a 'good' mother but social action theorists think that social roles are not clearly defined. They believe that the mother will interpret what that means for her in the context of her family, her relationship with her children, and her links with the wider society. There is no blueprint. For the social action theorist, the main aim is to understand how people interpret situations and behave in small-group face-to-face situations.

Reflect

Try to analyse the social dynamics at work or on work placement. Are some people more powerful than others? Do some people have power and influence even though they are not managers or supervisors? Do some clients or customers have more power than others. If so, can you analyse why?

Criticisms of interactionism

Social action theorists, although they emphasise individual choice, accept that social roles exist – even if they are not clearly defined. They do not, however, study where the social roles come from. They are criticised for paying insufficient attention to issues of power in society. Although they would say that social roles are only vaguely defined, they do not explain where these roles come from and they do not explain why people largely behave in very predictable ways.

In addition, they are sometimes criticised for describing social behaviour 'in a vacuum'. They describe behaviour in delinquent gangs or the relationship between staff and patients in a hospital ward but they do not describe the wider social factors that have influenced this, or the historical factors that

might have defined or caused the situation. Social action theorists tend to focus on the interactions within the group, rather than these wider issues.

Postmodernism

Postmodernism is an approach to sociology, or understanding society, that focuses on the rapid change and uncertainty (some would even say chaos) in our society. Postmodernists would suggest that we can no longer talk about established institutions like the family, religion or the economy because nothing stays the same. Domestic arrangements are so varied these days that it is no longer possible to talk about the 'typical' family. Postmodernists hold the view that, because of the constant change, structuralist perspectives like functionalism and Marxism no longer help us to understand society. The social institutions have become fragmented. Individuals and groups of people now make their own lifestyle decisions, choosing from the many leisure activities and consumer goods that are available.

Activity 12: Is there a 'typical' family?

In groups:

1 Identify and list the different types of family in our society.
2 Is there a typical family type in our society?
3 Are the postmodernists right – these days 'anything goes'?
4 Discuss the possible consequences for the individual and for society of one change in family life. You may consider:
    - Fall in the number of marriages
    - Introduction of civil partnerships
    - High levels of divorce
    - Smaller families
    - Higher proportion of lone parent families
    - Increased number of much older relatives
5 Report back to the whole class and compare issues.

Collectivism

Collectivism is an approach to providing health and social care services that is underpinned by a government commitment to provide care and support for the vulnerable, funded through taxation and National Insurance. This contrasts with the New Right (see page 319), who consider welfare to be the responsibility of the individual and their family and believe that the state should play a minimal role.

Collectivism and the New Right are examples of political responses to the role of government in our society and, for our purposes, their response to meeting identified areas of welfare need. In all societies there are groups of people who are potentially vulnerable. These may include children, older people, people with physical impairments and those with mental health needs. In some societies the care of these people will be seen as the responsibility of the individual or their family; in other societies it will be seen as the responsibility of religious groups, the commune or the local community.

The state has played a role in the care of the vulnerable in Britain since the passing of the Poor Law in 1601. However, it was not until the nineteenth century that governments took a significant role in the support of the vulnerable (many would say this did not happen until after the Second World War with the 'birth of the Welfare State'). The Beveridge Report, in 1942, provided the political foundation for a comprehensive range of welfare services. Lord Beveridge, in his *Report on Social Insurance and Allied Services*, identified five giant evils that urgently needed to be challenged.

There was cross-party agreement that the state should take collective responsibility for:

- addressing poverty through a wide range of welfare benefits including Family Allowance, Unemployment and Sickness Benefit and retirement pensions
- fighting disease through the National Health Service

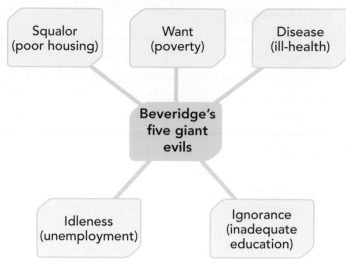

Fig 7.4: Beveridge's five giant evils

- combating ignorance through the expansion of secondary education for all
- eradicating squalor through the building of council houses
- removing idleness by supporting policies of full employment and the development of labour exchanges.

This placed the provision of key services in the hands of the state, working co-operatively with families and voluntary organisations, and was to be financed by taxes and National Insurance.

Activity 13: Yesterday's evils today

In five groups, design posters to identify services that are in place today which address each of Beveridge's 'giant evils':

- Want – Poverty
- Squalor – Poor housing
- Disease – Ill-health
- Idleness – Unemployment
- Ignorance – Inadequate education.

PLTS

Independent enquirer: This activity may help you demonstrate your ability to plan and carry out research and analyse and evaluate information.

The New Right

The post-war collectivist approach to welfare remained largely in place for over a generation and was not seriously challenged or questioned until the election of Margaret Thatcher's Conservative government in 1979. The view of this government was that the state should play as small a role as possible in welfare provision. They believed that welfare should be largely seen as the responsibility of the individual and their family. The New Right regarded state support as intrusive and supporting a dependency culture. Mrs Thatcher and her government thought the welfare state produced a society in which people relied on state benefits rather than planning for the future and taking responsibility for their own needs and those of their families.

Assessment activity 7.1

Produce an information booklet explaining the principal sociological perspectives: functionalism, Marxism, feminism, interactionism, collectivism, postmodernism and the New Right.

Grading tips

P1 To achieve a pass grade, you will need to use the sociological terms introduced at the beginning of the chapter, such as culture, values, beliefs, norms, socialisation, social status, social roles, diversity, and social class. You may also find it helpful to refer to your table of perspectives (see page 312).

Around 150–200 words for each perspective would be a good guide to length. Provide examples from your personal or placement experience to show your understanding of, for example, the functions of the family, the place of women in the home or the range of services provided by the state in a collectivist society.

---

2 Understand sociological approaches to health and social care

2.1 Application of sociological perspectives to health and social care

The functionalist approach

The functionalist approach to considering health and illness derives from the work of Talcott Parsons. Using the traditional functionalist approach, he described how, for society to function efficiently, its members need to be healthy. He described illness as a form of deviance and ill members as performing a form of social role – the sick role. This became a very powerful concept in the sociology of illness. In his view, if people declared themselves ill, specific rights and responsibilities came with their new role.

The rights associated with the sick role were:

- to be exempt from normal social obligations, for example, to go to school, college or work, and from meeting normal family obligations
- to be cared for.

Parsons would see it as one of the key functions of the family to care for the sick and other dependent members of the family group.

The responsibilities of the sick role included the individual:

- taking all reasonable steps to get better and seeking to resume their normal place in society as soon as possible
- co-operating with medical professionals, particularly doctors and their staff.

The functionalist view (and the view of most governments) is that illness has social consequences. The ill are not normally at work and they may need to be cared for, and this must, whenever possible, be swiftly dealt with, in order for society to run smoothly.

The Marxist approach

Marxist approaches believe that the definitions of health and illness, and the health and social care services provided, serve the interests of the more powerful dominant social classes. Doctors are seen as agents who ensure that people go back to work as soon as possible, working in the interests of the employers rather than those of the patient. Their job is to provide the company owner with a healthy workforce. In addition, the government allows companies to make profits from products that cause ill-health, such as tobacco and junk food. Firms and factories continue to produce toxic waste and large cars pollute the atmosphere.

Unlike the functionalists, who regard ill-health as something that occurs almost randomly, conflict theorists see levels of illness as being related to differences in social class. For example, there is a higher level of illness and lower life expectancy in areas of poverty, high unemployment and environmental pollution. The government does not do enough to tackle the issues that lead to illness, as this costs money, which would have to be found by the most advantaged in society.

Reflect

Why do you think there is more illness in areas of poverty and high unemployment?

The interactionist or social action approach

Interactionism is probably the theoretical approach that has devoted the most attention to issues of health and illness. It is concerned with:

- the processes that lead a person to define themselves as ill – people with the same 'complaint' vary as to whether they will call themselves ill and certainly vary as to whether they will seek professional help. Some people with very serious illnesses do not regard themselves as ill.

- the interaction between the professional and the patient in agreeing how ill they are. Although they understand that there are sometimes quite clear diagnoses, interactionists are interested in the negotiation that takes place with the professional in trying to agree on the impact of the illness. Should the patient be signed off work or not? How far should someone's bad back limit their daily activities?

- the impact on people's self-image and on their relationships if they are labelled as 'ill'.

Interactionists, in studying the sociology of health and illness, do not look at structures and institutions but study the complex relationships between people, their family and friends and their links with the professional services. They think that these relationships have as much influence as any medical diagnosis on whether or not people declare themselves to be ill.

Critics of the interactionist approach say that, in concentrating on these relationships and the negotiations that take place, it ignores the 'real' causes of ill-health. These include medical explanations and environmental factors such as pollution, stress and poverty.

The feminist approach

Feminist writers have focused on male domination in the medical professions and its impact on women. They have been particularly concerned with the way in which pregnancy and childbirth have been regarded as medical issues (even sometimes as illnesses), rather than as natural processes. Feminist writers also comment on the way in which the medical profession and the related pharmaceutical industries have given relatively low priority to the development and promotion of the male contraceptive pill (which arguably has fewer harmful side-effects than the contraceptive methods used by women). In considering issues of mental health, anxiety and depression, and the fact that relatively higher numbers of women suffer from these conditions, feminists would see this partly as a result of their exploited position in society and especially in the family. These issues are, however, defined as a medical problem, for which medicines are a solution. This shifts attention away from the fact that a woman's day-to-day circumstances may be the cause of stress.

Marxist and other socialist feminists have been more concerned with the impact of social inequalities on women's health. In *What Makes Women Sick?* Lesley Doyal (1995) particularly highlights the increasingly dual role of women, or the 'double day' as she calls it: women often have full-time jobs outside the home and then also take most of the responsibility for domestic life.

2.2 Understanding different concepts of health and ill-health

Concepts of health

It will come as no surprise that sociologists have great difficulty in agreeing on a definition of what it means to be healthy. Health can be defined in negative terms, as 'the absence of disease'. This is contrasted with a positive definition such as that provided by the World Health Organization (WHO) in 1974: 'not merely an absence of disease, but a state of complete physical, mental, spiritual and social well-being'.

A negative concept of health (as the absence of disease) is therefore opposed to a positive concept of health as being concerned with people's physical, intellectual, social and emotional well-being.

In the health and social care sectors, care professionals usually adopt a holistic approach to care and support. They see their role as addressing the needs of the 'whole' person, rather than single issues or identified problems.

Activity 14: Who is healthy?

1 In groups try to agree a definition of 'good health'. Then compare your definition with those of other groups in your class

2 Think of someone you regard as being very healthy. What makes you think that they are healthy? Do they fit your definition of 'good health'?

PLTS

Self-manager: This activity will require you to agree the key points to share with the rest of the group.

A person with complex needs, such as a young mother with multiple sclerosis, may be supported by a range of professionals. These would include a GP, a community nurse, an occupational therapist, a social worker and a health visitor, often referred to as a multi-disciplinary team. They will each have their particular roles and responsibilities for her care and support but they will also want to carry out a **holistic assessment**, recognising the importance of the young woman's wider needs when providing their specialist care.

Key term

Holistic assessment – An approach to care that addresses the individual's physical, social, emotional and spiritual health, attempting to meet the needs of the 'whole' person.

Fig 7.5: A holistic approach to care

Mildred Blaxter (1990) interviewed almost 10,000 people in her large-scale study, *Health and Lifestyles*. She identified three strands to people's understanding of health and well-being:

- a positive definition, regarding health as feeling fit and well

- a negative definition, regarding health as being free from pain or discomfort

- a functional definition, regarding health in terms of being able to perform certain, often day-to-day, tasks.

Defining health, then, is not easy and there is certainly no clear agreement on it among scholars.

In fact, most sociological research concerned with studying and comparing levels of health within and between societies actually focuses on issues of ill-health. For example, sociologists use a great deal of information about death rates, visits to GPs' surgeries, incidence of serious diseases, admissions to mental health units and suicide statistics. This data is often analysed by social class, occupation, ethnicity, gender, age and geographical location.

This type of information can be measured statistically and is generally clearly defined. It is much more difficult to measure the positive indicators of health (people's physical, intellectual, social and emotional well-being), as in the WHO definition on page 321.

Models of health

Biomedical model

The model of health that has dominated Western industrialised societies, certainly since the industrial revolution of the mid-nineteenth century, has been the **biomedical model**. This view of health underpins the policies and practice of the National Health Service (NHS). According to this model, health is largely regarded as being the absence of disease, and the intervention of health professionals is necessary in times of illness. The main purpose of the health services is to cure disease, and health professionals will use scientifically tested methods to address diagnosed illnesses. Sociologists believe that the focus on the individual patient for whom a cure should be found is a limitation of this model. Little regard is paid to environmental and social factors that may have led to ill-health. The causes of illness may be many and varied, but the biomedical approach tends to focus on the individual while largely ignoring the environmental factors that might cause disease.

The biomedical model fits well with the functionalist perspective discussed earlier (on page 317), in which illness is regarded as in itself dysfunctional for society. If people are ill they cannot make their normal contribution to the smooth running of society. For the functionalist, if people adopt the sick role and are exempt from their usual social responsibilities, they also have a responsibility to co-operate with health professionals and take all reasonable steps to get better.

Socio-medical model

The **socio-medical** model of health focuses on the social factors that contribute to health and well-being in our society. Research indicates that life expectancy rose and death rates began to fall, especially infant mortality rates, with improvements in sanitation and the provision of clean water, the building of new council houses and generally improved standards of living during the late-nineteenth/early-twentieth centuries. This was long before 1948 and the introduction of universal free personal health care through the NHS. This sort of evidence supports the view that environmental and social conditions are a significant source of disease, and the causes of ill-health are not solely located in the individual.

The socio-medical model sits more easily with the conflict theorists than the functionalists. The conflict theorist would explain the shorter life expectancy and the relatively higher rates of ill-health among the poor as consequences of the inequalities in society and the life circumstances of the disadvantaged. The poor, they would say, are more likely to have an inadequate diet and live in damp houses, often in inner-city areas where unemployment and environmental pollution tend to have the most impact. The ruling groups in society, the politicians and the owners of industries, are not willing, they would say, to make the changes needed to protect the poor from ill-health and disease.

The biomedical model of health has a clear focus on individual diagnosed illness, and the socio-medical model is concerned with the environmental causes of illness. They can be seen as two complementary approaches to the study of health and illness.

Activity 15: Social factors linked with poor health

Draw a spidergram or similar diagram that summarises the range of social and environmental factors that may lead to ill-health.

Key terms

Biomedical model – An approach to health and illness that identifies health as 'the absence of disease' and focuses on diagnosing and curing individuals with specific illnesses.

Socio-medical model – An approach to health and illness that focuses on the social and environmental factors that influence our health and well-being, including the impact of poverty, poor housing, diet and pollution.

Case study: Life expectancy

The Child Poverty Action Group reports that life expectancy at birth varies significantly according to social class, with professional men expecting to live to around 80 years and unskilled manual men to 72.7 years. For women, the figures are 85.1 and 78.1 years respectively.

Poorer children on average experience poorer health during their childhoods and the effects of this last throughout their lives. Three-year-olds in households with incomes below about £10,000 are 2.5 times more likely to suffer chronic illness than children in households with incomes above £52,000.

The risk of infant mortality is higher for poor children. In the lower social group (routine and manual occupations) infant mortality is 5.9 infant deaths per 1,000 live births. This is 20 per cent higher than the average 4.9 per 1,000.

Source: Child Poverty Action Group
Facts and Figures
www.cpag.org.uk/povertyfacts

1   In three groups explain why levels of the following vary by social class:
   • life expectancy
   • health and well-being
   • infant mortality rates.
   Be prepared to feed back your views to the rest of your class.

2   Discuss the view that this evidence supports the socio-medical model of health.

Assessment activity 7.2

Aziz and Tamsela have four young children. Tamsela's elderly parents live with them. Their three-bedroomed house is in a deprived and rather depressing area of London. Their house is in a poor state of repair; it is damp and very expensive to keep warm in the winter. Neither Aziz nor Tamsela is currently in paid work.

The family is in poor health. In the winter the children seem to have permanent colds. Tamsela suffers from asthma and her father has bronchitis. Tamsela's mother is depressed and has been prescribed drugs for this condition.

Write an essay of 800–1000 words that explains different sociological approaches to health and ill-health P2 and include in the essay an assessment of both the biomedical and socio-medical models of health M1. Use the case study of Azis and Tamsela and/or other examples from those known to you or from placements to illustrate points you make in the essay.

Grading tips

P2 • If using examples from placements or others known to you, respect the confidentiality of individuals and their contexts.

• You should apply the perspectives introduced in Assessment Activity 7.1 when explaining the different sociological approaches.

• Include an explanation of different concepts of health and different definitions of health and illness in the essay.

M1 • To assess the two models of health, you will need to weigh up the relative strengths and weaknesses of each when considering health and illness.

• Apply a range of sociological perspectives when comparing the two models of health as part of the assessment of each.

• Consider the extent to which each model takes into account any environmental and social issues that should be considered when assessing the needs of individuals in health and social care.

Concepts of ill-health

Disability and impairment

The related ideas of **disability** and **impairment** are very closely linked to the medical and social models of health. Like many of the other sociological terms introduced in this unit, the words 'disability' and 'impairment' can be used in different ways, and the term 'disability' is not easy to define. It is important that you are absolutely clear on how you are using these terms when considering the issues. Tom Shakespeare (1998) formalised a helpful distinction between disability and impairment.

Impairment focuses on the individual and refers to the day-to-day restrictions that may arise because of a long-term physical or mental condition, such as the loss of a limb, a sensory impairment or depression. This has similarities to the biomedical model of health and illness. From this point of view, the patient would need to co-operate with the health and social care professionals to limit the restrictions caused by the impairment. They will have similar social obligations to a person in the 'sick role' discussed earlier.

Disability, in contrast, is seen by Tom Shakespeare as a problem that arises when a society does not take into account the needs of people with impairments. For example, there may be no ramps into buildings, and doorways may be too narrow for people who use wheelchairs. A person with a hearing impairment may only be disabled if they do not have access to a hearing aid or have not been taught to lip-read. Disability, from this point of view, is seen as a restriction on the opportunity to take part in the normal life of the community because of physical, social or attitudinal barriers. In this context writers will sometimes refer to the **disabling environment** – an environment where facilities are not in place to ensure that people with impairments can take full part in a social life; this is a social model of disability.

Activity 17: The enabling environment

Write a short report describing:

* either how accessible your college is for people who are wheelchair users
* or how easy it is for wheelchair users to do their shopping in your local high street.

In your opinion are these enabling environments?

Case study: Impairment and disability

Mohammed is 45 years old and has multiple sclerosis. He needs considerable help with daily living activities. He is a wheelchair user and he is unable to leave his house without a carer. Mohammed lives alone, he speaks very little English and he feels socially very isolated.

Mohammed has recently been assessed by the local social services department for a range of community care services. He is going to receive a direct payment so that he can choose his own care provider and he will be able to pay them directly. He is quite confused by this arrangement and does not know where to go for help.

1 Explain what is meant by the terms 'impairment' and 'disability' in this context.

2 Briefly discuss the view that Mohammed lives in a disabling environment.

3 Evaluate the usefulness of the distinction between impairment and disability.

Key terms

Disability – Sociologists will often refer to disability as the restrictions that arise for a person with an impairment because of the attitudes and the lack of appropriate services and facilities to meet their needs.

Impairment – The restrictions on day-to-day activity caused by a physical or mental dysfunction or abnormality, such as the loss of a limb, a sensory impairment or a learning difficulty such as Down's syndrome.

Disabling environment – A social context where adaptions and other facilities are not in place to ensure that people with impairments can take a full part in social life.

Yasmin Johnson
Nurse practitioner

Yasmin is the nurse practitioner at a busy GP's surgery in a northern town. The practice has a lot of elderly patients and Yasmin runs regular 'well man' and 'well woman' clinics for the over-sixties. Among the couples who come to her clinics are the Tattons and the Bensons, and she has got to know them quite well over the years.

Mr and Mrs Tatton both worked as solicitors and had a very good income all their working lives. They were able to save and now have a very good occupational pension. They have a beautiful home by the sea, and they play tennis and golf all year. They go on holiday abroad most winters and have their grandchildren to stay every summer.

They just don't seem to age, and hardly ever come to the surgery for treatment. Their daughter Sally married John Benson, the Bensons' eldest son, and John and Sally settled down in London.

The Bensons have lived very different lives. Mr Benson was a miner and was made redundant in the 1970s. He managed to get other work but the jobs were all poorly paid. He now has to rely on his state pension. Mrs Benson has worked part-time all her life in unskilled jobs. She doesn't have a works pension and she never paid into the state pension scheme. They still live in the three-bedroomed council house they moved into when they got married. It is damp and difficult to heat. In the winter they have to choose between eating well and keeping warm. They do manage to get away for a week in the summer but they have never been on holiday abroad. Some would say that they are rather proud and will not accept financial help from their grown-up children. Mr Benson has angina and Mrs Benson has suffered from asthma for about ten years. They both attend the surgery frequently so Yasmin tends to see them every few weeks.

Think about it!

1 List the factors that might contribute to and detract from the health and well-being of the Tattons and the Bensons.

2 What services will be available to each couple in their later lives?

3 Are there additional services that might be available to the Tattons?

4 How have changes in the family made it more difficult for children to look after their ageing parents? What are the implications for families, social services and government finances?

5 There is evidence that people in socio-economic class 1 have a greater life expectancy than those in socio-economic class 8. Using the Internet or other sources, check the current statistics for life expectancy by socio-economic class.

6 Which factors mentioned in the case study could indicate that the life expectancy of the two couples might be different?

2.3 Understanding patterns and trends in health and illness among different social groupings

Measuring health

Statistical trends in the levels of health and illness are generated from three main sources:

1 **Government statistics**

   The Office of National Statistics (ONS) provides current data on a wide range of health and care issues. Publications include *Social Trends*, *Population Trends* and, for more detailed information on health issues, *Health Statistical Quarterly*. These publications (available in hard copy and electronically) provide a wide range of statistics on birth rates and death rates, **infant mortality rate** and suicide rates, as well as appointments at GPs' surgeries and hospital admissions, and these are often analysed by social class, gender, geographical location and age.

2 **Charitable organisations and pressure groups**

   Many charitable groups and special interest groups also collect and publish statistical and other information which informs the discussion on issues of health and illness. For example, Mind (www.mind.org.uk) and YoungMinds (www.youngminds.org.uk) are charities that support people and young people with mental health needs, and www.youreable.com (formerly www.disabilitynet.co.uk) is a website that provides a disability-related news service on the Internet. All provide ongoing and up-to-date information relating to their areas of concern.

3 **Academic researchers and other authors**

   Largely based in universities, researchers and authors also contribute to the evidence and debate on a wide range of health and social care issues.

Throughout this book you will find references to evidence drawn from all these sources.

Government statistics not only include **mortality rates** (death rates) in the population but also the **morbidity rates**, the number of people who have particular diseases during a specified period, usually a year. These trends will be compared over periods of time. Have rates increased or decreased? They may be analysed by sex, age, geographical location or social class. Are mortality and morbidity rates higher in some parts of the country than in others? Is there a difference in mortality and morbidity between social classes? Specific morbidity rates may be measured in terms of the prevalence of a disease. **Disease prevalence** is the total number of cases of a specific disease in a population during a specified period of time. **Disease incidence** is the number of new cases of a specific disease occurring in a population during a specified period of time.

Mortality rates, especially infant mortality rates, are often used as an indicator of the health and well-being of the population as a whole. If they are higher or rising in a particular location, or among a particular social group compared to others, this is seen as a sign that levels of general health and well-being may be declining within those groups and that the causes of this may lie in their social and economic environment – perhaps inadequacies in a range of social and economic services and higher levels of poverty and economic hardship.

Mortality rates are collected from the official and required registration of deaths, and the causes of death from the legally required death certificates. Information on morbidity rates is drawn from a wide range of sources including GP and hospital appointments, hospital admissions and the registration of notifiable diseases (certain infectious diseases). There have also been more general studies measuring levels of ill-health. These studies are not related to

Key terms

Infant mortality rate – The number of deaths occurring in infants under one year old per 1000 live births.

Mortality rate – The number of people who have died in the population in a given year. The crude death rate is expressed as the number of deaths in a year per 1000 of the population.

Morbidity rate – This refers to the number of people who have a particular illness during a given period, normally a year.

Disease prevalence – The total number of cases of a specific disease in a population during a specified period of time.

Disease incidence – The number of new cases of a specific disease occurring in a population during a specified period of time.

a specific condition; instead they use self-reported measures of health, which ask people to describe or rank on a scale of 1 to 10 how healthy they feel.

Difficulties in measuring health

When referring to statistics and using them in your work, it is always important to quote the source of the data. Were they collected by a particular group in order to persuade and gather support? Should you also consult data from an organisation with an opposing view? Was the information published in a newspaper to satisfy the views and prejudices of their readers? Does the newspaper support a particular political party? Statistics must be treated with caution!

Furthermore, statistics gathered from official sources may not provide an accurate picture of patterns of health and illness. For example, some people who are ill may not go to the doctor; and conversely some people who visit the doctor may not really be ill.

Two doctors presented with similar symptoms may suggest different diagnoses. For example, a patient describing persistent fatigue with no interest in life and no energy may be described by one doctor as depressed, while another doctor may diagnose ME or post-viral fatigue syndrome. Another doctor might decide that they are a malingerer who simply does not want to go to work. This would certainly distort the official figures of the number of people with a specific illness.

Ken Browne (2006) provided a useful framework to explain this problem:

'For people to be labelled "sick" – and also to be recorded as a health statistic – there are at least four stages involved:

- Stage 1: Individuals must first realise that they have a problem.
- Stage 2: They must then define their problem as serious enough to go to the doctor.
- Stage 3: They must then actually go to the doctor.
- Stage 4: The doctor must then be persuaded that they have a medical or mental condition capable of being labelled as an illness requiring treatment.'

Official statistics on levels of illness are sometimes described as 'the clinical iceberg' because it is thought that the 'true' levels of illness are largely concealed. This is because, for a wide range of reasons, people who are ill do not necessarily visit their doctor.

Similarly the reasons for death (as recorded on death certificates) may not always be accurate or reflect the 'real' causes of death. The cause of death of a street person dying in freezing conditions may be stated as 'hypothermia' but it could be argued that the 'real' cause of death was years of malnutrition, substance abuse and inadequate or no housing. A person with AIDS may die of liver failure but it is probably AIDS that gave rise to the liver condition. The cause of death recorded on the death certificate will depend on the doctor's interpretation of the symptoms. Sometimes the doctor may record a condition that is one of a number of contributory reasons, but they choose the one that will cause least distress to the relatives of the deceased. Statistics drawn from death certificates therefore need to be used with care and an understanding of their limitations.

Social class and patterns of health and illness

Although official statistics must be treated with caution, there is overwhelming evidence that health, ill-health and life expectancy vary according to social group and especially according to social class. Members of the higher social classes are living longer and enjoying better health than members of the lower social groups. The most influential modern studies that consider the reasons for this difference are *The Black Report* (Townsend *et al*, 1980) followed by *The Acheson Report* (1998). They provide detailed and comprehensive explanations of the relationships between social and environmental factors and health, illness and life expectancy.

In fact, the findings of *The Black Report* exposed such vast differences in the levels of health and illness between different social classes that the government of the time suppressed its publication. A small number of duplicated copies were circulated and made available just before an August Bank Holiday weekend, when they would expect to get very little press coverage. Nevertheless, this study has been extremely influential and the explanations offered in it are still used by sociologists today when examining and considering these issues.

The Black Report considered four types of explanation that might account for the differences in levels of illness and life expectancy experienced by different social classes. The researchers were persuaded that the differences in health and well-being were an effect of the level of people's income, the quality of their housing and the environment in which they lived and worked.

The four possible sociological explanations were:

1 the statistical artefact explanation
2 natural or social selection
3 cultural or behavioural explanations
4 material or structural explanations.

The statistical artefact explanation

Here the researchers working on *The Black Report* suggested that the differences could be explained by the fact that the statistics themselves produced a biased picture. They argued that the people in the lowest social classes had a higher proportion of older people and people working in traditional and more dangerous industries and so it would be expected that they would have higher levels of illness than the more prosperous, younger people working in offices, call centres and other service industries. This explanation suggests that it is not really social class but the age structure and patterns of employment of people in the lowest social classes that really explain the differences. However, more recent studies have shown that, even when the researchers account for this bias in employment and age, they still find a link between low social class and high levels of illness, and lower life expectancy.

Natural or social selection

This explanation suggests that it is not low social class and the associated low wages, poverty and poorer housing that *cause* illness, higher infant mortality rates and lower life expectancy for adults – it is, in fact, the other way round. People are in the lower classes *because* of their poor health, absenteeism and lack of energy needed for success and promotion. This explanation has been rejected by sociologists because there is evidence to show that ill-health is caused *by* the deprived circumstances rather than causing it.

Cultural or behavioural explanations

This explanation focuses on the behaviour and lifestyle choices of people in the lower social classes. There was evidence that people in the lower social classes smoked more, drank more heavily, were more likely to eat junk food and take insufficient exercise. Their poor lifestyle choices were linked to a range of chronic illnesses including heart disease, some forms of cancer, bronchitis and diabetes. However, the fact is that many people in economically deprived circumstances use smoking and alcohol to help them cope with their difficult circumstances. It is their difficult circumstances that lead to their lifestyle choices – not the other way round.

Material or structural explanations

Material explanations claim that those social groups for whom life expectancy is shorter, and for whom infant mortality rates are higher, suffer poorer health than other groups because of inequalities in wealth and income. Poverty and persistently low incomes are associated with poorer diets, poor housing in poor

Why do you think people's lifestyle choices, such as the amount of exercise they take, can have such a dramatic impact on their health?

environments, and more dangerous and insecure employment. It is these inequalities and the associated deprivation that lead to the differences in health and well-being – an explanation that can be traced back to the work of Marx and Engels in the nineteenth century. The writers of *The Black Report* (Townsend *et al*, 1980) presented very persuasive evidence to support the materialist explanation. Shaw *et al* (1999) completed a major review of all the research in this area and concluded that the major factors that contributed to these differences in health and illness were social factors. Put simply, a consequence of poverty in a community is poor health and lower life expectancy.

Gender and patterns of health and illness

Although women's life expectancy is higher than that of men (with women in our society typically living some five years longer than men and with the infant mortality rates for boys being persistently higher than those for baby girls), studies consistently report higher levels of illness for women than for men. The social factors that contribute to these differences can be identified as:

- risk factors

- economic inequalities

- the impact of the female role, especially in the family.

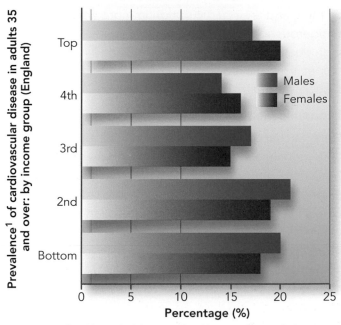

1 Equivalised household income has been used to rank the households into five groups of equal size. The bottom fifth, or bottom quintile group, is then the 20 per cent of households with the lowest incomes.

Fig 7.7: Prevalence of cardiovascular disease by household income and sex, *Social Trends* (2006)

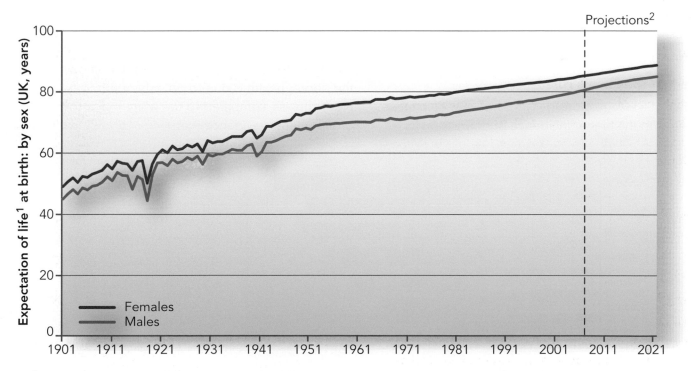

[1]Expectation of life. The average number of years a new-born baby would survive if he or she experienced age specific mortality rates for that time period throughout his or her life.
[2]2006 based projections for 2007–2021.

Fig 7.6: Expectation of life at birth by sex, *Social Trends* (2006)

Risk factors

The higher death rate for men can be linked with the higher levels of cigarette smoking and drinking by men, and their participation in more risky and dangerous sports and other activities. The relatively high death rate of young men between 17 and 24 is specifically linked with this risk-taking and the associated deaths from road accidents.

Economic inequalities

Despite changes in the law, women still earn less than men. In a recent survey by the Higher Education Statistics Agency, women who have degrees, for example are paid, on average, less than men. Men earn £1,000 more than their female college classmates within three years of leaving university. They are much more likely to go straight into high paid jobs with 40 per cent of men earning over £25,000 a year compared with 26% of women three years after graduating.

A higher proportion of women than men are in low-paid part-time work. They are also far more likely to be the main carer in a lone-parent family and are more likely to be on means-tested state benefits. In older age they are more likely to be in poverty because they are less likely to have an employer's pension and may not, because of family responsibilities, have a full state pension either. As discussed earlier in the unit, there are clear and direct links between poverty and poor health.

Impact of the female role

Women still take responsibility for housework in most homes, and the higher incidence of depression in women may be linked with the dull repetitive nature of this work. Popay and Bartley (1989), studying the hours spent on domestic labour in 1700 households in London, found that women spent up to 87 hours per week on housework and that women with children spent 64 hours per week even if they had a full-time job. Often women will be managing on a limited budget, working long hours, and will have little time to themselves. Nevertheless, it may be that the higher rates of diagnosed stress-related illness for women are due to their willingness to discuss mental health issues with their doctor, rather than them actually having a higher rate of stress-related illnesses.

Did you know?

In England and Wales suicide rates for men aged 25 and over are three times higher than the suicide rates for women. Source: *Social Trends* (2009)

Ethnicity and patterns of health and illness

Evidence for a link between race (or ethnicity) and illness is difficult to study systematically because there are difficulties in defining a person's racial type, particularly in the context of the increasing numbers of people who are of mixed race. In addition, a high proportion of people from minority ethnic groups live in areas of deprivation in inner-city areas with associated poor housing, pollution and relatively high unemployment. It is therefore difficult to know whether the poorer health is due to poverty or ethnicity. Nevertheless, compared to the white majority ethnic group, there is evidence that:

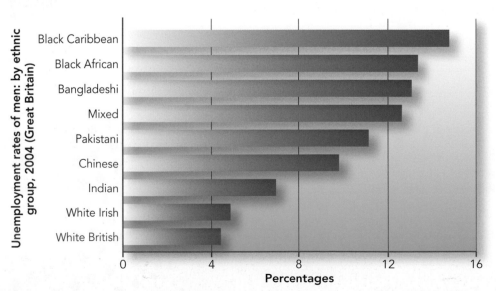

Fig 7.8: Unemployment rates of men by ethnic group, *Social Trends* (2006)

Source: *Annual Population Survey, Office for National Statistics*

- there is a higher incidence of rickets in children from the Asian sub-continent because of a deficiency of vitamin D
- most minority ethnic groups have a shorter life expectancy
- most minority ethnic groups have higher infant mortality rates.

In addition to the health implications of higher levels of poverty, there are issues of access to the health services. Language problems and other cultural barriers may limit full use of the health services. Asian women are often reluctant to see a male doctor, many of them speak little English and, despite improvements, translators are in short supply and much important information is not translated into minority languages. In addition, racism, or the fear of racism, is stressful. Unless health and social care workers understand the religious and cultural beliefs and practices of minority ethnic groups, their care needs are unlikely to be fully met, leaving them vulnerable to higher levels of ill-health.

Age and patterns of health and illness

Many people over retirement age are fit, healthy and making valuable contributions to our society through paid work, voluntary activities, and caring for their families. In fact, the 2001 census revealed that 342,032 people aged 65 and over provided 50 hours or more unpaid care per week. However, it is also true that

there are higher levels of illness among the older population and particularly those people over the age of 75. During a three-month period in 2003, 24 per cent of people over the age of 75 had attended the casualty or out-patient department of a hospital, compared with 14 per cent of people of all ages (General Household Survey 2003). The Alzheimer's Society in 2007 estimated that one in 20 people over 65 and one in five people over the age of 80 suffered from dementia.

Locality and health and illness

There are also regional variations in patterns of health and illness. Mortality and morbidity rates vary in different parts of the country and also within towns and cities in the UK. It is probably no surprise to learn that it is in the poorer regions and the poorer parts of cities that higher levels of illness are recorded.

For example, research has shown that there are regional trends in the incidence of lung cancer across the UK. Within England, the rates for lung cancer are higher than average in the north-west, northern and Yorkshire regions and below average in the south-western, southern and eastern regions.

Reflect

Can you think of reasons why these regional differences in health and well-being might exist?

Assessment activity 7.3

 BTEC

You have been asked by your employer to investigate which social groupings are most in need of health and social care services. In order to assist in the planning of care provision, write a report or an extended essay that will:

1 explain patterns and trends in health and illness among different social groups

2 discuss patterns and trends of health and illness using sociological perspectives

3 evaluate different sociological explanations for patterns and trends in health and illness in two different social groups.

Grading tips

To achieve P3, you will need to explain the different patterns and trends in health and illness in social groupings identified according to factors such as gender, social class, geographical location, ethnicity and age.

To illustrate your answers you may, for example, consider differences in life expectancy, morbidity and mortality rates, incidence of disease and suicide rates, and suggest reasons for these differences.

You will need to refer to statistical data from a range of sources to explain the patterns of health

continued on page 332

Assessment activity 7.3 *continued*

and illness in the range of different social groups. When quoting statistics, make sure that you clearly identify and reference reliable and up-to-date sources for your data.

To achieve **M2**, you may develop material used in your response to **P3**. You need to use the language and tools of sociology to examine trends in health and illness in two different social groups. Make sure that you plan your work carefully. You are not required to apply all sociological perspectives to each group. That would be a textbook in itself!

When examining the patterns of health and illness you may consider, for example, the difficulties involved in defining health and issues relating to the reliability of statistical data. Introduce the sociological approaches as they are relevant to the groups you have chosen.

To achieve **D1**, you will need to evaluate, for

both of your chosen social groups, the quality of the evidence for the differences in health and well-being. You will need to consider the strengths and weaknesses of the evidence and come to your own conclusion. For example, you could ask: 'Is there sufficient reliable evidence to suggest that there is a difference in the health and well-being of people in higher social classes as compared with the lower social classes or between men and women?' and 'Is there sufficient evidence to claim that infant mortality rates vary between countries and different social classes?'

Having weighed up the evidence, you may present your evaluation as a final section to the work presented for **M2**. You will not yet have all the evidence required to reach a definitive conclusion. Further research is always needed. However, you have to make a judgement and come to a conclusion based on the evidence you have found.

Resources and further reading

Abbott, P. & Wallace, C. (1997) *An Introduction to Sociology: Feminist Perspectives*, second ed. London: Routledge

Acheson, D. (1998) *Independent Inquiry into Inequalities in Health London*: HMSO

Blaxter, M. (1990) *Health and Lifestyles* London: Routledge

Browne, K. (2006) *Introducing Sociology for AS Level* Cambridge: Polity Press

Doyal, L. (1995) *What Makes Women Sick?* London: Macmillan

Engels, F. (1845) *The Conditions of the Working Class in England* London: Panther Books

Illich, I. (1976) *Limits to Medicine* Marion Boyars: London

Lines, Clifford (1990) *Companion to the Industrial Revolution* Facts on File Ltd: Oxford

Murdock, G.P. (1949) *Social Structure* New York: Macmillan

Oliver, M. (1990) *The Politics of Disablement* London: Macmillan

Parsons, T. (1951) *The Social System* New York: The Free Press

Popay, J. & Bartley, M. (1989) 'Conditions of labour and women's health', in C. Martin and D. McQueen *Readings for a New Public Health* Edinburgh: Edinburgh University Press

Shakespeare, T. (1998) *The Disability Reader: Social Science Perspectives* London: Casssell

Shaw, M., Dorling, G. & Davey, G. (1999) *The Widening Gap* Bristol: Policy Press

Singh, J.A. & Zingg, R.N. (1942) *Wolf-children and the Feral Man* New York: Harper

Social Trends, Vol. 36 (2006) London: HMSO

Townroe, C. & Yates, G. (1995) *Sociology*, 3rd ed. Harlow: Longman

Townsend, P., Davidson, N. & Whitehead, M. (1980) *Inequalities in Health: The Black Report* Harmondsworth: Penguin

World Health Organization (1974) *Alma-Ata Declaration*

Useful websites

Age Concern www.age.org.uk

Alzheimer's Society www.alzheimers.org.uk

disabilitynet www.youreable.com

Equality and Human Rights Commission www.equalityhumanrights.com

General Household Survey www.statistics.gov.uk/ssd/surveys/general_household_survey.asp

King's Fund www.kingsfund.org.uk

Just checking

1   Define the following key terms: socialisation, culture, norms, ethnicity, social role and social class.
2   Provide a definition for the following sociological perspectives: functionalism, Marxism, feminism, postmodernism, interactionism, collectivism and the New Right.
3   Explain the following concepts of health: negative concept, positive concept and the holistic concepts of health.
4   Explain the biomedical model of health and the socio-medical model of health.
5   Identify and give examples of three main sources of statistical information about trends in health and illness.
6   Why may statistical evidence be unreliable as a measure of the nation's health?
7   Identify five social groups who, according to research, have a higher level of illness than the population as a whole.

Assignment tips

1   The sociological terms introduced at the beginning of the unit (such as socialisation, culture, social class, gender and ethnicity) should be used in class discussion of sociological issues and in your written assignment tasks.

2   To achieve the pass grade in this unit, you are required to **explain** ideas and issues, such as different sociological perspectives, different sociological approaches to health and ill-health, and trends in health and illness among different social groups. Explanations require more detail than a definition or a description. In this case, the grades can be achieved by using appropriate examples to illustrate the concepts introduced. As a rule, you should devote one or two paragraphs to each sociological perspective or approach that you are explaining.

3   To achieve **merit** grade, you are required in **M1** to **assess** the biomedical and socio-medical models of health described in **P2**. When assessing ideas you are should consider the strengths and weaknesses of the approaches or ideas, in this case the two models of health. **M2** requires you to discuss trends of health and illness in two different social groups e.g. gender, social class or ethnic group. This requires you to develop further and in more detail two of the groups introduced in **P3**, presenting clearly the evidence for the patterns and trends explained. You may, further, refer to the difficulties in defining health and to issues relating to the reliability of statistical data. Ensure that you use the sociological terminology accurately and appropriately when considering these topics.

4   To achieve the distinction grade for this unit, you are required, in addition to meeting all other grading criteria, to **evaluate** patterns and trends in health and illness among two social groupings. Draw on the evidence presented earlier, in particular commenting on the strengths and weaknesses of the evidence, and in the final paragraph present your conclusion.

8 Psychological perspectives for health and social care

Psychology is a science devoted to the study of the mind and behaviour. There are different 'schools' of psychology, which have grown up around different ways of understanding the mind and behaviour, called perspectives. A perspective is a point of view or a way of considering how certain ideas can be linked together and their relative importance.

In this unit you will be introduced to several of these psychological perspectives and encouraged not only to understand them but also to apply them to a work setting. Each has its merits but no one perspective can explain all behaviour. For example, the biological perspective explains behaviour in terms of brain and bodily functions, such as the influence of brain chemicals and hormones. By contrast, the psychodynamic perspective sees behaviour as originating in early childhood experiences and being motivated by unconscious forces. You will therefore be encouraged to think critically about the strengths and weaknesses of each one, and to use more than one perspective to explain different types of behaviour in individuals.

Learning outcomes

After completing this unit you should be able to:

1   understand psychological approaches
2   understand psychological approaches to health and social care.

Assessment and grading criteria

This table shows you what you must do in order to achieve a **pass**, **merit** or **distinction** grade, and where you can find activities in this book to help you.

To achieve a **pass** grade, the evidence must show that you are able to:	To achieve a **merit** grade, the evidence must show that, in addition to the pass criteria, you are able to:	To achieve a **distinction** grade, the evidence must show that, in addition to the pass and merit criteria, you are able to:
P1 Explain the principal psychological perspectives. **See Assessment activity 8.1, page 353** *achieved*	**M1** Assess different psychological approaches to study. **See Assessment activity 8.1, page 353** *achieved*	
P2 Explain different psychological approaches to health practice. **See Assessment activity 8.2, page 363** *achieved*	**M2** Compare **two** psychological approaches to health and social care service provision. **See Assessment activity 8.2, page 363** *achieved*	**D1** Evaluate **two** psychological approaches to health and social care service provision. **See Assessment activity 8.2, page 363** *achieved*
P3 Explain different psychological approaches to social care practice. **See Assessment activity 8.2, page 363** *achieved*		

How you will be assessed

You will be assessed by means of two written assignments. The first assignment requires you to show understanding of the different psychological perspectives; the second to show that you can apply these perspectives to health and social care provision.

Tara, 18 years old

When I first started this unit I thought it would be really hard. There was so much jargon and all the different perspectives seemed so confusing. I found class discussions really useful and made notes each time we had a discussion, and made notes on arguments for and against them, which helped me to get the M and D grades. I also found that the jargon wasn't so bad when I started to keep a glossary. This helped me to meet the P grades.

I found I knew much more psychology than I had realised – I just didn't know the terminology. For example, all the theories of learning made sense to me because I had watched my mum and older brother 'reinforcing' my little sister, Patti, when she was good, and seen Patti imitating people she saw on television, so I could understand about role models. I found the idea of the hierarchy of needs really useful for my work placement in a hospital, as it guided me in knowing how to help people better by identifying where on the hierarchy they were. I also found the ideas of self-concept, self-esteem and self-fulfilling prophecy really useful as they could be applied directly to patients. I have gained a lot of insight into behaviour, which I can use in my own life and in my future career as a nurse.

Over to you!

1   What do you think you will find most interesting about this unit?

2   Do you think keeping a glossary will help you remember the terminology?

3   How do you think you might use the knowledge you gain in this unit in your future career?

1 Understand psychological approaches to study

What kind of psychologist are you?

Consider the following scenario and discuss reasons for Aisha's behaviour.

Five-year-old Aisha's parents divorced a year ago. Today her dad is taking her out for the day. He arrives at the house to find his ex-wife flustered and upset because her new baby has been up all night and Aisha has refused to wear the clothes she laid out for her. The trip starts with a visit to McDonald's, with a breakfast of chicken nuggets, chips and Coke. Aisha throws a tantrum when they leave because she wanted ice-cream and her dad refused so he promised she could have a packet of Smarties in the car if she behaved well. Her mum has specifically asked him not to give her Smarties because they are so sweet and sugary. Towards the end of the day, Aisha's dad needs to get some food from the supermarket and once again Aisha throws a tantrum. He tells her if she behaves he will give her some sweets in the car on the way home.

1 Could Aisha's tantrums be in any way linked to her parents' divorce? Make some suggestions about how and why their divorce may influence her behaviour.

2 What would you say to Aisha's dad about giving her Smarties when her mum has asked him not to?

1.1 The behaviourist perspective

In the introduction to this unit it was explained that perspectives in psychology explain behaviour based on a particular set of beliefs and ideas. The key idea of the behaviourist perspective is that we can understand any type of behaviour by looking at what the person has learned. This will include personality traits such as shyness, confidence, optimism or pessimism, as well as more fleeting behaviours such as offering to help with the washing up.

Behaviourist psychologists explain all human behaviour as resulting from experience. Two key thinkers associated with this perspective are Pavlov (classical conditioning) and Skinner (operant conditioning). Although these two theorists believed that different processes were involved, they both explained all types of behaviour as being the result of learning – everything from shyness to aggression, from happiness to depression. This is quite different from, say, the psychodynamic or biological approaches, which are explored later in this unit.

Classical conditioning

The first theory of learning we shall investigate is called classical conditioning. This theory was developed by a Russian physiologist called Ivan Pavlov (1849–1936). He was working with dogs to investigate their digestive systems. The dogs were attached to a harness, as shown opposite, and Pavlov attached monitors to their stomachs and mouths so he could measure the rate of salivation (production of saliva).

He noticed one day that a dog began to salivate when the laboratory assistant entered the room with a bowl of food, but before it had actually tasted the food. Since salivation is a reflex response (which until then was thought to be produced only as a result of food touching the tongue), this seemed unusual. Pavlov speculated that the dog was salivating because it had learned to associate the laboratory assistant with food. He then developed his theory in the following way.

Food automatically led to the response of salivation. Since salivation is an automatic (not learned)

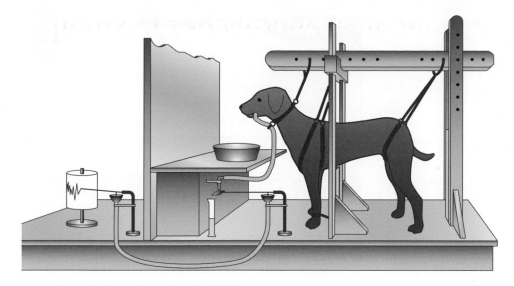

Fig 8.1: The harness used by Pavlov while conducting his conditioning experiments with dogs

response, he called this an **unconditioned response** (UR). 'Unconditioned' means ' not learned'. As food automatically leads to this response, he called this an **unconditioned stimulus** (US). Pavlov then presented food at the same time as ringing a bell (a neutral stimulus), to see if the dog would learn to associate the bell with food. Over several trials the dog learned that the bell was associated with food and eventually it began to salivate when only the bell was rung and no food was presented. It had thus learned the **conditioned response** (CR) of salivation to the **conditioned stimulus** (CS) of the bell.

Operant conditioning

This type of learning is associated with the theories of Burrhus Frederic Skinner (1904–1990). (For a fuller description of the work of Skinner and other

Case study: Sandra

Sandra is 25 years old and is due to have an anti tetanus booster. She is absolutely terrified of this and asks her GP to prescribe her a tranquilliser. The doctor is, naturally, reluctant to do so and questions her a bit about why she is so afraid. Sandra reveals that she remembers having an injection when she was seven (she doesn't consciously remember her earlier immunisations), which resulted in her fainting. She has never been able to bear injections since that time.

1 Identify the unconditioned stimulus, unconditioned response, conditioned stimulus and conditioned response in Sandra's case.

2 Do you think this theory explains Sandra's fear well?

Key terms

Unconditioned response – A response that regularly occurs when an unconditioned stimulus is presented, e.g. the startle response resulting from a thunderclap.

Unconditioned stimulus – A stimulus that regularly and consistently leads to an automatic (not learned) response from, e,g, a clap of thunder.

Conditioned response – A new, learned response to a previously neutral stimulus that mimics the response to the unconditioned stimulus.

Conditioned stimulus – A neutral stimulus that, when paired with the unconditioned stimulus, produces a conditioned (learned) response, just as the unconditioned response used to.

behaviourists, consult the book *Learning and Behaviour* by L. Barker – see page 365 for details.) Skinner was an American psychologist who worked mostly with rats and pigeons, to discover some of the key principles of learning new behaviours. He used a very famous device, called a Skinner box, illustrated below. The box contains a lever which, when pressed, releases a food pellet into the box, thus reinforcing lever-pressing behaviour.

When the rat is first placed in the box it will run around, sniff the various items and at some point it will press the lever, releasing a food pellet. After a while, when the rat has repeatedly performed this action, it will learn that this behaviour (pressing the lever) is

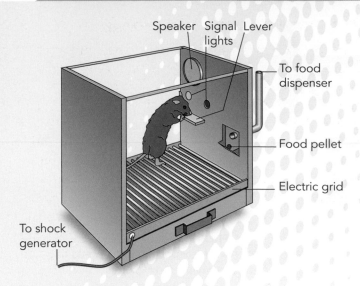

Speaker Signal Lever
        lights

To food
dispenser

Food pellet

Electric grid

To shock
generator

Fig 8.2: A rat in a typical Skinner box

automatically followed by the release of a food pellet (the consequence). Because the pellet is experienced as *reinforcing* (something the rat would like to have more of), this consequence increases the probability of the behaviour being repeated. There are two types of reinforcement: **positive reinforcement** and **negative reinforcement**.

Skinner investigated negative reinforcement by running a very low electrical current on the floor of the Skinner box. The current could be de-activated if the rat pressed the lever. The behaviour of lever pressing was thus negatively reinforcing. For humans, this can be demonstrated by the example of using pain relief. For example, if you have a headache and you take a painkiller, which results in the headache going away, you are negatively reinforced for taking a painkiller.

Punishment occurs when behaviour is followed by a consequence that is experienced as unpleasant. Skinner investigated this by giving the rat a small electric shock when it pressed the lever. The consequence of lever pressing (the electric shock) was experienced as unpleasant, so the rat learned to stop pressing the lever.

Key terms

Positive reinforcement – This happens when the consequence following a particular behaviour is experienced as desirable.

Negative reinforcement – This happens when behaviour results in a consequence that removes something unpleasant.

Case study: Sean

Sean is known for his kind behaviour. His friends think this is a bit over the top because he seems to get involved with every needy person in the college. If he is out on the street he almost seems to search out homeless people and gives away more money than he can afford.

One day, in discussion with a group of friends who are curious about his behaviour, he explains that when he was a small child he was out in a shopping precinct with his father, who gave money to a homeless person. His father asked him to give some money out of his pocket money but he refused. The disapproving response from his father was experienced by him as punishing (he felt bad). Next time they were out together, he gave all his pocket money (50p) away and his father praised him.

Ever since that experience, he learned that not being kind made him feel guilty and uncomfortable, whereas being kind led to feelings of pleasure and pride and took away any initial feeling of guilt. He thus felt that the punishment for not being kind was removed by giving money (negative reinforcement). The act of giving in itself had therefore developed his sense of worth and was thus positively reinforcing.

1 If Sean hadn't felt guilty about refusing to give money, would the consequence have changed his later behaviour?

2 Do you think Sean's kindness and generosity can be fully explained in terms of operant conditioning?

1.2 Social learning theory
The effects of other individuals on behaviour

We do not live in a vacuum and there are many influences on our behaviour – from peers, siblings, parents, television, sports personalities and other celebrities, as any parent of a teenager can tell you!

According to social learning theory, role models are very important. While we may learn new behaviours from anyone, the likelihood of imitating such behaviours is strongly influenced by the way we perceive the person performing the behaviour (the model).

If we observe someone we admire behaving in a particular way, we are more likely to imitate such behaviour. If, for example, a sports personality such as Cristiano Ronaldo is shown on television recommending wearing a cycle helmet, we are much more likely to feel motivated to imitate such behaviour ourselves because this will bring us closer to being like this admired model. On the other hand, if cycle helmet wearing is associated with a model we look down on (e.g. someone we regard as a 'geek') then we are much less likely to imitate it. The diagram below illustrates factors associated with a model that influence whether we will imitate him or her.

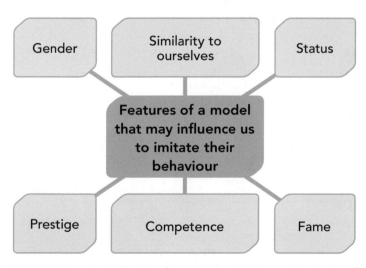

Fig 8.3: Certain attributes of a model make it more likely that their behaviour will be imitated

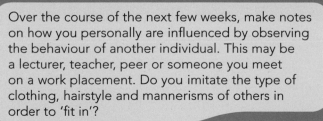

Activity 1: How much are you influenced by observing others?

Over the course of the next few weeks, make notes on how you personally are influenced by observing the behaviour of another individual. This may be a lecturer, teacher, peer or someone you meet on a work placement. Do you imitate the type of clothing, hairstyle and mannerisms of others in order to 'fit in'?

The effects of groups on behaviour

Our behaviour is dramatically influenced by the presence of others, however much we may believe ourselves to be truly individual in our beliefs and behaviour. Nowhere is this more clearly demonstrated than in the experiments conducted in the 1950s by social psychologist Solomon Asch. He was interested in a concept called **majority influence**. This is when the presence of other people causes us to change our public behaviour or opinions because we do not want to stand out from the crowd. We have a powerful desire to belong and will 'go along' with what others in our group say, think or do in order to fit in. This is what he did to test this idea.

A group of six stooges or confederates of the experimenter (people who were play-acting according to instructions) were joined by a naïve participant (a genuine participant who knew nothing about the nature of the experiment) in a task that supposedly tested visual perception. The experimenter explained that the task involved stating whether a target line shown matched the length of one of a set of three

Key term

Majority influence – A type of influence exerted by groups that is associated with the individual's desire to be accepted. Behaviour, beliefs and views are changed publicly in order to be in line with the norms of a group, although privately they are unchanged.

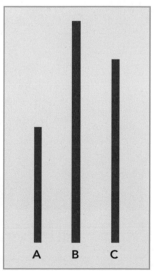

Target line   Comparison lines

Fig 8.4: The target line and comparison lines used in Asch's experiment

lines (a, b and c) similarly shown to all participants. An example of this task is given in Fig 8.4.

As far as the genuine participant was concerned, all those taking part in the experiment were similarly naïve (i.e. didn't know what was happening and were genuine participants). The group was seated in a horseshoe arrangement, with the naïve participant always last but one to be asked to make a judgement. The procedure began with the first participant stating out loud whether the target line was equal in length to one of the specified comparison lines. The next person in the horseshoe then answered, and so on, right through to the end. This 'perceptual trial' was repeated 18 times but on 12 of the 18 trials the confederates all gave the same wrong answer when the correct answer was obvious. Astonishingly, out of 123 naïve participants, 28 per cent gave an incorrect answer eight or more times. This shows clearly how an individual can be influenced by a group.

The effects of culture and society on behaviour

Culture refers to the shared values, norms, language, customs and practices of a group. Although we tend to think of culture as being specific to different countries, it also refers to different sub-groups within society. For example, people from different socioeconomic groups within the UK will share different aspects of culture, such as the value placed on eating at a table rather than on your lap in front of the television; the way in which money is spent; how to talk to your elders, and so on. It is important to understand how culture affects our behaviour in order to gain a full understanding of the people we encounter and those we work with. Watson (1970) found that the average amount of eye contact made varied between countries, with high degrees of eye contact being seen as insolent by some Africans and East Asians, whereas among Indians and Latin-Americans this was seen as desirable.

Fig 8.5: The participant is always the last but one person to give his or her judgement out loud

The extent to which we value individualism is also heavily dependent on culture. Generally speaking, in European cultures and the USA, self-reliance, assertiveness and individualism are highly valued traits and parents see it as part of their duty to enable children to grow up with these characteristics. In many Eastern and Asian cultures, by contrast, the emphasis is on collectivism: the child is socialised to put the needs of the group before his or her own needs. Thus, a 40-year-old American male living at home with his parents would perhaps be seen as a 'mummy's boy' and disparaged as such, whereas in parts of Africa, India and China this would be seen as normal, admirable behaviour and as showing respect for parents.

My behaviour: I am sullen, aggressive, unfriendly and hostile

Other people's response to me: They are cool, distant and perhaps even unfriendly or hostile

My thoughts and beliefs: I think I am worthless; the world is full of people out to get me

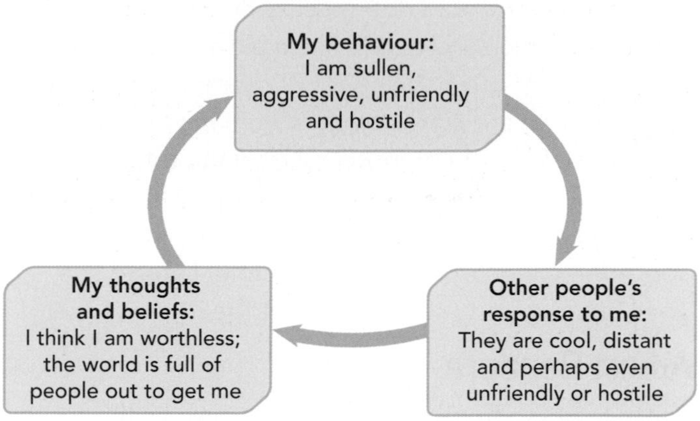

Fig 8.6: The way we think and feel about ourselves influences the way others respond to us

Activity 2: Investigating social and cultural norms

Do you always join a queue at the back and stand in line until you get to the front? Is your language and speech more formal with teachers and people in authority than with friends and family? Think of how your upbringing has influenced your behaviour. Discuss with others whether their experience is the same or different, and think of three more examples of norms that may differ across social and cultural boundaries.

The self-fulfilling prophecy

This is an important concept in psychology that has a big impact on the way we behave towards others and expect them to behave towards us. If we believe ourselves to be worthwhile, pleasant and likeable then we will almost certainly be polite and cheerful towards those we meet, thus creating a favourable impression. In response, those who come into contact with us perceive us favourably and behave in a positive way towards us, with the result that our positive self-beliefs are confirmed. If, on the other hand, we are angry, full of resentment, believe the world is against us and so on, then we are likely to behave in a more aggressive, confrontational or argumentative way, in which case that is how we will be responded to, which will confirm our views of ourselves and the world. An example of this is illustrated in Fig. 8.6.

Case study: Ruby

Ruby has just begun her work placement at a residential care home for the elderly, and her supervisor, Janine, is giving her a brief description of the people she will be working with. When describing 85-year-old George, Janine says:

'Well, George… What can I say? He's just trouble, from start to finish. He moans and grumbles all the time, annoys the other residents, and is attention-seeking. Lots of people are much worse off than he is, but he causes the most disruption.'

1 What sort of expectations do you think Ruby will have of George?

2 Do you think Janine's negative attitude to George affects his well-being, and if so, how?

3 Do you think it is possible to break the self-fulfilling prophecy?

Role theory

There is a similarity between role theory and the self-fulfilling prophecy, in that role theory suggests that, because we live within a particular culture, society and social group, we are influenced by other people. This influence helps lead us to adopt certain roles and try to live up to the expectations that go with this role. For example, a nurse is expected to be level-headed, warm and competent. However, whereas we might expect a surgeon to be similarly level-headed and competent, we would not necessarily expect him or her to be particularly warm. Since we all take on many different roles, our behaviour will change according to the role we are currently in. A woman visiting the zoo with her children will take on the role of a mother; whereas when she goes to work she may be a colleague, a supervisor or a subordinate and she will adopt the expectations of her job role. Later, if she goes out to a party she may adopt the role of a friend.

Albert Bandura

Social learning theory explains behaviour as the result of learning from people we are exposed to in our environment. We can also learn new behaviours from people we observe, either in real life or in the media. This is known as **observational learning** and this theory was developed by the American psychologist, Albert Bandura.

The person we learn from is known as a **role model**, and the process of imitating is called **modelling**. However, we do not imitate all behaviour we observe and remember. Whether or not it is in our interests to imitate particular behaviour is influenced by characteristics of the model (see Figure 8.3 on p. 341). If we see a model being punished for a certain behaviour, we are less likely to imitate it than if we see him or her being positively reinforced.

Reflect

What features of a model would influence you to imitate that person?

Key terms

Observational learning – This occurs when we observe someone behaving in a particular way and we remember this behaviour. We can learn positive and negative behaviours from observing others. For example, we may observe someone going to the aid of a person who collapses.

Role model – An individual who has characteristics that inspire us to copy their behaviour (for example, because they are prestigious, attractive or have high status).

Modelling – The process of basing behaviour, attitude, style of speech or dress on someone we admire or want to be like.

1.3 The psychodynamic approach

This approach is associated with the Austrian psychologist Sigmund Freud (1856–1939), who developed the theory of psychodynamic psychology and the treatment known as psychoanalysis. A key follower of Freud was Erik Erikson (1902–1994), who adapted aspects of Freud's approach.

The importance of the unconscious mind: Sigmund Freud

Freud described the occasion when a Member of Parliament was referring to the MP for Hull, with whom he disagreed about some policy. Instead of saying 'the honourable member from Hull' he started to say, 'the honourable member from Hell'. What do you think caused him to say Hell when he should have said Hull?

Freud was one of the earliest thinkers to bring to public attention the idea that we are not always aware of all aspects of ourselves. He suggested that what we are aware of is represented in our conscious mind but that many of our memories, feelings and past experiences are locked up in a part of our mind he called the 'unconscious'. We cannot access the contents of our unconscious, but they often 'leak out' in dreams and slips of the tongue. Freud believed that the conscious mind was like the tip of an iceberg – only a small part being available to awareness. Part of the unconscious that we can easily access he called the pre-conscious. This contains information not yet in consciousness but that can easily be retrieved (e.g.

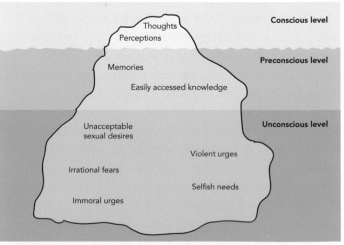

Fig 8.7: According to Freud, the conscious mind represents the 'tip of the iceberg'. Most of our experiences and memories are either pre-conscious or unconscious

the name of Aunt Edie's cat). The rest, well under the surface, consisted of the unconscious. This is illustrated in Fig 8.7.

The importance of early experiences

The importance of early experience in determining later behaviours is clearly illustrated by Freud's developmental theory of psychosexual stages. He believed that we all go through several stages of psychosexual development. At each stage, the individual's libido (energy) is focused on a part of the body that is particularly relevant at that stage. If the needs of the developing child are met at each stage, it moves on to the next developmental stage. If, however, there is struggle or conflict or some unsatisfactory experience, the individual becomes 'fixated' (stuck) at this stage. This results in certain ways of being, or personality traits, which are carried through into adulthood and which can explain behaviour later in life.

The earliest stage is the 'oral stage'. The focus here is on the mouth and activities such as sucking, biting and licking. (You will probably have noticed that young babies seem to put everything in their mouths.) Freud believed that there could be two reasons for fixation. If the infant was weaned too early, it would feel forever under-gratified and unsatisfied and would develop into a pessimistic, sarcastic person. If, on the other hand, it was over-gratified (weaned too late) the individual would develop a gullible personality, naively trusting in others and with a tendency to 'swallow anything'. This stage lasts from birth to approximately 18 months.

If the infant successfully passes through the oral stage without becoming fixated, the next stage is the 'anal stage', which lasts from approximately one to three years. Here the libido is focused on aspects to do with potty training. If there is a battle with parents about potty training, with the child feeling forced to use the potty before they are ready, or feeling over-controlled in various areas, they may rebel by retaining their faeces: the child refuses to 'go', thus holding on to control and withholding satisfaction from the parent. This type of fixation is called 'anally retentive' and is associated with later personality characteristics such as obstinacy, miserliness and obsessive traits. The alternative scenario is that the child is not given enough boundaries over potty training so they take excessive pleasure in excretion and become a messy, creative, disorganised sort of person.

During the ages of four to five the child passes through the 'phallic stage'. Fixation at this stage is associated with anxiety and guilty feelings about sex and fear of castration for males. If this stage is not resolved, the theory suggests that a boy may become homosexual and a girl may become a lesbian. Freud thought these were abnormal fixations; however most people today would not view them in this way.

Between the ages of five to seven and the onset of puberty, the child enters the 'latency stage', which is not strictly speaking a developmental phase but a time when the focus is on social pursuits such as sport, academic excellence and the development of friendships.

The final psychosexual stage is the 'genital stage', which begins at puberty. Freud believed that the less fixated the individual has become during the earlier

Think about how, if fixated at this stage, this person may become a smoker in later life.

stages, the more easily this stage will be negotiated, resulting in the ability to form strong heterosexual relationships with an ability to be warm and loving as well as to receive love in a new, mature fashion.

A second important feature of early experience is the development of **ego** defence mechanisms. The use of a defence mechanism allows us to block out events that threaten to overwhelm us. Examples of these are given below.

Table 8.1: Examples of defence mechanisms

Name of defence mechanism	Explanation	Example
Repression	The person forgets the event	Forgetting a traumatic event in childhood (e.g. a car crash)
Regression	Reverting to an earlier stage of development	Wetting the bed when a sibling is born, having been dry before
Denial	Pushing an event or emotion out of consciousness	Denying that a loved one has died
Displacement	Redirecting desires onto a safe object	Kicking the cat at home because your boss gave you a hard time at work

A final influence is that of the mind. Freud suggested that the mind (which he called the **psyche**) is divided into three dynamic parts. The **id** is a part of the mind which is totally unconscious and which exists at birth. It is focused on getting what it wants and consists of aggressive, sexual and loving instincts. It is the part of us that says 'I want it now!' The **superego** is formed as a result of socialisation and consists of all the instructions, morals and values that are repeatedly enforced as we are growing up. It takes on the form of a conscience and also represents our view of our ideal self. The main role of the superego is to try to subdue the activity of the id. The ego tries to balance the demands of the id and the superego. It is the rational part of the mind, always seeking to do what is most helpful for the individual. Different behaviours can be understood by trying to infer which part of the psyche is dominant at any time.

Key terms

Ego – The part of the mind whose function it is to moderate the demands of the id and prevent the superego being too harsh. It operates on the reality principle.

Id – Part of the psyche we are born with. It operates on the pleasure principle.

Psyche – The structure of the mind, consisting of three dynamic parts.

Superego – Roughly equivalent to a conscience, the superego consists of an internalisation of all the values of right and wrong we have been socialised to believe in. It also contains an image of our ideal self.

A person who is very submissive, guilty and always wanting to please may have a very strong superego.

A person who is impulsive, careless of other people's feelings, doesn't think through the consequences of their actions and is perhaps inclined to aggression, either verbal or physical, probably has a dominant id.

A person who can be submissive and assertive when necessary, who is able to think about other people's feelings but also consider and value their own needs, has probably got a strong enough ego to balance the demands of the id and the superego. They are likely to have quite a rational and realistic outlook on life.

Erik Erikson

Erik Erikson was a psychologist who agreed with much of Freud's theory in so far as he thought that we developed through a series of stages. However, he thought that these continued throughout our lifetime and were essentially social in nature. He also believed that Freud put too much emphasis on our desire for individual gratification and not enough on our need to be accepted by society and lead a meaningful life. Erikson suggested that we move through a series of psychosocial crises with a different social focus at each stage. For example between birth and the age of one, the life crisis concerns developing trust or mistrust in self and others. The social focus at this stage is the mother.

Reflect

Identify which stage you are in, as outlined by Erikson. As you work through the following section, make notes on whether you think he is correct in his explanation of this stage. Is there anything you disagree with?

Key terms

Trust – A sense of hope and faith in others.

Autonomy – Faith in one's ability to influence the environment through one's own actions.

Doubt – Lack of self-belief; a sense of shame associated with failure.

Initiative – A sense of purpose and belief in one's abilities to pursue appropriate goals.

Guilt – The result of trying to follow goals that conflict with those of family members.

Industry – An application of skills and abilities to projects in the world, including at school.

Inferiority – A sense of being a failure.

Identity – A consistent sense of sameness, associated with occupational choice and social roles.

Role confusion – The inability to find a social role; indecision about occupational choice and the lack of a continuous sense of self.

Case study: Word association

One method used by Freud to access the contents of the unconscious is known as word association. He would say a word and the patient would respond with the first word that came to mind. The speed of response and lack of conscious editing produced some curious responses. One example was a man who replied 'shroud' in response to the word 'white'. Upon further probing, Freud uncovered his client's fear that he would soon die from heart failure and be covered with a shroud. It emerged that a relative of this man had died at the age he now was, as a result of heart failure. The patient, being overweight himself, had developed a deep fear of dying at this same age but had buried the fear in his unconscious.

1 Do you agree that much of what motivates our behaviour is, indeed, unconscious? Can you think of examples?

2 Can making the contents of the unconscious accessible to the conscious mind really help us deal with our innermost fears? How and why?

Table 8.2: Psychosocial stages

Stage	Key focus of stage	Positive outcome	Negative outcome
Stage 1 (0–1 year)	How the infant is parented	Dependable, responsive, caring parenting leads to a sense of **trust**	Parenting that lacks warmth and affection or is inconsistent leads to mistrust
Stage 2 (1–3 years)	Being enabled to do things by yourself	Being supported in growing independence leads to a sense of **autonomy**	Being criticised and over-controlled leads to a feeling of **doubt** about your own competence
Stage 3 (3–6 years)	Interaction with the world	Being encouraged to try out new skills and explore the world leads to a sense of **initiative**	Being hampered in the desire to find things out (e.g. criticised, told not to be silly) leads to a sense of **guilt** and a lack of confidence
Stage 4 (6–12 years)	Understanding how things are made and how they work	The ability to succeed at realistic tasks leads to a sense of **industry**	Being pushed to take on tasks they are not ready for leads to a sense of **inferiority**
Stage 5 (12–18 years)	Developing a consistent sense of identity by experimentation	Experimentation leads to a secure sense of **identity**	The inability to experiment and develop a sense of identity leads to **role confusion** and a negative identity

How does belonging to a group help us to experiment with a new identity?

1.4 The humanistic perspective

Humanistic psychology looks at human experience from the viewpoint of the individual. It focuses on the idea of free will and the belief that we are all capable of making choices. Two psychologists associated with this approach are Abraham Maslow and Carl Rogers.

Abraham Maslow

Maslow (1908–1970) was an American psychologist who believed that we are all seeking to become the best that we can possibly be – spiritually, physically, emotionally and intellectually. He called this **self-actualisation**. He constructed a theory known as the hierarchy of needs, in which he explained that every human being requires certain basic needs to be met before they can approach the next level. This hierarchy of needs is shown in Fig 8.8.

Key term

Self-actualisation – An innate tendency we all possess as human beings to become the best that we can be in all aspects of personality and intellectual, social and emotional life.

Self-actualisation
needs
(achieving full potential)

Self-esteem needs
(respect, including self-respect)

Love and emotional needs
(affection from others, being with others)

Safety and security needs
(freedom from anxiety and chaos,
stability, predictability)

Basic physical needs
(oxygen, food, drink, warmth, sleep)

Fig 8.8: Maslow's hierarchy of needs – according to Maslow, we need to progress through each level before we can reach self-actualisation

As the diagram shows, Maslow believed that, until our basic physiological needs are met, we will focus all our energies on getting them met and not be able to progress further. When we are well-housed, well-fed and comfortable physically, we begin to focus on our emotional needs, such as the need to belong and be loved and to feel **self-esteem**. When our lives are such that these needs are also met, we strive to self-actualise. As Maslow said, 'A musician must make music, an artist must paint, a poet must write, if he is to be ultimately at peace with himself. What a man can be, he must be. This need we may call self-actualisation.'

blonde or brunette, tall or short, as well as personality traits such as being kind, humble, assertive, hard-working. The self-concept is formed from an early age and young children **internalise** other people's judgements of them, which then become part of their self-concept. If a child is told they are silly, naughty and will come to no good, part of their self-concept will contain these aspects. If, on the other hand, a child is praised, encouraged to succeed and told they are valued, they will have a positive self-concept and see themselves as someone who is worthwhile and competent.

Case study: Amina

This case study shows how the hierarchy of needs can be applied to the case of an asylum seeker.

Amina is a refugee from Somalia. She arrived in the UK at the age of 16, having been given a place on a lorry after both her parents were killed. When she reached the UK she applied for asylum. She was housed in temporary accommodation for the first 18 months and was then granted leave to remain and given a bedsit. She is being supervised by a multi-disciplinary team, including Helen, an outreach worker from Connexions. Helen is due to visit her to assess her needs, and suggest an educational route that could enable Amina to gain qualifications, so she can eventually support herself. Helen's supervisor advises her to familiarise herself with Maslow's hierarchy of needs before she meets Amina for the first time.

1 At what stage of Maslow's hierarchy of needs was Amina when she first arrived in England?

2 What needs may she satisfy by entering education?

3 Suggest some questions Helen might ask in order to find out whether or not Amina is yet ready to benefit from education.

Key terms

Self-esteem – How valuable we feel; literally, the amount of esteem we give to ourselves. Someone with high self-esteem will believe they are loved and lovable and that they are important and valued. By contrast, an individual with low self-esteem may feel themselves to be worthless, of no value to anyone else, unloved and unlovable.

Self-concept – The way we see ourselves. In early life this comes from what we are told about ourselves (e.g. 'you're so pretty', 'you're a good footballer', 'what a kind girl you are'). As we grow older, our ability to think about ourselves develops and we begin to incorporate our own judgements (e.g. 'I did well at that test – I'm good at maths', 'I wasn't invited to that party – I must be unpopular').

Internalise – This is to do with the way we take in information from the outside world and build it into our sense of self. It then becomes part of our feelings, thoughts and beliefs about who we are and what we expect from the world around us.

Activity 3: Investigating your own self-concept

Write down 20 statements about yourself. How many of these are positive and how many negative?

Consider the influences there have been on your self-esteem. How much praise/criticism did you receive from others when you were growing up?

Are you able to feel good about your achievements, and accept praise from others or do you tend to brush it off? People with high self-esteem and a positive self-concept are able to accept praise.

Carl Rogers

Rogers (1902–1987) was particularly interested in the concept of self. There are many aspects of the self but two are especially important here. **Self-concept** refers to the way we view ourselves. This includes physical and biological attributes such as being male or female,

Rogers believed that we also hold a concept of self, called the ideal self. This represents a view of ourselves as we feel we should be and as we would like to be. When there is incongruence (a mismatch) between our actual self and our ideal self we become troubled and unhappy.

1.5 The cognitive/information processing perspective

This psychological perspective has gained enormous ground since the 1960s, when the influence of behaviourism began to wane. With the development of computers came the idea that brain activity was like the operation of a computer. A great deal of research has been devoted to understanding cognitive processes such as attention, memory, perception, information processing, problem solving, thought, language and other aspects of cognition. However, to understand this perspective as it relates to health and social care, we shall concentrate on just two theorists: Jean Piaget and George Kelly.

Jean Piaget

Jean Piaget (1896–1980) was a Swiss psychologist who initially worked on measuring intelligence. During his research he noticed that children of the same age made the same mistakes in logic, however bright they were. He came to the conclusion that cognition develops through a series of stages, each new stage building on the previous one. The stages and key associated features are described below. (For more information on these stages, see Unit 4.)

How does this photo show that a baby is only able to experience the world through sense perceptions and motor activity – the sensori-motor stage?

Table 8.3: Piaget's stages of development

Stage	Age	Key features
Stage 1: Sensori-motor	0–2 years	The world is experienced through motor activity and the senses
Stage 2: Pre-operational	2–7 years	Language develops along with memory. The child is egocentric and unable to conserve
Stage 3: Concrete operational	7–11 years	The child can now understand conservation but cannot yet solve problems mentally
Stage 4: Formal operational	11+	The child can now use abstract thoughts and represent problems mentally

George Kelly

George Kelly (1905–1966) developed a unique psychological theory known as the Psychology of Personal Constructs. He saw the individual as a scientist, making predictions about the future, testing them and, if necessary, revising them according to new evidence. A construct is a way of construing (interpreting and making sense of) reality and the environment. For example, if an individual develops deafness in middle age they may construe this as a disaster, withdraw from the world and become socially isolated. Alternatively, if they construe this as a challenge, they may seek out new, exciting opportunities, work around their deafness and continue to live a rich, fulfilling life.

Kelly believed that we do not have to be constrained by our past history but can seek out new, alternative, more positive meanings.

1.6 The biological perspective

Maturational theory

The theory of maturation holds that the effects of the environment are minimal. The child is born with a set of genetic instructions passed down from its parents, and its cognitive, physical and other developmental processes merely unfold over time, rather than being dependent upon the environment to mature. It is, in effect, a theory which states that development is due to nature not nurture. This is quite a contrast to learning theory or humanistic theory, where the effects of nurture are paramount.

Gesell's theory of maturation

Arnold Gesell (1880–1961) believed that development occurred according to a sequence of maturational processes. For example, development in the womb follows a fixed set of stages: the heart begins to form first, along with a rudimentary nervous system. Bones and muscles develop next and over time the organism develops into a fully functioning human being, ready to be born. As the child develops from birth onwards, its genes allow it to flower gradually into the person he or she is meant to be. The environment should provide support for this unfolding of talents, skills, personality and interests but the main thing driving this development is the maturational process.

Genetic influences on behaviour

Genes can affect behaviour in many ways. Some disorders, such as Huntington's disease, are caused by a single dominant gene, which either parent can pass on to their child. Others, such as cystic fibrosis and sickle cell anaemia, are caused when both parents pass on the gene for the disorder.

Disorders that occur regardless of environmental influences, such as those listed above, are genetically determined disorders. This means that the individual who inherits the gene or genes is certain to develop the disorder, regardless of environmental factors. An example of this is Huntington's disease. This disorder usually begins to show when the individual is aged between 30 and 50. Symptoms of dementia appear and the individual is likely to die about 15 years after the onset. Some of the changes in behaviour are listed below, though this list is not comprehensive:

- hallucinations and delusions
- severe confusion
- progressive memory loss
- inappropriate speech; use of jargon or wrong words
- personality changes including anxiety and depression, withdrawal from social interaction, decreased ability to care for oneself and inability to maintain employment.

Did you know?

Out of 23 pairs of identical twins affected by autism, both twins had the disorder in 22 cases. For a sample of 17 non-identical twins affected by autism both twins had the disorder in only 4 cases. This demonstrates that the environment is also responsible for this disorder.

Ritvo, Freeman *et al* (1985)

Disorders that are not genetically determined, but where an individual's genes may leave them with a vulnerability to developing the disorder, are far more common. A classic way of measuring the contribution of genes to any type of behaviour is through twin studies. There are two types of twins. Monozygotic (or identical) twins share 100 per cent of their genetic material since they are formed from only one fertilised egg, which has divided into two. Dizygotic (or fraternal) twins share only 50 per cent of genetic material since they occur when two eggs are fertilised by different sperm at the same time. If, the reasoning goes, one of a pair of monozygotic twins has a disorder, it would be expected that, if genes are the only influence, the second twin *must* also have the disorder.

Activity 4: The contribution of genes

Research the genetic component in susceptibility to one of the following diseases:

- breast cancer
- bowel cancer
- diabetes
- stroke.

PLTS

Team worker: If you work in a group on this activity, you will show your team working skills by collaborating with others to work towards common goals.

The influence of the nervous and endocrine systems on behaviour

For more information on the nervous system, see Unit 5.

The autonomic nervous system produces its effects through activation of nerve fibres throughout the nervous system, brain and body or by stimulating the release of hormones from endocrine glands (such as the adrenal and pineal glands). Hormones are biochemical substances that are released into the bloodstream and have a profound effect on target organs and on behaviour. They are present in very small quantities and individual molecules have a very short life, so their effects quickly disappear if they are not secreted continuously.

There are a large number of hormones including:

- melatonin, which is released by the pineal gland and acts on the brainstem sleep mechanisms to help synchronise the phases of sleep and activity
- testosterone, which is released in the testicles and may influence aggressiveness
- oxytocin, which is released by the pituitary gland and stimulates milk production and female orgasms.

Some hormones are released as a response to external stimuli. For example, the pineal gland responds to reduced daylight by increasing production of melatonin. Other hormones follow a circadian rhythm, with one peak and one trough every 24 hours. (Circadian means 'about a day' and refers to a 24-hour rhythm.) For instance, levels of cortisol rise about an hour before you wake up and contribute to your feelings of wakefulness or arousal.

Central nervous system	Autonomic nervous system	
Consists of the brain and spinal cord	Regulates organs of the body and processes such as heart rate and blood pressure; only one branch is activated at any time	
	▼	▼
	Sympathetic branch	**Parasympathetic branch**
	Associated with arousal and the fight or flight response	Associated with rest and relaxation
	Person may appear agitated, with a fast pulse and heavy, rapid breathing	Person will appear calm and relaxed, with a slow pulse

Fig 8.9: A representation of the nervous system

Assessment activity 8.1

Produce an information booklet including:

1 an explanation of the principal psychological perspectives

2 an assessment of the different psychological approaches to study.

Grading tips

P1 To achieve P1, you need to explain the principal psychological perspectives. When you do this, remember to use the appropriate terminology for each perspective. For example, explain 'unconditioned' and 'conditioned stimulus' for the behaviourist perspective; and outline what is meant by the 'psyche' and 'ego defences' for the psychodynamic perspective.

M1 For M1, you need to assess different psychological approaches to study. When doing this, you could consider how well the different approaches explain behaviour. Do they miss out alternative explanations? For example, does everyone who has an injection develop a needle phobia? Why do we not always perform a behaviour we have learned by observing others?

PLTS

Self manager: By completing this assignment you may be able to gain evidence that you can organise your time and resources, prioritising your actions.

Independent enquirer: Analysing and evaluating evidence, judging its relevance and value, may enable you to obtain evidence for this skill.

Functional skills

English: By researching textbooks and websites regarding psychological perspectives and approaches, you can show evidence of being able to compare, select, read and understand texts and use them to gather information, ideas, arguments and opinions. Producing an information booklet for this assignment may also enable you to demonstrate that you can write documents, including extended writing pieces, communicating information, ideas and opinions effectively and persuasively.

2 Understand psychological approaches to health and social care

2.1 Application of the behaviourist perspective

The behaviourist perspective is extremely useful in explaining learned behaviours, as we can look at a particular behaviour and trace its origin, using the concepts of association (classical conditioning) or reinforcement or punishment (operant conditioning). The case study below gives an example of this.

Case study: Understanding challenging behaviour

Farai is 13 years old and was recently admitted to a local authority children's home after her foster placement broke down. She has fierce rages, during which she smashes windows and shouts at people. It turns out that Farai used to behave in exactly this way at her foster home and that everyone ran around trying to please her.

1 Explain, using the terminology of learning theory, how and why Farai may have learned the undesirable behaviours.

2 Do you think an explanation that relies entirely on learning is sufficient to explain Farai's behaviour?

Changing behaviour

For some people, there may be aspects of everyday life that are simply impossible to cope with. A small boy may be unable to go to school or to the park because he has an overwhelming fear of dogs, which he is likely to encounter in the vicinity of school or the park. An elderly woman may never leave her home and be isolated and depressed because her agoraphobia (fear of going out) is so severe that it dominates her life. Fortunately, as well as explaining the development of phobic behaviours, classical conditioning is also useful in helping to change such behaviours.

We can apply the principles of classical conditioning to everyday life in a very practical way. A commonly used method of changing phobic behaviour uses a method of treating acquired fears known as 'systematic

desensitisation'. This involves first creating a 'hierarchy of fear'. Supposing the feared object is hospitals. The individual would create a list of aspects associated with going to hospital. It might look something like this:

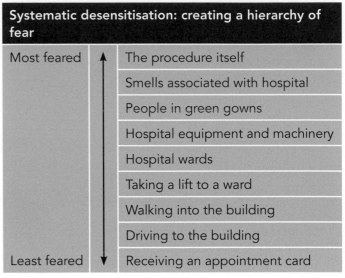

Systematic desensitisation: creating a hierarchy of fear	
Most feared ↑	The procedure itself
	Smells associated with hospital
	People in green gowns
	Hospital equipment and machinery
	Hospital wards
	Taking a lift to a ward
	Walking into the building
	Driving to the building
Least feared ↓	Receiving an appointment card

Fig 8.10: A patient's hierarchy of fear in relation to hospitals

The principle of this procedure is to help the person achieve a state of very deep relaxation – on the assumption that relaxation and anxiety are incompatible. The aim is to replace the anxiety and fear with a state of calm and relaxation. An image of the least feared object or situation is then shown to the individual and they are encouraged to relax until they are able to view this without fear or anxiety. This may take more than one session. When this level of fear has been satisfactorily overcome, the person moves to the object or situation at the next level, again working on relaxing until they are able to contemplate the object or situation without a trace of anxiety. Over a period of time the procedure is repeated until the final, most feared, object or situation can be faced without worry.

With some treatments, the patient is encouraged to practise some of the lower level fear-inducing situations (for example, opening an envelope containing an appointment card or driving as close to the hospital as is tolerable without arousing too much anxiety).

The principles of classical conditioning are also used in a common treatment for alcoholism. Individuals are given a drug which, when mixed with alcohol, leads to extremely unpleasant physiological effects including nausea and vomiting. The person thus learns to associate alcohol with an aversive rather than desired response.

Did you know?

Phobias are culturally specific. In Japan a syndrome known as *tai-jin-kyofu-sho* is a fear of embarrassing other people by, for example, glaring at their genitals while blushing in their presence, or making odd faces. (McNally, 1997, cited in Davison and Neale, 2001, p.129)

Shaping behaviours

Just as we can learn inappropriate or unhelpful behaviours, so we can use the principles of operant conditioning to create new, more helpful, behaviours and eliminate the unhelpful ones. Using the principles of reinforcement and punishment is a very powerful way to change someone's behaviour: this is sometimes called behaviour modification.

This technique has been used with autistic children to help them interact socially. **Target behaviours**, such as making eye contact, are identified. The child is initially reinforced (e.g. with a sweet) for looking in the general area of the adult. Once this behaviour is established, more specific behaviours (e.g. looking at the face) are reinforced, until finally the target behaviour of making eye contact is achieved. This is known as shaping behaviour.

Key term

Target behaviours – Those behaviours that have been defined as being of benefit to the individual's well-being.

2.2 Application of social learning theory

Promotion of anti-discriminatory behaviours and practices

Earlier in this chapter (on p. 344) we discussed the way people can learn new behaviours by observing others. We also noted that the model's characteristics influence whether we are likely to

Activity 5: Investigating the use of role models to promote behaviour change

Take note of television adverts you see over the next few weeks and ask yourself why a particular individual was chosen to promote a product or service. What are the features they have that might appeal to viewers? What influence might they have on your behaviour or that of others?

PLTS

Independent enquirer: By carrying out this activity you may be able to gain evidence for the skill of considering the influence of circumstances, beliefs and feelings on decisions and events.

imitate the behaviour. An example of a model who was prestigious, of high status, attractive and most definitely a 'celebrity' was the late Princess Diana. When she visited patients with HIV and AIDS at a hospital in 1987 and shook hands with a patient with AIDS, she not only broke a taboo on the subject, but also helped remove a great deal of prejudice and misunderstanding about this illness.

Inaugurated in 2009 as the first African American President of the United States of America, Barack Obama is an inspirational role model to all.

Another example of how a model can be influential in promoting anti-discriminatory behaviours and practices is provided by the President of the United States, Barack Obama. When lifting the ban on entering the USA, which had previously applied to individuals with HIV/AIDS, he stated that it was important for the United States to be a good role model as a country – if the overall intention was to take the lead globally in reducing the stigma associated with this disease.

The use of positive role models in health education campaigns

As explained above, role models can play a powerful part in influencing the behaviour of those who observe them. For example, celebrity chef Jamie Oliver has had a huge impact in terms of getting local authorities to re-introduce freshly cooked school meals (as opposed to pre-cooked meals, which were much less healthy). His celebrity status greatly influenced the likelihood of his message being taken on board and acted upon.

On a more practical, everyday level, modelling is an excellent way of helping patients overcome anxieties. For example, Melamed et al (1983) found that children in hospital suffer reduced stress and recover better from surgery if the procedures they are about to undergo are modelled, for example using films or video tapes (cited in Sarafino, 1990, p. 149).

2.3 Application of the psychodynamic perspective to health and social care practice
Understanding challenging behaviour

The basic tenet of this perspective is that much of our behaviour is driven by unconscious forces. It is therefore important to recognise that we may not be able to understand behaviours using question and answer techniques, as the individual may not be aware of what is troubling them. It is necessary to delve a little deeper and try to interpret behaviour, on the assumption that the behaviour is in some way a symptom of what is going on in the unconscious.

Understanding and managing anxiety

When we are anxious we often have fears about events that have happened or might happen, about things we have done or might do, and about whether the world is a safe or unsafe place. We often try to control anxiety using a variety of strategies. Sometimes we use denial – the ostrich approach where we bury our heads in the sand and pretend the object of our anxiety doesn't exist. Sadly, for most of us, the anxiety still seeps through, and may present itself in the form of physical symptoms.

Case study: Juliet's dilemma

Juliet is the eldest of three children. When she was 11, her mother died, and since that time her father has depended on her more and more to look after the younger children and help run the household. Juliet is a naturally conscientious and dutiful daughter and she misses her mother terribly but hides this, as she can see all too well how much she is needed by other family members. She doesn't feel able to confide in her father about her own grief but instead puts a smile on her face and busies herself with daily tasks. When she is 13, she begins to get paralysing headaches, which are so incapacitating that she has to stay in bed for up to three days at a time. Despite optical and neurological tests, there is no physiological explanation for the headaches, which do not resemble migraines either.

Juliet's GP refers her to Aisha, a clinical psychologist with a particular interest in psychodynamic psychology. After several sessions, Aisha concludes

that Juliet has repressed her grief about her mother's death, that she is resentful that her father is not taking better care of her needs, and also that she is effectively having to 'mother' her younger siblings. Juliet's extreme conscientiousness also suggests that she has a dominant superego and a weak id. Although she at first denies these suggestions, Juliet gradually comes to realise that all these feelings were being buried, and the symptom of headaches served the purpose of preventing her from looking after other family members and allowed her to receive some much-needed care herself.

1 Aisha has identified that Juliet is using certain defence mechanisms. What are these?

2 Are there other explanations for Juliet's behaviour that Aisha may have missed by focusing solely on the psychodynamic perspective? Discuss these.

2.4 Application of the humanistic perspective to health and social care practice

Carl Rogers is famous for developing a particular type of counselling based on **unconditional positive regard** from the counsellor, to help the individual develop a more positive sense of self. Unconditional positive regard refers to the idea that the therapist supports and validates the person's experiences, feelings, beliefs and emotions unconditionally (i.e. without making a judgement about whether they are good or bad). In this way, over time, the person comes to accept themselves as they really are and to see themselves as worthy. The incongruence between the actual self and the ideal self dissolves as the two become closer, or the individual lets go of unrealistic expectations associated with the ideal self.

Empathy

One crucial feature of this approach to helping others is to develop empathy. Unlike sympathy, where we feel sorry for someone, empathy requires us to really listen to the other person, be in tune with their emotions and respect them for who they are. This is not always easy, as we do not always understand why someone feels so bad about an issue that we could easily dismiss. However, if we try to respect the individual we are working with and understand that the issue is of crucial importance to them, we can come closer to demonstrating empathy. True empathy requires us to put aside judgements about another person and do all we can to 'put ourselves in their shoes'.

Tips for achieving empathy

Suppose you are working with a client or patient who is terrified that eating more than three grains of rice will make them obese and ruin their lives. You are probably aware that this is factually incorrect. You may find it difficult to understand, let alone feel empathy for such an extreme view.

Now try really listening to them. Observe their body language. They may be so frozen with fear that they appear calm and indifferent. Or they may be so anxious that they are pale and sweaty with huge fearful eyes almost bulging out of their head.

Next, think of something that brings you out in a cold sweat of paralysing fear. This may be something 'real' such as having been buried under an avalanche of snow and fearing for your life, or something imaginary. Recollect this fear. Did it help for people to tell you, 'Well, you were all right, weren't you? You didn't die! Here you are – as well as anything!'? Now put aside all judgement about the individual's fear or terror. Recognise that what they are feeling makes sense to them. It is painful, agonising, terrifying. Tune in to those feelings and you will be much closer to feeling true empathy.

Understanding

Rather like empathy, understanding is of crucial importance when applying this perspective to health and social care practice. In fact, Rogers often refers to more than just understanding at an intellectual level: he talks about empathic understanding, which involves using your own emotions and sensitivity to become a more effective helper. All too often we allow our own personal experience or judgements to dominate the way we relate to others. We think 'Well, that's not a problem – they should just pull themselves together! I've dealt with worse myself!' This is a major barrier to understanding and will not help the client or patient. Instead, we need to listen carefully to what is being said and to ask probing questions that enable the individual to break down the problem and recognise its component parts. Useful questions might include:

- 'How does that make you feel?'
- 'Can you identify what it is you are afraid of?'
- 'Could you tell me a bit more about that?'
- 'That seems to have upset you?'

Key term

Unconditional positive regard – This refers to a totally non-judgemental way of being with and viewing a client. The therapist does not like or approve of the client at some times and disapprove of them at others: they value the client in a positive way with no conditions attached.

Sanjay Bashir
Psychiatric nurse

Sanjay is a community psychiatric nurse who is visiting Irene, a 35-year-old teacher, for the first time. Irene lives in a beautiful five-bedroomed house in a leafy suburb of a university town. Her three children are all at private school and her husband is a respected university professor of biochemistry. Irene has been referred to the outreach team after a suicide attempt and is receiving medication for depression.

Sanjay himself comes from a high-rise in an inner-city suburb and has worked hard to get where he is. During the course of his visit, he finds himself feeling irritated with Irene. What has she got to be depressed about? Her life is the envy of many.

She should just pull herself together and get on with things – many people are far worse off than she is.

Sanjay is, fortunately, aware that his attitude to Irene is unhelpful so he books an appointment with his supervisor, who encourages him to identify where his judgemental feelings are coming from, and to challenge his negative perceptions of Irene. When he next visits her, he is able to use active listening and gentle probing questions to help her express her feelings, and finds that he is feeling empathy and understanding and is in a much better position to help her. He recognises that his own upbringing and experiences have left him with a tendency to be judgemental about others more fortunate than himself in material terms, and that active listening and the tips for empathy described above help him to 'see' Irene more clearly and to hear the pain in her story and thus be more understanding.

Think about it!

1 Explain how Sanjay's own upbringing was at risk of interfering with his ability to adopt a non-judgemental approach

2 Do you think the fact that Sanjay was a man and Irene was a woman might have made a difference to Sanjay's ability to show empathic understanding?

3 How might the humanistic perspective explain Irene's unhappiness?

Active listening

For more information on active listening, see Unit 1.

Another key feature of the humanistic approach is that of active listening. All too often in our interactions with others, what we think of as a conversation is merely two or more people 'queuing up to talk'. We just wait for the other person to finish what they are saying so we can have our own say. This is the opposite of active listening, which involves a very focused approach. We need to avoid daydreaming and distractions and listen sensitively to the meaning and emotions behind the other person's words. Attention is also paid to the person's body language and facial expressions. The active listener suspends all judgement about what is being said and seeks to use empathic understanding. When the listener does intervene, it is not to pass judgement but to interpret what the other person is saying, or to check understanding.

Respecting other individuals and adopting a non-judgemental approach

Giving people respect may seem an obvious feature of a helping relationship but in fact it can sometimes be quite difficult to achieve. If we find it hard to identify with the other person, for example because there are differences in gender, social class, ethnicity, religious beliefs, language, culture and so forth, then we may find ourselves taking a judgemental stance. This is a major barrier to respect. The workspace opposite illustrates this problem.

2.5 Application of the cognitive perspective to health and social care practice

Supporting individuals with learning difficulties

Individuals with learning difficulties can experience enormous frustration in their daily lives as they seek to make sense of what can be bewildering experiences. The cognitive approach can be used to help people who misread situations. By identifying irrational thoughts, an individual can be guided to change them, with consequent benefits for their emotions and behaviour. Cognitive work of this type can improve self-esteem and reduce outbursts, which may be triggered by lack of understanding of the requirements of a given situation (for example, having to wait in turn for a meal).

Consider how a cognitive approach can be used to help people with learning difficulties

Assessment activity 8.2 *continued*

 M2 For M2, you need to compare two psychological approaches to health and social care service provision. Choose just two psychological perspectives and focus on these in detail, as they relate to the new centre you are proposing. You may find it helpful to suggest how practitioners from the two perspectives would work in such a venue and the type of individuals they would help.

D1 To achieve D1, you need to do all of the above but, in addition, you have to evaluate the two approaches, making an informed judgement on which aspects of each perspective are most or least useful, justifying your conclusions.

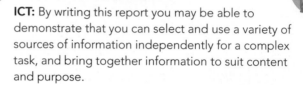

PLTS

Independent enquirer: By focusing on both health provision and social care provision, you may be able to provide evidence for exploring issues, events or problems from different perspectives.

Creative thinker: In applying your knowledge and understanding of the potential uses of this new venue, you may be able to demonstrate creative thinking skills: asking questions to extend your thinking and questioning your own and others' assumptions.

Self manager: By planning and writing this report, you may be able to show evidence of organising time and resources, and prioritising actions.

Functional skills

ICT: By writing this report you may be able to demonstrate that you can select and use a variety of sources of information independently for a complex task, and bring together information to suit content and purpose.

As this is your second assignment, you may also be able to provide evidence that you can produce two different assignments in different formats for different purposes.

English: This assignment may also allow you to demonstrate your research and writing skills.

Resources and further reading

Barker, L.M. (1997) *Learning and Behaviour: Biological, Psychological and Sociocultural Perspectives*, second ed. New Jersey: Prentice Hall

Bettleheim, B. (1967) *The Empty Fortress: Infantile Autism and the Birth of the Self* New York: Macmillan Publishing

Birch, A. and Malim, T. (1988) *Developmental Psychology: From Infancy to Adulthood* Bristol: Intertext Limited

Davison, G.C. and Neale, J.M. (2001) *Abnormal Psychology*, eighth ed. New York: John Wiley and Sons

Ewen, R.B. (1993) *An Introduction to Theories of Personality*, fourth ed. Hove: Lawrence Erlbaum Associates

Eysenck, M.W. (1994) *Perspectives on Psychology* Hove: Psychology Press

Kalat, J.W. (1995) *Biological Psychology*, fifth ed. Pacific Grove: Brooks/Cole Publishing Company

Kelly, G.A. (1970), cited in Ewen, R.B. (1993) *An Introduction to Theories of Personality*, fourth ed. Hove: Lawrence Erlbaum Associates Ltd

Melamed, B.G., Dearborn, M. and Hermecz, D.A. (1983), cited in Sarafino (1990)

Nolte, D.L. & Harris, R. (1998) *Children learn what they live: parenting to inspire values* New York: Workman Publishing

Ritvo, E.R., Freeman, B.J. *et al* (1985), cited in Kalat, J.W. (1995) *Biological Psychology*, fifth ed. Pacific Grove, California: Brooks/Cole Publishing Company

Rogers, C.R. (1961) *On Becoming a Person* London: Constable & Robinson Ltd

Sarafino, E.P. (1998) *Health Psychology: Biopsychosocial Interactions*, third ed. New York: John Wiley & Sons

Sarafino, E.P. and Goldfedder, J. (1995), cited in *Asthma and Genetics* http://acc6.its.brooklyn.cuny.edu/~scintech/asthma/Genetics2.htm

Shaffer, D.R. (1993) *Developmental Psychology: Childhood and Adolescence*, third ed. Pacific Grove: Brooks/Cole Publishing Company

Watson (1970) cited in Smith, P.B. & Bond, M.H. (1993) *Social Psychology across Cultures: Analysis and Perspectives* New York: Harvester Wheatsheaf (p. 103)

Useful websites

Circadian rhythms www.guardian.co.uk/science/2003/dec/04/lastword.health

Cognitive behavioural therapy (Royal College of Psychiatrists) www.rcpsych.ac.uk

Gesell's assessment scale: www.gesellinstitute.org

Health Education & Behavior journal www.sph.umich.edu/hbhe/heb

Infantile autism (NARSAD – The Brain and Behavior Research Fund) www.narsad.org

Mind www.mind.org.uk

Stages of prenatal development www.babycenter.com

Just checking

1 Which psychologist is associated with the theory of classical conditioning?
2 What perspective in psychology uses the terminology of positive reinforcement, negative reinforcement and punishment?
3 Why are features of the model important in observational learning?
4 Can the self-fulfilling prophecy be positive as well as negative? Explain your answer.
5 List three ego defence mechanisms.
6 Which theorist developed a scale to assess normal development in infants and children?
7 List three aspects of circadian rhythms.

Assignment tips

1 You can carry out further research by accessing the following websites:

Behaviourist and social learning theory
http://psychology.about.com/od/behavioralpsychology/a/introopcond.htm (operant conditioning)
http://psychclassics.yorku.ca/Pavlov/
http://psychclassics.yorku.ca/Bandura/bobo.htm

Freud and Erikson
http://www.freudfile.org/theory.html
http://psychology.about.com/library/bl_psychosocial_summary.htm

The humanistic perspective
http://webspace.ship.edu/cgboer/rogers.html
http://www.businessballs.com/maslow.htm

The cognitive perspective
http://webspace.ship.edu/cgboer/piaget.html
http://webspace.ship.edu/cgboer/kelly.html

2 Preparing for assessment: Copy out the following table and complete each section as you work your way through this unit. You will find it helps you to work on the merit and distinction grade material.

Perspective	Strengths	Limitations	My opinion
Behaviourist	*Classical conditioning explains phobias*	*Not everyone develops a phobia*	*There must be other factors, e.g. genes or family influences*
Social learning			
Psychodynamic			
Humanist			
Cognitive developmental			

3 See Unit 4 for more information on aspects of developmental psychology covered in this unit. For more details on how to carry out research, see Unit 22 (Research methodology). You may also want to look at Unit 10 Caring for children and young people and Unit 29 Applied psychological perspectives for help with this unit.

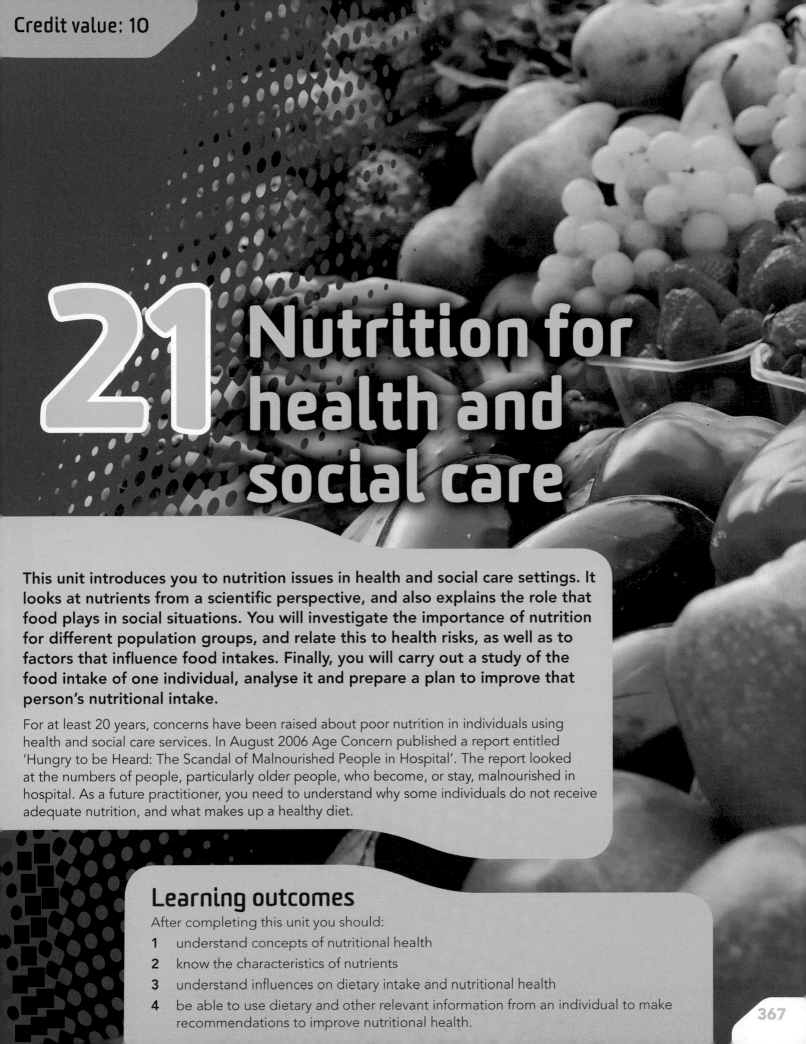

21 Nutrition for health and social care

This unit introduces you to nutrition issues in health and social care settings. It looks at nutrients from a scientific perspective, and also explains the role that food plays in social situations. You will investigate the importance of nutrition for different population groups, and relate this to health risks, as well as to factors that influence food intakes. Finally, you will carry out a study of the food intake of one individual, analyse it and prepare a plan to improve that person's nutritional intake.

For at least 20 years, concerns have been raised about poor nutrition in individuals using health and social care services. In August 2006 Age Concern published a report entitled 'Hungry to be Heard: The Scandal of Malnourished People in Hospital'. The report looked at the numbers of people, particularly older people, who become, or stay, malnourished in hospital. As a future practitioner, you need to understand why some individuals do not receive adequate nutrition, and what makes up a healthy diet.

Learning outcomes

After completing this unit you should:

1 understand concepts of nutritional health
2 know the characteristics of nutrients
3 understand influences on dietary intake and nutritional health
4 be able to use dietary and other relevant information from an individual to make recommendations to improve nutritional health.

Assessment and grading criteria

This table shows you what you must do in order to achieve a **pass**, **merit** or **distinction** grade, and where you can find activities in this book to help you.

To achieve a **pass** grade, the evidence must show that you are able to:	To achieve a **merit** grade, the evidence must show that, in addition to the pass criteria, you are able to:	To achieve a **distinction** grade, the evidence must show that, in addition to the pass and merit criteria, you are able to:
P1 Explain concepts associated with nutritional health **See Assessment activity 21.1, page 380**		
P2 Describe the characteristics of nutrients and their benefits to the body **See Assessment activity 21.2, page 389**	**M1** Discuss similarities and differences in the nutritional and energy requirements of two groups of individuals **See Assessment activity 21.2, page 389**	
P3 Explain possible influences on dietary intake **See Assessment activity 21.3, page 399**	**M2** Assess how influences on dietary intake may affect the nutritional health of individuals **See Assessment activity 21.3, page 399**	**D1** Make realistic recommendations for minimising negative influences on the individuals in a specific health and social care setting **See Assessment activity 21.3, page 399**
P4 Carry out a quantitative analysis of daily intake of nutrients and energy by one individual. **See Assessment activity 21.4, page 402**	**M3** Assess how the plan will meet the nutritional needs of the chosen individual **See Assessment activity 21.4, page 402**	
P5 Prepare a one-week plan for improving the nutrition of the chosen individual. **See Assessment activity 21.4, page 402**		**D2** Evaluate how the nutritional plan might improve the health of the chosen individual **See Assessment activity 21.4, page 402**

How you will be assessed

This unit will be internally assessed by your tutor. Various exercises and activities are included to help you understand all aspects of nutrition in health and social care environments, and prepare for the assessment. You will also have the opportunity to work on some case studies to further your understanding.

Charlene, 17 years old

I have to admit my diet was terrible before I did this unit. I never sat down for a proper meal except on a Sunday, when my Dad cooks me an enormous roast dinner! I used to get up late and rush out of the house without any breakfast. Then I would grab a chocolate bar from the vending machine. At lunch it was a quick trip to the chippy, and then some evenings I was either going out or going to work, so again I was grabbing a quick snack.

This unit has really made me think. Although I am not overweight, I do value my health. My mum died of bowel cancer when I was 12, and my grandad died of a heart attack, so there is certainly a bit of family history to consider. I hadn't realised these things run in families.

So when it came to Assessment activity 21.4 I looked at my own diet, which gave me plenty of food for thought!

What I really enjoyed was learning about all the things that can affect what you choose to eat. I notice the supermarkets' little tricks now, trying to tempt me to buy the wrong things. I sometimes do the shopping and even Dad has commented that I am choosing better things – and our food bill has gone down.

So now I get up a bit earlier, make some sandwiches and have breakfast before college – and guess what – I can concentrate better now as well!

Over to you!

1   Why do you think nutrition is important in health and social care?

2   Which part of this unit do you think you will find most difficult and why?

3   Which aspects of health and nutrition do you find most interesting?

1 Understand concepts of nutritional health

Food, glorious food

How much do you know about healthy eating? Divide into small groups and see which team knows the most about foods that promote good health. Perhaps your tutor will have some healthy prizes for the team that knows the most!

1.1 Concepts

Food

Food is any substance eaten to nourish the body. Food can be solid or liquid, and can be taken by mouth, by tube or even directly into a vein, if a person is unable to eat or drink normally.

Diet

A diet refers to the types of food eaten regularly by an individual. The word diet does not necessarily refer to a weight loss diet. A person's diet means all the meals and snacks they eat.

Meals and snacks

The traditional pattern of eating three meals a day still exists in some households, but a significant number of people gain a lot of their food intake from snacks. Some people have snacks between meals if they feel hungry, and sometimes just because the food is there. Snacks are not necessarily unhealthy.

Nutrients

Nutrients are the specific chemical constituents of food that provide energy or support growth, repair or normal functioning of the body. Protein, carbohydrates, vitamins and minerals are all nutrients.

1.2 Nutritional health

Malnutrition

Malnutrition is any condition in which the body does not receive enough nutrients to function properly. Malnutrition can include undernutrition or **overnutrition**.

Did you know?

Care settings have a unique opportunity to ensure that individuals are well nourished, yet the Nutrition Screening Survey (BAPEN 2007) found that between 19 and 30 per cent of all people admitted to hospitals, care homes and mental health units were at risk of malnutrition. According to Age Concern, six out of ten older people are at risk of becoming malnourished or dehydrated or their situation getting worse. Patients who are malnourished stay in hospital for longer, require more medication, and are more likely to suffer from infections.

Undernutrition

Undernutrition is a deficiency of calories or nutrients and results from eating insufficient food or an inability to digest nutrients from the diet because of a medical condition such as ulcerative colitis (in which food passes through the digestive tract very quickly, preventing nutrients being absorbed into the bloodstream). A body mass index (see page 372) of less than 18.5 is considered underweight by the Department of Health.

Deficiency

A deficiency is the absence of a particular nutrient in the body. This may be due to a lack of the nutrient in the diet, or a medical condition that prevents certain nutrients being absorbed from the diet.

Key term

Overnutrition – A condition that results from eating too much, eating too many of the wrong things, or taking too many vitamins or other dietary supplements.

Overweight

The Department of Health define overweight as having a body mass index greater than or equal to 25. Being overweight increases the risk of arthritis, Type 2 diabetes and high blood pressure.

Obesity

According to the British Nutrition Foundation, obesity is a condition in which abnormal or excessive fat accumulation in adipose tissue impairs health. A person with a body mass index greater than or equal to 30 is considered to be obese.

The National Audit Office warns us that being obese can take up to nine years off our lives. In addition to the social and psychological problems linked to being overweight, people who are obese are far more likely to develop health problems such as cancer, cardiovascular disease, osteoarthritis, gallstones, infertility and depression.

1.3 Nutritional measures

Nutritional and energy balance

The body needs energy to function. Even when you are resting, your body uses energy for all the processes going on inside it. This is known as the basal metabolic rate and depends on your gender, size, and the climate you live in. The amount of extra energy you need depends on your lifestyle. It is important to balance the amount of energy being used and the amount of calories eaten. Too many calories will lead to weight gain, and too few, to weight loss.

Of course, it is not just calories that we need to think about, but the types of foods we eat. You will learn about a balanced diet later in the chapter, but nutritional balance just means having the right proportion of different types of foods.

You can find out more about energy balance on the British Nutrition Foundation website:

www.nutrition.org.uk/nutritionscience/energy

Growth charts

Babies and young children should be taken to the health centre regularly to monitor their weight gain, so that action can be taken if they are not gaining weight or they are putting weight on too quickly. Weight is recorded on a chart which has lines printed on it to show the range of weights for children according to age, so babies can be compared to others of the same age. The range of normality is quite large. The most important thing is the rate of increase, and just because a baby is within the normal range for their age does not mean that all is well. For example, it is worrying if a baby at the top end of the scale stops gaining weight.

Weight for height and gender

When monitoring people's weight, it is important to consider their height (Fig 21.1). Someone weighing 12 stone 7 lb (80 kg) would be very overweight if they were 4 ft 9 in (1.45 m) tall, but normal weight if they were 6 ft 2 in (1.9 m). Men are slightly heavier than women of the same height as they have more muscle.

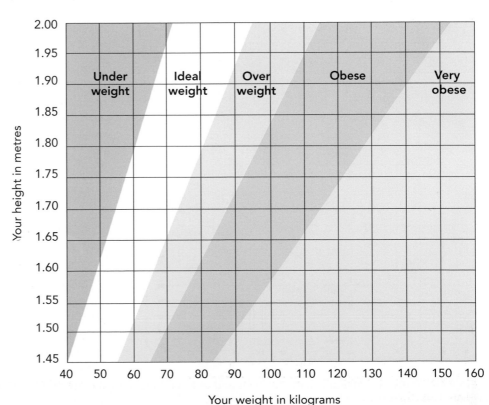

Fig 21.1: This chart is an easy way to check if a person is a healthy weight for their height

Activity 1: See how they grow

Look at the two charts in Fig 21.2. Using the Internet or a child development book, find out what the different lines mean. Compare the difference between the expected height at 5 and 18 years between boys and girls. Contrast the growth patterns of boys and girls.

school entry screen and body mass index [BMI]

The National Screening Committee recommends that the height and weight of every boy in the United Kingdom be measured at, or around, school entry and the data stored for the calculation of BMI for public health and the National Minimum Dataset purposes. A boys BMI centile chart [birth – 18yrs] is available. It also features waist circumference centiles as a second measurement to confirm fatness more conclusively. The International Obesity Task Force definitions of paediatric overweight/obesity [from 2 – 18yrs] are superimposed over the UK centiles to facilitate international comparison. A BMI chart can of course be used to monitor under-nutrition as well as over-nutrition. The charts may be purchased in packs of 20, 50 and 100 upwards.

growth assessment at school

If two growth assessments have not been recorded pre-school, two further assessments should be made after the school entry check and preferably within the next 12 months to establish normal/abnormal growth. Approximately 20% of growth-related disorders may not be identifiable until the school years because of their late onset or their association with puberty.

school entry screen and body mass index [BMI]

The National Screening Committee recommends that the height and weight of every girl in the United Kingdom be measured at, or around, school entry and the data sorted for the calculation of BMI for public health and the National Minimum Dataset purposed. A girls BMI centile chart [birth – 18yrs] is available. It also features waist circumference centiles as a second measurement to confirm fatness more conclusively. The International Obesity Task Force definitions of paediatric overweight/obesity [from 2 – 18yrs] are superimposed over the UK centiles to facilitate international comparison. A BMI chart can of course be used to monitor under-nutrition as well as over-nutrition. The charts may be purchased in packs of 20, 50 and 100 upwards.

growth assessment at school

If two growth assessments have not been recorded pre-school, two further assessments should be made after the school entry check and preferably within the next 12 months to establish normal/abnormal growth. Approximately 20% of growth-related disorders may not be identifiable until the school years because of their late onset or their association with puberty.

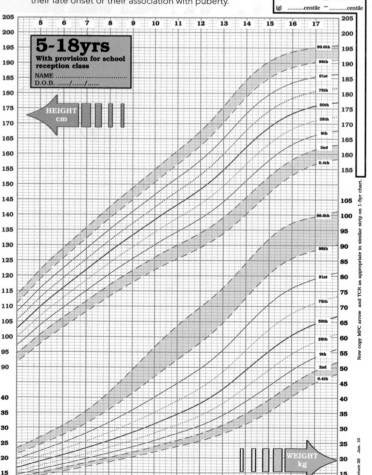
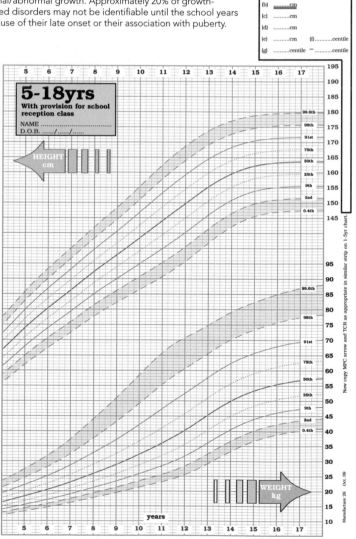

Fig 21.2: There are different charts for boys and girls, and the normal patterns of gaining weight are different according to gender. © Child Growth Foundation

Body mass index

The body mass index is used to decide whether people are the right weight for their height. The ideal BMI is between 18.5 and 24.9.

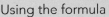

Activity 2: Overweight or obese?

Using the formula

$$BMI = \frac{\text{weight in kilograms}}{(\text{height in metres})^2}$$

calculate the BMI of the following individuals:

- Stewart – weight 50 kg, height 1.7 m
- Shabnam – weight 78 kg, height 1.6 m
- Claude – weight 85 kg, height 1.8 m

Actual food intakes

Sometimes there is a difference between what people think they eat and what they actually eat. For example, a diet may consist of only healthy foods, but if portion sizes are large, an overweight person may be puzzled as to why they are not losing weight. Some people do not realise how often they are eating high-fat, high-sugar foods. A food diary can be quite revealing if it is completed honestly, and is a good starting point for someone who is trying to improve their diet.

Recommended intakes

The Food Standards Agency has produced simple, easy-to-follow guidance on healthy eating, in the form of eight tips:

1 Base your meals on starchy foods.

2 Eat at least 5 portions of fruit and vegetables a day.

3 Eat 2–4 portions of oily fish a week.

4 Cut down on saturated fat and sugar.

5 Try to eat less salt, no more than 6 g a day.

6 Get active and try to be a healthy weight.

7 Drink plenty of water.

8 Don't skip breakfast.

You can find out about recommended intakes of specific types of food later in the chapter.

Dietary Reference Values

Dietary Reference Values (DRVs) are estimates of the amount of energy and nutrients needed for good health. Again, this will vary according to age, size and gender.

Table 21.1: Examples of the information you would expect to find for two different cereals

Cereal A		
Typical values	Per 100 g	Per 30 g serving with 125 ml of semi-skimmed milk
Energy	368 kcal	169 kcal
Protein	8.0 g	6.5 g
Carbohydrate of which sugars	69.1 g 26.5 g	26.7 g 13.9 g
Fat of which saturates	6.6 g 3.6 g	4.0 g 2.4 g
Fibre	7.7 g	2.3 g
Sodium equivalent as salt	0.29 g 0.7 g	0.16 g 0.4 g
Iron	11.9 mg	3.6 mg
Cereal B		
Typical values	Per 100 g	Per 30 g serving with 125 ml of semi-skimmed milk
Energy	327 kcal	157 kcal
Protein	10.8 g	7.4 g
Carbohydrate of which sugars	66.7 g 17.2 g	26.0 g 11.1 g
Fat of which saturates	1.9 g 0.4 g	2.6 g 1.3 g
Fibre	13.6 g	4.1 g
Sodium equivalent as salt	0.57 g 1.4 g	0.24 g 0.6 g
Iron	16.1 mg	4.9 mg

Reference Nutrient Intakes

Reference Nutrient Intakes (RNIs) are used for protein, vitamins and minerals, and are an estimate of the amount that should meet the needs of most of the group to which they apply. They are not minimum targets.

Nutrients per portion and per 100 g of food

When buying packaged foods, the nutritional value has to be displayed on the label. The label explains the amount of calories, protein, fat and carbohydrates provided per serving and per 100 g, and will state how much a 'serving' weighs for that product. Some also list the vitamins and minerals found in that food, and the percentage of the recommended daily amount (RDA) provided. If you want to compare one product with another, compare the amount per 100 g on each product.

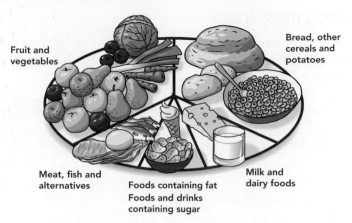

Fig 21.3: The Eatwell Plate – a pie chart like this can help people to visualise the proportion of their daily intake that should come from different types of foods

Activity 3: Choosing foods for good health

Look at the tables on the previous page. Which product would be best for:

- someone with anaemia needing to increase their iron intake?
- someone suffering from constipation who needs a high-fibre diet?
- someone trying to eat fewer calories to lose weight?
- someone with high blood pressure trying to reduce salt intake?

Activity 4: A balanced diet

Look at the Eatwell plate below and estimate what proportion of your diet should be made up of the following types of foods:

- Fruit and vegetables:
- Bread, cereal, potato, rice and pasta
- Milk and dairy produce
- Meat, fish and alternatives, such as soya
- Foods containing fat and sugar.

You could give your answer as a fraction or a percentage, whichever makes most sense to you.

How does this compare with your own intake?

1.4 Dietary intake guidelines

The dietary intake of an individual is simply the food they consume.

Food groups

The Balance of Good Health illustrates food in groups; this is a simple way of categorising foods. The five food groups are:

1 Fruit and vegetables
2 Bread, other cereals and potatoes
3 Milk and dairy products
4 Foods containing fat and foods containing sugar
5 Meat, fish and alternatives.

It is easier for people to plan a healthy diet if advice is not made too complicated. Even children can usually understand these food groups.

Functional skills

Maths: By estimating the proportion of the diet that should come from different types of foods you can provide evidence of mathematical skill, as you will need to understand and use percentages, fractions and angles at the centre of a circle.

Five-a-day

The five-a-day programme promotes the message that people should eat at least five portions of a variety of fruit and vegetables. Fresh, frozen, canned and dried vegetables, fruit and pulses all count. The programme includes health education initiatives to increase public awareness and inform people of the benefits of fruit and vegetable consumption. There are also direct schemes to increase access to fruit and vegetables, such as the Healthy Start programme and the school fruit scheme.

Effect of food preparation/processing methods

The nutritional value of food can be affected by the way food is prepared. Fresh vegetables served raw provide a high nutritional value. Cooking vegetables destroys some of the vitamins, but some cooking methods cause less damage than others. When vegetables are boiled the vitamins are lost in the water, and the longer they are boiled the more vitamins are lost. A study carried out by Professor Paul Thornalley at Warwick University, published in 2007, found that the anti-cancer substances found in green vegetables are much reduced by boiling.

If you use the vegetable water to make gravy, you can save some of the vitamins, or vegetables can be steamed instead of boiled to retain much of their nutritional value. Stir-frying is also a good cooking method for retaining vitamins, and only requires a minimal amount of fat.

Frying food retains nutrients, and dry-frying (frying without adding fat to the pan) is a useful method if you wish to have a quick, healthy meal.

The nutritional value of food is also reduced by keeping food hot, so whenever possible food should be served up as soon as it is cooked.

Food manufacturers use various methods to prevent food from deteriorating. Canning, freezing, and sealing in vacuum packs are all ways of commercially preserving foods.

Canning involves heating food to very high temperatures to destroy bacteria, and, although carbohydrate and protein are not affected by this, some vitamins are – in particular, vitamins B_1 and C. Canned food does not deteriorate for years, so it is better to eat canned foods than vegetables that are deteriorating, or meat that is past its use-by date. Canned food has been criticised as being less nutritious than fresh food, and often having high salt

or sugar content. However, many manufacturers have responded to these criticisms and it is now possible to buy fish and vegetables in spring water and fruit in natural juice.

Freezing foods is an excellent way to preserve goodness.

Vacuum-packed foods, including bacon and fish, can be kept in the fridge for two or three weeks. The majority of bacteria found in food need air to reproduce, so vacuum packing will slow down the rate at which food goes off. The fridge should be kept below 3°C for these foods, as this will prevent bacteria that can breed without air from multiplying. Vacuum-packed foods are sometimes also heated for a short while, or preserved in salt solution, to increase their shelf life.

UHT stands for Ultra-High Temperature. UHT milk is briefly heated, for one or two seconds, to 135°C, which kills off any bacteria and spores in the milk. The milk is then cooled quickly and packaged in sterile cartons. The milk will not deteriorate for six to nine months, as it is the bacteria in milk that cause it to go off.

Pasteurisation also involves heating milk, but only to 73°C for 15 seconds. It kills most bacteria, but not all, so after a week or so the milk will start to go off. Most people prefer the taste of pasteurised milk to UHT.

1.5 Current nutritional issues
Food labelling

Falsely describing food is an offence. The Food Labelling Regulations 1996 require food to be marked or labelled including the following information:

* the name of the food
* a list of ingredients (including foods often linked to allergies)
* an appropriate 'best before' or 'use by' date
* any special storage instructions and cooking instructions
* the name and address of the manufacturer, packer or retailer
* the country of origin.

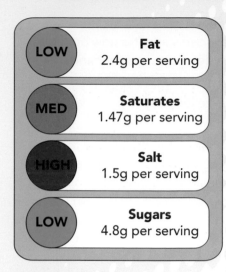

LOW	**Fat**	2.4g per serving
MED	**Saturates**	1.47g per serving
HIGH	**Salt**	1.5g per serving
LOW	**Sugars**	4.8g per serving

Fig 21.4: The Food Standards Agency recommends 'at a glance' information on food packaging, giving consumers information about the nutritional content of foods through the use of traffic light colours

Functional skills

English: You could provide evidence of your English skills by making a significant contribution to the group discussion, and helping to formulate the key points.

PLTS

Creative thinker: You can demonstrate your creative thinking ability by examining the issues from different angles.

Self-manager: Self-management skills are required to organise your research and work with other members of your group.

Organic food

Organic farming involves restrictions on the use of fertilisers and pesticides to control pests and diseases. Organic food products must use ingredients that were produced organically, and organic ingredients must make up at least 95 per cent of the food. There are only a limited number of additives used in organic food production.

Genetically modified foods

Genetically modified food involves altering the genetic make-up of a plant or animal, or inserting one from another organism – that is, a living thing. Genes carry the instructions for all the characteristics that an organism inherits. They are made up of DNA. Food is genetically modified for several reasons: to produce higher yields; to make them poisonous to pests that

previously damaged the crop; to make them more nutritious; or to make foods deteriorate more slowly.

You can find out more about genetic modification on www.bionetonline.org (or refer to Bionet 2009).

Environmental aspects of food production

Modern methods of food production can affect the environment in many ways. Pollution problems are caused by the use of pesticides and fertiliser. There are also links between meat production and global warming because it has been estimated that meat production is responsible for nearly one-fifth of emissions of greenhouse gases (UN Food and Agriculture Organization 2008). This is because cows release methane, which causes substantially more global warming than carbon dioxide.

Another related issue is deforestation. Meat production is a good source of income in less developed countries, and unfortunately this encourages farmers to increase the amount of land used for growing soy, which is used for cattle feed. This has led to the destruction of vast areas of forest in South America. In addition, the use of hazardous pesticides to spray the soy crop sometimes causes health problems for local people.

Self-prescribed health supplements

According to the Food Supplements (England) Regulations 2003, food supplements are defined as 'food sold in dose form whose purpose is to supplement the normal diet, and which is a concentrated source of a vitamin or mineral or other substance with a nutritional or physiological effect, alone or in combination'.

Activity 5: Finding out the truth about food production and the environment

Look on the Internet and investigate the following topics:

- pesticides
- fertilisers
- global warming
- deforestation.

1 In small groups, look at the sources you find and, in each case, consider the writer's viewpoint. Is the article sensationalist or factual, or a bit of both?

2 Draw up a list of six key factual points for each topic.

There is a huge range of products marketed to supplement our diet. These range from vitamin and mineral supplements to unusual substances like gingko biloba, green-lipped mussel and devil's claw, which are sold with carefully worded claims about their health-improving properties.

Activity 6: What's the evidence?

Research on the Internet what gingko biloba, green-lipped mussel and devil's claw are reputed to do. Look at the way the claims are worded, and investigate any scientific proof about the benefits of taking these supplements. Then consider what care workers should do if asked for advice about alternative therapies.

Functional skills

ICT: Finding out information about supplements from secondary sources will show that you can select and use appropriate sources of ICT-based and other forms of information that match requirements.

Some people struggle to consume sufficient amounts of important vitamins and minerals due to their diet. This can include fussy eaters, those on a special diet, and people with conditions leading to poor absorption or frequent attacks of diarrhoea. Some people need to consume high quantities of particular nutrients; for example, a woman who suffers from heavy periods may benefit from iron supplements.

Under the Food Supplements (England) Regulations 2003, the supplement container must state:

- the name of the substance
- the recommended daily amount
- a warning not to exceed the stated recommended daily dose
- a statement to say that food supplements should not be used as a substitute for a varied diet.

There are a number of foods that have recently been given the status of 'superfoods'. These include blueberries, strawberries, goji berries, walnuts and watercress. Generally these foods are high in **antioxidants**.

In October 2009 the European Food Safety Authority brought in regulations to ban the use of health claims that could not be scientifically proven.

Treatments for obesity

Reducing diets

The first method most people try is a reducing diet, which is lower in calories than those being used by the individual. By doing this, the person has to use energy stored by the body as fat to provide energy not obtained through eating, so they should lose weight. Many 'fad' diets have been created over the years, but the principle remains the same: eating less than the energy you use.

Exercise

Along with reducing the number of calories being eaten, increasing exercise will use more energy up, and has the added benefit of improving heart health and mental well-being.

Surgery

Surgery is only considered in the case of people who are classed as **morbidly obese**, with a BMI of 35 or more. At this size, people have significant health risks, such as heart disease and diabetes. If they have been unable to reduce their weight through diet and exercise, surgery may be considered. Patients will only be accepted for this treatment if they are fit for anaesthetic, and if they are prepared to commit to follow-up care, to ensure that the cost can be justified.

Surgery is performed to reduce the amount of food that can be eaten or digested.

There are three operations widely used in weight-loss surgery:

- gastric band (also known as stomach stapling)
- gastric bypass
- intra-gastric balloon.

Medication

It is now recognised that obesity is a complicated disorder, and that weight loss is very difficult for some people to achieve.

Key terms

Antioxidants – Substances that are especially good at destroying free radicals (harmful molecules that damage cells and DNA and can contribute to ageing, heart disease and cancer). Antioxidants are therefore thought to lower the risk of developing cancer and heart disease.

Morbidly obese – When a person's weight is causing disease, and likely to shorten their life.

Currently there are two drugs approved to help with weight loss, Orlistat (Alli) and Sibutramine (Reductil). They still require the person to eat a healthy diet and exercise, but make it a little easier to lose weight.

To find out more, you can visit www.nationalobesity forum.org.uk (National Obesity Forum 2009).

Advertising food

There has been a lot of media coverage on the topic of obesity in children, and food advertisers have been heavily criticised for influencing children to pester parents to buy unhealthy foods. Of course, this only applies to children. Adults are expected to be able to understand the basics of healthy eating and not be so easily influenced by advertisements.

Case study: Georgia

Georgia is 18 years old. When she was 8 she already weighed 10 stone (63 kg). She was being teased at school. Her mum and the school nurse put her on diets, but Georgia comfort-ate when they weren't looking, and her weight continued to rise. Now she is 18 and her weight is nearly 28 stone (177 kg). She has difficulty walking, high blood pressure, and sleep apnoea, which means that her breathing keeps stopping during the night.

1 Investigate and discuss with your peers the options available to Georgia.

2 What are the pros and cons of each of the treatments available for morbidly obese individuals?

3 Discuss whether these treatments should be available on the NHS, trying to see both sides of the argument.

Did you know?

In 2003, Ofcom, responsible for standards on TV and radio, was asked to consider restricting the advertising of junk food. As a result, since December 2008 foods containing high levels of fat, salt and sugar may not be advertised at times when children are likely to be watching TV.

Restrictions on advertising in non-broadcast media, such as children's magazines, are even stricter, and only fresh fruit and vegetables may be promoted in this way.

It is also not permitted to use recognised cartoon characters to promote unhealthy foods.

To find out more, visit www.asa.org.uk (Advertising Standards Authority).

Using psychology, might it be possible to tempt people to buy healthy foods in the same way as they are attracted to high-fat, high-sugar foods?

Jackie McMahon
Community project worker

Jackie works at a community project set up in a former mining village in South Yorkshire. It is part of the Health Action Zone set up to improve the health of the local community. The obesity rates in the village are much higher than average and Jackie has been researching the eating habits of the local community. She wasn't surprised to find a high consumption of high-fat, high-sugar foods and a poor intake of fruit and vegetables.

Jackie decided to try to gain more understanding of the psychology used by shops to persuade customers to buy certain goods.

The project opened a community shop in the centre, so they could try the same techniques to persuade people to buy healthy foods.

Jackie found out that retailers have become very skilled at persuading consumers to spend their money. In supermarkets the smell of freshly baked bread is often pumped out to draw people to the in-store bakery, or just to make shoppers feel hungry.

Products the retailer is trying to persuade shoppers to buy on impulse are placed at the entrance and at the ends of aisles.

The large supermarket chains produce own-brand products, which have a higher profit margin than branded ones, so they often position them near well-known brands, hoping the consumer will buy the cheaper alternative.

The products that give the highest profit are often stacked at eye-level, as it is known that consumers are more likely to buy products in their line of sight.

Think about it!

1 What are the major influences on your own family's food consumption? Think about the last week. Why did your family buy the food it did?

2 Discuss with other people in your group reasons for making particular food purchases.

3 Devise a plan for Jackie to use in the new shop. Think about different types of consumers, including children, teenagers, adults and older people, males and females.

Global food inequalities

According to the International Food Policy Research Institute, 'Twenty-nine countries around the world have alarming levels of hunger, and thirteen countries have actually seen increases in their hunger levels since 1990'. At the other end of the scale, the World Health Organization reports that there are more than a billion overweight adults in the world and 300 million of these are obese. Why do these differences exist?

Assessment activity 21.1

Task A

Produce a booklet suitable for patients in a health centre to improve their understanding of nutrition.

- Start with a page explaining the terms: food, diet, meals and nutrients.
- Explain what nutritional measures and dietary guidelines could be used to identify a person who was malnourished, undernourished, deficient in certain nutrients, overweight or obese.
- Use illustrations and examples to make the information easier to understand.
- Explain the dietary intake guidelines that are published to help individuals to have a balanced diet.

Task B

Carry out research to extend your knowledge about *one* of the nutritional issues discussed in Section 1.5. Then prepare a wall display or presentation to explain how that issue impacts on the nutritional content of food.

> **Grading tip**
>
> To achieve P1, you need to explain concepts associated with nutritional health. Take care to use clear, simple language. This will show your understanding and your ability to explain the concepts of nutrition to other people.

---

2 Know the characteristics of nutrients

2.1 Characteristics of nutrients

This section will help you to understand which foods are important sources of particular nutrients, and the functions of those nutrients in the body. This will enable you to offer suitable foods to ensure that nutritional needs are met. You also need to understand the way in which processing (such as heat and storage) can affect the nutritional value of foods, so you can avoid the destruction of nutrients.

2.2 Carbohydrates

Carbohydrates provide energy for the body. Even when you are asleep, your cells need oxygen and nutrients to function. Your heart needs to beat, your brain needs energy to maintain your vital functions and you need to replace cells. This is known as basal metabolism. When you are active you need energy for movement. About 50 per cent of the total dietary intake should come from carbohydrates. There are two different types of carbohydrate, simple carbohydrates (or sugars) and complex carbohydrates (starches and fibre).

Sugars

Sugars occur naturally in foods, such as fruit and milk, or can be added. Some of the simplest forms of sugar are glucose and fructose (found in fruit). These are monosaccharides, single molecules, and are easily digested by the body. Glucose can be absorbed into the bloodstream and transported around the body to provide energy.

Disaccharides are formed when two monosaccharides combine. Common disaccharides include sucrose, lactose and maltose. Sucrose is table sugar, and is a combination of glucose and fructose; lactose is the natural sugar in milk and is a combination of glucose and galactose. Maltose comes from grains and is a combination of two glucose molecules.

Sugars are added to many types of foods. Biscuits and cakes contain added sugar, but you may not be aware that there is sugar in tomato ketchup, beer, high-fibre snack bars and some tinned vegetables. It is recommended by the British Nutrition Foundation that no more than 11 per cent of an adult's diet should be sugar.

Fig 21.5: Sugar is in many foods and drinks, not all of which taste particularly sweet

Starch

The Food Standards Agency recommends that a third of the food we eat should come from starchy foods like pasta, rice, bread, potatoes, and chapattis. Starchy foods, sometimes referred to as complex carbohydrates, release energy more slowly than sugars, so they will keep you satisfied longer. Starches are polysaccharides, made of many monosaccharide molecules combined together.

All carbohydrates have to be broken down into glucose before the cells can use the energy. If the body doesn't need all the glucose in the bloodstream the hormone insulin is released from the pancreas, which converts the excess glucose into glycogen. This is stored in the liver and muscles. Excess glucose may also be stored as body fat.

Eating insufficient carbohydrates may result in protein being used for energy instead of for growth and repair.

If a person's diet is seriously deficient in carbohydrate the body starts to break down muscle and other tissue to produce glucose. This causes a state known as ketosis, and is more often associated with people with diabetes, who are unable to use glucose in the bloodstream in the absence of insulin. Another group where this may be seen is those with anorexia nervosa.

A diet low in carbohydrate is likely to be low in fibre, vitamins A, B group, and E, calcium, magnesium, iron and potassium and antioxidants. Such a diet could increase the chances of a person developing cancer and other diseases.

Non-starch polysaccharides

Non-starch polysaccharides (also known as fibre) are an important component of a healthy balanced diet obtained from vegetables and cereals. There are two types of fibre: soluble and insoluble.

Soluble fibre can be partially digested and is important in reducing cholesterol in the blood. It also helps to control blood sugar levels, which in turn control appetite. Pulses, such as peas, beans and lentils, are a good source of soluble fibre, as are oats.

Insoluble fibre is contained in vegetable stalks, wholemeal cereal and brown rice, for example. It is also known as cellulose. Insoluble fibre is not absorbed by the body and therefore contains no usable calories. It is important because it forms the bulk in our faeces, preventing constipation, and is thought to help prevent bowel cancer and other bowel conditions. Fibre makes people feel full, so they are less likely to overeat.

Sugar substitutes (e.g. artificial sweeteners, sorbitol)

Artificial sweeteners allow food to be sweetened without the use of sugars, which are high in calories and cause tooth decay. Saccharin was the first sweetener to be developed in 1879. Aspartame was approved in 1982, and has the advantage of being suitable to use to replace sugar in recipes, which is not possible with saccharin. Sorbitol is used to produce sugar-free products. Artificial sweeteners are 200 to 300 times sweeter than sugar, so only a tiny amount is needed. Every time you use sweetener instead of sugar in drinks you save 15 calories per level teaspoonful. A diet soft drink has very few calories, whereas a normal version has about 150.

2.3 Proteins

Protein is a vital nutrient used by the body for growth and repair, so it is particularly important for infants and children, and people who are ill or injured. Proteins are made up of amino acids.

Amino acids all have the same basic molecular structure: a carbon atom, with four groups of atoms attached. One of the four groups is always one nitrogen and two hydrogen atoms, and this is the amino group. Another is always one carbon, one hydrogen and two oxygen atoms, and this is the acid group. The third is a single atom of hydrogen, and the fourth is a variable side chain and is the part that distinguishes one amino acid from another.

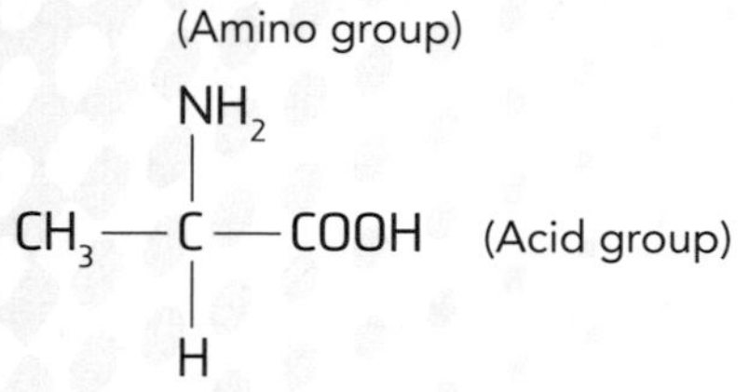

(Amino group)

$$CH_3 - \overset{\overset{\displaystyle NH_2}{|}}{\underset{\underset{\displaystyle H}{|}}{C}} - COOH \quad \text{(Acid group)}$$

Fig 21.6: The amino acid alanine

Polypeptides, essential and non-essential amino acids

Proteins are formed when amino acids join together in chains, known as polypeptides. They are linked by peptide **covalent bonds**. The amino end of one amino acid links with the acid group of another. There are 20 different amino acids, which can combine to form

Key term

Covalent bond – A bond in which two atoms are connected to each other by sharing two or more electrons.

different polypeptides, eight of which must come from the food we eat. The rest we can make ourselves. Complete proteins provide all the eight essential amino acids and include meat, fish, poultry, eggs, milk, soya and cheese.

Protein is used in the body in a variety of ways. All tissues in the body contain protein, including hair and bone. Enzymes and hormones are also proteins. Proteins are used in all activities taking place inside the body, such as messages travelling along nerves, digesting food, and muscles contracting.

The recommended daily intake of protein, according to the Food and Agriculture Organization of United Nations (2009), varies according to age, size, gender and how active a person is. For example, a baby boy weighing 4 kg needs approximately 10 g of protein per day – about 2.5 g per kg body weight. An adult only needs about 0.6 g of protein per kg body weight, so if you weigh 60 kg you need about 36 g of protein a day.

It is unusual for people in the UK to be short of protein in their diet, and it certainly should not be the case in a residential care setting, although people receiving daycare may not receive an adequate diet at home. If someone is following a vegan or vegetarian diet you must make sure it is varied, so that all the eight essential amino acids are eaten. Don't worry too much, as the body can store amino acids for a short time, so as long as the diet is varied and well-balanced there shouldn't be a problem. Good vegan sources of protein include nuts, seeds, lentils, beans and soya. In fact 2 oz (56 g) of kidney beans, chickpeas and lentils contain as much protein as 3 oz (85 g) of steak. These nutritious foods are low in fat and loaded with fibre so they will keep you feeling full for a long time.

Foods we consider as protein foods are not pure protein. For example, 100 g of lean beef contains about 23 g of protein.

2.4 Lipids

The term 'lipids' means fats and oils. Lipids are insoluble in water. About 95 per cent of lipids in our diet are triglycerides, which are made up of three fatty acids attached to glycerol. Bile is secreted from the gall bladder into the digestive tract, and lipase is secreted from the pancreas into the jejunum. These two substances split the fatty acids and glycerol apart.

Fatty acids can be used as energy in most cells.

Glycerol can be converted into glucose by the liver and can be used for cellular respiration. We need to have some fat in our diet, as it is an important source of vitamins A, D, E and K. We also need to eat fat to make hormones, to keep our skin healthy and to prevent loss of body heat. If we eat too much fatty food it is stored as adipose tissue, leading to obesity.

Monounsaturates, polyunsaturates, and saturates

Fatty acids are made up of carbon, hydrogen and oxygen. They are arranged as a carbon chain with hydrogen atoms attached and an identical COOH acid group to protein at one end. Each carbon atom has the potential to bond with four other atoms. There are two main types of fat: saturated and unsaturated. In saturated fats the carbon atoms are joined in a chain by single bonds, and the remaining bonds are with hydrogen atoms, apart from the last carbon atom, which is attached to the acid group. Monounsaturated fatty acids have two fewer hydrogen atoms than the carbon atoms could hold, and instead there is one double bond between two of the carbon atoms. Polyunsaturated fats have four or more less hydrogen atoms and consequently two or more double bonds between carbon atoms.

The monounsaturated and polyunsaturated molecules are too big to fit on the page, so the illustrations below show the principle rather than a specific molecule.

Most saturated fat, such as lard, cream, butter and the

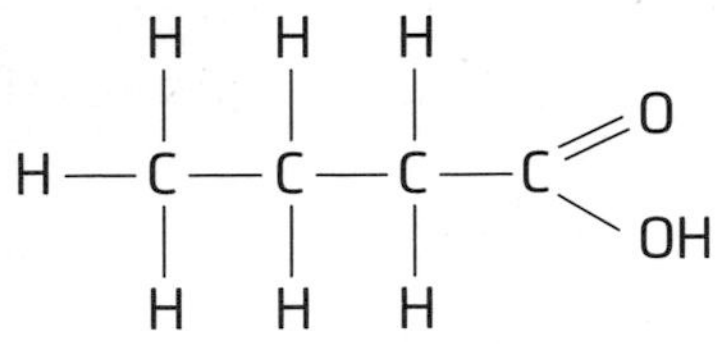

Fig 21.7: Butyric acid (saturated)

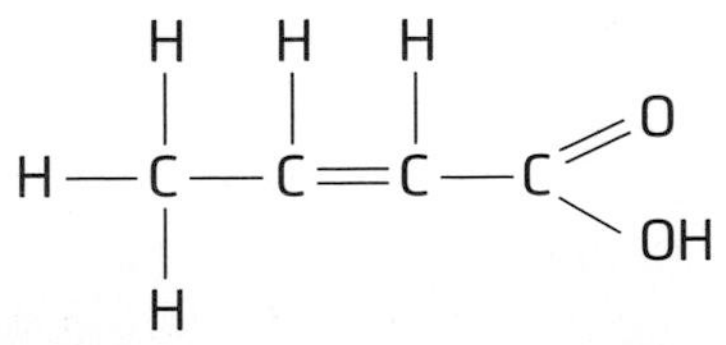

Fig 21.8: An example of a monounsaturated fatty acid molecule

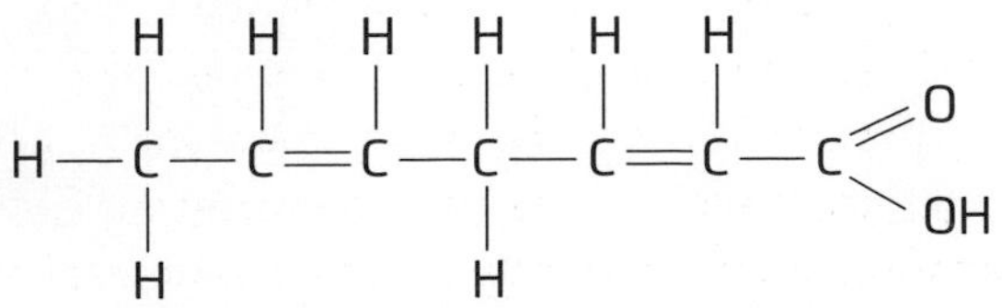

Fig 21.9: An example of a polyunsaturated fatty acid molecule

fat on meat, comes from animal sources. Saturated fat is generally solid at room temperature. Most unsaturated fat is from vegetable sources, and it is usually liquid at room temperature.

Unsaturated fats contain essential fatty acids that cannot be manufactured by the body so we need to get them from food. Unsaturated fat in the diet can lower the levels of low-density lipoproteins (LDLs), known as 'bad' cholesterol in the blood, and raise the levels of high-density lipoproteins (HDLs), known as 'good cholesterol'. HDLs protect against heart disease. Saturated fat is blamed for the high rate of heart disease and strokes in the UK. There is also some evidence that a diet high in saturated or unsaturated fat can increase the risk of cancer.

Cis and trans fats

Unsaturated fats can exist in two different forms, as cis fats or trans fats. Most of the fats found in plants exist in the form of cis. Cis fats are monounsaturated or polyunsaturated, but have a short shelf life. Hydrogenation is the process of adding hydrogen to cis fats to change them into trans fats, which makes them saturated. It increases the shelf life, but the resulting products have been found to increase the risk of heart disease, and many food manufacturers have stopped using them in their products.

Cholesterol

We naturally make a certain amount of cholesterol ourselves, and some people make more than others. Cholesterol can build up in the artery walls, narrowing the lumen (the channel within the artery). If this happens in the coronary arteries it may eventually lead to angina or a heart attack. If arteries in the brain are affected the risk of stroke is increased. People who naturally make a high amount of cholesterol need to be particularly careful to eat a diet low in saturated fat. They can be prescribed tablets called statins, which reduce the cholesterol in the blood, thus reducing the chances of a heart attack or stroke. Some people are lucky and have a naturally low cholesterol level.

It is recommended that adults and children over five years, have a low-fat diet. Children under five years may struggle to get sufficient calories to meet their energy needs if their diet is low in fat. You cannot dictate to people what they eat, but it is important to offer healthier alternatives and ensure that individuals are aware of healthy eating advice.

Table 21.2: The major vitamins, their functions, sources and characteristics

Vitamin and RDA	Functions	Food sources	Effects of shortage	Water/fat soluble	Notes
A 800 μg	Night vision; keeps skin and linings of nose, mouth, lungs and gut healthy; antioxidant	Fish oil, liver, butter, cheese, eggs, milk, fruit and vegetables	Night blindness, itching, dry and thickened skin	Fat soluble	Stored in liver; excess can be harmful
D 5 μg	Absorption of calcium in intestine; regulates calcium and magnesium in bone tissue	Fish liver, oily fish, eggs, milk, margarine, sunlight	Rickets, osteomalacia, fractures	Fat soluble	Produced in skin by sun; stored in liver
E 12 mg	Maintains healthy muscles; antioxidant; protects cell membranes	Eggs, cereal oils, vegetable oils, nuts, seeds	Poor muscle, circulatory and nerve performance	Fat soluble	
K 75 μg	Blood clotting	Leafy vegetables (especially spinach and celery), cheese and liver, asparagus, coffee, bacon and green tea	Rare, bleeding into brain in newborn babies	Fat soluble	Widely given by injection to babies at birth; can be made by intestinal bacteria
B group (see table below for RDA)	Release of energy from carbohydrates; metabolism of fats and proteins; health and maintenance of nervous system	Liver, yeast, leafy green vegetables, nuts, milk and whole grains.	B_1 Beri-beri, B_3 Pellagra B_9 Megaloblastic anaemia, neural tube defects (Spina bifida and Hydrocephalus, which occur during development of unborn baby) B_{12} Pernicious anaemia	Water soluble	
C	Formation of bones, teeth and blood; wound healing; fighting infection, healthy skin and gums; antioxidant	Blackcurrants, citrus fruits, green vegetables, peppers, tomatoes	Scurvy, poor healing, easy bruising	Water soluble	Not stored in body so daily dose needed; lost in cooking

2.5 Vitamins

Vitamins are essential nutrients that your body needs in small amounts to work properly. There are two types of vitamins: fat-soluble and water-soluble. Fat-soluble vitamins can be stored in the body and therefore do not have to be eaten daily, whereas excess water-soluble vitamins are excreted in the urine, so a daily intake is necessary. Soaking vegetables in water for long periods before cooking results in vitamins being lost in the water. Chopping vegetables too small creates a larger surface area, and more nutrients will be lost. If you do boil vegetables, use the water to make gravy. Vitamins are also lost when food is kept hot after cooking.

Table 21.2 shows the main vitamins, their functions, food sources and deficiency diseases, based on information from the Food Labelling (Nutrition Information) (England) Regulations 2009. The recommended daily allowance (RDA), of vitamins is shown in Table 21.3.

Table 21.3: RDAs for B group vitamins

Vitamin	RDA
Thiamin (B_1)	1.1 mg
Riboflavin (B_2)	1.4 mg
Niacin (B_3)	16 mg
Pyrodoxine (B_6)	1.4 mg
Folic Acid (B_9)	200 µg
Cyanocobalamin B_{12}	2.5 µg
Biotin (B_7)	50 µg
Pantothenic acid (B_5)	6 mg

2.6 Minerals

There are six major minerals and eight trace minerals found in food. Major minerals include iron, calcium, magnesium, sodium and potassium. Even though some are only required in tiny amounts, they are needed for chemical processes in the body and our health suffers if we do not get them.

Iron

Iron is essential for the production of haemoglobin in red blood cells. It also helps the immune system and growth in childhood. Haemoglobin is the oxygen-carrying part of the cell, so without sufficient haemoglobin a person will become anaemic. They will be breathless, feel tired and cold, may be dizzy and may have headaches. The pulse will be fast. It can also affect concentration.

Good sources of iron in the diet are dark green leafy vegetables, red meat, liver, apricots, dried fruit and many breakfast cereals. Vitamin C increases absorption of iron. Taking iron supplements may cause constipation, nausea, vomiting and stomach ache. If someone is taking iron supplements their faeces will be black, and people should be warned of this so as to avoid alarm. The recommended intake of iron for adults is 14 mg per day.

Calcium

A good calcium intake is needed to develop strong bones and teeth. Vitamin D is required for the absorption of calcium from the small intestine. Calcium is laid down in the bones up to early adulthood, so it is particularly important for young females to eat lots of calcium-rich foods to reduce the risk of osteoporosis in later life. Calcium is also essential for blood clotting, and helps the heart, muscles and nerves to work properly. Calcium activates certain enzymes. Good sources of calcium include milk, bread, flour, cheddar cheese, skimmed milk, green vegetables, sardines (with bones) and tofu. Insufficient calcium in the diet causes rickets, osteomalacia, osteoporosis and muscle cramps. The recommended intake of calcium in adults is 800 mg per day.

Other major minerals

The tables on the next page (adapted from Food Standards Agency, www.eatwell.gov.uk) give you information about other important minerals.

Trace elements

Trace elements are minerals that are only required in very tiny amounts, so unless a person has a specific condition, such as a genetic abnormality, it is highly unlikely that a deficiency will occur. Trace elements include zinc and selenium.

2.7 Energy
Dietary sources and measurements

The main dietary sources of energy are fats and carbohydrates. Energy is measured in both kilocalories and kilojoules, with both being displayed on food labels.

Table 21.4: Magnesium, sodium and potassium: functions, sources and characteristics

Mineral and RDA	Function	Food sources	Effects of shortage	Notes
Magnesium 375 mg	Needed for storing, burning and using energy; keeps all the minerals in balance; helps muscles to work properly and keeps bones and teeth strong; it has an important role in reducing blood pressure	Green leafy vegetables, nuts and grains	Symptoms include insomnia, muscle cramps, palpitations, cold hands, soft or brittle nails and depression	High levels of magnesium also cause symptoms such as nausea, muscle weakness, low blood pressure and an irregular heartbeat
Sodium 1600 mg	Helps maintain fluid balance (sodium works with potassium); regulates blood pressure; aids muscle contraction and nerve transmission	Occurs naturally in eggs, meat, vegetables, milk; added to many processed foods	Dizziness, confusion, tiredness, muscle cramps	Salt lost by body in diarrhoea and sweating; restriction needed in renal disease and high blood pressure
Potassium 2000 mg	Helps maintain fluid balance (with sodium); needed for cells and nerve function; controls pH of blood	Found in most foods; good sources include potatoes, fruit (especially bananas), vegetables and juices	Irregular heartbeat, muscle weakness	Most is absorbed; excess is excreted by kidneys; excess can cause heart failure

Table 21.5: Selenium and zinc: functions, sources and characteristics

Mineral and RDA	Function	Food sources	Effects of shortage	Notes
Selenium 55 µg	Selenium plays an important role in the immune system's function, in thyroid hormone metabolism and in reproduction; it is also part of the body's antioxidant defence system, preventing damage to cells and tissues	Good food sources include Brazil nuts, bread, fish, meat and eggs	Keshan disease, a potentially fatal form of cardiomyopathy (disease of the heart muscle)	Too much selenium causes selenosis, a condition that in its mildest form can lead to loss of hair, skin and nails
Zinc 10 mg	Helps make new cells and enzymes; helps process carbohydrate, fat and protein; helps with healing of wounds	Meat, shellfish, milk and dairy foods such as cheese; bread, and cereal products such as wheatgerm	Hair loss, loss of taste, poor wound healing, diarrhoea, and failure to thrive in children	Taking high doses of zinc reduces the amount of copper the body can absorb; this can lead to anaemia and to weakening of the bones

(Information in tables adapted from Food Standards Agency, www.eatwell.gov.uk)

We normally work in kilocalories in the UK, but confusingly refer to them just as calories.

1000 calories = 1 kilocalorie = 1 kcal = the energy it takes to raise the temperature of 1 kg of water by 1°C

1 kilocalorie = 4.2 kilojoules

The Food Standards Agency currently recommends an average daily intake for adults as 2000 calories for women and 2500 for men.

Energy values for protein, fat, carbohydrate and alcohol

The energy density for proteins and carbohydrates is 4 calories per gram, compared to 9 calories per gram for fat, so you should avoid fat to lose weight.

Alcohol provides 7 calories per gram of alcohol, so the calories in alcoholic drinks depend on the percentage of alcohol they contain. Drinks with high-percentage alcohol, like spirits, have more calories for their volume than lower-percentage alcoholic drinks like beer and lager. For example, 50 ml gin has just over 100 calories, whereas 50 ml lager has 20 calories.

2.8 Other diet-related consumption

Water

Water is not only found in drinks, but is also a component of many foods. For example, fresh celery is 94 per cent water. Water makes up 70 per cent of the body's weight. It is very important that people have an adequate intake of fluids because most of the chemical reactions that take place in our cells need water. Water is also required to carry nutrients around the body.

Water has several very important functions including:

- regulating body temperature
- improving bowel function
- enabling chemical reactions to take place inside cells
- helping the exchange of oxygen and carbon dioxide in the lungs
- aiding the action of medicines.

There is medical evidence to show that water is helpful in preventing or reducing the effects of a wide variety of conditions, including constipation, blood clots, low blood pressure, kidney stones and incontinence.

Opinions vary about the amount of fluid that adults should drink daily, but the average recommendation is about 2 litres a day. Most of the fluid we consume comes from drinks, but we also get fluid from foods such as lettuce and cucumber, soups and jelly.

Children and older people are particularly vulnerable to dehydration as they sometimes don't recognise thirst, or don't ask for a drink when they need one. Older people often restrict their fluid intake, wrongly assuming that this will reduce the likelihood of incontinence.

Dietary fibre

Dietary fibre is made of non-starch polysaccharides. You can read about this in the section on carbohydrates on page 381.

Alcohol

Alcohol plays a significant part in British culture, and therefore cannot be ignored when exploring diet. As well as its effect on overall calorie intake, alcohol can affect health in both negative and positive ways.

The current government guidance is that we should limit our weekly intake of alcohol to 21 units a week for women and 28 units for men, spread over the week, rather than in binges.

Excessive alcohol consumption can lead to an increased risk of liver damage, known as cirrhosis. Some cancers are linked to alcohol, particularly liver, mouth, oesophagus, breast, bowel and larynx. Alcohol can also affect mental health, increasing depression, anxiety and aggression, and it can cause dementia.

In moderation alcohol is thought to reduce the risk of heart disease, in particular red wine, which contains **flavonoids** that reduce **atherosclerosis**.

Key terms

Flavonoids – The pigments in plants that function as antioxidants.

Atherosclerosis – A thickening of the artery wall caused by cholesterol deposits.

2.9 Groups

Young children and young people

Growth and development is fast during this phase, and children should be very active. Protein and carbohydrates are therefore very important. The diet should follow the Food Standards Agency guidelines outlined on pages 373–374. If children are hungry between meals, healthy snacks should be offered, such as fruit or toast. Crisps and sweets will increase the risk of obesity and tooth decay.

Adults

Once growth has stopped, adults need to maintain their weight, but should try to avoid putting on extra weight. High-fat foods should be kept to a minimum, as they raise cholesterol. Being overweight can also increase the chances of developing arthritis, diabetes and cancer. To reduce the risk of developing high blood pressure. salt should be limited to 6 g per day, which is about 1 teaspoonful. High-sugar foods should be a treat rather than a regular part of the diet. Ideally, alcohol consumption should be limited to 1 unit a day for women and 2 units a day for men.

Did you know?

1 unit of alcohol is:

- half a pint of 3.5 per cent proof beer, cider or lager
- or a 125 ml glass of 9 per cent proof wine
- or a 25 ml measure of spirits

Older people

The dietary needs of older people do not change and they should follow the basic guidelines for a healthy diet in order to avoid poor nutrition.

In August 2006 Age Concern published a report entitled 'Hungry to be Heard: The Scandal of Malnourished People in Hospital'. The report looked at the numbers of people, particularly older people, who become, or stay, malnourished in hospital. There were several reasons suggested including:

- insufficient help being offered to those who are unable to feed themselves independently
- staff failing to notice when patients were persistently leaving meals
- food being placed out of reach
- failure by staff to ensure that personal preference is taken into account.

You can access the report by visiting the Age Concern website: www.ageconcern.org.uk

Similarly, the Royal College of Nursing, with the *Nursing Standard*, launched a campaign on 18 April 2007 entitled 'Nutrition Now', following a survey of over 2000 nurses to find out the main barriers to helping patients to get good nutrition. The main reasons given were the lack of availability of food outside mealtimes and the lack of staff available to support patients during mealtimes. Many hospitals have now introduced **protected mealtimes**.

Pregnant and breast-feeding mothers

Extra folic acid should be taken during the first three months of pregnancy, as this is recommended to prevent **spina bifida**.

During the last three months of pregnancy a woman needs about an extra 200 calories a day. While breast-feeding, she will need an extra 500 calories. Extra calcium should be eaten as the developing baby will take what it needs, leaving the mother deficient. This is why women often have to have more dental treatment during pregnancy and for the first year after having a baby.

Pregnant women are advised to avoid certain foods that are known to be a potential risk to the unborn child. These include soft and blue vein cheeses, pâté, unwashed raw fruit and vegetables, raw or undercooked meat, unpasteurised goats' milk or goats' cheese, and liver. It is also recommended that pregnant women eat no more than four medium-sized tins of tuna per week, as tuna has been found to contain traces of mercury.

Key terms

Protected mealtimes – A policy whereby patients must not be disturbed from their meals for treatments and tests.

Spina bifida – A condition in which the backbone is not properly formed. It can result in paralysis.

Assessment activity 21.2

Task A

Produce a set of wall charts, one for each of the following nutrients, which demonstrate your understanding of the characteristics of the nutrients and their functions:

- carbohydrates
- proteins
- lipids
- vitamins
- minerals.

Make the charts as attractive as possible, using images to create visual stimulation.

Task B

Choose two of the following groups of individuals:

- young children
- young people
- adults
- older people
- pregnant women and breastfeeding mothers.

Produce one booklet that discusses nutritional and energy requirements, comparing and contrasting similarities and differences between the two groups for each nutrient, and for energy.

Grading tips

P2 To gain P2, you must describe fully the characteristics of nutrients and their benefits to the body. A list of bullet points or a table is not sufficient. Avoid copying out the charts from the book.

M1 To achieve M1, you have to examine similarities and differences in the nutritional and energy requirements of two groups of individuals. You need to show your understanding of the fact that people need different amounts of certain nutrients at each life stage, depending on whether they are growing, very active, or if they need to actively prevent certain disorders. You can also discuss differences within the group – between male and female, or active or sedentary jobs, for example.

PLTS

Independent enquirer: The activity requires you to carefully check the differences in nutrient requirements at different life stages against reliable sources of information about nutrient content of foods.

Creative thinker: You can demonstrate this skill by researching carefully and not relying on your assumptions.

Self-manager: This activity requires you to work carefully and thoughtfully to produce an accurate set of fact sheets and a professional-looking booklet within a specified timescale.

Functional skills

ICT and **English:** You can use your ICT skills to find and select information about the nutrients, and you can use writing skills to produce the booklet.

3 Understand influences on dietary intake and nutritional health

3.1 Health factors

So far, this chapter has concentrated on the diet of healthy people, but there are many underlying health conditions that result in specific nutrient needs, and influence what people can and cannot eat. It is always important for individuals to eat a healthy diet, and include all the essential nutrients, but it can be more complicated – when you have to avoid certain foods – to ensure that you eat a balanced diet.

Diabetes mellitus

Diabetes mellitus is a condition in which the hormone insulin is either not being produced by the pancreas, is being produced in insufficient quantities or is not being used properly by the body. There are two types of diabetes mellitus. If left untreated, the most severe type of diabetes would lead to certain death due to lack of glucose in the cells and vital organs.

The most severe type is IDDM (insulin dependent diabetes mellitus). It is sometimes known as Type I diabetes. The less severe form is NIDDM (non-insulin dependent diabetes mellitus). It is sometimes known as Type 2 diabetes. IDDM is treated with insulin injections, whereas NIDDM is treated either by diet alone or with a combination of diet and tablets.

Anyone with diabetes should see a registered dietician. A healthy diet is important, as poorly controlled diabetes can lead to some very serious complications, including blindness, kidney failure, strokes, and gangrene, leading to amputation of lower limbs.

Coeliac disease

This is **intolerance** to the protein gluten, which is found in wheat, barley and rye. Gluten causes the immune system to produce antibodies, which attack the lining of the bowel. This can affect the body's ability to absorb nutrients from food, and can lead to

Key term

Intolerance – A condition in which a specific food causes unpleasant symptoms such as diarrhoea, bloating and wind. An intolerance is not the same as an allergic reaction.

anaemia and osteoporosis. It can also increase the risk of bowel cancer.

Symptoms include abdominal pain, diarrhoea, constipation, bloating, failure to gain weight in childhood, weight loss in adulthood, and anaemia.

People with coeliac disease need to eliminate all foods containing wheat, rye and barley from their diet. Gluten-free products are available, but are very expensive to buy. If a person has been medically diagnosed with coeliac disease some gluten-free products can be obtained on prescription. Food lists are available from Coeliac UK, and some information is available on the Internet at www.coeliac.org.uk.

Case study: Sonia

Sonia works as a carer, visiting people who require help at home. One of the people she visits is Mrs Hannaway, a lady in her eighties, who has a number of health problems including gluten intolerance. Sonia has to bear this in mind when she does the shopping and cooking for Mrs Hannaway.

1. Make a list of foods that contain gluten.
2. Design a menu for one day for a person who has to avoid gluten; try to make it as tasty as possible.
3. Next time you are in a supermarket look at the range of foods available to customers who are intolerant to particular food components. It is useful to see what you can buy in case you ever need to get some at short notice. Compare the prices of these products to other foods in the supermarket.

Irritable bowel syndrome

Irritable bowel syndrome (IBS) is a condition where the bowel function is easily disturbed, causing abdominal pain, flatulence, bloating and either constipation or diarrhoea, or even both. However, on examination there is no apparent abnormality in the bowel. The cause is not clear, but there seems to be overactivity in the nerves in the gut, and some people can identify particular foods that cause their symptoms. Sometimes IBS develops following a bout of diarrhoea caused by an infection, and continues after the infection has gone. Some people find that they have these symptoms after a course of antibiotics, which kill the normal bacteria that should be present in the bowel. There is a lot of varied advice given to people with IBS, but the best thing is to experiment with the diet to try to identify which foods make it worse, and avoid them. Probiotic yogurt drinks may also help.

For more information, visit www.patient.co.uk/sitemap.asp/ and look up Irritable Bowel Syndrome under 'I'.

Lactose intolerance

Lactose, the natural sugar in milk, is a common intolerance. It can be mild or severe. Children who are lactose intolerant do not produce lactase, an enzyme that is used to break down lactose into glucose and galactose before being absorbed during digestion. Children with this condition in its severest form have difficulty putting on weight and suffer from diarrhoea. The lactose ferments inside the bowel, causing bloating. Lactose is present in a wide variety of foods, including chocolate, cheese, ice cream, mayonnaise and cakes. Anyone eliminating all these products from their diet is at risk of calcium deficiency, which can lead to rickets and osteoporosis, so it is important to make sure that sufficient calcium is still eaten.

Food allergy

Some people may have an allergy to particular foods. A food allergy is sometimes confused with food intolerance, but, in fact, is much more serious. An allergic reaction can be severe and life-threatening. In adults, the most common food allergies are to nuts, fish and shellfish. In children cows' milk, eggs, soya, and wheat are common **allergens**, but any food can cause allergies.

Symptoms

Following contact with the allergy trigger food, the person will develop one or more of the following signs and symptoms within minutes or hours:

- itchy mouth
- swollen lips, mouth, tongue and/or throat
- rash
- wheezing
- vomiting and/or diarrhoea
- red itchy eyes.

Key term

Allergen – A substance that can cause an allergic reaction in sensitive people when their immune system recognises it as 'foreign'. These substances cause no response in most people.

Some people develop a severe reaction called anaphylactic shock. This is a rare but potentially fatal allergic reaction where the symptoms develop all over the body, causing swelling, a rash (hives), loss of consciousness, low blood pressure and breathing problems. Every effort should be made to ensure that the person is never given food containing the substance to which they are allergic. Anyone who is known to have a severe food allergy should be prescribed an Epipen, which they should carry with them at all times. Both the person and anyone who cares for them should be trained to use the Epipen.

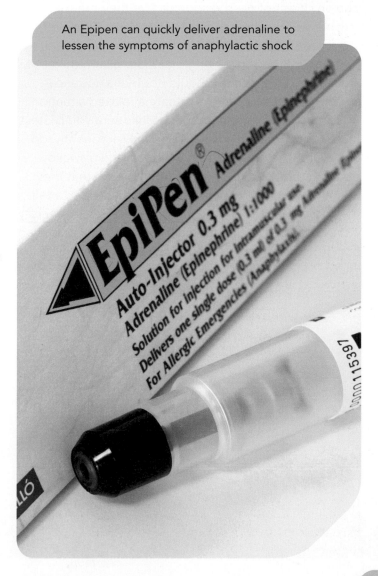

An Epipen can quickly deliver adrenaline to lessen the symptoms of anaphylactic shock

Loss of ability to feed independently

Unfortunately some people are unable to feed themselves independently, either throughout their lives, or following an accident, leading to paralysis, or development of a debilitating condition. A further reason may be that they are unable to take food in through the mouth and have to be fed by tube.

If some degree of independence can be maintained, then it should be. There are a wide variety of gadgets available to assist people who are having difficulty in feeding themselves. Some of these include wide-handled cutlery, plate guards and non-slip mats.

Another way of maintaining independence is to cut up food before serving it, enabling a person to manage without further help.

Sometimes there is no possibility of an individual feeding themselves. This may be because of cognitive impairment, such as advanced dementia, where a person does not even recognise that their meal has arrived, or know how to feed themselves. Whatever the reason for needing full support with eating and drinking, it is important that meals are given while they are still hot. The person should not feel a nuisance, so you should sit down and create a relaxed situation where the meal can be enjoyed. Make sure you protect the clothing with a napkin. Offer drinks frequently, do not overfill the person's mouth and let them swallow one mouthful before offering more. Ensure that they are offered enough to eat. It may be necessary to tell the person what you are going to feed them, especially if they have a visual impairment or are confused. It is an opportunity for some social conversation as well.

The face and hands should be washed at the beginning and end of the meal.

Some people may need to be fed via a tube. This is usually due to problems with the digestive system. Swallowing difficulties, known as dysphagia, can cause a person to choke frequently, or be unable to eat sufficient food to maintain nutritional health. A stroke or cancer of the oesophagus can cause dysphagia. Liquid feeds can taste unpleasant. Sometimes a tube is passed up the nose and down the throat, but if it is a permanent problem a gastrostomy can be created – a hole through the abdomen straight into the stomach (sometimes called a PEG or Mic-Key button).

Tube feeding is potentially very unsociable. Children may be happy to be fed at the table and play with utensils, but teenagers and adults may be self-conscious, and prefer to be fed in private. You should always respect privacy and dignity.

A gastrostomy may be created for someone who has problems swallowing food

What problems do you think these items could help with?

3.2 Dietary habits

Meal patterns

'Meal patterns' refers to the way a person takes their food. Some people stick to the traditional three meals a day. However, there are many possible variations. Some households do eat together, but in an increasingly busy world mealtimes have changed in many families, with individual family members eating separately, people eating frequent snacks, and microwave meals all being normal patterns. According to the website www.disordered-eating.co.uk, 'It is thought that eating meals regularly together as a family may help to prevent the onset of eating disorders in children and adolescents'.

There has been an increase in the habit of 'grazing' over recent decades, and this pattern of eating is one of the factors blamed for rising obesity levels in the UK.

Snacking

Eating between meals, once discouraged, is now normal behaviour in the UK. If the snacks consist of healthy foods, such as fruit, and do not push the daily calorie intake above energy use, then there is no problem with this. However, snacks often consist of high-fat, salty and sugary foods so this can be a problem. Occasional unhealthy foods are of no consequence, but people who consume several packets of crisps a day or several bars of chocolate are significantly increasing their risk of obesity, high blood pressure and heart disease as they age.

Personal tastes

Most people have likes and dislikes in foods, and very few people like absolutely every food offered to them. Some people feel it is morally wrong to eat animals, and therefore wish to follow a **vegetarian** diet. Some people extend this to a **vegan** diet, where no animal products are eaten at all. Religion can also impose restrictions on dietary intake. When providing food and drink for individuals these considerations need to be taken into account, as you also need to ensure that the diet provided is nutritionally balanced. So it is not enough just to serve the same meal to everyone, omitting the foods that are not wanted. They must be replaced with foods of equal nutritional value.

Food availability

Another influence on the diet taken is the food that is available. You can probably think of many occasions when you have eaten a chocolate bar just because it was in the house, and if it had not have been you might have had toast instead! It is important that healthy food is readily available for people using health and social care services, or they too will not eat a healthy diet. National Minimum Standards for Care Homes for Older People require that residents should have access to cooking facilities. Drinks should be readily available. Water should be available at all times, perhaps by leaving jugs of water for people to help themselves.

For those who live in their own homes, but who are unable to cook or shop independently, planning is needed to ensure that food and drink are available when needed and desired. Lunchtime can usually be accommodated by the local meals service, which is organised through social services. Hot meals are delivered daily, even at weekends in cases where there is no realistic alternative. Some local authorities provide a choice of meal, which has to be ordered in advance; others will just deliver meals without offering a choice. Special diets will be catered for. If the meal arrives too early, it can be kept hot in the oven, although this will reduce the nutritional value as vitamins levels soon start to drop as food is kept hot. The food should be kept above 63°C to prevent food poisoning (Food Standards Agency, 2005). It is less risky to keep the food hot than reheat it, but if food is being reheated after being allowed to cool it must be piping hot all the way through.

For other meals, people may be able to manage independently as long as the food is in the house. Shopping can be done by a home care assistant, a relative, a neighbour or by ordering on the Internet. For those who cannot prepare any meals independently, a home care assistant, relative or neighbour might help. If a cooked lunch has been provided, many people will be happy with a flask of hot drink or soup and a light evening meal left in the fridge, covered to keep it fresh.

Key term

Vegetarian – A diet that omits all meat and fish, but includes dairy produce.

Vegan – A diet that omits all animal products.

3.3 Lifestyle

Eating at home

Eating at home means that you can have total control over what you eat. Cooking from raw ingredients can be a real eye opener when you find out exactly what goes into particular recipes, and is likely to make you eat a healthier diet. However, the sales of ready meals have rocketed in recent years. Research conducted by Mintel estimated that Britons spent £1.9 billion on ready meals in 2006 and 30 per cent of adults in the UK eat at least one ready meal a week.

The 2008 Tesco survey on home cooking, which was reported in *The Daily Telegraph*, found that people in the UK were cooking more foods that originate from abroad (such as spaghetti bolognaise) than traditional British dishes like Lancashire hotpot. Of course, many traditional British meals are high in fat and sugar, so this trend is not necessarily a bad thing.

The social services meals service ensures that older people and those with disabilities get at least one cooked meal a day

Social eating and drinking

According to the Office of National Statistics, the amount of money spent on eating outside the home more than doubled between 1992 and 2004. The risk of eating out frequently is that it is tempting to choose high-fat, salty and sugary foods, which is fine for occasional treats, but not on a regular basis. The Food Standards Agency website gives advice on making healthy choices when eating out.

Exercise/activity levels

People who participate in strenuous activity will have different dietary needs. Professional athletes usually have a dietician to advise them on the most appropriate diet for their sport.

The International Conference on Foods, Nutrition and Sports in Lausanne (1991) agreed the following optimum nutrient intakes for most sports:

- 60–70 per cent of calories in the diet from carbohydrates
- 12 per cent from protein
- and the remainder (18–28 per cent) from fat.

This in effect means eating a diet far higher in carbohydrate, and lower in fat and protein, than the average.

Carbohydrate is important for athletes, as it provides fuel. Carbohydrate is stored as glycogen in the liver and muscles, and released when needed during exercise. It can be quickly broken down to provide energy, but only limited amounts can be stored, so during prolonged periods of exercise glycogen will become depleted, leading to an increased risk of injury. The other source of energy is fat, but this cannot be converted into energy as quickly as glycogen.

The other crucial component of the diet for athletes is fluids. Water is usually adequate, but for intense activity isotonic and hypotonic drinks are useful to speed up the process of water transferring into the bloodstream.

Activity 7: Calorie calculator

There are several websites that enable you to calculate how many calories are burnt up by doing different types of exercise.

Experiment with all the different types of sports and fitness activities you participate in to see which ones burn the most calories.

PLTS

Independent enquirer: You can provide evidence of independent enquiry by demonstrating your appreciation of the potential effects of choosing different types of activities.

Occupation

Another influence on the diet needed is your occupation. It will be no surprise to you that a building labourer will use up far more calories than an office worker. Just like athletes, manual workers should gain the extra calories they need from starchy carbohydrates rather than from fatty foods.

As people get older, they may do less physical activity, so if this is the case, their energy needs reduce. If they do not reduce their calorie intake they will start to gain weight, which will put strain on ageing joints.

When trying to decide whether an older person is eating sufficient amounts of food, it is important to keep an eye on their weight. Weighing someone monthly should soon tell you if they are starting to lose or gain a significant amount of weight, and action can be taken to rectify this.

If a person is losing weight they are obviously not eating enough calories. This might be because they have lost their appetite. The food being consumed will need to be a good source of protein, vitamins and minerals. The highest-calorie foods are fats but, of course, you cannot just feed people on high-fat food, as this could raise their cholesterol levels. Plant foods, such as nuts, seeds, olives and avocados, have unsaturated fats that are less harmful than animal fats, so these could be one solution.

Leisure pursuits

The way people spend their leisure time can also influence what they eat. Eating out and sporting activities have already been discussed. Most people eat differently on holiday, and this can be a time when people eat unhealthily and justify it to themselves. Some destinations can pose risks due to poor food hygiene, and some parasitic diseases can cause long-term health problems.

3.4 Economic factors
Cost of food

It is generally accepted that a healthy diet costs more than an unhealthy one. Supermarkets have been criticised for focusing on high-fat, salty and sugary foods when running promotions. The Low Income Diet and Nutrition Survey (LIDNS) was commissioned by the Food Standards Agency and published in 2007. It looked at the eating habits, nourishment and nutrition-related health of people on low incomes. You can see a summary of its results on:

www.food.gov.uk/science/dietarysurveys/

Activity 8: Diet and low income

Have a look at the results of the Low Income Diet and Nutrition Survey to help you understand more about the effects of low income on diet.

Make a table to compare the nutritional intake of people on a low income with the average for the general population.

PLTS

Creative thinker: You can demonstrate creative thinking by trying to explain objectively why people on low incomes usually eat a particular diet.

Not all healthy foods are expensive so you may be able to advise people on healthy foods that they can afford. For example, chicken and pork tend to be cheaper than beef and lamb, and are healthier foods, because they are lower in fat.

Larger supermarkets often produce own-label products with very similar nutritional value to branded ones.

Some supermarkets have two ranges of own-label products, with the more expensive one usually being of a similar quality to the branded ones. Budget own-label foods are sometimes higher in fat, salt and sugar, with poorer-quality ingredients. However, some of the budget own-label foods are still nutritious. As a rule, unprocessed foods, such as raw meat and vegetables, from the budget range are a good buy.

Access to shops

The food you are able to eat may depend on how easy it is for you to access shops. Supermarkets usually provide the best value for money, with a better choice and more competitive prices. Most supermarkets can be accessed by public transport. If you live in a rural location and do not have a car, you may have to shop at a small local shop, which can be expensive with a limited range. Internet shopping has helped those with access to the Internet and the skills to use computers.

Food supply

At one time, fruit and vegetables were sold only when they were in season. Now we are in a global market and produce travels many thousands of miles around the world. This means that most fruit and vegetables are available most of the year, which has had a big influence on menus. In developing countries and remote areas there will be much more seasonal variation affecting what people eat.

The fact that we expect to be able to buy all types of food all year round has had a dramatic effect on some food supplies. One example of this is fish.

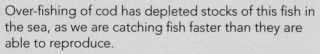

Activity 9: Pollock and chips, please!

Over-fishing of cod has depleted stocks of this fish in the sea, as we are catching fish faster than they are able to reproduce.

1 Find out what other species of fish are now being used to make products like fish fingers.

2 Design a campaign to persuade customers that they should try other fish.

PLTS

You can show your creative thinking abilities by devising an imaginative campaign.

3.5 Socio-cultural issues

One of the biggest influences on diet is the family. You will have developed your first eating habits from your carers and it is they who have guided you about what you should and should not eat. This may have been directly through teaching you about healthy eating or religious rules, or indirectly through the foods that you have been served and your carers' own preferences and tastes.

Fasting and feasting feature in many religions, along with beliefs about certain animals being sacred or unclean.

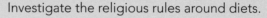

Activity 10: Religious rules on eating and drinking

Investigate the religious rules around diets.

1 Choose a religion, find out which foods are prohibited and why.

2 Consider whether the religious restrictions could affect health.

As children are brought up, they are socialised into the norms of their culture. Mealtimes are more important in some cultures than others. Where they *are* important, a mealtime is a good opportunity to introduce good manners and the ability to make social conversation. Being a guest at another family's mealtime can be awkward for young children, as they are faced with unfamiliar foods. It is an opportunity to introduce children to a variety of foods and to encourage them to take risks by trying them.

Some religious occasions involve food rituals. For example, in Hinduism there is a ceremony called Annaprasana for a baby's first meal of solid food.

3.6 Education

A substantial amount of money is spent on educating the population about healthy eating, and food hygiene, and this education has had a considerable influence over the foods we choose to eat, and how we prepare them.

Public health

The environmental health department of each borough council is responsible for monitoring anyone preparing food for public consumption to ensure that the food they serve is fit to eat, and prepared in a hygienic way. Any food that is found to be unfit is confiscated and destroyed. If unsafe food hygiene practice is identified, improvement notices are issued, and organisations can be temporarily or permanently closed. Inspections are carried out both with and without warning, and good practice is rewarded through a scheme awarding between 0 and 5 stars.

Health education

In recent years there have been a number of prominent campaigns to improve public awareness of healthy eating. The five-a-day campaign began in 2003, when a £150,000 Big Lottery grant was awarded to improve the consumption of fruit and vegetables in Primary Care Trusts. The success of the campaign has been monitored, but by 2008 only 12 per cent of the UK population was managing to achieve this target. However, the report did say that children's lunch boxes now contain 16 per cent more fruit and 25 per cent more vegetables than a year before.

Other health education campaigns include 'Eat Well, Be Well' and 'Change 4 Life'.

Food hygiene

Food hygiene is crucial for the provision of food that will benefit health. It doesn't matter how fresh or high quality the food is, if good hygiene is not practised it will make people ill and could even kill them. Good food hygiene involves frequent hand-washing, correct storage of food, and thorough cooking. More information can be found about food hygiene in Unit 3 Health, safety and security in health and social care, and by visiting the Food Standards Agency website (www.food.gov.uk).

Marketing and labelling

Food labels allow people to make choices about the food they eat. If a person is trying to choose a healthy diet they need to know whether food is high or low in different components.

Many foods are marketed as healthy options, and some food manufacturers make claims about their health benefits. There are rules governing this. Manufacturers cannot call foods 'reduced calorie', for

Table 21.6: The Food Standard Agency's 'traffic light' guide to what is regarded as high or low quantities of sugar, fat, fibre and salt and sodium

	High per 100 g	Low per 100 g
Sugars	10 g	2 g
Fat	20 g	3 g
Saturated fat	5 g	1 g
Fibre	3 g	0.5 g
Salt	1.25 g	0.25 g
Sodium	0.5 g	0.1 g

example, unless the food is much lower in calories than the standard version. There are no legal definitions for terms such as 'low-fat'; however, producers would not be allowed to describe a high-fat food as 'low fat'.

If a food label has an image on it of an ingredient, that ingredient must be contained in the food.

Role of health professionals

Dieticians

Dieticians work with patients who need a special diet, and they try to enable the individual to eat within the restrictions of their medical condition while maintaining a healthy balanced diet.

Public health nutritionists

Public health nutritionists do not work with individuals, but advise the government about healthy eating messages that can inform policy makers. Their advice forms the basis of public health campaigns.

Doctors

General practitioners (GPs) are in an ideal position to discuss diet during consultations. Many of the people they see do not regularly see any other health professional. They may have come to discuss a minor ailment, but the GP can take the opportunity to check their weight or blood pressure, or order blood tests for diabetes or cholesterol levels. Advice about avoiding saturated fat or high-salt foods can be given, and a referral made to a dietician if necessary.

Nurses

Nurses also need a good understanding of both healthy diets and special diets. They are expected to know what foods to suggest and what to avoid for a range of medical conditions. They are involved in administering tube feeds and ensuring that those who are unable to eat independently receive adequate food and drink. The 'Better Hospital Food' programme was introduced during 2001, and included the requirement for hospital wards to introduce protected mealtimes (during which non-urgent treatments are not allowed if they will disturb patients from eating their meals). The initiative also introduced 24-hour catering, meaning that patients can ask for hot food, snacks and drinks at any time of the day or night.

Carers

Care workers in both residential and community settings should understand healthy eating and special dietary requirements. However, this has not always been the case. In response to a 1998 survey, which revealed serious problems with nutrition in care homes and hospitals, *Skills for Care*, the sector skills council for the care industry, devised a set of knowledge sets, setting out the minimum level of understanding that care workers should have in a variety of topics, including nutrition and well-being. It is hoped that this will address the poor understanding of some care workers and improve their ability to advise individuals on good diet.

Sports nutritionists

A sports nutritionist will work with athletes to devise a diet that maximises their strength, stamina and fitness to enable them to perform at their best. The nutritionist prepares a diet plan that considers different needs according to whether the person is training for an event, recovering from an event, or resting. The diet usually includes powder supplements as well as normal foods to match the requirements of the particular sport they participate in.

Health and fitness instructors

These staff work at gyms and leisure centres and include personal trainers who work with people who are trying to improve or maintain their fitness levels, but are not athletes. These instructors have a good understanding of diet and healthy eating, as this is part of their training.

3.7 Social policy
Legislation, regulations and policies

There have been several attempts to improve the diet of the population through social policy. This is a different approach to health education, and involves creating more opportunities for people to choose healthy foods.

Every Child Matters was a government Green Paper published in 2003, following the death of Victoria Climbié, aiming to improve the well-being of all children, and was the forerunner of the Children Act 2004. One of the intended outcomes of *Every Child Matters* is 'being healthy' and the quality of food that children eat is one aspect of this outcome. The outcomes were revised in 2008.

In Scotland the Early Years and Early Intervention Policy has much the same aims for improving child health. For more information on this, visit the Scottish government website (www.scotland.gov.uk).

The government publication *Healthy Weight, Healthy Lives: One Year On* looks at progress towards reducing childhood obesity. It states that, 'Our ambition is to be the first major nation to reverse the rising tide of obesity and being overweight in the population by ensuring that everyone is able to achieve and maintain a healthy weight. Our initial focus will be on children: by 2020, we aim to reduce the proportion of overweight and obese children to 2000 levels.'

In 1996 the Scottish government launched 'Eating for Health: a Diet Action Plan for Scotland'.

In 2004 'Eating for Health: Meeting the Challenge' was published, reviewing the strategies.

The Food Standards Agency launched the Healthy Food Code of Practice, encouraging clear labelling on packaging indicating the levels of saturated fat, salt and sugar in foods (*Every Child Matters* 2008). The Scottish Executive Health Department and the Food Standards Agency Scotland jointly established the *Scottish Food and Health Alliance* to support further the implementation of the Scottish Diet Action Plan.

The School Food Trust (SFT) was set up by the government in 2005 to improve the nutritional quality of food served in schools and the cooking skills of children and their parents.

Research carried out by the SFT found that there had been an improvement in school lunches, but not in packed lunches brought from home.

Nutritional Standards for School Lunches were agreed by the School Meals Review Panel and implemented in 2006. The standards require that:

- high-quality meat, poultry or oily fish are regularly available
- at least two portions of fruit and vegetables should be available with every meal

- bread, other cereals and potatoes are regularly available
- deep-fried food is limited to no more than two portions per week
- fizzy drinks, crisps, chocolate and other confectioneries are removed from school meals and vending machines
- children and young people must have easy access at all times to free, fresh drinking water in schools.

Under the National Minimum Standards for Care Homes for Older People, the registered manager is required to ensure that individuals receive a varied, appealing, wholesome and nutritious diet, which is suited to their assessed and recorded requirements, and that meals are taken in a pleasant setting and at flexible times.

Residents should be offered a choice of three meals a day, at least one of which should be cooked. Drinks and snacks should always be available. Foods should be nicely presented and appetising. Special diets should be catered for, including religious and cultural diets. Menus should be available in different formats. Diet should be assessed on admission and recorded on the care plan.

Assessment activity 21.3

 **P3 M2 D1** **BTEC**

Using a case study approach, explain how the following factors have influenced four individuals' diets:

- medical disorders
- personal preference
- lifestyle
- socio-cultural factors
- economic
- social policy.

For M2, assess how influences on dietary intake may affect the nutritional health of individuals.

Choose a setting, such as a residential home, a day centre or a Sure Start nursery, and make realistic recommendations about how you could compensate for negative influences on diet in that setting.

Grading tips

P3 To achieve P3, you need to explain how each of the factors influences what people choose to eat.

M2 To achieve the merit, you need to make a link between the factors that influence the food choices people make and how this can increase or decrease risks to their health. Try to balance positive and negative influences.

D1 To achieve the distinction, you need to think creatively about what you could do to help people overcome the effects of negative influences. This will usually involve giving people skills and knowledge, and changing their attitudes, away from feeling helpless and towards taking personal responsibility to improve a situation.

PLTS

Self-manager: You can demonstrate self-management skills by working carefully and thoughtfully to produce innovative case studies showing how negative influences can be overcome and by submitting your work within the timescale given.

Why do you think encouraging children to enjoy cooking at school can have a positive impact on healthy eating at home?

4 Be able to use dietary and other relevant information from an individual to make recommendations to improve nutritional health

4.1 Recording food intake

In order to assess a person's actual diet, it is often necessary to keep an accurate diary of everything eaten and drunk over a period of a few days. This can be a real revelation, and many people are surprised when they see exactly what they have been consuming. The record needs to cover all food eaten including meals, snacks, sweets, drinks and food supplements. It should indicate the portion size as well, as it is not just *what* a person eats but *how much* that is important when assessing intake.

A comprehensive nutritional analysis method involves recording the frequency of eating specific foods, categorising them as in the example below. This type of table can be used to analyse food intake over a long period of time without the need for a detailed record of everything eaten.

You could clearly see from this type of chart whether a person was eating a healthy diet, and if not, which nutrients they were eating too much or too little of, by comparing their intake to the recommended healthy balanced diet for that person according to age, gender and activity level. Of course you would also need to take into account any dietary restrictions.

4.2 Sources of nutritional information

Information about the recommended intake of nutrients is available. Some of these sources are more complicated than others. The Food Standards Agency's 'Eat Well, Be Well' campaign offers dietary guidance in a way that is fairly easy to follow, although, apart from fruit and vegetables, it does not provide much help on portion sizes.

In section 2 of this unit you will find information about the recommended daily amounts of components of diet to help you analyse a person's food intake. You can also look at the British Nutrition Foundation website (www.nutrition.org.uk).

Many food manufacturers now give indications of portion sizes on the package, and also include information about the amount of specific nutrients in the food, both as a portion and as 100 g.

4.3 Quantitative analysis

When analysing a person's diet, you need to identify how much of each nutrient they are consuming daily, including energy in calories, and the proportion

Table 21.7: Frequency of eating chart

Food and amounts	Never/less than once a month	1–3 times a month	Once a week	2–4 times a week	5–6 times a week	Once a day	2–3 times a day	4–5 times a day	6+ times a day
Fruit and vegetables								✓	
100 g meat/fish						✓			

gained from fat, protein, iron, vitamin C, and fibre intake. These measures can then be compared to recommended intakes to enable you to analyse the diet in terms of health, and risk of ill-health.

4.4 Strengths and weaknesses

The strengths of a person's diet would relate to foods they eat that are known to maintain good health and prevent ill-health. The weaknesses would include foods contributing to risks of ill-health such as deficiency diseases, heart disease or obesity. Look back at section 2 to remind yourself of recommended intakes and the health risks related to eating too much or too little of particular nutrients.

Reflect

Unfortunately, when asked to record food intake, some people may present a plan that is not really representative of their normal diet. What impact would this have on the benefits of the exercise for the person being assessed?

4.5 Nutritional plan

When devising an improved menu for a person, you should include their total intake for the day, including drinks and snacks, and give advice on the portion size. For example, seven cherry tomatoes are considered to be one of your five-a-day portions. Likewise, recommendations about protein intake should give details of the weight of meat or volume of milk.

People who exercise a lot will need more calories than those with sedentary lifestyles

4.6 Activity

As you know from earlier in the chapter, nutritional needs vary according to how active you are, so your plan needs to take into consideration whether or not the person participates in any exercise, and if so how much and what sort of activity they do. You can then take that into account when suggesting a diet plan.

You will need to ask them to complete another diary about their exercise patterns to find out how long they sleep, how much of their day is spent sitting, and how much time being active. You will need to know what exercise they have taken, such as fast or slow walking, or particular sports and fitness activities.

4.7 Lifestyle influences

Finally, in order to create a realistic diet plan, you need to know about a person's lifestyle. It is no good recommending foods that they do not like, or that are forbidden by their religion. Suggestions should not be too expensive if a person is on a limited budget, nor should they include time-consuming recipes if the person works long hours or has a busy lifestyle.

If your diet plan is going to include the weekend you may need to consider differences in their lifestyle compared to weekdays. They may have more time at the weekend, or wish to eat out.

Assessment activity 21.4

Identify a person who would be willing to keep a detailed food and activity diary for three days. This person should ideally be yourself, although it could be someone you know in a private capacity, e.g. a relative or a friend prepared to share the necessary information with you. Design a chart to capture the information you need. It is important that the diary is accurate and includes every meal, drink and snack that has been eaten, including portion sizes (i.e. weight) and cooking methods, and describes the type and duration in minutes of all activity undertaken, including sleeping, sitting, walking, dancing, sports, etc.

1 Carry out a quantitative analysis of daily intake of nutrients and energy by the individual chosen.

2 Once the chart has been completed, analyse the strengths and weaknesses of the diet in relation to energy, protein, fat, iron, and vitamin C intakes.

3 Calculate the additional energy used for physical activities, on top of the basal metabolic requirements, so you can compare energy intake with energy expenditure.

4 Prepare a one-week plan for improving the nutrition of the chosen individual, based on their lifestyle, beliefs and preferences.

5 Assess how the plan will meet the nutritional needs of the chosen individual. This will involve justifying your choice of foods recommended to provide all the nutrients they need.

6 Evaluate how the plan might improve the chosen individual's health. You need to consider the health benefits of the foods you have chosen for reducing risks of ill-health.

Grading tips

P4 To achieve this, you need to find a comprehensive source of information about the composition of foods, such as the Food Standards Agency Manual of Nutrition, or the FSA website (www.food.gov.uk). You are expected to analyse in detail the nutrients consumed in the food diary and the energy expended on activity during the three days. You will need to record labelling information from food packaging and weigh unpackaged food. The results could be recorded on a spreadsheet to help you to calculate intake and energy expenditure more easily.

P5 The seven-day nutritional plan should include all meals, snacks and drinks, with portion sizes and cooking methods. You should also include information about lifestyle changes, and take into account the beliefs and preferences of the chosen individual.

M3 To achieve the merit, you have to be able to explain how the menu and lifestyle changes you have devised will maintain the health of the chosen individual. Refer to the person's age, gender, lifestyle, beliefs and preferences when justifying your choices in the improved menu.

D2 To achieve the distinction, you will need to show your understanding of how particular foods can prevent illness in the short, medium or long term. Short term might be preventing constipation; medium term might be preventing tooth decay; and long term might be preventing cancer. You will need to explain how the foods actually work inside the body to create health benefits, or how foods you have eliminated cause ill-health.

PLTS

Reflective learner: You can demonstrate reflective learning by analysing the daily intake of nutrients and the daily amount of energy expended.

Resources and further reading

Aldworth, C. (2008) *Knowledge Set For Nutrition and Well-being* Oxford: Heinemann

Arnold, A. and Bender, D. (1999) *Food Tables and Labelling* Oxford: Oxford University Press

Barasi, M. (2003) *Human Nutrition: A health perspective* London: Arnold

Byrom, S. (2002) *Pocket Guide to Nutrition and Dietetics* London: Churchill Livingstone

Donnellan, C. (ed) (2004) *Food and Nutrition* Cambridge: Independence

Food Standards Agency (2008) *Manual of Nutrition* London: Stationery Office

Webb, G. (2008) *Nutrition, A Health Promotion Approach*, third ed. London: Hodder & Stoughton

Neumark-Sztainer *et al* (2004) 'Are family meal patterns associated with disordered eating behaviors among adolescents?' *Journal of Adolescent Health* Minnesota: University of Minnesota

Useful websites

The Official Documents Archive www.archive2.official-documents.co.uk

Age Concern www.ageconcern.org.uk

The Advertising Standards Authority www.asa.org.uk

BAPEN (British Association for Parenteral and Enteral Nutrition) www.bapen.org.uk/

BBC Health www.bbc.co.uk/health/

Bionet – New discoveries in science www.bionetonline.org

Bupa www.bupa.co.uk/

Coeliac UK www.coeliac.org.uk

Disordered Eating www.disordered-eating.co.uk

The Food Standards Agency www.eatwell.gov.uk, www.food.gov.uk

The Environment Agency www.environment-agency.gov.uk

The Food and Agriculture Organization of the United Nations www.fao.org

International Food Policy Research Institute www.ifpri.org

National Obesity Forum www.nationalobesityforum.org.uk

NHS Choices www.nhs.uk

British Nutrition Foundation www.nutrition.org.uk

Patient UK www.patient.co.uk

Peak Performance – Sporting excellence www.pponline.co.uk

Online Publications – Every Child Matters http://publications.everychildmatters.gov.uk

School Food Trust www.schoolfoodtrust.org.uk

UK Government public services www.direct.gov.uk

Weight Loss for Good www.weightlossforgood.co.uk

Just checking

1 What sources of information are available to assist people in selecting foods to provide a balanced diet?
2 Why has general dietary advice become simpler over time, when more people are educated to a higher standard?
3 What are the current guidelines for a healthy diet?
4 What are the main factors that have a negative impact on the nutritional value of the diet eaten by individuals?
5 What initiatives have been launched in recent years to improve the diet of people in the UK?
6 Why are people in residential care settings at greater risk of malnutrition?
7 In what ways have eating patterns changed in the UK over the last 30 years?
8 What health risks are associated with obesity?

Assignment tips

1 To get the best out of this unit, you need to really get to grips with nutrition, so that you can advise confidently on specific foods and preparation methods to provide the most nutritious diet for people you are caring for.

2 You need to understand the huge range of influences on what people choose to eat, and take these factors into account when planning menus for individuals, who may have to work around medical conditions, religious restrictions and budget as well as personal taste or constraints on time. Only if you can do this will your recommendations stand any chance of being adopted. This is the way dieticians and nutritionists have to work.

3 There are some fantastic resources available on the Internet to support this unit, written at a level that is both in-depth and readable. The Food Standards Agency is particularly good on nutrition, and the Food and Agriculture Organization of the United Nations gives an excellent overview of international aspects of nutrition (see the 'Useful websites' on page 403).

4 To achieve the highest grades, you need to think for yourself about how to apply the knowledge you gain from this unit to improving the diet of people receiving support from the health and social care sector. This is the way effective professionals work, so if you can do this you have the potential to become an excellent practitioner in the future.

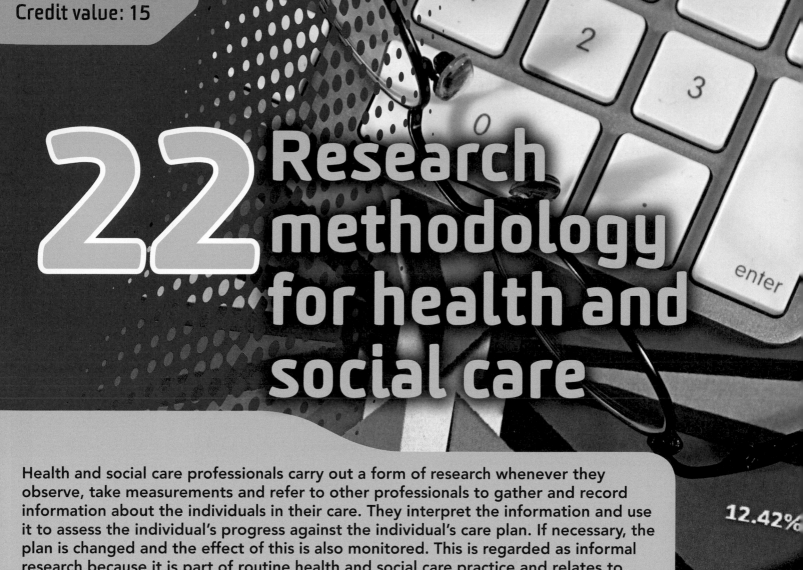

22 Research methodology for health and social care

Health and social care professionals carry out a form of research whenever they observe, take measurements and refer to other professionals to gather and record information about the individuals in their care. They interpret the information and use it to assess the individual's progress against the individual's care plan. If necessary, the plan is changed and the effect of this is also monitored. This is regarded as informal research because it is part of routine health and social care practice and relates to the care of individuals. However, all new advances in health and social care are tested using a formal research process, which involves specific planning, collecting relevant information, interpreting it and publishing the results of the research.

This unit investigates different functions of health and social care research and the principles that underpin it. You will explore ethical and legal issues relating to health and social care research and different techniques that may be used to gather research data. You will plan a small-scale research project on a topic relating to health and social care, subject to consent from your centre and the assessment requirements of the unit. The plan will include a justification of your choice of methods to gather new information in the context of existing knowledge of the subject gathered from a literature review. You will carry out the research and produce a report in which you present your results, interpret them and evaluate the research methodology you used in the project.

Learning outcomes

After completing this unit you should:

1 understand the function of research in health and social care
2 understand ethical issues relating to research in health and social care
3 understand research methodologies relevant to health and social care
4 be able to plan for a research project
5 be able to conduct research relevant to a health and social care context
6 be able to interpret research findings.

Assessment and grading criteria

This table shows you what you must do in order to achieve a **pass**, **merit** or **distinction** grade, and where you can find activities in this book to help you.

To achieve a **pass** grade, the evidence must show that you are able to:	To achieve a **merit** grade, the evidence must show that, in addition to the pass criteria, you are able to:	To achieve a **distinction** grade, the evidence must show that, in addition to the pass and merit criteria, you are able to:
P1 Explain the function of research in health and social care. **See Assessment activity 22.1, page 413**	**M1** Discuss the function of research in chosen area of interest. **See Assessment activity 22.1, page 413**	
P2 Discuss ethical issues relating to research in the health and social care sectors. **See Assessment activity 22.2, page 424**		**D1** Assess research methodologies with regard to ensuring validity of findings. **See Assessment activity 22.4, page 446**
P3 Compare different research methodologies for health and social care. **See Assessment activity 22.3, page 440**	**M2** Justify the research methods chosen for the project. **See Assessment activity 22.4, page 446**	
P4 Plan a research project. **See Assessment activity 22.4, page 446**		
P5 Carry out the planned research project. **See Assessment activity 22.5, page 448**	**M3** Assess strengths and weaknesses of the research project in meeting the aims or hypothesis. **See Assessment activity 22.6, page 456**	
P6 Report findings and conclusions from research project. **See Assessment activity 22.6, page 456**	**M4** Assess findings of the research project in relation to the original hypothesis. **See Assessment activity 22.6, page 456**	**D2** Evaluate how the research project could have been improved. **See Assessment activity 22.6, page 456**

How you will be assessed

This unit will be assessed through assignment tasks that you will complete in stages over the duration of the unit. Your assessment will include written assignments, a detailed action plan for your own research project, and a report on the findings from your project.

Dave, 17 years old

I chose swine flu as the topic for my project because there were lots of scary headlines in the news at the time and I wanted to find out why everyone was worried.

Because I chose my topic quickly, I had plenty of time for my project. I found the Internet most useful for research, especially as the information on swine flu was changing all the time. Information about other types of flu helped me decide on the questions and answer choices for my questionnaire. It took quite a long time to get the questionnaire right but the pilot study was worth it because I got good data from the survey. I interviewed a practice nurse and got lots of information about vaccination because I had planned my questions in advance. I also found the latest government statistics about swine flu on the Internet so I was able to use these in the discussion of all my results.

Although I had to alter the timescales (I had to rearrange the interview because the nurse was ill and I got a bit behind), my plan helped me stick to what I had to do and I handed in the report early. I concluded from my results that the public is very confused about swine flu, partly because of the news stories. By the time I had finished, the government was saying that there was no swine flu epidemic after all, even though they were predicting an epidemic when I started my project.

Over to you!

1   What will you choose to investigate for your research project?

2   How could you use the research skills you learn in this unit to help you with other units on the programme?

3   Why do you think research is important in health and social care?

1 Understand the function of research in health and social care

Get started

How has research affected your health and well-being?

In pairs, discuss how your own experiences of health and/or social care, or of others known to you, could have been influenced by research. You could think about changes in procedures introduced in recent years, either nationally or locally. Why were these changes introduced? What sort of research do you think might have been carried out, both before the change was made and after it was implemented?

Share your examples in a small group and list as many different purposes for research as you can.

1.1 What is research?

Research is a planned process in which information is collected systematically for a specific purpose, analysed and reported. The processes of research will be explored in detail in this unit but key features are presented in Table 22.1 to provide an introductory overview.

1.2 Functions of research

Research can have many different functions or purposes: identifying needs, highlighting gaps in provision, planning provision, informing policy or practice, extending knowledge and understanding, improving practice, aiding reflection, allowing progress to be monitored, and examining topics of contemporary importance.

Table 22.1: A summary of key features of research

Purpose	The overall aim of the research
Rationale	The reasons for the research (e.g. its value to health and social care)
Audience	The people interested in the research findings
Literature search	Finding out what is already known about the subject of the research
Ethical issues	Ensuring that the research does not cause any harm
Research proposal	The plan for the research
Methodology	The strategy and techniques used to conduct the research
Participants	The individuals who provide research information about themselves or their experiences
Research data	New information obtained from carrying out the research
Interpretation	Analysing the research data to gain new understanding of the topic
Evaluation	Making judgements on the quality of the data, etc.
Conclusions	A summary of the key points that have been learned from the research
Recommendations	Suggestions for further research or ways in which the research findings might be applied
Research report	A detailed, full (usually written) account of the research, sometimes also accompanied by an oral presentation by the researcher, who is questioned by experts about the research

Identifying needs

All health or social care workers who are involved in care planning use research principles to identify the needs of individuals. A doctor takes a medical 'history' of a patient in an initial consultation and may take measurements such as the pulse rate or blood pressure and require blood samples to be analysed. A care home manager observing an individual resident may identify that they may need more assistance with personal care and discuss this with the individual. The information gathered enables the professional to make decisions about treatment or care to meet the individual's needs.

The specific needs of one individual may be similar to those of others but, before a new treatment or care routine is introduced for everyone, it is necessary to carry out a specific study, or research project, to investigate the benefits to others. There are many organisations, often charities, which are dedicated to improving the care of individuals with specific diseases and disorders through research. Their research may focus on better diagnosis so that needs can be identified earlier or more specifically, e.g. through screening or by researching the physiological aspects of the disease so that treatment can be more carefully targeted to interact with the body's systems and tissues to slow the progress of the disease or to cure it. For example, 2.5 million people in the UK have Type 2 diabetes and Diabetes UK spent over £6 million on research in 2009 (Diabetes UK, 2009a). Its website has considerable information about its diabetes research (Diabetes UK, 2009b). Health professionals, commercial companies and others who work in the NHS frequently contribute to this type of research.

Did you know?

In 2008/09 UK medical charities invested over £935 million in research relating to medical conditions such as cancer, heart disease and arthritis.

Source: Association of Medical Research Charities (AMRC), 2009

Highlighting gaps in provision

The health and social care needs of communities change over time with the rise and fall of local employment; young families moving in and growing up; and young adults moving on, leaving older adults in the family home. The services needed for a new housing estate, with lots of young children, are usually different from those needed on a well-established estate with a greater proportion of older adult residents. In addition, risks to health also change. Government and local authorities continually gather data at local and national levels to monitor whether health and social care services are adequate to meet the needs of the local population. In the UK, the proportion of older people in the population is increasing steadily as people live longer and much attention is being given to how best to provide services to meet their needs effectively and efficiently. Support for adolescent mental health needs, the predicted swine flu epidemic and maternity care are some other examples of services where gaps in provision have been highlighted in recent years.

Planning provision of services

Provision of services for health and social care is expensive and a new service can take several years to develop. Strategic health authorities, primary care trusts (PCTs) and local authorities, which are responsible for planning health and social care service provision, have to be sure that any decision to invest public money in developing new services is justified. Their decisions need to be based on information that is accurate, recent and reliable. They may carry out the research themselves or they may **commission** others, such as universities or organisations, to do it for them.

Research reports about various aspects of service provision are available online, for example on the NHS Direct (2009) service.

Key terms

Provision of services – This refers to health and social care services which are provided, and how they are organised, in communities (e.g. hospitals, care homes, Sure Start centres, etc.).

Commission – The process by which an organisation requests and funds another organisation to carry out work on their behalf. For example, the Department of Health may commission a university to conduct research on a specific topic. In the UK public sector, the commissioning process usually requires the organisations to tender competitively against others.

residential homes and now deliver more home-based care. Similarly, some doctors' surgeries are now based on out-of-town business or industrial parks because research has shown that workers take less time off if they can see a doctor near their workplace, rather than taking a day's leave to get to a surgery near where they live. To assist in developing health and social care policy, the government commissioned a major review of the NHS, known as the Darzi Review (DH, 2008), to identify priorities for health care over the next ten years or so.

Practice

Research into health and social care practice may be associated with, for example:

- the needs of individuals
- improving the quality of care
- ensuring that resources are used efficiently, without waste
- addressing specific problems that have arisen
- reducing risks, e.g. of acquiring infections such as MRSA.

Improvements to practice might involve, for example:

- modifying care routines
- changing how care teams work together
- reorganising the layout of a care space
- developing better communication for visitors
- increasing choice
- enabling more autonomy.

If a health or social care professional identifies that the care received by the individuals they are responsible for could be improved, they may carry out **action research** within their everyday duties that leads to improvements to practice being made.

The professional would research published literature on the subject, plan a simple project to introduce a change in practice, collect information to measure

Informing policy and practice

Policy

Research shows that older people stay healthier for longer if they remain in their own homes so local authorities have reorganised their social services departments (see also Unit 6, Personal and Professional Development), closed down many of their

Key term

Action research – Research in which the researcher is a participant in a situation that occurs, regardless of the research, but from which information is collected systematically. The purpose is to gain a better understanding of the situation so that knowledge, understanding or practices in that context can be enhanced.

Sally Knowles

Early years practioner

Sally has worked as an early years practitioner for about ten years and has noticed that an increasing number of children are coming to the nursery with delayed speech development. She is completing her degree to gain early years professional status. For her dissertation, she has chosen to research how the nursery could better support these children and their parents/carers to help the development of their speech. Sally discusses her ideas with her tutor, gains consent from the nursery's governors and plans her project. From her literature search, she realises there are a range of schemes and support programmes available but she is not sure which one is best.

She also wants to gain a better understanding of why the children in her nursery are not developing age-appropriate speaking skills.

Sally decides to survey the parents of all the children in the setting to find out what interactions the children usually have with adults when they are not at nursery. She realises from her initial research that it would also be useful to know how long the children spend watching television and playing with other children. She knows the questionnaire needs to be simple to complete because some of the parents have limited English and others have limited reading skills. Another aspect of her project is to observe parent–child interactions when the parents come into the setting. Sally also researches, critically analyses and evaluates reviews of six specific language support strategies. As a result of her research, she makes several recommendations for actions the nursery can take to promote speech development in all the children and particularly those with language delay. These include:

- inviting a speech therapist to take a two-hour evening CPD training session for staff to raise their awareness of speech and language difficulties
- nominating two staff members to work with the therapist as specialist support workers for the children with speech delay
- presenting a request to the governors for an early years practitioner to be sponsored to undertake specialist training in supporting speech and language development.

Think about it!

1 What type of research is Sally carrying out?
2 How could Sally's recommendations improve practice in the nursery?
3 What can you find out about delayed speech and language development in young children?

its effects, and then analyse and interpret it. If the results show positive or negative effects on individuals, the professional could recommend that the change becomes standard practice in the care unit. Publishing a report of the research in a health or social care journal could encourage similar care units to adopt the improved practice.

Extending knowledge and understanding

Science and technology research leads to the development of new knowledge and understanding of materials and the living world. Although some scientific research may appear quite far removed from health and care needs, health and social care is a very important area in which scientific knowledge and discovery can be applied. New drugs, techniques and equipment (such as MRI scanners) are all products of laboratory-based science research. For example, when the 'pacemaker', to regulate the heartbeat, was introduced, it had a huge impact on many individuals, enabling them to live a near-normal life. Other computerised devices allow continuous monitoring of the body so that critically ill patients have an improved chance of surviving previously fatal conditions.

Did you know?

Survival rates for leukaemia, a cancer of the blood, have doubled since 1971. This is largely because of research into finding new drugs to treat the cancer, how the drugs are given, and the testing that can be done to see how the body is responding to treatment.

Source: Cancer Research UK, 2009

Sometimes research in apparently unrelated areas may have consequences for people's health, well-being and care. For example, research into climate change has highlighted the fact that there will be a shortage of food and that some communities may be displaced by rising sea levels. Action research following previous natural disasters suggests that major disruption to communities affects basic amenities such as safe drinking water and adequate food, both important for individuals' health.

Aiding reflection

The concept of reflection is explored in Unit 6 Personal and professional development. Research can provide you with **data** on which to reflect. Data obtained using a research methodology is likely to be more objective and reliable than information obtained by casual, unplanned observations, etc.

Monitoring progress

When any major change has been introduced it is important to find out what the effect of the change is. On an individual level, a care worker in a care home makes regular observations and checks to see that a new resident settles in well. A PCT manager wants to know that a newly introduced practice or service is working well. If the change is complex, such as using a new building and staff team, monitoring systems and processes would help assess whether the service is effective in benefiting individuals. Monitoring involves research, for example:

- using questionnaires to investigate perceptions of individual users of a new service
- interviews or questionnaires with staff
- gathering quantitative data, e.g. the number of individuals using the service, how quickly they are seen or that their needs are met
- reviewing the data to see whether there are any weaknesses in the service
- developing and then implementing an action plan to address problem areas and enable further improvements.

Examining topics of contemporary interest

New, or contemporary, issues relevant to health and social care continually emerge both at national and local levels and become the subject of debate among the public and professionals. Before the debate can give rise to changes in services or practice, research is needed to explore the extent of the issue and possible benefits to individuals and society. Examples of issues that have emerged in recent years include:

- the role of alternative therapies in health and well-being

Key term

Data – A plural word for 'information'. Strictly, a single piece of information, fact or statistic is 'datum' but because data usually consists of more than one piece of information, this term is rarely used.

- the likelihood of a global epidemic of influenza (flu)
- the strategy to focus accident and emergency cover in fewer larger hospitals and downgrade more local emergency departments to 'minor injuries' units.
- whether individuals with terminal illnesses should be assisted in ending their life
- concerns about global warming and climate change and its impact on populations and their needs for survival
- whether genetically modified crops are harmful to man and the environment.

More examples of different purposes for research are given in Table 22.2 on the next page.

Most of us will have experienced new health or social care developments introduced as a result of research. For example, advances in development of new materials mean that dental fillings are now plastic and white, rather than the more visible metal (amalgam or gold) used for most of the last century. At the same time, other research into the chemistry of the teeth and dental decay means that the chemicals included in toothpastes also make it less likely that people will need fillings.

Activity 2: Contemporary issues

Can you think of other contemporary issues that are relevant to health and social care both nationally and locally?

Spend 20 minutes researching the issues above, or your own choice of issues, on the Internet and share your findings with others in your group.

Activity 3: Current research

Use the Internet, journals and newspapers to find specific research that illustrates each of the examples in Table 22.2.

Go back to the starter activity at the beginning of the unit and match your ideas about how research has influenced your experiences of health and social care with the purposes identified in the table.

Assessment activity 22.1

Write an essay:

- *explaining* the function of research, using a range of examples you have researched
- *examining* the function of research, using the examples you have researched.

Grading tips

P1 Before you start your task, review research reports from a range of health and social care sources. Make notes on the purpose of the research reported in each case.

M1 Use Internet research to investigate a range of different points of view on the examples of research you select, and discuss these in your assignment task.

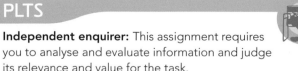

PLTS

Independent enquirer: This assignment requires you to analyse and evaluate information and judge its relevance and value for the task.

Functional skills

ICT: In this assignment you will be navigating and discriminating between sources to meet the requirements of the task.

Table 22.2: Examples of how different purposes might apply in health and social care research

Purpose	Examples
To find an explanation for a phenomenon	• Why there is an increase in the incidence of hospital-acquired infection
To improve an outcome from a process	• So that older people discharged from hospital can be rehabilitated in their own homes more successfully
To improve practice	• To enable an operation to be carried out without the need for a general anaesthetic • To identify support that will enable carers to communicate better with relatives of people with dementia
To develop new equipment, tools and devices for use in health and social care	• The development of MRI scanners • The development of microscopic nanotechnology devices circulating in the blood that continually monitor changes in levels of specific circulating chemicals, together with computers that pick up the signals from the microchip and process the data onto a monitor screen
To describe new knowledge	• Finding out more about the ways in which people are using a newly opened drop-in centre • Describing the way a gene works to control a particular metabolic process in a cell or tissue
To measure the effect of a change	• Finding out whether a day centre for those with mental health difficulties reduces the amount of medication these individuals need to take
To criticise a theory/practice/opinion	• Gathering evidence to disprove the theory that there is an association between the MMR vaccine and autistic spectrum disorders
To explore the effects of different variables on a phenomenon	• How specific socio-economic factors influence the health and well-being of a community • How different activity levels affect individuals' ability to lose weight
To apply new knowledge and understanding to a previous interpretation of a phenomenon	• Applying advances in medical genetics to identify young women at risk of developing breast cancer at a particularly young age
To predict an outcome	• Moving individuals into sheltered housing will enable them to live independently for longer
To assess perceptions of an experience	• Assessing young people's perceptions of their experience of school health education lessons • Assessing the public's understanding of the nutritional information provided on food packaging
To find out attitudes	• Examining students' attitudes to behaviours that may damage their health • Examining workers' views of people who experience stress in their workplace
To answer a question	• Is there an association between being overweight and education? • What causes myalgic encephalomyelitis (ME)?
To test a hypothesis	• Proving (or disproving) that intensive support for families with children under three will increase the children's life chances as adults

2 Understand ethical issues relating to research in health and social care

2.1 Ethical principles of research

Ethics are written statements that reflect the **morals** of society. Whereas morals are unwritten codes setting out what is deemed to be acceptable or unacceptable behaviour, ethics are written codes and reflect society's views of what is right or humane. There are internationally recognised guidelines in place that provide a framework for ethical research and this influences the codes of ethics that apply to research carried out in the NHS and universities in the UK. Codes of conduct or practice (see Unit 6, Personal and Professional Development) for health and social care professionals do not explicitly include research but the underlying principles of professional practice would be consistent with expectations for ethical research.

Did you know?

The conduct of modern medical research is based on the principles stated in the Nuremberg Code of Human Rights in Experimentation published in 1947. This code was introduced to prevent any repeat of the abuse suffered by concentration camp prisoners during the Nazi era, who were subjected to degrading and inhuman experiments in the name of research.

The ethical principles that underpin all research include clauses:

- protecting individuals
- ensuring that individuals only participate **voluntarily**
- ensuring that any personal information relating to the research is treated confidentially
- stipulating that the plan for any research project is subject to independent scrutiny by experts.

Although codes of ethics are written, they are not rules, but serve to set the boundaries of what is, and is not, an acceptable way to conduct research.

Protecting individuals from harm

This principle ensures that researchers consider the possible effects of their research on the participants. For example, participants' rights and feelings should

Activity 4: What is acceptable research?

There are two research projects relating to teenage behaviour being proposed. The first involves 14- to 16-year-old participants using sun beds and the second, with 16–18-year-olds taking part in a physical exercise activity.

1 What are your views as to the acceptability of each project? What would your reservations be?

2 What safeguards would you want to put in place?

be considered when planning the project and collecting the data from the individuals. Research should not cause harm, or **maleficence**, but this should be considered in the context of the research being undertaken. Thus it might be unacceptable for a researcher to cause a patient with mental illness to become very distressed when being asked questions about mental health. However, if tests for an anti-cancer drug cause a patient's hair to drop out, this might be seen as acceptable harm under the principle of **beneficence**, if the drug destroys the cancerous growth and the patient survives the cancer.

Key terms

Ethics – Written statements, relating to what is acceptable and unacceptable, that reflect the morals of a society. Morals may be modified over time, so ethical codes tend to evolve to reflect these changes.

Morals – The unwritten codes of what a society considers to be acceptable or unacceptable. The morals of a society tend to change over time.

Voluntarily – Doing something of your own free will, without being forced, or coerced, into doing it.

Maleficence – Causing harm.

Beneficence – Something that does good or has a beneficial effect.

Informed consent

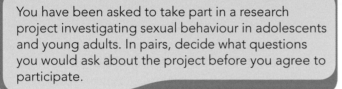

Activity 5: Would I participate?

You have been asked to take part in a research project investigating sexual behaviour in adolescents and young adults. In pairs, decide what questions you would ask about the project before you agree to participate.

Getting **informed consent** means telling participants how their contribution will advance the research. They should receive all the information they need *before* agreeing to participate, including:

- the overall purpose of the research
- what is expected of the participants if they take part in the research
- what, if any, risks are involved in participating, e.g. possible side-effects, how severe these might be, how data generated from participation will contribute to the research
- an entitlement to be able to withdraw from the research at any time.

Researchers should tell participants explicitly about their rights. In the examples above, the distressed patient could therefore withdraw from the research, and the cancer patient should be warned beforehand of possible effects. Participants may withdraw from the research while the study is in progress or have their own data withdrawn from any report of the study. Participants should be free to use their personal judgement about whether to participate according to their own perception of the risks associated with participation.

Occasionally, it may be necessary to withhold some information from participants in order to avoid knowledge about the research affecting how participants respond. This can arise particularly in behavioural studies, when knowledge of what behaviour is being studied might affect how participants respond in the research. Another example would be the double-blind trials that are used to test the effectiveness of new drugs. The doctors who administer the test drug to patients do not know whether they are giving the patient the drug or a placebo (an apparently identical dose that does not contain the drug). This ensures that the doctor remains totally objective in monitoring the patient's progress in response to the treatment.

Confidentiality

Researchers must ensure that data from participants cannot be identified or be traceable back to specific individuals. The researcher needs to establish appropriate systems to ensure **confidentiality** and prevent data about individuals being accessed by unauthorised people. This can be achieved by designing systems for collection and processing of the data that do not reveal the identity of the participants, yet enable all the data from any one participant to be linked. Usually, this involves representing each participant by a unique code reference, rather than by name, so the **anonymity** of individuals is maintained.

Maintaining anonymity is an important protection for participants. It is also important for maintaining the integrity of the study because it helps to reduce the risk of bias. As a consequence, any analysis and interpretation of the data from the project would be less objective or comparable.

Key terms

Informed consent – Being provided with all relevant information that may influence the decision to give consent to participate.

Confidentiality – Keeping information, such as research data, confidential or hidden, so that only the information needed for the purpose of the research is made available to the health or social care researchers.

Anonymity – Keeping the identity of an individual hidden from others.

Case study: Janice

Janice is a nurse in a psychiatric research team investigating dementia. The research protocol requires her to make observations of patients with dementia while they are undertaking specific tests of memory and cognitive function. One of the patients does not complete the research tests and, although Janice saw this patient doing something almost identical earlier in the day, she did not make the observation under the conditions set for the research test, so she realises she cannot include the observations in the research.

1 Why couldn't Janice include her observation from earlier in the day?

2 In what way was Janice demonstrating her awareness of ethical principles?

Ethical approval

All research carried out in the NHS, care settings, the community or in university departments requires ethical approval. The research should not commence before the approval has been received and, if it does, any data collected prior to the approval date has to be discarded.

Organisations such as the NHS, charities and university departments have formal procedures for the ethical approval process. The researcher submits a specially designed form to present the relevant information about the proposed research project to the ethical committee.

Did you know?

The ethical guidelines from the Medical Research Council, which is funded by the government, include sections among others, on data sharing, use of animals, use of human tissue and global bioethics.

A research ethics committee consists of a panel of individuals who critically evaluate each proposal in relation to the ethical implications of the planned research. An ethics committee may accept, reject or ask for modification and resubmission of a research proposal. NHS ethics committees are made up of health and care professionals and scientists, who contribute technical and research expertise to the discussion, and lay members contributing as representatives of the general public. Universities, for whom research is often a major part of their activity, will have a research ethics committee and publish guidelines for researchers.

Did you know?

Each NHS Strategic Health Authority operates an ethics committee for its own region. Information about all these committees and dates for submitting proposals to be considered at monthly intervals are available online from the National Research Ethics Service (NRES), via the National Patient Safety Agency (NPSA) website.

Gaining ethical approval for a research project is time-consuming, often taking many months. Any research involving vulnerable individuals (such as patients, children or individuals using care services) or a health or social care setting, would only be approved if the study was being carried out by professionals. It is not acceptable for students to carry out a research project in health or social care settings for these reasons.

Fig 22.1: Why are research proposals scrutinised by an ethics research committee?

2.2 Ethical issues and research

Ethical codes for research are only guidelines, not legislation. While it may be straightforward to make a judgement about what is, or is not, acceptable for many projects, the judgement for some research may be much less clear. Over time, the boundaries of knowledge are continually extended by research, particularly in science. Society's understanding of what is acceptable is based on existing knowledge. Research that is breaking through existing boundaries of knowledge, into the unfamiliar, creates ethical **dilemmas**.

Examples of dilemmas relating to research that have arisen in recent years include:

- using stem cells in research to better understand certain diseases
- investigating genetically modified crops as a way of increasing food production to support increases in the human population.

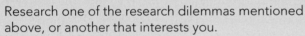

Activity 6: Research dilemmas

Research one of the research dilemmas mentioned above, or another that interests you.

1 Identify the different arguments in relation to the ethical issues raised by the research dilemma.

2 What would *your* decision be, if you were a member of an ethical committee discussing whether or not to give consent to similar research?

3 Compare your judgement with that of other members of the class.

Dilemmas such as the examples above make news headlines because they affect society. Resolution of the dilemma may involve changes in the law and in the interpretation of the ethical codes that govern research.

Key term

Dilemma – Arises when it is difficult to choose between different choices.

Human rights

Individuals in European Union countries have, among other rights, a right to life, to be free from torture, degrading treatment, and discrimination and to have their privacy respected. All research must respect these rights. Stem cells are retrieved from embryos that are a few days old, and it is this that creates the ethical dilemma in relation to research using this type of tissue.

Role of the media

The media, whether print, broadcast or Internet, are powerful influencers of public opinion. For example the media were very influential in publicising the contents of the 1998 research report on MMR and autism. In 2002, the media publicised destruction by protestors against experiments in which genetically modified crops were being grown in fields to investigate any potential effects on the environment. This research trial was subsequently abandoned because it was impossible to protect the research sites.

News media are mostly controlled by private companies, which often think it more important to print spectacular headlines that will maximise profits for their shareholders, rather than take care to present a fair and objective report of all the uncertainties and weaknesses the researchers may have discussed in their full research report. However, there are other examples where the media have campaigned vigorously to benefit groups who would otherwise not be in a position to influence opinion and social policy. The Thalidomide case, for example, led to major changes in the ways new drugs are tested before being prescribed.

Activity 7: The Thalidomide story

In the late 1960s and early 1970s, the *Sunday Times* ran a vigorous campaign on behalf of children born with limb deformities after their mothers took the drug Thalidomide for morning sickness. As a result the Distillers Company, which marketed the drug, set up a trust fund in 1973 to support the needs of the Thalidomiders, as they now prefer to be called.

1 Use the Internet to research the role of the *Sunday Times* in influencing research on drugs.

2 Extend your research to investigate how the Thalidomiders are coping with life, now that they are in their middle years.

Use and misuse of data

Researchers have a duty not only to protect participants from harm but also to ensure that the project is carried out with integrity. Integrity in research involves:

- carefully considering the methods used to carry out the research
- ensuring the accuracy of the data
- ensuring the accuracy of generalisations derived from the results and the analysis
- ensuring that the contributions of participants are not wasted because the research is of poor quality due to flawed methodology. (This is not the same as research that does not prove its underlying hypothesis or does not provide an answer to the question posed by the research.)

Research methods

Methods of research are described in the next section but, in relation to ethics, it is important to design the project with care and select methods that are appropriate for the purpose of the research. A flawed methodology reduces the validity of the research findings, lessens the usefulness of the research and devalues the participants' contributions.

Research accuracy

Inaccuracies due to equipment faults and sloppy practice or carelessness in taking measurements would be considered unethical because they abuse the commitment participants make to the research project. Changing data or ignoring unexpected or 'rogue' results is unethical because it is falsifying evidence. Sometimes a rogue result could indicate an important difference. The researchers should investigate the cause of the rogue result before dismissing it.

Deliberately presenting data to exaggerate or downplay research findings is also unethical. This can be done, for example, by taking measurements with an accuracy that is inappropriate for what is being measured, or by setting the scale of a chart or graph in such a way that it makes the difference between two measures look proportionately greater (or smaller) than it is. For example, recording the body weight of 60–70 kg adults to the nearest 0.01 kg (i.e. the nearest 10 grams), while very accurate, would be relatively meaningless because a 0.01 kg difference in weight would not be significant in relation to normal hour-by-hour fluctuations in body weight. However, it might be appropriate to record the weight gain of a premature baby weighing less than 2 kg to the nearest 0.01 kg.

Generalisations

A common strategy for researchers, when interpreting their results, is to use **inductive reasoning** to apply their findings from the specific results obtained under the specific methodology of their particular research project to make a more general claim. Similarly, in a wide-ranging project, **deductive reasoning** could be used to make claims about more specific situations.

If the researchers have sufficient valid evidence from their research, preferably combined with other evidence published in the literature, inductive or deductive reasoning may be acceptable when making claims about the value of their research findings. However, if the logic of the arguments put forward in support of the reasoning is flawed and not supported by reliable and valid evidence, then making either inductive or deductive claims is not valid and the data is being misused. For this reason, researchers use very tentative language when drawing conclusions about their research. For example, they may emphasise that their conclusions only hold for their particular research methodology, for their particular participants, or use language such as 'the results suggest that' or 'are consistent with those found in other studies'. (This means they do not disagree with the other studies but cannot be more certain than that.)

Did you know?

The discovery of the antibiotic Penicillin came from a chance contamination of a culture of bacteria being grown in a laboratory by Alexander Fleming.

Key terms

Inductive reasoning – Arguing logically from the specific to the general.

Deductive reasoning – Arguing logically from the general to the specific.

These are some of the reasons why it is rare for researchers to claim they have 'proved' a theory or claim. However, when introduced to the implications of research, e.g. in relation to the effectiveness of a new treatment, the public may find it easier to understand certainty, rather than a balance of probabilities.

Vulnerability of individuals

Research involving vulnerable individuals is important if health and social care services and practice are to meet their needs. However, their vulnerability, perhaps from learning disability or acquired cognitive impairment (e.g. brain injury or dementia), means that as participants, individuals may find it difficult to understand the information about the research, to ask questions about it or to answer questions (e.g. in a questionnaire) without help. There is a risk that anyone helping the participant to answer questions could influence the responses given or change them, either deliberately or unintentionally. Also, researchers could exploit the vulnerability of the participants by omitting to check that the participant has understood the information they have been given or possibly not being truthful about the research. Omitting individuals from a sample because they are vulnerable is also not ethical. Researchers should make provision to avoid exploitation or abuse of vulnerable people when they participate in research.

2.3 Implications of research

Who commissions research?

Research costs money by taking up professionals' time, or because they require particular equipment and other resources. It also requires specialist research skills, which an organisation may not have – either because they are too small or because they do not have sufficient use for such skills. These considerations mean that research is often commissioned from another organisation.

Research carried out by an organisation is likely to reflect that organisation's interests. The Alzheimer's Society will therefore commission research, or carry it out itself, relating to that disorder. However, if the organisation paying for the research is a commercial company, it may only be interested in the findings of the research if they promote the company positively, e.g. if they boost sales or enhance the public's perception of the organisation. As the commissioner of research, the organisation has the power to influence the research by:

- setting up the research methodology so that it deliberately only investigates a selected aspect of the subject
- only comparing its own findings with those from other research projects that also support the arguments in favour of its own interests and ignoring contradictory evidence
- suppressing, by not making public, any research findings that are against the company's interests in promoting its activities.

Not all research carried out by private organisations is necessarily poor quality. Nevertheless reports based on commercially sponsored research should be evaluated critically so that any possible **bias** is clearly identified; and the results of the research should then be used with appropriate care to take account of this.

Did you know?

Research commissioned by the government, the NHS and other public sector organisations is usually won through a competitive tendering process whereby each organisation interested in carrying out the research submits a proposal and budget for the research.

Activity 8: Who's paying?

Several companies relevant to health and social care carry out extensive research, which they publish in relevant journals. Just because a commercial company has commissioned research, it does not necessarily mean that the research will not conform fully to ethical principles and be conducted and reported openly and objectively.

Look at a selection of research reports and note the name of the organisations involved in the research, either as researchers or through funding (sponsoring) the research project.

1 To what extent do you think the organisations may benefit from the research?

2 Is there anything in the research methodology and findings that suggests the research may be biased?

Functional skills

English: In this activity you will be reading a range of texts and understanding the detail in order to detect meaning and identify the purpose of the research when considering bias.

Authenticity

Research aims to add new knowledge and understanding either by:

- generating new data
- or interpreting or applying existing knowledge in a new way.

Research is based on the principle that the researcher is a neutral observer of a **phenomenon** and does not distort or alter observations made of the natural world.

Key terms

Bias – A situation in which an investigation produces results that are influenced by *unacknowledged* factors, perhaps because of the way the investigation was designed, errors were ignored or how the results were interpreted.

Phenomenon – A term used to describe an event or observation, e.g. the rise in hospital-acquired infections. The plural is phenomena.

However, due to pressures on a researcher, such as:

- the need to produce results by a deadline
- wanting to gain prestige for career advancement
- inappropriate influence of others (e.g. the sponsors of the research)

there may be a temptation to alter results from those actually recorded. This is unethical and can have serious consequences for the researcher involved.

Did you know?

A health or social care professional may be charged with professional misconduct if they are involved in unethical research practice.

Validity

Validity depends on what *claims* are made about a piece of research and how well the claims are supported by the evidence or results from the research. Various factors, listed below, may affect the validity of research.

- The *methods* used to conduct the research should be appropriate for the purpose of the research. This might include the underlying premise of the method, the accuracy of the equipment used to make measurements, whether any tests for reliability of the research instruments/equipment used were carried out, the care with which the conditions of the experiment or investigation were carried out, how the results were analysed and any assumptions made in doing this.

- The presentation of the *findings*, for example what arguments are used to explain the relationship between the results and the conclusions, assumptions or bias in the arguments presented, ignoring some results and/or over emphasising others.

- The *conclusions* should be an automatic outcome from a discussion of the results. Conclusions that have been evaluated against evidence from other sources apart from that being reported (see also triangulation, page 449) have greater validity than those that are not evaluated against existing knowledge and understanding of the subject. Conclusions that have very little relationship with the results reported would have very limited, if any, validity.

Reliability

Reliability is about the extent to which the research can be reproduced. Reliable research when repeated by another researcher using exactly the same methods, produces the same results. Researchers often test the reliability of equipment used in experiments before they conduct a long, complex series of tests. In a laboratory, experiments may be repeated several times. Once the scientists have perfected their techniques and equipment, an average value may be used, or if the variations between results are unavoidably great, then many measurements may be required and statistical tests applied to the results. It is much more difficult for social scientists to repeat a survey. Even if they use exactly the same participants, the circumstances could not be exactly the same because participants' second contributions could be influenced by their previous experience of participating.

Did you know?

Good practice in social research is to conduct a pilot study on a small sample of participants beforehand, to test the reliability and validity of research instruments such as the questions combined together in a questionnaire. This enables possible sources of error to be identified and steps can then be taken to reduce them before starting the main study.

Apart from conducting a pilot study, social science researchers take great care to keep as many aspects of the research methodology as constant as possible. In a large study, several different researchers may be involved in carrying out interviews. In this situation all the interviewers should take part in trial interviews, compare the results, discuss the differences and agree the actions they will take to reduce the differences when carrying out the research interviews. This process is sometimes called standardisation.

Did you know?

The National Child Development Study (NCDS) is a longitudinal study of all the people born in England, Scotland and Wales in one specific week in March 1958. The numbers of people in the original sample have decreased slowly over the years since then, because people die or emigrate. Source: IoE, 2009

In social science research, one way to maintain the validity of data over a long period is to start with large numbers of participants. In the above study, over 17,600 babies were born in that week in 1958 but, although nearly two thousand were no longer traceable, there were still well over 15,000 participants remaining in 2004. Research that involves unstructured interviews may only report fewer than ten case studies but if the interviewees were selected because they have a very rare disease, the findings – even from such a small sample – could still be valuable in improving the care sufferers from the disease receive. A survey using a questionnaire enables many more people to give information for the research and, provided that all reasonable care is taken with the methods, the results should be reasonably reliable. Each method used in social science research is limited by the reliability of the data it generates.

Impact of key reports

The government and other reputable organisations, such as The King's Fund and the Nuffield Trust, commission or produce research reports on health and social care topics.

Activity 9: Independent research organisations

Explore the websites of The King's Fund and The Nuffield Trust to find out about each organisation.

1 How do they contribute to health and social care?

2 Investigate one health and social care report from each organisation.

Reports that are based on high standards of research tend to be influential, often giving rise to significant changes in policies that benefit individuals. Influential in health and social care reports include:

- The Beveridge Report 1942
- The Black Report 1980
- The Griffiths Reports 1984, 1988
- The Acheson Report 1998
- The Laming Reports 2002, 2009
- The Darzi Review 2008.

Activity 10: Influential reports

Find out the full titles of these reports and what their key recommendations were.

1 What social policy initiatives have resulted from these reports?

2 What reports relating to health and social care have been published in the last year? Write a summary of what each is about in no more than two sentences.

Functional skills

English: This activity will involve reading to understand key points and ideas presented in the reports.

Publication of many reports on health and care matters is highlighted in public news bulletins. Sometimes reports of research carried out by journalists themselves, and published in newspapers, draw public attention. Green papers are consultation documents in which the government outlines their thinking on policy issues, and these documents can result in the drafting of legislation in a white paper, which is then debated in Parliament.

Did you know?

Not all reports are influential in a beneficial way. In 1998 a report was published in the highly respected medical journal *The Lancet*, which made a link between the MMR vaccine and autism. As a result of the publicity this report received, large numbers of parents refused to have their children vaccinated so that by 2005 the incidence of measles showed a very sudden rise. The scientific evidence for the claim was found to be seriously flawed and, in 2007, the doctors involved were charged with professional misconduct by the General Medical Council. In January 2010, after lengthy investigation, the GMC announced that 30 charges of unethical research practice were proven against the doctors. *The Lancet* had already published an apology regarding the publication of the flawed research in February 1998, and retracted the paper in January 2010. Despite the major flaws in the research that invalidate the findings, some parents still believe there is an association between MMR and autism.

Access to information

Participants in research should have access to all the information held about them (see next section). Also, researchers may consider that some information would be valuable for their research but they may not have the right to see, or access, it. Under the Freedom of Information Act 2000, any individual is entitled to apply to see information held by public authorities but this Act does not apply to information held by private companies. Without access to information that may be important to the research, the validity of the findings could be reduced.

2.4 Legislation, policy and research

The Human Rights Act

The Human Rights Act 1998 embodies in UK law the rights enshrined in the European Convention on Human Rights. The Act makes clear statements about the rights of individuals, which include:

- the right to life
- the right to freedom from torture or degrading treatment
- the right to privacy (and family life)
- the right to freedom of expression.

All research should respect these rights.

The Data Protection Act

Any information held about an individual by others is subject to the Data Protection Act (DPA) 1998. There are greater restrictions on sensitive information, such as ethnicity, beliefs, health and sexual life. Organisations (e.g. employers that hold personal information about individuals) have to register with the Information Commissioner's Office, the public body that enforces the Act. The DPA means that if information is held, it can only be used for specific declared purposes and the information can only be held for a specified period of time. For a researcher, this means that under the DPA:

- only data relevant to the project can be collected
- the data can only be processed according to the stated purpose so a researcher could not use the data collected for one project in another project, unless consent for the second project had also been obtained from each participant
- it would be illegal to change the information so that it is no longer accurate
- the information must be processed in such a way that it does not breach an individual's legal rights, or cause them harm or distress. This would include revealing the person's identity either directly or indirectly. Thus it would contravene the DPA if, in a case study using a pseudonym, the information given still enabled the individual to be identified
- all information gathered from participants should be kept securely
- after the data is analysed, each individual's personal records would need to be destroyed
- the individual data cannot be taken outside the UK unless it is protected (e.g. encrypted).

Any participant could request to see the data you have collected on them under the principle of 'right of subject access' laid out in the DPA. All organisations collecting and using personal information are legally required to comply with these principles and you, as a researcher, should also respect them throughout the period of your project. Once you have completed the project, you should destroy the original records such as the completed questionnaires (e.g. by shredding them). If information relating to an individual's ethnic background, political opinions, religious beliefs, health or sexual life is gathered, you need to be particularly careful about the security and anonymity of the data.

Codes of practice

All professional bodies associated with the health and social care professions have codes of practice. Any researcher in health and social care would be expected to comply with the code of practice of their professional body. All those whose work is in any way associated with the NHS must conform to the NHS National Patient Safety Agency's (NPSA) guidelines for Research Ethics Committee review.

Activity 11: The NPSA

Research the guidance produced by the NPSA, the British Psychological Society and the Medical Research Council regarding their codes of practice for the conduct of ethical research.

Policies and procedures

All research involving staff or individuals using services, either in a health or social care setting or in individuals' own homes, must comply with the policies and procedures of the care organisations involved. In some settings (e.g. early years), parents sign a general consent for staff, including students on placement, to observe children as part of their routine care. However, observations carried out for a research project would require additional specific consent.

Assessment activity 22.2

P2 **BTEC**

Prepare a piece of writing that discusses how ethical issues influence health and social care research.

Grading tip

P2 Before you complete the task, take part in a discussion or debate with your peers about

examples of ethical issues associated with health and social care research. Practical issues, such as how a confused older person could give consent to participate in a research project, or when it might be ethical to withhold information about the research from participants, could also be considered.

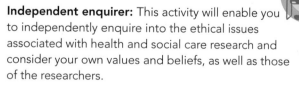

PLTS

Independent enquirer: This activity will enable you to independently enquire into the ethical issues associated with health and social care research and consider your own values and beliefs, as well as those of the researchers.

Effective participator: You can show effective participation by discussing different viewpoints and dilemmas about the ethics of research and seeking resolution of these.

3   Understand research methodologies relevant to health and social care

Activity 12: Participating in research

Have any of your class group ever filled in a questionnaire or been interviewed? Use the following questions to explore your experiences:

1   How did the interviewer or person who distributed the questionnaire choose or find you?

2   Did you know what the purpose of the questionnaire was or why you were being interviewed?

3   How did you know this?

4   Did you have an opportunity to agree to being interviewed or to complete the questionnaire (or not to complete it)?

5   How easy was it to understand what was expected of you, e.g. how much to say in response to the interviewer's questions or how to fill in the questionnaire?

6   Did the interviewer or the questionnaire enable you to give the answer you wanted to give, e.g. did the interviewer give you enough time to answer or did the questionnaire give you answer options that enabled you to provide a fair answer?

7   What were your feelings at the end of the interview or after you had completed the questionnaire? Why did you feel this way?

Functional skills

English: This activity requires you to make a range of effective contributions and to listen to those of others, presenting ideas clearly and appropriately for the context of this activity.

3.1 Types of research

Research in health and social care tends to adopt the methods of social science research because the projects often involve investigating people's feelings, perceptions, attitudes etc., which do not lend themselves to investigation by scientific methodology.

Laboratory-based research into diseases and disorders, using tissues and chemicals, is likely to be based on scientific method until such time as the research needs to involve people. Your project for this unit is most likely to follow a social science approach.

Quantitative research

Quantitative research involves numbers and measuring quantities or amounts. Scientific method often involves quantitative data – for example, measuring changes in the body's physiology in laboratory analyses of blood or urine samples. Measures of weight and height can be used to calculate body mass index (see Unit 21) to find out whether an individual is a healthy weight.

Key term

Quantitative – Describes information that is directly measurable; quantitative data usually involves number values and units of measurement, e.g. number of breaths per minute or weight in kg.

Activity 13: Measuring health status

List other measurements that may be taken to investigate whether the body systems are functioning normally or not. Identify the units of measurement used for each measure listed.

Quantitative research may also involve finding out, for example:

• frequency or how many times something happens in a given period, usually expressed as per minute, per hour, per day, and so on (e.g. minutes of exercise per day or number of falls per year or population data such as the number of deaths in a year from stroke)

• how many individuals there are in a particularly category (e.g. smokers or non-smokers)

• information involving more complex equipment and processes such as analysing a sample of blood to measure its haemoglobin content to assess whether a patient is anaemic or not (see also Unit 5 Anatomy and physiology for health and social care).

Quantitative research requires the use of specific measurement instruments. Measurements gathered routinely are sometimes recorded on charts, which can reveal how small variations between individual measurements may add up to a more noticeable change over a longer period. Body temperature, for instance, may change over a day or body weight over a few weeks. Multiple-choice questions, with specific answer options, can generate data that can be analysed quantitatively; questionnaires are often used for this purpose.

Qualitative research

Qualitative research involves gathering data that cannot be easily quantified and instead can only be recorded using language. Qualitative data tends to be collected using unstructured interviews, audio recording of conversations or narrative observations. An individual's feelings or emotions may be evident through observing facial expression (see Unit 1 Developing effective communication) but can really only be fully understood by letting the individual describe how they feel.

Did you know?

Patients who experience a heart attack most often describe the experience of the pain as if someone has clenched their fist around their heart. This description is so often used by patients that it can enable paramedic teams to diagnose the heart attack before they even get to the scene in the ambulance.

In routine practice, health professionals gather both qualitative and quantitative data and use both types of information to make judgements about the individual's care and treatment. Every conscious patient admitted to a hospital ward is interviewed by a doctor, who takes notes about the patient's experience of their illness – their medical 'history'. The doctor may have received information second-hand (e.g. from a GP's letter or from the accident and emergency team) but the doctor who is overseeing the patient's care on a ward needs to hear the patient themselves describe their experience of their illness, even if the doctor supplements this information by obtaining quantitative data from blood samples and other investigations, often called 'tests'. Only the patient can describe their symptoms; pain is only experienced by the sufferer and can therefore only be described by that individual. If the patient is not conscious, then the health worker has to rely on descriptive information provided by relatives or whoever is available.

A doctor interviewing a patient as part of the process of being admitted to hospital. What sort of questions is this doctor likely to ask?

Key term

Qualitative – Data that cannot be 'measured' quantitatively but can only be described using words.

In a research study, researchers often attempt to express qualitative data about individuals and their experiences in quantitative ways. Examples of this might be:

- using a rating scale to quantify the severity of pain
- completing a questionnaire to find out an individual's experience of using a health or social care service
- recording how often a specific event or behaviour happens (its frequency).

Primary research

Primary research involves seeking new knowledge that has not been previously published. The researcher gathers new data from **participants** or by examining objects, materials or data in a different way from previous studies. For example, interviewing individuals in their twenties about their experiences of health education in school as teenagers could help devise a new policy for health education. A study repeating one carried out thirty years previously would be primary research that was relevant to young people now, rather than young people as the world was for an earlier generation. Using a new technique that enables traces of a specific chemical to be identified in blood or urine samples might produce new understanding of a disease.

Primary research in health and social care often involves gathering data from individuals. Surveys using questionnaires and interviews are commonly used techniques and participants may be users of services, staff working in the services or members of the public.

Secondary research

Given that research is about finding out *new* information or understanding, a researcher needs to know what the *existing* information and understanding about the topic is, as published in books, journals and on the Internet. **Secondary research** is essential for any research project. All researchers need to read widely around their subject of interest so that they are aware not just of long-established knowledge but also of new knowledge that is emerging while they are doing their own research. Research carried out by researchers in universities and other research establishments may take several years to complete and report in full. Small-scale research projects can be completed more quickly but need to be clearly defined in order to produce results that can be analysed and reported within a few months.

Did you know?

Sharing research 'publicly' does not necessarily mean that the findings get into the daily newspapers. Research work is often very specialised so reports of the research are therefore published in specialist magazines, or journals, which may only be read by others with a similar specialist interest. University libraries hold stocks of many specialist journals. However, these days most researchers access journals online.

Activity 14: What's in the library?

Go to a library and look at the magazine rack. What specialist publications relevant to health and social care are available? What sort of articles do they contain? Who is writing the articles? You might find different types of publications available in your school or college library compared with those available at a public library.

1 Repeat the exercise looking at the book stock.

2 Can you access any e-books from your school or college library? If so, find out how to use e-books.

Did you know?

A PhD (Doctor of Philosophy) is the post-graduate qualification expected of professional researchers. Usually a full-time PhD student takes three years to complete the research and submit the thesis (i.e. the report of the research) for examination by the university.

Key terms

Primary research – Research that generates new data from sources.

Participant – An individual who contributes information about themselves to a research project; the information may be qualitative or quantitative.

Secondary research – Research in which data is obtained from sources that are already in the public domain, i.e. sources that have been published in journals, books, magazines, etc.

3.2 Primary sources

Research techniques that can be used to generate primary data include questionnaires, structured and unstructured interviews, formal and informal observations, measurements and scientific experiments.

Questionnaires

Research in health and social care often relies on obtaining information from individuals using social research methodologies. Questionnaires are convenient for obtaining information from many individuals in a **survey** and those answering them are sometimes known as respondents. A questionnaire asks questions of participants but, usually, also only enables answers to be given according to options constructed in advance by the researcher using a **response frame**. The response frame usually only allows a limited choice of different responses.

In small surveys, questions may be put to the respondent orally by the researcher, who then ticks a box corresponding to the answer given and also records the responses provided. Market research carried out in the street usually follows this approach. In health and social care, this method may be the only way to capture information from a frail older person about the care they receive, for example.

Reflect

In research about care for older people, what potential ethical issues could arise when asking a frail 90-year-old, who is partially blind, unable to hold a pen or understand the questions to complete a questionnaire? How could the risk of unethical research practice be reduced?

In a self-completion questionnaire, **respondents** fill in the answers themselves. The questionnaire may be distributed to individuals directly by hand, by post or online, provided the organisation or researcher has a means of making contact through an email address or information held on a database.

You may well have been asked to complete a customer satisfaction questionnaire but being asked to complete a questionnaire is not the same as actually doing so. The respondent may ignore it, only answer some of the questions or not return the questionnaire to the researcher. The **response rate** to a questionnaire is an important measure of how representative the

Activity 15: Questionnaires

Examine a selection of questionnaires gathered from a range of sources, e.g. those your school or college distributes to learners. What is the purpose of each questionnaire? What sort of information was being sought? How was the questionnaire completed? Do you always complete questionnaires when asked to do so?

responses actually received by the researcher are, compared to the number of individuals originally asked to complete the questionnaire.

The **sample population** should be defined when the research is planned, as it will influence what information can be obtained from a survey. The method for selecting the participant **sample** from the sample population should also be considered at the planning stage.

Some frequently used sampling techniques include:

- random sampling, in which individuals are selected randomly; researchers may use random numbers selected by a computer or from a table of random numbers

- systematic sampling, which involves selection of the individual at a regular interval, e.g. distributing a questionnaire to, say, every sixth student who enters the college canteen, or every other patient who presents with diabetes

Key terms

Survey – A systematic process of gathering information from several people, often using a questionnaire.

Response frame – The menu of answer options to an individual question provided in a questionnaire.

Respondents – The individuals in the selected sample who actually complete the questionnaire and return it to the researchers.

Response rate – The percentage of respondents from the selected sample. For example, a 30 per cent response rate is good in a survey in which individuals are sent a questionnaire by post.

Sample population – The group of individuals in a population who are targeted for investigation, e.g. older people, college students, etc.

Sample – In social research, the individuals selected to participate in the research from the sample population.

- quota sampling, which requires the researcher to select a pre-determined number of individuals from representative groups (e.g. according to age, area of the country, socio-economic profile, male and/or female etc.); opinion pollsters use this method

- opportunity sampling, which involves researchers handing out questionnaires to individuals who happen to be passing by at the time. Standing in a college canteen on a particular day and handing out questionnaires to anyone who will take a copy would be opportunity sampling.

The sampling technique and sample size chosen for a research study affect the validity of the research and the conclusions that may be drawn from it.

Reflect

The more complex or varied the information being sought from the survey sample, the larger the number of respondents that are required to ensure the validity of the data obtained. Why do you think this is?

Who your respondents are could affect the interpretation of the results so it is usual to gather factual information about them that your secondary research has suggested might be significant. Questionnaires usually request information on age, or age group and gender. However, requesting information that is not relevant to the research (e.g. about marital status) would be unethical because it invades individuals' privacy. Ethical approval may involve removing some questions if this were the case.

The simplest questionnaires have response frames that offer only straightforward choices and require all responses to be indicated entirely by ticks. More complex questionnaires may have:

- more questions
- more options in each response frame
- require respondents to provide written comments.

Questionnaires with only closed and open questions are probably the simplest response frame for the researcher to construct but provide more limited data, which can be more difficult to interpret, especially when working with a small sample.

Closed questions only offer two alternative answers: usually 'Yes' or 'No'.

Open questions require the respondent to answer freely, either orally or by writing in a blank space provided on the questionnaire. The respondent has to write the answer (or the researcher, if it is not a self-completion questionnaire).

Other response frames enable more specific and detailed information to be obtained. Examples include:

- ranking scales, which require respondents to rank different statements in an order, often using a number scale, where, for example '1' is very important and '5' is not at all important (see Figure 22.2)

Q. Which of the following is most important to you when you finish your current course?

In the right hand column, enter one number per line according to how important each statement is to you with 1 representing the most important and 5 the least important.

Getting the highest grades I can for my Level 3 qualification(s)	
Passing my level 3 qualifications(s)	
Getting to university	
Getting a job	
Moving away from home	

Fig. 22.2: In this ranking questionnaire the statements assume that the respondent is on a Level 3 programme. Unless the sample population is selected for this reason, how would the response options prevent other respondents from answering the question?

- Likert scale response frames, which gather respondents' opinions of carefully worded statements using a five-point scale such as 'strongly agree, agree, neither agree nor disagree, disagree, strongly disagree'. Other descriptor words may be used (see Figure 22.3).

Examples of other response frames are presented in Figures 22.4 and 22.5 on page 431. Constructing a questionnaire takes time if it is to yield good-quality research information. Questionnaires are very useful when finding out about people's opinions, perceptions, experiences, or to find out how much knowledge and understanding they have of a topic. Surveys undertaken for a student project are likely to focus on this type of information because of the ethical constraints on students regarding research in health or social care settings or with users of services.

The drawback of using response frames is that the answer options offered may not include the answer the respondent thinks is right for them. One way round this is to include an option such as 'none of these', 'all of these' or 'other', with a space for the respondent to provide an alternative answer.

What is your experience of using your GP surgery?

Please enter one tick per statement

	Strongly disagree	Disagree	Neither agree or disagree	Agree	Strongly agree
1 I can get an appointment with the doctor I choose within two days		✔			
2 The surgery offers evening appointments					
3 The surgery has male and female doctors					
4 The doctor will visit me in my home if I am too ill to go to the surgery					
5 I can have prescriptions made up at the surgery					
6 Staff at the surgery are helpful					
7 Staff at the surgery are friendly					

For Q4 the respondent may never have been ill enough to need this service in which case the Likert scale on its own does not give a sensible answer option; inserting a 'don't know' column on the right, could get round this problem.

In Q6 and Q7, by separating these two apparently similar questions, it enables respondents to acknowledge helpfulness even if the staff are not friendly and vice versa.

Fig. 22.3: What other questions could you include in this Likert scale patient questionnaire?

Did you know?

In the UK, the government carries out a survey of all households, called the National Census. It is compulsory by law for Census forms to be completed. The Census has been carried out every ten years since 1851 (with the exception of 1941, when the country was at war). The next Census is due in 2011. The data gathered in the National Census is analysed by government statisticians and computers and provides valuable information about the population that is used to formulate social policy. Census forms are particularly long and complicated questionnaires.

Reflect

Why is it important to hold the respondents' interest throughout the questionnaire, rather than getting them bored or annoyed by the questions and the answer options?

Partly completed questionnaires reduce the quality of the data from a survey and therefore limit the validity of any interpretation and conclusions drawn from the research. Factors to consider when designing a questionnaire include:

- a clear understanding of the contribution the data respondents will make to the research
- the abilities and experience of the respondents, e.g. their understanding (avoid jargon), literacy skills, etc.
- how you will address ethical issues (e.g. providing information about the research)
- what the document looks like; does its layout, font size and style help the respondent complete the questionnaire?
- what instructions the respondent will need to complete the questionnaire
- the order of the questions, e.g. simple questions at the start and more complex ones later; questions probing personally sensitive information are best placed towards the end of the questionnaire

Are you affected by any of the following common chronic disorders?

Please tick only those that apply.

Asthma	☐	Irritable bowel	
Eczema	☐	Crohn's Disease	☐
Psoriasis	☐	Rheumatoid arthritis	☐
Diabetes (Type 1)	☐	None of these	☐
Diabetes (Type 2)	☐	Other chronic disorder	☐
		(Please specify below)	

Other (*please state*): _____

_____

The term chronic may need to be explained to respondents

The last two options enable respondents to provide information other than that given in the response frame and to indicate if they have no chronic disorders at all

Fig. 22.4: This response frame requires respondents only to indicate those responses that apply to them

How important are each of the following social contacts to you?

Circle one number per statement.
1 = very important, 5 = not important at all

Others living at my home	1	2	3	4	5
Relatives not living at my home	1	2	3	4	5
Work or college/school colleagues	1	2	3	4	5
Neighbours	1	2	3	4	5
Friends outside of home and work/study that I first met face-to-face	1	2	3	4	5
Social networking on the Internet with people I have never met	1	2	3	4	5

Fig. 22.5: In what ways could you use a response format that enables the respondent to quantify a statement using a numbering system?

How often do you exercise?

Enter one tick per line for each statement (a)–(e)

Construct the statements carefully; meanings should be unambiguous

'at least' is easier to understand than 'a minimum of'

This option enables a respondent who does not exercise regularly to enter an answer rather than leave the line blank

Define the frequency of an event or activity rather than using relative descriptors such as often or very often because 'often' may mean different things to different individuals

	Every day	3–4 times per week	Once a week	Once every 2–3 weeks	Once a month	Less often than this
(a) Walk at a steady pace uninterrupted for 20 mins						
(b) Walk briskly for 1 hr uninterrupted						
(c) Attend yoga or similar session for at least 1 hr						
(d) Participate in moderate specific activity, resulting in mild sweating, for 1 hr minimum						
(e) Participate in energetic activity e.g. squash, rugby, resulting in substantial sweating, for at least 40 mins						

Fig. 22.6: How could you use a response frame like this to find out the frequency of other behaviours and lifestyle habits such as diet?

- how you will hold the interest of the respondent so they answer all the questions
- the distribution method and how long the questionnaire will take to complete, e.g. will respondents have a hard surface available for the writing involved?
- how the completed questionnaires will be returned.

Distributing questionnaires by email or post means that you need the email or postal addresses of the participants. This information is confidential and may not be known by the researchers. All such information would be subject to the DPA. The aim of any survey is to get as many of the completed questionnaires returned as possible; the **return rate** is an indicator of the reliability of the data generated from the survey. To calculate the return rate, you need to record exactly how many questionnaires are printed and distributed, as well as how many are returned.

Interviews

Interviews involve an interviewer interacting with participants in the research. Sometimes there

Activity 16: Distributing questionnaires

In groups discuss the advantages and disadvantages of different methods of distributing questionnaires for research projects investigating:

a) the alcohol consumption of university students
b) how older people manage their finances
c) the exercise habits of busy professionals.

Key terms

Return rate – The number of questionnaires returned, relative to those distributed, expressed as a percentage.

Interview – An interaction or conversation between a small number of people for the purpose of eliciting information.

may be more than one interviewer or two or three interviewees. Interviews may take place:

- face-to-face
- over the telephone
- using text messaging
- online
- using video-conferencing facilities so those involved are not in the same location but can see each other
- via social networking websites
- in a focus group, where several interviewees respond to questions.

An interview is a useful research method for example, when:

- detailed information is required
- knowledge and understanding are being sought from a specialist
- the population sample is very small
- participants may have difficulties completing a questionnaire
- a wide range of experience is being investigated
- the information being sought is not sufficiently predictable to be gathered using a structured questionnaire.

Structured interviews

In a structured interview, the interviewer has pre-prepared questions, which are put to the interviewee. The interviewer writes down the answers given by the interviewee, possibly using a structured template, which may involve ticking boxes and recording a summary of what the respondent is saying.

Unstructured interviews

An unstructured interview is not constrained by pre-prepared questions. Instead the interviewer will have identified some broad topics to ask the interviewee about but will then use follow-up questions, according to the answers provided by the interviewee. This approach enables the interviewer to probe specific aspects in detail, to check understanding, return to points already mentioned, etc. Unstructured interviews are therefore time-consuming and it is more difficult to standardise the technique if several interviewers are involved. Also, it is difficult for the researcher to concentrate on what responses the interviewee is giving, if these have to be written down at the same time. It is therefore quite common for such interviews

to be audio-recorded but there the interviewee would need to give explicit consent for the interview to be recorded. Alternatively, a scribe could be present solely to record what is said but this may affect the interviewee's responses. After the interview is over, the interviewer listens to the tape again and prepares a **transcript**.

Scientific experiments

The scientific method involves making an investigation to establish factual information. Its origins are in making careful observations of different phenomena in the natural world.

Key term

Transcript – An exact word-for-word written record ('ums' and 'ers' included) of what is said, both by the interviewer and the interviewee, taken from an audio record of the interaction.

On his 1831–36 voyage on *HMS Beagle*, Charles Darwin filled 37 notebooks with observations of thousands of different species and their environment. These detailed records formed the core of the evidence from which Darwin developed his theory of evolution. He eventually published his theory in 1859. This drawing, which he made in an 1837 notebook, is the first sketch of the evolutionary tree.

The scientific method involves testing a **hypothesis**, which is a statement about a phenomenon. The statement is based on prior knowledge and is an 'educated guess' about the relationship between factors influencing an observed phenomenon.

Factors that influence a phenomenon are called **variables**. A scientific **experiment** is a test specifically designed to investigate the nature of the influence of a single variable on the phenomenon.

The phenomenon is the **dependent variable** and the factor influencing it is the **independent variable**. A single experiment is only valid if it tests the effect of just one dependent variable against one independent variable, so making it a 'fair' test. Both variables need to be measurable, as far as possible using quantitative measures.

An experiment may prove or disprove a hypothesis. Either outcome is equally positive. If a hypothesis is disproved, the scientist will analyse and evaluate the results, construct a modified hypothesis and conduct a further experiment to test it. Scientists may pose a hypothesis that requires knowledge and understanding of a whole range of factors or variables. The scientists break up the main hypothesis into individual hypotheses and investigate a single pair of variables for each of these in turn so that the main hypothesis is not fully tested until a series of experiments is completed.

Human beings are complex organisms and their behaviour and physiological responses are influenced by very many variables. Ethical considerations mean that researchers have very limited scope to control

these variables, as expected in a scientific experiment. While experimental work is used in some psychology research, much other social science research can only be based on scientific principles as far as is permissible within ethical frameworks. Sometimes the research strategy mixes scientific method and social research. For example, an investigation of the effect of an exercise routine on individuals' health could measure some aspects (e.g. changes in pulse rate, respiration rate, blood pressure, etc.) under scientific conditions but would then have to adopt a social science methodology, such as a questionnaire, to investigate how the exercise made the individuals *feel* about their health.

Activity 17: Experiments

In groups, discuss the following questions:

1 What experiments have *you* carried out, and where? The most likely place will have been in a science laboratory.

2 What was the hypothesis?

3 What were the variables in these experiments?

4 Which was the dependent variable and which was the independent variable?

5 Were you measuring quantitative results or making qualitative observations?

6 Did you have a control and, if so, why?

Observations

An observation involves gathering information visually, and is not necessarily dependent on verbal content. Observations are valuable for understanding behaviour, and for recognising the degree of mastery of practical skills and how people interact with each other and their environment and events as they happen. Observations can be made in 'live' situations or from recorded visual media. Consent is always required from the participants who are being observed and, for good practice, from the organisation on whose property the observation is being made. Observations made in public spaces may not need consent, on the grounds that anyone can observe others as a passer-by. Recording events and activities (e.g. on mobile phones or video cameras) for research purposes would also require explicit consent from participants.

Key terms

Hypothesis (plural: hypotheses) – A hypothesis is a statement that predicts an association between two variables.

Variable – An entity or factor that can have a range of values that can be measured.

Experiment – A test designed specifically to test the validity (truthfulness) of a hypothesis.

Dependent variable – A variable whose value is dependent on that of another variable. The dependent variable is associated with the phenomenon being measured.

Independent variable – A variable whose value is not dependent on that of another variable. Time and temperature are common independent variables in scientific experiments.

If the observer is actively engaged in the event or activity being observed, then they are a **participant observer**. For example, a care worker might be stimulating an individual with profound and multiple learning needs to respond to various stimuli by moving objects, talking and otherwise interacting with the individual and at the same time making a record of the individual's reactions. Alternatively, if *another* care worker was observing the interaction between the carer and the disabled individual and noting the responses, this care worker would be a **non-participant observer** because they would not be involved in the interaction between the two people and would be observing it as an outsider.

Formal observations

Formal observations can provide specific information for a research project. A formal observation is a planned event in which the observer watches a specific activity for a period of time and makes a record of what goes on during that time.

Did you know?

The Early Years Foundation Stage curriculum introduced in England in September 2008 requires early years workers to observe young children regularly to record their progress in meeting specific developmental objectives.

Techniques for making formal observations include narrative, time sampling, checklists, event sampling and sociograms. The observation may be documented on a specific form but should always record the date, time, duration and context of the observation. In childcare, observations are a routine aspect of the early years practitioner's work and information from observations helps the practitioner plan activities to promote the development needs of the children in their care.

Formal observations are not limited to observations of individuals. They may involve observations of staff and

Key terms

Participant observer – The individual doing the observation is part of the process being observed.

Non-participant observer – The individual is an onlooker and not part of the situation being observed.

of the environment. A health and safety audit is a form of routine research that involves close examination of equipment, décor and furniture to see that it is still in a good state of repair and not a risk to people. The health and safety officer might use a checklist to record what has been observed and note any signs of wear and tear that might be a danger.

Informal observations

Informal observation is an important aspect of all care. Carers should always be watchful of the individuals they care for. In this context, an informal observation could simply mean noticing changes from normal patterns. For instance, a person might be uncharacteristically aggressive, or quiet and not participating in a group activity, or look pale and unwell. Informal observations are often the only means of gathering information about unplanned events or incidents (e.g. a violent outburst or a patient collapsing). Informal observations may have a place in a research, and they have greater validity if the person making the observation is a health or social care professional.

Reflect

Gathering information through informal observation, i.e. being observant, may provide valuable information. What ethical issues might arise in relation to using informal observation in a research project? How should you present findings acquired in this way in a report of the research to take account of these?

Measurements

Research may be based on changes to the values of measurements. For example, a study exploring levels of stress experienced by individuals may involve measuring their blood pressure and possibly pulse rate. Measurements usually generate quantitative data.

3.3 Secondary sources

In the twenty-first century, information that has already been published can now be obtained through a variety of different media. Books, journals and magazines are traditional sources but, increasingly, researchers use digital media to access secondary sources for their research. However, to do this successfully, researchers need:

- the technological resources to access them (e.g. access to the Internet, to a library that subscribes to online journals, etc.)

- the skills and understanding to use the software required to access and use the resources effectively

- to be able to establish the validity of any secondary source accessed via the Internet

- to understand the legal expectations regarding copyright, confidentiality, etc. when using secondary sources.

Information literacy

Information literacy means understanding the limitations of different information sources so that data from them can be used appropriately to maintain validity for the purpose for which the information is being used. Factors to consider when using secondary sources are highlighted in Unit 6 Personal and professional development page 251.

Secondary sources accessed for a research project are likely to reflect the specialist focus of the research. They may contain advanced text that is less fragmented by headings than a Level 3 textbook and they may discuss complex ideas and detailed factual data. Here are some strategies for making the best use of secondary sources:

- ask yourself what the heading tells you

- skim-read to identify the type of text (e.g. research report, critical analysis, review article) and its structure (e.g. headings, referencing, sources)

- scan-read to identify key words and judge the relevance of the text for your purpose

- target more detailed reading on the abstract/ summary (if there is one, it may be in a feature box or sub-heading), conclusions (at the end), discussion (towards the end), introduction (start of main text), results and method, in that order

- make notes in your research notebook

- record all details needed for later referencing.

Reflect

Why would it be particularly important to pay attention to the country to which a secondary source related when carrying out research relating to health, social care or education in your local area or region?

Examples of secondary sources that could be a source of relevant data for a research project include:

- websites

- specialist journals that are relevant to health and social care and the research topic

- media (e.g. newspapers, radio, television, Internet news pages)

- books

- e-books

- government reports

- reports from other reputable bodies (e.g. charities and research foundations).

Websites

Activity 18: Websites

a) Search the websites of:

- a government department

- a voluntary organisation

- your local authority

- a local primary care trust.

b) Find one document from each website that is relevant to health and social care, open it and summarise what the document is about in no more than 50 words. Share this with your peers.

c) Make a list, with brief notes of the sort of information each website contains, to use later in your research project.

Websites are a useful means of accessing government documents and important reports. The details for the government departments most relevant to health and social care research are listed at the end of this unit. Websites for charities that provide health and social care services or carry out medical research can also be useful sources of data.

The amount of information available on the Internet is vast, and can be accessed via many different websites, which can make it difficult to find an article again at a later date. Good discipline is valuable, not only for your research project, but for all study. Here are some useful tips for Internet research:

- *always* save *all* the details you need to compile a reference list for the research report; these should include a) the URL (*full* web address details as taken from the textbox at the top of your Internet screen), b) the day/month/year date you accessed the webpage and c) if possible, the year the document was posted on the website or published

- save web addresses on the personalised 'Favourites' directory of your Internet Service Provider (ISP) so you can return to the same site with a single click

- download documents you may want to return to later, saving them to a data stick or hard drive on your computer

- avoid printing out whole documents unless they are difficult to read on screen, or contain complex information you wish to annotate or return to repeatedly; sometimes printing selected pages is sufficient, combined with saving an e-copy.

Journals

Journals are specialist publications published at regular intervals for specialist groups such as professionals, scientists and other researchers. Academic journals publish reports of research. The publication of research in a journal is an important aspect of the research process. Indeed, in the UK, government funding of research partly depends upon publication this way and in future will also be dependent on how often other people read the research reports. Some weekly or monthly journals may be available for reading in your school or college library or in placement settings. These days, libraries subscribe to online versions of journals so those registered with the library can access them online.

Media

Print and broadcast media can be a valuable source of information, particularly in relation to news but also on other topics of broad interest to the public.

Newspapers

Newspapers are a traditional source of information about what is going on in the world and individual customers tend to purchase the same paper every day. Newspapers can be influential in developing opinions among the public (e.g. about controversial topics or at election time). However, each UK newspaper is written to appeal to its particular group of customers and they can show their bias by:

- what they present as the main news (e.g. on the front page)

Activity 19: Newspapers

Work in a group of 6–8 for this. Each group member should obtain a copy of a different daily or evening newspaper on a day when there is a story relevant to health and social care in the news. Bring the newspapers to class and investigate how each paper has reported the story.

1 Each newspaper will have presented the health and social care news differently. What key message is each putting across in its headlines? What factual information do they present? Where is the story located in the newspaper? Has the paper sought the views of different people? What is the newspaper's opinion? (You may need to look at the 'comments' or 'editorial' page to find this out.) What is the style of writing?

2 When you have compared the way each newspaper has covered the story, you need to think about how the information has influenced your own perspective. What have you learned about the story? Which newspaper do you think has given the fairest (most balanced) coverage to the news story? What are your reasons for this? What is your opinion of the story now? How important do you think the story is in relation to health and social care? What has influenced your judgement on this?

3 Now consider where you may find out more about the story – to check the accuracy of the information you have read in the newspapers. Is there a report that you could read? What does the government say about it? Where could you get other opinions on the story? If you investigate these sources, to what extent does additional information confirm or alter your own opinion and conclusions about the health and social care story?

PLTS

Effective participator: You can participate effectively in this activity by collaborating with other group members when sharing out the tasks across a range of newspapers and enabling each group member to contribute.

- what they decide to write about it
- from what perspective they write (e.g. that of business or the private individual, etc.).

Professionals and researchers should be aware of this when using newspapers as a source of information for research. Some newspaper publishers are beginning to restrict free access to news stories online so that people have to pay a subscription in order to read them.

Broadcast media

Radio and television provide news, information and discussion of different opinions on a wide range of topics. The rigour of the broadcast content can vary across channels but several television and radio programmes frequently discuss topics relevant to health and social care including, for example, long-standing favourites such as *Panorama*, *Horizon* and *Regional News* on television and *The Today Programme*, *You and Yours*, and *Woman's Hour* on Radio 4.

Books

Books are the traditional means of publishing information. Social science theory tends to be published in books, whereas science-based research reports are usually published initially in journals. New knowledge and understanding from research gets incorporated more widely into specialist textbooks later so recently published textbooks have greater credibility than books published several years ago. In health and social care, continual policy change can mean a textbook is soon out of date. However, a book published a long time ago may be the original book written by a particular theorist. When quoting the theory in your own writing, you need to reference the source in such a way that it is clear whether you have read the original book or journal article or just read about the theory (or research) in a more recently published textbook.

Reflect

Can you think of some famous theories you have studied (in other units) that were originally published a long time ago?

School, college or university libraries tend to stock textbooks and other books for study. In contrast, public libraries tend to stock books of more general interest,

including books about specific disorders and health and care issues.

e-resources

Apart from the Internet itself and online academic journals and newspapers, an increasing number of books are available as e-books, either by direct purchase or if you are a member of a library.

Activity 20: e-books

Find out what e-books you can access through your school, college or public library that could be relevant to your BTEC course. Arrange to view an e-book and experiment with the software capabilities for using the book for study.

Literature review

The literature review is carried out at the start of a research project to enable the researcher to find out what is already known about the topic so that the research does not simply repeat work already done by others. The review involves reading around the immediate topic of the research to acquire knowledge and understanding relating to the context of the research. A literature review also helps to narrow down the research topic and identify the specific aspects that will be the focus of the research project.

The review is likely to involve accessing a range of secondary sources. It is important to be systematic in recording all the details needed to construct a reference list from every source used. The details you need to record are listed on page 444. You could expand a literature review by following up items from bibliographies and reference lists in the sources you have already viewed. Sources where sufficient information is provided to make a judgement about their reliability should be used in preference to poorly validated sources, such as online encyclopaedias, or where there is no named author or other identifier to enable reliability or validity to be established. It is usual to return to the literature review and sources used when writing up the report of research.

Once you have established the usefulness of a source, you can go back and read it more carefully.

Table 22.3: Stages in a literature review

Extracting information	• skimming and scanning for preliminary judgement on relevance • identifying key words for exploration in text • establishing type of information, e.g. research report, essay, comment, quantitative/ qualitative, etc. • detailed reading in order: 1 Abstract or summary; 2 recommendations; 3 introduction; 4 discussion; 5 results and methodology
Interpretation	• understanding what is being said in the source • understanding the reasons for the interpretation presented • how objective is the interpretation? • identifying the relationship with research topic/your purpose
Analysis	• what are the arguments presented in the source? • to what extent are they supported by valid and reliable evidence? • what **assumptions** are being made? • what are the similarities to, and differences from, your own research? • how does the source compare with other secondary sources? • who are the participants? • what methodology was used? • how objective is the data? • exploring other factors relating to the data, e.g. when and where it was collected
Synthesis	• bringing together the knowledge and data from all the sources to develop a new or different perspective on the topic • possibly identifying gaps in the knowledge • acknowledging similarities and disagreements between your own findings and information in the literature • possibly suggesting explanations, influences, etc. • defining the limitations of the source in relation to your own project

Analysis

Analysis means a detailed exploration of a text to better understand different aspects of the information it contains. Analysis involves dissecting the text of the source, or breaking it down, by exploring and discussing each detail. An important part of analysis is to identify any **arguments** being proposed by the authors. Strengths and weaknesses in the evidence or arguments should be discussed as part of a critical analysis.

Key terms

Assumption – Conditions that apply to a situation but which are not investigated in the research. It is good practice to be explicit about the assumptions being made.

Argument – A point of view that aims to persuade others to the same view by presenting supporting evidence. An argument is more than a statement of fact.

Synthesis

Synthesis is the process of constructing or developing a new/different argument or perspective, based on the issues revealed by the preceding analysis. Once each source in the literature search has been critically analysed individually, the researcher will have a different perspective on the research topic and be able to identify more specifically how further research could contribute new knowledge and understanding. The researcher can then decide on exactly what aspect of the topic to research, formulate a suitable hypothesis or research question and plan their project.

Data

Quantitative data, in the form of graphs, tables and statistics, often features in health and social care research.

Tables enable data to be viewed systematically, without the need for a lot of text. They are most frequently used to present numerical data, but can also be used to summarise qualitative information concisely and for clarity.

Graphs and charts present quantitative data visually, which usually assists interpretation of the data. They also enable large quantities of data to be presented in a manageable format.

Reflect

How confident are you about reading and interpreting quantitative data presented within text, in tables or in graphs and charts? Discuss any concerns you have with your tutor who may be able to arrange specialist support during your project.

Demographic statistics collected by government departments or agencies, local authorities and health trusts are valuable for comparison with data gathered in your project.

The Office for National Statistics (ONS) publishes a range of demographic statistics that are categorised under health, social care, education, etc. They provide national data as well as a breakdown of the data for each of the UK regions. They also present comparisons with similar data from earlier years.

The ONS website has several reports that present health and social care data through its link to the NHS Information Centre. Statistical information may be presented in various formats such as tables, graphs and charts.

Activity 21: Statistics

Go to the ONS website (www.statistics.gov.uk) and note the type of data that can be retrieved from each site and the different types of graphs and charts used to present the data.

Note all the information provided with the data, e.g. headings, keys, scales, units, etc.

Select one table and two different types of chart, all unrelated to each other and describe orally to each other, the results shown in each. You could do this activity in pairs. Use questioning to each other to clarify any uncertainty or misunderstanding you have in interpreting the data.

Check your own interpretation of the statistical data by reading the descriptions of it given in the text accompanying the visual representations of the data.

Functional skills

Mathematics: This activity enables you to demonstrate your understanding of statistical information presented in different formats and communicate this to others.

Key term

Demographic statistics – These are statistics relating to populations. In the UK, statistical information is collected continuously by various agencies but particularly by government departments through information about UK residents gathered from e.g. tax collection, driving licences, passports, the ten-yearly Census, schools, GPs' records, etc.

Assessment activity 22.3

P3 BTEC

Present a comparison of different research methodologies as they might be used in health and social care research.

Grading tip

P3 You could present your comparison in a summary form, e.g. as a detailed table, giving examples of where each method could be used in health and social care research, and submit it with the evidence for your research project plan.

PLTS

Creative thinker: The questions you ask in order to make the comparisons will demonstrate your creative thinking skills.

4   Be able to plan for a research project

Please note: you may wish to cover the content in Section 5, Topic selection (pages 443–447) first, before covering this section on Planning.

4.1 Planning

Methodology

The methodology is the overall approach you select to conduct your research – for example, whether you will use a scientific or social science methodology. It includes the specific methods you will use and the literature search to contextualise your project within existing knowledge and understanding of the subject.

Activity 22: Selecting your subject

Once you have selected your research topic, carry out some further reading. At the same time, you should start to compile a reference list of the sources you use.

Draw a mind map to break down the subject into different aspects and decide:

- whether your research will be based on a research question or a hypothesis and then what it will ask or propose
- which information could be gathered qualitatively, which quantitatively, and what questions you could ask to generate relevant data.

Consider whether you could gather relevant data from formal and/or informal observations.

These decisions should be influenced by the knowledge and understanding you have gained from your literature search, supported by advice from your tutor and, at this stage, the aims and the hypothesis proposed or research question posed. Designing a questionnaire that is **fit for purpose** is very time-consuming and you should therefore allocate sufficient time in the action plan to do so.

If you have time, you may be able to trial your questionnaire to see whether the questions, and instructions for answering them, enable respondents to complete the questionnaire as fully as you intended.

This is a **pilot study**, which is good practice in research. A few, carefully worded questions and well-thought through response frames may provide more valuable and reliable data than several, poorly thought out questions consisting only of closed answer options.

You should indicate in your action plan if you intend to carry out a pilot study and should get any amendments made checked by your tutor before starting the full-scale study.

Action plan

Once you have decided on your methodology, you can construct a detailed plan for your project. The action plan you will submit for your research project may follow a similar format to the action plan for personal development you prepared for Unit 6. The plan should be sufficiently detailed to give you all the time needed for different tasks. If the plan is not detailed, it is more likely that the time needed will be seriously underestimated and you will get behind with your overall plan.

The details of your action plan should include time needed for the literature search, gaining ethical approval, developing the research tools, gathering the data, interpreting it, and preparing your report on the findings. Ethical approval for your project will be organised internally at your centre and you should follow your tutor's instructions. The approval process could be part of the assessment process for P4.

Timescales

Most professional research projects are time limited. In this unit, the timescale will be determined by the submission date set by the unit tutor. You will need to work backwards from this deadline to plan how you

Key terms

Fit for purpose – A product or object that performs its intended function well.

Pilot study – An initial, small-scale (perhaps only 10 per cent of the full sample number planned) exercise, in which you use your research tools to see if they are fit for purpose. It is acceptable to make small amendments to improve the reliability and validity of the data gathered in the main, full-scale study.

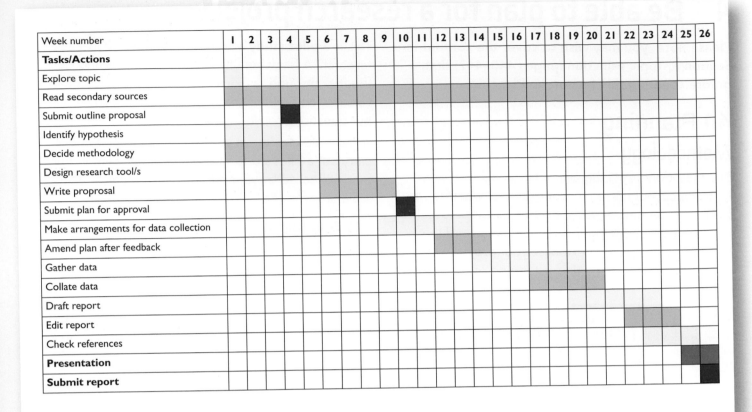

Week number	1	2	3	4	5	6	7	8	9	10	11	12	13	14	15	16	17	18	19	20	21	22	23	24	25	26
Tasks/Actions																										
Explore topic																										
Read secondary sources																										
Submit outline proposal																										
Identify hypothesis																										
Decide methodology																										
Design research tool/s																										
Write proprosal																										
Submit plan for approval																										
Make arrangements for data collection																										
Amend plan after feedback																										
Gather data																										
Collate data																										
Draft report																										
Edit report																										
Check references																										
Presentation																										
Submit report																										

Fig 22.7: Would you use a project action plan like this to identify and monitor the overall goals, deadlines and outcomes of the project and the practical tasks required to meet them?

will use the time available. This means you need to allocate time for each of the actions you identify in your action plan. Developing a questionnaire that has well-focused, clear questions and carefully constructed answer frames takes time, especially if you carry out a pilot test on it. If you aim to have a large participant sample, then you may need to factor in time for printing the questionnaire. Depending on the overall timescale, you may be able to build in some slack time to allow for the slippage that often occurs when planning over several weeks and months.

Target group

The target group is the sample population from which the participant sample is selected. As you are a student on a course that in itself does not lead to a professional qualification, in almost all cases it would be unethical for your participants to be sampled through contacts in health or social care settings. To do so would require ethical approval from external organisations such as the local strategic health

authority, something which is unlikely to be granted, given your unqualified status.

It is ethically acceptable to involve your peers as participants in a student project. Since most students on a BTEC Level 3 course will be studying in a college or sixth form, their peers would be fellow students at the same institution. However, you should be aware that only students over the age of 16 years should be included in your sample because involvement of individuals younger than this would require written consent from their parents/guardians. If based in a college, you may need to consider this, as some learners at Key Stage 4 may also attend college.

It might be possible to include friends, family and acquaintances as participants *provided* they know you through your private life rather than through work or a college placement *and* you can interview them away from a setting. Sampling from the general public in a public space could expose you to personal risk, and your centre would be unlikely to give consent for this method of accessing participants.

Consent

In addition you need to plan how you are going to gain informed consent from each individual participant and be explicit about this in your project plan. You also need to consider how your questionnaires will be distributed so that participants have privacy while they complete them. Peers may ridicule respondents, which would be a form of harm. They may also influence their responses, which would greatly reduce the accuracy of the data and the validity of any findings.

You will need consent or approval from your school or college to carry out the overall project and this consent should be included with your project plan. You should always remember to gain consent for the project *before* you involve *any* participants in the research.

This would also apply for any pilot study to trial your research tools. Remember too that you should obtain written consent from an appropriately senior manager to hand out questionnaires or carry out observations on the premises of any other organisation apart from your school or college.

Informal observations of general practices and behaviours observed in placements or in public spaces might be included but, because the information has not been collected formally, it has only limited validity in a research project. However, data collected this way may be better than having no data. Informal observations (e.g. from placements) may support the rationale for selecting the topic of the project in the first place.

5   Be able to conduct research relevant to a health and social care context

5.1 Topic selection

Activity 23: Narrowing down a topic

1   List *five* aspects of health and social care that interest you.

2   For each topic, draw a spidergram to highlight anything at all related to it.

3   In groups of 2–3, quiz each other about each topic and discuss possible primary methods you could use to investigate each.

4   After 20 minutes' discussion, narrow down your choice of topics to *three* and justify your selection to your group.

Now work in your group to consider the following:

1   What factors influenced your selection of three topics from the original five? To what extent did each member of your group identify similar or different influences?

2   Have the discussions with your group altered your selection? If so, why?

3   What possible project topics have other groups explored? What factors influenced their choices? Has the class discussion altered which three topics you have chosen? If so, why?

4   Spend no more than 60 minutes in total conducting a preliminary search for information on each of the three topics.

5   Which *one* topic do you think is the most appropriate one to select for your research project? Why? Record your reasons in a notebook.

Subject

The subject, or focus, of your research project will be the specific aspect of the topic you eventually decide to investigate. Selecting a suitable subject can be likened to a filtering process. Some of the factors that should be considered when selecting a topic are summarised below.

- Ethical constraints on who participants can be
- Accessibility of secondary sources in the subject and appropriate for Level 3 study
- Access to a sample population to whom you can distribute questionnaires
- How the topic relates to health and social care

- What hypothesis or research question could you propose?
- Can you test the hypothesis or is the question answerable?
- Time scale for duration of project and planning it
- Is the scale (breadth and depth) of the topic manageable with the time and other constraints?
- Sensitivity of topic for participants
- Making the data you can collect, given the constraints, relevant to the topic
- Travel accessibility e.g. to conduct interviews, time and cost factors
- Access to specialist equipment and resources
- Personal safety when doing the primary research.

Some of the influences may be specific to the circumstances of your school or college. For example, if you are in a rural area, the cost of transport when making visits to interview a specialist might be more of an obstacle than if you lived in an urban area.

Some of the factors to record when reviewing the topic for your research project and carrying out a literature search are:

- full surname (last name) plus first name initials of *every* author
- if an edited book, *also* note full surname and first name initials of all the editors
- year of publication or day/month/year for newspapers and broadcasts
- full title of the book (as on the cover), journal, Internet/newspaper article or broadcast programme
- if using/referencing an edited book, full title of book, *plus* the title of the chapter read, *plus* its start and end page numbers
- town/city of publication (books)
- name of publisher or broadcasting company
- for all sources from the Internet
  - the day/month/year accessed
  - full URL reference copied from the box at the top of Internet screen.

Note: you should include all the relevant information from each source used in a literature review and project report.

Your literature search will have highlighted different aspects of the topic you are interested in but you need to analyse the topic closely. Drawing a detailed mind map of the different aspects of the topic can help narrow your focus on a specific aspect that is sufficiently small to be manageable in the time you have available.

Research question

A research question is used when the research aims to investigate a topic without making any prediction as to what the research might discover. It enables the research to be broader than when testing a hypothesis. An example of an 'open-ended' research question might be 'How do college students cope with stress?'

Hypothesis

If you plan to test a hypothesis in your research, you will need to identify measurable variables and distinguish between the independent and dependent variable. You will then need to design a test to see whether the hypothesis is true (i.e. proven) or not (i.e. disproved). For example, you might want to find out whether people's drinking habits varied across the days of the week. The days of the week would be the independent variable and the alcoholic drinks they consumed on each day would be the dependent variable. You then need to construct a statement that identifies an association between the two variables. Your hypothesis might be, for example, *'people drink more alcohol at the weekend than they drink in the week'*. However, before setting up the test you would need to consider the statement more carefully.

- Who are the 'people'? This might be determined by what participants you can include in your sample. Would it be interesting to compare the drinking habits of different age groups, e.g. young people/ young adults compared with older adults with family responsibilities and a mortgage to pay? How could you distinguish between the different groups? By age? By gender? By whether they are a parent or not? How will you find this information out?
- Are you going to ask the respondents to tell you whether they drink more on particular days? Do you think they would know this reliably? Could you ask a less direct question that would enable you to calculate how much they drank? Would it still be valuable to ask the question because there is often a mismatch between people's *perceptions* of what they consume and what they *actually* consume. And would this mismatch be interesting to investigate in its own right?

Case study: Nazrul

Nazrul is interested in doing a project on lifestyle choices and health because he is aware that lifestyle factors have a negative impact on the health of his own family and community. He creates a spidergram that identifies diet, smoking, alcohol consumption, exercise and relaxation as relevant lifestyle factors. Starting with diet, he thinks of different aspects of the topic he could look at. He adds five-a-day, school lunches, omega 3, vitamins, obesity, BMI, dieting and food allergies around the word 'diet'. He ends up with over 30 different topics about lifestyle.

Nazrul chooses school lunches, thinking he could go into his younger sister's school to do his primary research. However, his tutor points out that it would not be ethical for him to carry out a survey of schoolchildren and instead he can only survey his fellow students at college. Nazrul then finds some government statistical data on the Internet and an organisation called the School Food Trust, which has lots of information. He still wants to investigate school meals but is not sure what relevant information he can get from his college friends

when they are no longer at school. He wants to test the hypothesis 'school meals are unhealthy'. His tutor asks him lots of questions such as 'What does being "unhealthy" mean?', 'How will you measure it?', and 'How are you going to get hold of school meals to make a measurement?'

After some discussion with his tutor and a group of his classmates, Nazrul decides it would be better to use a questionnaire to find out what his fellow college students eat at lunchtimes and then draw his own conclusions as to whether or not they eat healthily. He also decides to interview the catering manager about the college's lunchtime menus and a practice nurse who is a friend of his mum's to find out about dietary issues affecting young people's health in the local area.

1   How have ethical constraints affected Nazrul's original idea for his project?

2   Can you think of a suitable hypothesis for Nazrul to test in his project?

- Could you recall what you drink (alcoholic or non-alcoholic) each day? If you cannot, then are your respondents likely to remember? Could you ask them a more specific question or, rather, give them some answer options that enabled them to give you more accurate information about their drinking habits?

- What do you mean by an alcoholic drink? Do all alcoholic drinks contain the same amount of alcohol? Does it matter? Do you need to know what people drink more specifically? How could you get this information from your survey questions? Do you need to know the size of the drink as well as what type it is (e.g. wine can be served in a range of different-sized glasses)?

- What about students who are under 18? It is illegal for them to consume alcohol other than in their home. Does this mean you should ask respondents where they drink their alcohol? Do you think under-18s might not give you a truthful answer because they are drinking illegally? Do you think people might not give you a truthful answer because they are aware they probably drink too much? How could you ask the questions so that you reduced respondents' concern about giving you this information? What are the ethical issues that might be relevant here specifically?

- What is 'the weekend'? Friday, Saturday and Sunday nights or just Saturday and Sunday? Would a different combination of days be more representative of the days when you suspect people drink most? Do you think all your respondents will think of the weekend as being the same days? How could you make sure in your questionnaire that there was no confusion about how you were defining a 'weekend'?

This sort of questioning can be relevant to any project but it is important to be clear about what you are actually measuring when testing a hypothesis, otherwise the validity of the test may be considerably reduced. For example, you may end up with an amended hypothesis such as 'people consume most alcohol at the end of the week'.

Rationale

The rationale is the reason why you have selected the topic and the particular aspect of it that you have chosen to investigate – for example, the research question posed or the hypothesis proposed. Explaining the reason for your choice by referring to a wider context would be helpful. Maybe your research has been triggered by current interest in the media, your wider reading or a specialist interest or because you wanted to follow up in more detail something studied in another unit. For a more complete justification, good practice would be to support your explanation by referring to some secondary data from your literature search.

Relevance to sector

Your project should be relevant to health and social care and the research could be relevant because it relates to health care needs, raises awareness of health risks from particular behaviours, or relates to changing policies and practices.

Identifying relevance at this stage can support your rationale and aid interpretation, analysis and evaluation of your results in your project report.

Achievable and realistic

In order to make your project manageable, so that you can obtain sufficient results to enable you to meet all

the grading criteria within the time limits set for you, it is important to establish clear boundaries for the project. This means defining what it is you *are* going to investigate and also what you are *not* going to research. If you identify the boundaries at the planning stage, then it is much easier to stay within them as you conduct your literature search and develop your research instruments. In this way your research project should be achievable within the time and using the resources available to you.

A project that does not have a clear focus tends to generate such a wide range of data that it becomes difficult to analyse and evaluate your results and draw valid conclusions. This could make it difficult to meet the higher-grade criteria.

Assessment activity 22.4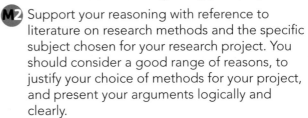

Produce an action plan for a research project investigating an aspect of health and social care that interests you.

Justify why you have chosen the research methods identified in your plan and rejected others.

Assess the value of different research methodologies in ensuring the validity of findings from health and social care research.

Grading tips

P4 Make sure your actions follow SMART principles (see Unit 6).

Remember that your research project needs to enable you to meet not just P4 but also P5, P6, M3, M4 and D2 so the plan you submit for P4 could consider *how and when* you are going to carry out the research, report the findings, and analyse and evaluate your findings and methods *as part of the plan*. However, you will not present the evidence for the other criteria until later in the project.

Keep a research notebook in which you record all notes and details regarding your project

M2 Support your reasoning with reference to literature on research methods and the specific subject chosen for your research project. You should consider a good range of reasons, to justify your choice of methods for your project, and present your arguments logically and clearly.

D1 In the first instance, you may find it easier to consider the value of the methodologies you are planning to use in your own project in ensuring validity, as you will already have thought about this in some detail and the evidence could be integrated with that for M2.

If your project does not enable you to assess all the methodologies, then you could consider health and social care research more generally if it enables you to make a more thorough assessment regarding their influence on the validity of research findings.

PLTS

Reflective learner: You will be demonstrating your skills as a reflective learner when planning the project and setting the aims of the research itself and success criteria and when you review your progress.

5.2 Conduct research

Secondary sources

The range of secondary sources and their use in the literature search have already been discussed. While you will start the literature search as you decide the topic of your research, and produce the written literature review at the same time as you research your action plan, you should also continue reading about your research topic while the project is ongoing. As you get more involved in the research, you will gain a better understanding of the subject and, by re-reading a source, you will understand more of the detail in the sources and therefore adapt your interpretation of it, possibly realising that it is more relevant than you originally thought, or less relevant. You may need to find new sources to support an unexpected finding from your primary data.

Data collection

It is now increasingly easy and economic to use information technology (IT) as a tool to make routine tasks easier. A mobile phone may be able to execute several useful functions to help you process data from your project, whether this is simple arithmetic on a calculator function, taking a photograph of your equipment as set up to take measurements, or possibly other functions such as recording an interview or accessing the Internet. You may also use specialist equipment that incorporates technology, e.g. a pedometer to record walking activity or an electronic counter to record a particular behaviour observed in people in a public space, etc.

Monitoring

An important aspect of any research project is to continually monitor your progress against your original research plan. There are two reasons for this: firstly to keep focused on the purpose of the research as stated in the research question or hypothesis; and secondly to monitor your progress against your action plan so that you complete the different stages of the project by the deadlines set. Research rarely proceeds exactly as planned. Regular monitoring of your progress against your plans should enable you to identify variations from the plan promptly so that you can make changes to overcome any problems before you have lost too much time.

As already discussed, disproving a hypothesis has as much validity as proving it. After you have gathered the data, you may realise that you are in fact testing a different hypothesis from the one you originally intended. If this is the case, then this adjustment should be justified through the analysis and evaluation of the research when you write the report. If results from a pilot study indicate there is a problem, then it may be acceptable to make adjustments at this preliminary stage, before you commence the full primary research study, provided this is discussed with your tutor first. It is not acceptable to change your methodology after the pilot stage because any change will reduce the reliability of your results, severely limit valid comparisons between data and make it difficult to draw any conclusions. The validity of all findings will be reduced and it is better to persevere to the end and then address the issues in the evaluation (see pages 453–454). The risk of encountering such problems can, of course, be reduced by carrying out a pilot study to test the experimental method first.

Modification

Examples of possible changes to your project plan that may be necessary might include revising the order/sequencing of tasks, adjusting the timescales, altering how equipment is used so that measurements are more reliable, or even amending the scope of the study by amending the range or depth of detail that you investigate. If your primary research reveals more interesting results than anticipated, you may not have time to analyse them all before the end of the scheduled period for reporting on the project. Your tutor can advise you in these circumstances. However, it would be better to keep the project more narrowly focused from the start.

Reflect

What are the ethical implications associated with not using all the primary data gathered from your participants?

Assessment activity 22.5

P5 **BTEC**

Carry out your research according to the approved action plan.

Grading tips

 Remember to monitor your progress against the plan and record this on the plan.

Use your research notebook to record all the details relating to your project and summarise the main changes and progress points on your plan.

Record on the plan any amendments made to the research methodology. You will discuss these later and include the reasons for any amendments and the consequences for reliability of the data and validity of the interpretation, as part of M3.

Initial and date all monitoring and amendments made on the plan, according to good practice.

6 Be able to interpret research findings

6.1 Methods of analysis

In this section you will examine the data gathered from your research. Firstly, you will place all the original records from your primary sources in an order that will enable you to return to them easily at any time. Next, the data can be transferred (if necessary) into systematic formats as the 'results' of your research. Then you can interpret the data to find out whether your project has met its aims in answering the research question or testing the hypothesis.

Use of IT software

You may have used IT (e.g. a digital counter linked to a computer or an ergometer that produces a trace of an individual's responses to exercise) in which case you will need to download the relevant files to your own data stick or hard drive. However, remember that the DPA demands a higher order of security on electronically stored data, so do not store it on a shared drive on a networked system.

Once you have collated your raw data, you may have generated quantitative data that lends itself to being entered onto spreadsheet software. This will enable easy conversion of the data into an appropriate format for your report on the findings from your project.

Collecting data

The notes you make throughout the project from your literature research, records of measurements, experimental results, observations and interviews, as well as completed questionnaires, comprise the **raw data** from your research. The raw data needs to be sorted, collated and ordered systematically so that you can interpret all your findings.

Raw data may be collected in different forms, for example:

- as handwritten figures from a laboratory experiment entered on to a pre-designed tabulated template
- as graphical printouts from equipment, e.g. ergometers
- as images, e.g. scans, X-rays, photomicrographs, photographs (but not of individuals, for ethical reasons)

- digitally organised according to a specifically designed computer program, e.g. responses to online questionnaires
- on CD, an MP3 player, e.g. used as a pedometer.

A tally chart is the best way of collating data from the responses to each question on completed questionnaires. This could be done using a blank copy of the questionnaire. You should go through each questionnaire in turn and enter a tally of each response option the respondent has made. The numerical totals from the tally chart can then be entered onto a spreadsheet. If you have used an electronic questionnaire, this is done automatically. Responses to open questions should be transposed into a single location so they can be compared. You should also record where respondents have not entered answers.

For interviews that have been recorded, it is usual to make a transcript so you can study it more easily and include it as evidence The full transcript would be appended to a research report and this is expected for unstructured interviews. For structured or semi-structured interviews, a copy of the questions/prompts used and contemporaneous records of responses would probably be sufficient for this research study.

Collectively, your organised and collated data are your **results**.

Spreadsheets

Spreadsheets can be used in a variety of ways. They are most appropriate for collating numerical data because the software makes it easy to perform calculations involving the data, to rearrange data (e.g. in ascending or descending order of size, etc.) and to convert the data into charts and graphs. Which of these capabilities you use will depend on the data you have gathered and the way you interpret the data.

Presentation of data

There are conventions regarding the presentation of data, which should be followed, particularly within a research report. Data may be presented in a table, chart, graph or other diagram such as a flow chart, as already discussed. A set of data collected from a single experiment or from a group of individuals under the same conditions is called a **data set**.

Data may be either continuous or discrete. Time, weight and temperature are examples of **continuous data** because they can have any value. UK shoe sizes

are **discrete data** because they only come in definite and separate values e.g. 5, 5½ or 6 with no values in between. It is important to recognise which is which because this will determine what type of chart or graph should be used (see page 451).

Triangulation

Interpreting results from any research should be based on rigorous analysis and evaluation of your results. This is done by comparing the primary data you obtain with data from secondary sources accessed in your literature search. Good practice would be to make comparisons with several different sources, a process known as triangulation. In your project, you should aim to include at least one published source. However, it is acceptable to triangulate using two different types of primary data. For example, you might say that analysis of the survey data suggests that respondents had little accurate knowledge of the dangers of excessive alcohol consumption and this was confirmed by comments made by the nurse you interviewed, as well as by statistical data you found in a government report.

Graphical presentation

This is explored in the next section.

6.2 Data representation and interpretation

Interpretation of data involves understanding the raw data collected in the primary research in the context of either the research question or the hypothesis. Visual

Key terms

Raw data – Consists of the records of data collected from research in the form they were originally generated.

Results – Results from research are the data collected and collated into tables, graphs and charts.

Data set – A series of quantitative measurements of the same variable, recorded under the same conditions.

Continuous data – Data that can have any value. Weekly changes in body weight or changes in body temperature over a day would both generate sets of continuous data.

Discrete data – Factual information presented in numerical form; the data can only have specific values, e.g. male or female, smoker or non-smoker, those born in 1980, those born in 1981, etc.

formats for presenting data help to reveal patterns in the data that are difficult to identify just by looking at the raw data.

Tables, graphs and charts

Tables, graphs and charts (e.g. pie charts and histograms) are often used in data interpretation. The features of each of these formats are summarised in the table on the next page.

It is important to remember that, when presenting data in any format, including within the text of a report, it should be presented in accordance with mathematical conventions. The conventions ensure that all the necessary information required to interpret the data is provided within the table, graph or chart. This information is as follows.

- An overall heading, which identifies the format either as a 'table' or as a 'figure'. The item is numbered and followed by words describing the data presented in the item. For example, note how all tables and diagrams are titled in this book.

- Each column in a table should have a heading to identify what the data in that column is measuring. If it is a number, it will have no units. If it is a measurement, then the units should be given once only, in the heading title. The data should then be entered into the column *without repeating the units*.

- In graphs and charts, *both* the horizontal (x) axis and the vertical (y) axis should be labelled with a descriptive title and, as for columns, with the correct units if the variable is a measurement. If it is a number, then the axis will state 'number of …'

- A key should be provided to differentiate between different colours, shading, codes or any other visual device used to contrast the data presented.

You should remember to use all these conventions in every graph, chart or visual image you include in your project report, oral presentation or appendix.

Mean, median and mode

As indicated in Table 22.4, many biological measurements tend to follow a standard pattern called a normal distribution similar to that shown in Figure 22.8. The spread, or distribution of the measurements in a data set, is an indicator of how much the measurements vary from each other. The height of the histogram indicates how many measurements fall into each category or data group.

The mean, median and mode are different types of average.

- The mean is the arithmetical average of all of the actual measures making up the data set.

- The median is the middle value of all the individual measures when they are ranked, i.e. listed in increasing size order (lowest first and largest last).

- The mode is the value which occurs most frequently in the data set, (the most popular value).

Understanding the different ways in which data may be presented and analysed gives you a range of possible approaches for interpreting your primary data. Secondary sources may also include quantitative data and accompanying analysis, and comparing your data with independent data is helpful when evaluating your research to draw conclusions from it.

Activity 24: What can I learn from my data?

In groups of two or three, discuss your findings from the research each of you have carried out.

1 How could you present the primary data to help you understand what it means?

2 Construct tables, graphs and charts as appropriate and get a friend to check that you have presented each of these correctly.

3 Describe in words what each table, graph and chart shows, using the language introduced in this unit and especially in this section. In class, discuss each form of presentation with a partner.

4 To what extent does your data interpretation enable you to answer your research question or hypothesis?

5 How does your data compare with data from your literature searches? What are the similarities and differences?

Functional skills

Mathematics: You will be selecting and applying a range of mathematical solutions to your data, checking accuracy and interpreting the data in this activity.

Table 22.4: Features of different forms of data representation

Presentation	Features
Tables	• may be used for qualitative as well as quantitative data • can organise data systematically • may record several sets of measurements for one set of variables • may enable trends to be identified • can organise quantitative data in order of increasing or decreasing size • data may be continuous or discrete
Graphs (line graphs)	• for plotting continuous data only • for plotting changes in a dependent variable against a dependent variable (often time) • the dependent variable is usually plotted on the vertical axis and the independent variable on the horizontal axis • the values of individual measurements of each variable are plotted and joined together using straight lines (not a best-fit line) • can reveal trends, e.g. how the variable changes over time
Bar charts	• bars have identical width and vary in height/length • each bar is separated by a small space (the bars do not touch) • bars are usually drawn vertically but can be drawn horizontally • in complex bar charts, each bar may show more than one measurement • used to plot discrete data, e.g. data for males and data for females
Pie charts	• used to represent different categories within a larger group (segments of a pie) • each segment of the 'pie' is proportionate to the percentage of the whole that the category represents • each category of the 'pie' is calculated as a proportion of the whole group represented, i.e. as a percentage of a circle (360°)
Histograms	• a special type of bar chart with vertical bars with no spaces between bars (see also below) • used for large data sets of the same variable, usually of at least 50 measurements, e.g. blood pressure of 100 students • groups of possible values of the measurement are defined, each the same size • the possible measurement of the variable are categorised into equal sized groups, e.g. 1–4, 5–9, 10–14 etc., and each measurement recorded is allocated to the group in which the measurement falls and counts as 1 in that category • the boundaries for each category should not overlap • when all the measurements have been categorised into the right group, the numbers in each group are totalled • the totals in each category can be 0 or a whole number only • when drawing the histogram, the y axis is the number of measurement and the x axis shows each category of the measurement, all the same size • if no measurements are within the range of a group/category, then no bar is drawn and the space is left empty • histograms are useful to show the average and spread (range) of the values measured in the data set – the **distribution of data**

Key term

Distribution of data – An indication of the range or spread between the lowest and highest value of actual measures in a data set measuring the same variable.

What BTEC Level 3 learners at Sidson College do after completing their programme

Line graph showing changes in annual incidence of measles in England and Wales over a 10 year period

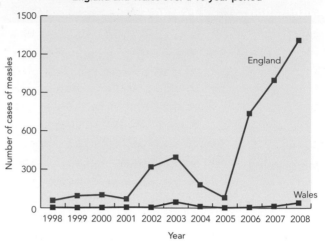

Bar graph to show the form of transport members of a BTEC class use to travel to college

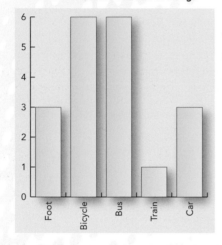

Graph to compare prevalence of underweight, healthy weight, overweight and obese men and women in a sample

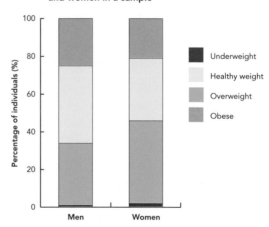

Fig 22.8: How could you use the various forms of charts and graphs to present your quantitative data?

Histogram to show BMI of 50 adults

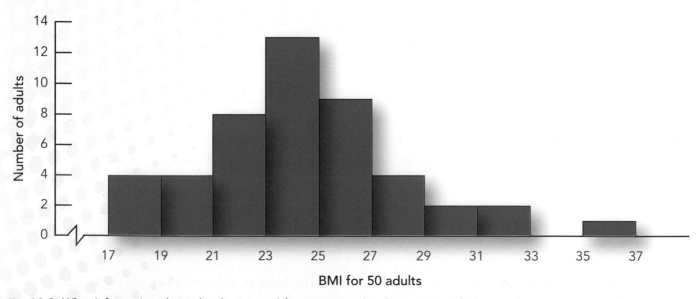

Fig 22.9: What information about distribution and frequency can be shown using a histogram?

6.3 Evaluation

Evaluation requires you to make a judgement about the worth, or value, of your research, based on the evidence you have generated from your primary and secondary sources and already interpreted. An evaluation involves examining *critically* all aspects of the work you have done on your project. This process should enable you to identify any weaknesses in your methodology that may have affected your results so you can estimate the reliability (see Section 2, pages 421–422) of your data, both primary and secondary. This evaluation is an essential part of the research because the critical review of the whole process enables you to place the results of the research in a context, and so formulate the **findings** of the research in your overall conclusions to the project.

Key term

Findings – The overall conclusions of an investigation.

Activity 25: Sources of error

- What are the possible sources of error in your data?
- What is the reason for each of these errors?
- How do the errors affect your interpretation of the results?

Comparison with the research aims

This aspect of the evaluation should analyse the extent to which the original aims of the research, as presented as part of the research plan, have been met. The focus will be the research question or the hypothesis. You should present arguments based on the evidence from your project to judge whether these have been fully addressed or only partly so.

Bias and error

Errors and bias occur in all research but it is important to examine how the errors and bias have arisen and assess the extent of their influence on the overall findings from the research. Errors can arise from, for example, weaknesses or flaws in questions or response frames that limit your ability to analyse and interpret

Activity 26: What are the findings?

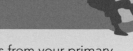

- What are the main findings from your primary data?
- How do these compare with your aims?
- To what extent does the secondary data validate the primary data?
- What reservations would you acknowledge about your findings and conclusions?
- Identify three conclusions you can draw from your research.
- What recommendations would you make for further research?

Functional skills

Mathematics: This activity could enable you to calculate the impact of the errors and bias on your data and draw conclusions about its reliability.

the data. Bias might come from factors such as inadvertently including a lot of sports students in your participant survey for a project investigating student fitness.

Ethical considerations

Because ethical considerations are so important in all social science research, and particularly when researching health and social care, your evaluation should include a thorough analysis of the steps taken to ensure that the research was conducted ethically. However, despite these measures, unforeseen issues may have arisen during the research, and discussion of how these were dealt with should also be included.

Relationship with current research

Your research report should include references to secondary sources throughout, as appropriate. Your ability to identify and discuss the extent to which your findings are supported by, or differ from, secondary evidence from your literature review should be particularly evident here, as well as in the introduction to the report, data interpretation and discussion.

Limitations of research

All research projects have limitations imposed upon them by external circumstances. Limitations may arise from practical difficulties, although you should have considered these at the planning stage. Limitations can arise, for instance, because of more restricted access to sources or more participants than anticipated. A small sample size or low return rate in a survey is a common limitation. Any factor that affects the validity of the research findings limits their value and this could be discussed here.

Strengths and weaknesses

Assessing the overall strengths and weaknesses of your research will mean reviewing all aspects of the project, including the planning stage. Firstly, identify the factors that contributed to the success of the project. You should discuss practical aspects, considering factors such as time, the sequencing of actions, communication limitations, as well as advantages and limitations that you have highlighted in earlier parts of the evaluation. Your assessment could be supported by evidence of similar experiences encountered by other researchers.

Areas for improvement

This aspect of the evaluation will be closely related to the previous section. Clearly any weaknesses, limitations arising from ethical considerations, methodological errors and bias should enable you to identify aspects of the project that you would do differently if you were to carry out a similar study again.

Implications for the sector

It may be appropriate to link your comments back to the research aims and the findings from the project when discussing the relevance of the project to health and social care for practice, individuals, service provision and topics that you have explored in other units. You could also discuss the extent to which the findings enable generalisations to be made about the limitations of the study. For example, your study is likely to involve your student peers and, depending on the nature of your project, it might not be realistic to suggest that the findings could also apply to older people, although they may apply to other young adults. By this stage of the evaluation you should have discussed the overall validity of your research data, as this is a significant influence on the conclusions that can be drawn from your findings. Your comments should be analytical and evaluative and could make an appropriate ending to your evaluation.

Conclusions

Conclusions identify concisely the main findings from your project and should be linked very clearly to the arguments and judgements made in the evaluation. They should only be statements, should not include any discussion and certainly not introduce new ideas. The conclusions should primarily be about the research subject but it may be appropriate to have one or two conclusions that relate to the methodology.

Recommendations

Recommendations relate to how the research findings could be used in the future. They may include suggestions of what further research is required, for example, to provide more robust evidence in order to fulfil the original aim of the project. There may also be general recommendations in relation to health and social care practice.

Reporting research findings

Reporting the findings of research is an important part of the research process because it enables your findings to be scrutinised by others. Research is reported using a formal report structure, which usually includes the following items.

- A title page with the project title, author name and the date of the report.
- A contents page (number the pages of the report).
- Abstract (usually only about 300 words) providing a summary of the key findings being reported.
- Introduction, including the literature review, updated.
- Methodology presenting a detailed description, with reference to sources that have influenced the methodology and preferably supported by a justification of why the methods were appropriate. (For assessment in this unit, the methodology and Introduction sections may be submitted in advance of the rest of the report.)
- Results described in the text and supported by tables, graphs and charts.
- Discussion – a substantial section presenting the analysis and the evaluation.
- Conclusions, which should be an obvious outcome from the discussion; no interpretation or new ideas should be introduced in this section. Conclusions should be succinct and to the point and may relate to the results and methodology,

- Recommendations – 3–5 recommendations that could be related to health and social care practice.

- References, presented in alphabetical order by surname of first author, preferably using a recognised academic style.

- Acknowledgements – optional, but a place to make a brief statement to thank participants publicly (but anonymously) as well as others who may have supported you.

- Appendices – number will vary but one should be a blank version of any questionnaire distributed (not the completed ones). Transcripts and context statements might also be appended. All appendices included should be there only because they are referred to in the text of the report.

It is usual for the researcher to answer questions on their research, often face to face, following a brief oral presentation of the findings. This scrutiny will involve critical analysis and evaluation from other perspectives apart from your own and so provides another check on the validity of your results. However, research presented as a written report has greater validity.

Another reason for reporting your research publicly is that it enables other researchers to benefit from

> **Did you know?**
>
> Professional researchers aim to publish their research in professional or academic journals. Publication in peer-reviewed journals is highly regarded because the report is scrutinised by experts in the same field before it is published. If the quality of the research is not of a good standard then the report will not be published. Some researchers publish the results of their research in books so they may only be reviewed by experts who review the book after it is published.

your results. From the information in your report, they may be able to repeat your research using your exact methodology, or take into account any weaknesses you have discussed so they can avoid the same problems in their research. This will have the effect of producing new, more reliable data from which future claims could be made with greater certainty. Also, the recommendations you make could help improve practice for individuals in health and social care. Thus your research report may become a secondary source for another research project.

Assessment activity 22.6

Write a report of the findings from your research.

Examine the strengths and weaknesses of the methodology of the project in addressing the research question or hypothesis.

Analyse your findings from the research in relation to answering the research question or proving/disproving the hypothesis.

Finally, evaluate how you could have improved the project.

Grading tips

P6 Present all the evidence for this assessment activity using a formal report format, as advised by your tutor, and including a reference list and appendices.

Remember that findings are based on an evaluation and that there are several aspects to consider when evaluating a research project.

M3 When examining the methodology, consider the type of research, the primary research techniques and secondary sources used and how well they enabled you to meet the project aim or test your hypothesis.

Consideration of errors and bias, ethical considerations and limitations on the research should also be included.

M4 The focus here is an analysis of whether the findings enabled you to prove or disprove your hypothesis or answer your research question.

Remember to take into account the aim of the research and its relevance to health and social care when discussing your findings, drawing conclusions and making recommendations.

D2 Your evaluation should be a thorough examination of all aspects of the project, with particular attention to errors, bias and weaknesses throughout.

Improvements should be clearly linked to the judgements made in your evaluation.

PLTS

Effective participator: Collating, interpreting and evaluating your research data and organising it effectively to present it in the research report will allow you to demonstrate your effective participation skills.

Functional skills

English: You will be preparing a formal report in which you will present information relating to your findings concisely, using formal English to express complex ideas.

Mathematics: The report will require tables, graphs and charts to present the results from your research.

ICT: You will develop a complex document using your ICT skills to produce the report, containing text and imported objects from a range of different files and applications.

Resources and further reading

Bell, J. (2005) *Doing Your Research Project — A guide for first time researchers in health, social care and early years* Maidenhead: Open University Press

Bowling, A. (2002) *Research Methods in Health: Investigating Health and Health Services* Maidenhead: Open University Press

Denscombe, M. (2006) *The Good Research Guide: For Small-scale Social Research Projects* Maidenhead: Open University

Lawrence, J. (2009) *"Thalidomiders": still fighting for justice'*, *The Independent Online*, Tuesday 26th May 2009

Michie, V. Baker, L. Boys, D. & McLeavy, J. (2008) *BTEC National Health and Social Care Book 2* Cheltenham: Nelson Thornes

Pears, R. Shields, G. (2008) *Cite them right: the essential referencing guide*, seventh edition, Durham: Pear Tree Books

Sennika, D. (2009) *'Incidence trends for childhood type 1 diabetes in Europe during 1989–2003 and predicted new cases 2005–20'. The Lancet*, Early Online Publications

Silverman, D. (2006) *Interpreting Qualitative Data*, third edition, London: Sage Publications

Smith, K, Todd, M. & Waldman, J. (2009) *Doing your undergraduate social science dissertation* Abingdon: Routledge

Stretch, B. & Whitehouse, M. (2007) *BTEC National Health and Social Care Book 1* Oxford: Heinemann

Walsh, M. (2001) *Research Made Real: A Guide for Students* Cheltenham: Nelson Thornes

Useful websites

Association of Medical Research Charities (AMRC) www.amrc.org.uk

BBC News http://news.bbc.co.uk/

Cancer Research UK http://info.cancerresearchuk.org

Channel 4 www.channel4.com

Daily Telegraph www.telegraph.co.uk

Department of Children, Schools and Families www.dcsf.gov.uk

Department of Health www.dh.gov.uk

The Guardian www.guardian.co.uk

Independent www.independent.co.uk

The King's Fund www.kingsfund.org.uk

Medical Research Council www.mrc.ac.uk

National Research Ethics Service www.nres.npsa.nhs.uk

NHS Direct www.nhsdirect.nhs.uk

Statistics Agency www.statistics.gov.uk

The Times www.timesonline.co.uk

UK government and public services www.direct.gov.uk

Just checking

1 What is research?
2 Identify five different purposes of research and give a specific example for each.
3 Why is ethical committee approval required to carry out a health and social care research project?
4 Distinguish between:
    a) validity and reliability
    b) results and findings
    c) continuous and discrete data
    d) analysis and evaluation.
5 What is:
    a) a hypothesis?
    b) a variable?
    c) triangulation?
    d) bias?
6 How does legislation affect research?
7 Explain when it is appropriate to use:
    a) a pie chart
    b) a histogram
    c) a line graph.

edexcel

Assignment tips

1 Make use of knowledge and understanding developed in Unit 6 because there are several links between these two units, e.g. planning, being organised and study skills.

2 At the start of this unit, create a Word document called 'References' on your data stick and every time you use a new secondary source type/copy and paste all the details needed for a reference list, including the access date if it is an online resource. Back it up regularly.

3 Get a spiral-bound A4 notebook (about 50 pages) to keep all your records for your research in one place. Date every entry and make notes on class discussions, observations, interviews, and more detailed ones from each of your secondary sources. Scan, copy or type up notes from it weekly as a back-up.

4 Do not be tempted to make your project too large. Have a well-defined aim and keep to it.

5 Test your questionnaire when you think you have a reasonable draft by distributing it to 5–10 members of your chosen sample population. Get them to complete it independently. Examine their responses and see whether all the questions have been answered as you intended. If there are gaps, errors or unexpected answers, review the questions, response frames and order of the questions, and make improvements before distributing the final version to the full participant sample.

Relevant legislation and organisational policy and procedures

This grid provides a list of some of the legislation and organisational policy and procedures relevant to health and social care. The content which is particularly relevant has been listed.

Legislation policy procedure	Website	Relevant content	EU directive implemented by the Act	Link to BTEC Level 3 National Health and Social Care
Adult Placement Schemes (Wales) Regulations 2004	www.wales-legislation.org.uk	Regulates placements for vulnerable adults over the age of 18 in the home of a person who is not a relative	2005/36/EC	**Unit 11** Safeguarding adults and promoting independence
Age Discrimination Act 2006	www.direct.gov.uk	Protects individuals from discrimination in employment on grounds of age in: • redundancy • unfair dismissal • unfair treatment	2000/78/EC	**Unit 2** Equality, diversity and rights in health and social care
Care Quality Commission	www.direct.gov.uk	The new health and social care regulator for England; the Commission replaces: • Commission for Social Care Inspection • Healthcare Commission • Mental Health Commission Regulates all health and adult social care services in England, (statutory, private and voluntary) Protects the rights of people detained under the Mental Health Act		**Unit 2** Equality, diversity and rights in health and social care **Unit 9** Values and planning in social care **Unit 11** Safeguarding adults and promoting independence
Care Standards Act 2000 (England and Wales)	www.opsi.gov.uk	This Act set up an organisation called the National Care Standards Commission. This was replaced by the Commission for Social Care Inspection which has now been replaced by the Care Quality Commission The Act sets standards all social care workers must meet. • standards can be found in the booklet '*General Social Care Council Code of Practice*' • ensures all care provision meets with the National Minimum Standards • sets standards of the level of care given to individuals requiring social care • requires that all staff have a thorough police check before they begin working with children and adults and a list is kept of individuals who are unsuitable to work with vulnerable adults	2005/36/EC	**Unit 2** Equality, diversity and rights in health and social care **Unit 3** Health, safety and security in health and social care **Unit 9** Values and planning in social care **Unit 11** Safeguarding adults and promoting independence

Legislation policy procedure	Website	Relevant content	EU directive implemented by the Act	Link to BTEC Level 3 National Health and Social Care
Children Act (2004)	www.ecm.gov.uk	Introduced Children's Commissioner, local Safeguarding Children boards and provided legal basis for Every Child Matters	2003/9/EC	**Unit 2** Equality, diversity and rights in health and social care **Unit 10** Caring for children and young people **Unit 21** Nutrition for health and social care
Children (Leaving Care) Act (2000)	www.ecm.gov.uk	Requires local authorities to plan for children leaving care. Local authorities must ensure children: • have support for housing and preparation for independence • have a personal adviser • can remain looked after in full time education until 21 years	2003/9/EC	**Unit 10** Caring for children and young people
Children (Leaving Care Act) (Northern Ireland) 2002	archive.nics.gov.uk	Provides a legal framework for those leaving care including: • an assessment of a young person's needs • personal advice • provision of a pathway plan • personal support and suitable accommodation for 16 and 17 year olds leaving care	2003/9/EC	**Unit 10** Caring for children and young people
Children Act (1989)	www.desf.gov.uk www.scotland.gov.uk	This brought about: • major change in childcare practice • concept of 'significant harm' • concept of 'parental responsibilities' rather than 'rights' It makes the wishes and interests of the child paramount	2002/58/EC	**Unit 2** Equality, diversity and rights in health and social care **Unit 10** Caring for children and young people
Control of Substances Hazardous to Health (2002) (COSHH)	www.hse.gov.uk	The details of this include: • storing cleansing materials correctly • labelling of hazardous substances correctly • appropriate handling of bodily fluids such as blood and urine • appropriate handling of flammable liquids/gases • appropriate handling of toxic/corrosive substances/liquids	67/548/EEC	**Unit 3** Health, safety and security in health and social care
Community Care and Health (Scotland) Act 2002	www.opsi.gov.uk	Introduced free nursing and personal care for older people in Scotland Older people who qualify receive payments of between £145 and £210 per week, depending on their needs		**Unit 9** Values and planning in social care
Convention on the Rights of the Child (1989)	eur-lex.europa.eu	Ensures the interests of the child are the primary consideration when making decisions concerning them Ensures children have the right to: • protection and care • express their views freely	2002/58/EC	**Unit 10** Caring for children and young people

Legislation policy procedure	Website	Relevant content	EU directive implemented by the Act	Link to BTEC Level 3 National Health and Social Care
Common Assessment Framework	www.dcsf.gov. uk	Provides a standardised approach to conducting assessment of children's additional needs and deciding how these should be met	2002/58/EC	**Unit 10** Caring for children and young people
Care Homes (Adult Placements) (Amendment) Regulations 2003	www.opsi.gov. uk	Applies to England only Regulates placements for vulnerable adults in the community	2005/36/EC	**Unit 9** Values and planning in social care **Unit 11** Safeguarding adults and promoting independence
Data Protection Act (1998) Date Protections (Amendment Act (2003) Access to Medical Records 1988	www.dh.gov.uk	Relates to the protection of the individuals' personal data with regard to processing and safe storage: <ul><li>storing confidential information</li><li>protection of paper based information</li><li>protection of information stored on computer</li><li>accurate and appropriate record keeping</li></ul>	95/46/EC	**Unit 2** Equality, diversity and rights in health and social care **Unit 9** Values and planning in social care **Unit 10** Caring for children and young people **Unit 22** Research methodology for health and social care
Disability Discrimination Act 2005	www.direct. gov.uk	Came into force in 1995 and was amended in 2005 It requires: <ul><li>providers of public transport to reduce the amount of discrimination on its buses and trains towards people with disabilities</li><li>public facilities and buildings to be made accessible to those who have disabilities</li><li>employers to make reasonable adjustments to allow an individual with a disability to gain employment</li></ul>	2005/75/EC	**Unit 2** Equality, diversity and rights in health and social care **Unit 9** Values and planning in social care **Unit 11** Safeguarding adults and promoting independence
Education (Nutritional Standards and Requirements for School Food) (England) (Amendment) Regulations 2008	www.direct. gov.uk	States the standards required for all aspects of meals for school children		**Unit 21** Nutrition for health and social care
Environmental Protection Act (1990, Section 34) and the Environmental Protection (Duty of Care) Regulations (1991)	www.dh.gov.uk	Section 34 of the Environmental Protection Act (1990) imposes a duty of care on persons concerned with control of waste; it places a duty on anyone who in any way has a responsibility for control of waste to ensure that it is managed properly and recovered or disposed of safely	2006/12/EC	**Unit 3** Health, safety and security in health and social care

Legislation policy procedure	Website	Relevant content	EU directive implemented by the Act	Link to BTEC Level 3 National Health and Social Care
European Qualifications (Health and Social Care Professionals) Regulations 2007	www.dh.gov.uk	These regulations extend the Care Standards Act 2000 in England and Wales Provides for mutual recognition of Diplomas, Certificates and other evidence of formal qualifications in order to assist the free movement of professionals throughout the European Union	2005/36/EC	**Unit 2** Equality, diversity and rights in health and social care
European Convention on Human Rights	eur-lex.europa.eu	Outlines basic human rights to which all European Citizens are entitled, for example: • safety and liberty • right to marry	2006/24/EC	**Unit 2** Equality, diversity and rights in health and social care **Unit 11** Safeguarding adults and promoting independence
Food Safety (General Food Hygiene) Regulations 1995	www.opsi.gov.uk	These regulations provide guidelines for safe handling and preparation of food. They include: • basic hygiene principles for handling and preparing food • food safety risks All staff who prepare food for users of services in day centres, residential settings and hospitals must follow the guidelines and be aware of the food safety risks	93/43/EEC 93/43/EEC	**Unit 3** Health, safety and security in health and social care
Freedom of Information Act (2000)	www.dh.gov.uk	Produced to promote a culture of openness within public bodies Allows anyone the right of access to a wide range of information held by a public authority Access to information is subject to certain limited exemptions, such as information about an individual Under this Act individuals can access their health records An individual can request the information to be provided in Braille; audio format; large type; or another language if necessary	95/46/EC	**Unit 9** Values and planning in social care
Freedom of Information (Scotland) Act (2002)	www.uk-legislation.hmso.gov.uk	In Scotland this Act established the office of Scottish Information Commissioner, responsible for ensuring public authorities maximise access to information		**Unit 9** Values and planning in social care
General Social Council Codes of Practice	www.gscc.org.uk	These codes set out six responsibilities for social care employers and six responsibilities for social care employees, stating the standards of conduct, performance and ethics expected of employers and staff	2002/58/EC	**Unit 9** Values and planning in social care **Unit 22** Research methodology for health and social care

Legislation policy procedure	Website	Relevant content	EU directive implemented by the Act	Link to BTEC Level 3 National Health and Social Care
Health and Safety at Work etc. Act (1974)	www.hse.gov.uk	Gives instructions for health and safety in the work place: • ensuring the environment is safe and free from hazards • assessing risks before carrying out tasks • checking equipment for faults before use • use of appropriate personal protective clothing • handling hazardous or contaminated waste correctly • disposal of sharp implements appropriately • shared responsibilities of employers and employees	89/391/EEC	**Unit 3** Health, safety and security in health and social care
Health and Social Care (Reform) Act (N.I.) 2009	www.opsi.gov.uk	Places a duty on each Health and Social Care Trust to 'exercise their functions' in order to improve the health and well-being of people who use the service and to reduce health inequalities		**Unit 2** Equality, diversity and rights in health and social care **Unit 9** Values and planning in health and social care
Health and Social Care Act 2008	www.dh.gov.uk	Established the Care Quality Commission for England and: • enables co-ordinated regulation for health and social care • helps to ensure better outcomes for people who use services		**Unit 9** Values and planning in social care
Human Rights Act 1998	www.opsi.gov.uk	Came into effect in October 2000 and allows people to take complaints about how they have been treated to a UK court • there are 16 basic human rights covering everyday things, such as what a person can say and do and their beliefs, as well as the more serious issues of life and death • human rights are rights and freedoms that all people living in the UK have, regardless of their nationality or citizenship • although everyone has these rights, they can be taken away from a person if that person does not respect other people's rights	2002/58/EC	**Unit 2** Equality diversity and rights in health and social care **Unit 11** Safeguarding adults and promoting independence **Unit 22** Research methodology for health and social care
Lifting Operations and Lifting Equipment Regulations (1998)	www.hse.gov.uk	Aims to reduce risks to people's health and safety from lifting equipment provided for use at work by ensuring it is: • strong and stable enough for the particular use and marked to indicate safe working loads	95/63/EC	**Unit 3** Health, safety and security in health and social care

continued

Legislation policy procedure	Website	Relevant content	EU directive implemented by the Act	Link to BTEC Level 3 National Health and Social Care
Lifting Operations and Lifting Equipment Regulations (1998) – continued		• positioned and installed to minimise any risks • used safely, that is the work is planned, organised and performed by competent people • subject to ongoing thorough examination and, where appropriate, inspection by competent people		
Management of Health and Safety at Work Regulations 1999	www.opsi.gov.uk	These regulations explain to managers and employers the measures they must take in order to keep staff and users of the service safe Main focus is risk assessment; regulations explain how to conduct a risk assessment and what the assessment should contain	1338/2008/EC	**Unit 3** Health, safety and security in health and social care
Manual Handling Regulations (1992)	www.hse.gov.uk	These regulations include: • preparing the environment before moving or handling anything • checking equipment is safe before use • safe moving and handling of patients • safe moving of equipment/loads	90/269/EEC	**Unit 3** Health, safety and security in health and social care
Mental Capacity Act 2005	www.opsi.gov.uk	This empowers and safeguards vulnerable people who are unable to make their own decisions Deals with the assessment of a person's capacity and protects those who lack capacity It created two new public bodies: a new Court of Protection and a new Public Guardian.	2005/36/EC	**Unit 2** Equality, diversity and rights in health and social care **Unit 11** Safeguarding adults and promoting independence
Mental Health Act 2007	www.opsi.gov.uk	This Act updates the Mental Health Act 1983 The main changes are: • 16 and 17-year-olds can accept or refuse admission to hospital and this decision cannot be overridden by a parent • patients who are detained in hospital under a section of the Act, are entitled to an independent advocate who will speak for them at a review to decide on their future • the introduction of Supervised Community Treatment Orders which mean that patients who are discharged will be visited at home by a mental health professional to ensure that they take their medication		**Unit 2** Equality, diversity and rights in health and social care **Unit 11** Safeguarding adults and promoting independence

Legislation policy procedure	Website	Relevant content	EU directive implemented by the Act	Link to BTEC Level 3 National Health and Social Care
Nursing and Midwifery Codes of Practice 2008	www.nmc-uk.org	These codes state the standards for conduct, performance and ethics required of qualified nurses and midwifes	2002/58/EC	**Unit 22** Research methodology for health and social care
Police and Justice Act 2006	www.homeoffice.gov.uk	This Act requires Police Authorities to monitor their forces in respect to Human Rights	91/477/EEC	**Unit 2** Equality, diversity and rights in health and social care **Unit 11** Safeguarding adults and promoting independence
Protection of Vulnerable Vulnerable Groups (PVG) (Scotland) 2007	www.scotland.gov.uk	A parallel scheme to the Safeguarding Vulnerable Groups Act 2006 in England and Wales which: • gives guidelines for the barring of individuals from working with vulnerable groups • provides protocols for the maintenance of registers of those barred from working with vulnerable groups	2005/36/EC	**Unit 9** Values and planning in social care **Unit 11** Safeguarding adults and promoting independence
Race Relations (Amendment) Act 2000	www.standards.dfes.gov.uk	Requires all public bodies, for example Health Authorities and Primary Care Trusts to: • review their policies and procedures • remove discrimination from these policies and procedures • remove the possibility of discrimination from their policies and procedures • actively promote equality In Health and Social Care, this means that all support must be designed and delivered in such a way that no individual will be treated less fairly because of their race or ethnicity	2000/43/EC	**Unit 2** Equality diversity and rights in health and social care **Unit 11** Safeguarding adults and promoting independence
Regulations of Care (Scotland) Act 2001	www.scotland.gov.uk	Regulates placements for vulnerable adults over the age of 18 in a home of a person who is not a relative	2005/36/EC	**Unit 11** Safeguarding adults and promoting independence
Reporting of Injuries, Diseases and Dangerous Occurrences Regulations (1995) RIDDOR	www.hse.gov.uk	This outlines procedures for: • reporting accidents and injuries objectively and accurately • reporting diseases to the appropriate bodies • reporting dangerous occurrences to the appropriate bodies • completion of relevant paperwork	89/391/EEC	**Unit 3** Health, safety and security in health and social care

Legislation policy procedure	Website	Relevant content	EU directive implemented by the Act	Link to BTEC Level 3 National Health and Social Care
Safeguarding Vulnerable Groups Act 2006	www.dh.gov.uk	Provides regulations to set out the very serious offences which will result in an individual being barred from working with vulnerable people The individual will not be able to appeal against the decision The individual cannot apply to have their case reassessed	2005/36/EC	**Unit 10** Caring for children and young people **Unit 11** Safeguarding adults and promoting independence
Sex Discrimination Act 1975 (Amendment) Regulations 2008	www.opsi.gov. uk	The Amendment expands the definition of gender harassment and gives: • greater rights to pregnant women who are employed • protection against transgender discrimination in employment • further protection against sexual harassment	2004/113/EC	**Unit 2** Equality, diversity and rights in health and social care
Vetting and Barring Scheme 2010	www.isa-gov. org	Extends the safeguards provided under the Safeguarding Vulnerable Groups Act 2006 in England and Wales, to include the barring of individuals from a wider range of activities and jobs Introduces a duty to share information about individuals who pose a threat to vulnerable groups, with prospective employers Introduces new criminal offences; it will become a crime for a barred individual to seek employment with vulnerable groups and to employ such a person	2005/36/EC	**Unit 10** Caring for children and young people **Unit 11** Safeguarding adults and promoting independence

Glossary

A

Absorption – The taking up of substances to be used by the body cells and tissues.

Abstract – A new piece of writing that brings together (or summarises) various points made in an existing piece of writing.

Abstract logical thinking – The ability to solve problems using imagination, without having to be involved practically; an advanced form of thinking that does not always need a practical context in order to take place.

Abuse – Treat with cruelty or violence, especially regularly or repeatedly.

Action research – Research in which the researcher is a participant in a situation that occurs, regardless of the research, but from which information is collected systematically. The purpose is to gain a better understanding of the situation so that knowledge, understanding or practices in that context can be enhanced.

Adenosine diphosphate (ADP) – A chemical left after ATP has released its stored energy to do work.

Adenosine triphosphate (ATP) – A chemical in mitochondria that is capable of trapping lots of energy in the last chemical bond: for example, A-P-P~P, where P is a phosphate group (an ordinary chemical bond) and ~ is a high energy bond.

Adolescence – A general stage of lifespan development that includes puberty.

Advocate – A person who speaks, or pleads, on another person's behalf, sometimes in court, or for a person who cannot defend themselves.

Allergen – A substance that can cause an allergic reaction in sensitive people when their immune system recognises it as 'foreign'. These substances cause no response in most people.

Anaesthetic – Used to cause unconsciousness during operations.

Anonymity – Keeping the identity of an individual hidden from others.

Antagonistic muscles – One muscle or sheet of muscle contracts while an opposite muscle or sheet relaxes.

Antioxidants – Substances that are especially good at destroying free radicals (harmful molecules that damage cells and DNA and can contribute to ageing, heart disease and cancer). Antioxidants are therefore thought to lower the risk of developing cancer and heart disease.

Argument – A point of view that aims to persuade others to the same view by presenting supporting evidence. An argument is more than a statement of fact.

Arterial blood – Blood flowing through arteries that are coming from the heart, usually carrying oxygenated blood to the tissues.

Artery – A blood vessel coming from the heart, usually carrying oxygenated blood to the tissues.

Assertion – Assertion is different from both submission and aggression. It involves being able to negotiate a solution to a problem.

Assumption – An idea that we think is true or correct without bothering to check. In relation to research, it is the conditions that apply to a situation but which are not investigated. It is good practice to be explicit about the assumptions being made.

Atherosclerosis – A thickening of the artery wall caused by cholesterol deposits.

Attitudes – Assumptions that we use to make sense of our social experience.

Autonomic nervous system – Part of the nervous system responsible for controlling the internal organs.

B

Baseline – A starting point against which to make comparisons.

Belief systems – The assumptions we use to make sense of our lives. Out belief systems often include our values.

Beliefs – An acceptance that something exists or is true, especially without proof.

Benchmark – A measure used as a standard against which comparisons can be made.

Beneficence – Something that does good or has a beneficial effect.

Bias – A situation in which an investigation produces results that are influenced by unacknowledged factors, perhaps because of the way the investigation was designed, errors were ignored or how the results were interpreted.

Bibliography – A list of all the sources that have been used to provide information and background knowledge about the topic.

Biological programming – It is argued that our genes can 'program' the amino acids which influence our body cells. Human development and behaviour are not 'programmed' by genes, although development may be influenced by genes.

Biomedical model – An approach to health and illness that identifies health as 'the absence of disease' and focuses on diagnosing and curing individuals with specific illnesses.

Body system – A collection of organs with specific functions in the body.

Bourgeoisie – In Marxist theory, the bourgeoisie are the powerful social class, who own factories, land and other capital and are able to organise the economy and other important social institutions to their own advantage.

Bullying – When an individual or group of people intimidate or harass others.

C

Capitalist – Another word for a member of the bourgeoisie.

Care Quality Commission – The independent regulator of health and social care services in England.

Caring presence – Being open to the experience of another person through a 'two-way' encounter with that person.

Cell – The basic unit of living material.

Central nervous system – The brain and spinal cord.

Charter – A written constitution, written by the legislative power of the country.

Chemotherapy – Treatment for cancer using drugs.

Chromatin network – The dark tangled mass seen in the nucleus of a resting cell.

Chromosomes – Long threads of DNA and protein seen in a dividing cell. They contain the genetic material or genes responsible for transmitting inherited characteristics.

Clinical waste – Waste contaminated with blood or other body fluids, which are potentially infectious.

Cognitive abilities – Ways in which you think, using your knowledge and experience.

Cognitive changes – Changes to a person's thinking, memory or mental abilities that influence their behaviour.

Cognitive impairment – Difficulty in thinking clearly and logically.

Collagen – A structural protein, generally in the form of fibres, for added strength.

Commission – The process by which an organisation requests and funds another organisation to carry out work on their behalf. For example, the Department of Health may commission a university to conduct research on a specific topic. In the UK public sector, the commissioning process usually requires the organisations to tender competitively against others.

Common Induction Standards – These standards cover all the training needed during the first few weeks working in a care setting.

Communication barrier – Anything that stops the development of understanding when people interact.

Communication cycle – Most important communication in care work involves a cycle of building understanding using an active process of reflecting on, and checking out, what the other person is trying to communicate.

Communication disability – A difference that may create barriers between people with different systems of communication.

Complex – Influenced by many inter-related factors.

Concrete logical thinking – The ability to solve problems providing you can see or physically handle the issues involved.

Conditioned response – A new, learned response to a previously neutral stimulus that mimics the response to the unconditioned stimulus.

Conditioned stimulus – A neutral stimulus that, when paired with the unconditioned stimulus, produces a conditioned (learned) response, just as the unconditioned response used to.

Confidentiality – Keeping information, such as research data or personal or hidden information. In relation to research, the information needed for the purpose of the research is only made available to the health or social care researchers.

Conflict model – A sociological approach first associated with Karl Marx, which sees the institutions of society as being organised to meet the interests of the ruling classes.

Continent – Able to control the bladder and bowels.

Continuing professional development (CPD) – This is learning acquired after qualifying as a professional.

Continuous data – Data that can have any value. Weekly changes in body weight or changes in body temperature over a day would both generate sets of continuous data.

Covalent bond – A bond in which two atoms are connected to each other by sharing two or more electrons.

Covert discrimination – Hidden discriminatory actions or words.

Cristae – Folds of the inner layer of mitochondrial membrane on which the enzymes responsible for the oxidation of glucose are situated.

Critical incident – An experience that enables significant learning. It may be a one-off emergency but may often arise from more routine activities that trigger specific learning or flashes of understanding (insight).

Cross-contamination – Germs being spread from one food to another.

Cultural variation – Communication is always influenced by cultural systems of meaning. Different cultures interpret verbal and non-verbal communication behaviours as having different meanings.

Culture – The collection of values, beliefs, behaviours language, rituals, customs and rules associated with a particular society or social group that might make it distinct from others.

Cytoplasm – The word means 'cell material'; the cytoplasm refers to anything inside the cell boundary and outside the nucleus.

D

Dangerous occurrences – These include fire, electrical short-circuit, needle-stick injury and collapse of lifting equipment.

Data – A plural word for 'information'. Strictly, a single piece of information, fact or statistic is 'datum' but because data usually consists of more than one piece of information, this term is rarely used.

Data set – A series of quantitative measurements of the same variable, recorded under the same conditions.

Decubitus mattress – A mattress designed to share the weight evenly and reduce pressure ulcers.

Deductive reasoning – Arguing logically from the general to the specific.

Delayed development – When a child's development lags behind the developmental norms or developmental milestones for his or her age.

Demographic statistics – These are statistics relating to populations. In the UK, statistical information is collected continuously by various agencies but particularly by government departments through information about UK residents gathered from e.g. tax collection, driving licences, passports, the ten-yearly Census, schools, GPs' records, etc.

Deoxyribonucleic acid (DNA) – A nucleic acid found only in the chromatin network and chromosomes of the nucleus. DNA is responsible for the control and passing on of inherited characteristics and instructions to the cell.

Dependent variable – A variable whose value is dependent on that of another variable. The dependent variable is associated with the phenomenon being measured.

Development – Complex changes including an increase in skills, abilities and capabilities.

Developmental norms – Description of an average set of expectations with respect to an infant or child's development.

Deviant – Someone who does not conform to the norms of a particular society or group.

Diagnosis – The medical condition a person has.

Dialect – Words and their pronunciation, which are specific to a geographical community. For example, people who live in the north of England might use a different dialect from Londoners.

Difference – A point or way in which people or things are dissimilar.

Diffusion – The movement of molecules of a gas or a liquid from a region of high concentration to a region of low concentration.

Digestion –The conversion of food into simple, soluble chemicals capable of being absorbed through the intestinal lining into the blood and being utilised by body cells.

Digestive disorders – Conditions affecting the stomach or gut leading to symptoms like nausea (feeling sick), vomiting, diarrhoea, wind and/or bloating.

Dilemma – The difficult decision between alternative choices.

Disability – Sociologists will often refer to disability as the restrictions that arise for a person with an impairment because of the attitudes and the lack of appropriate services and facilities to meet their needs.

Disabling environment – A social context where adaptions and other facilities are not in place to ensure that people with impairments can take a full part in social life.

Disadvantage – Unfavourable circumstance or condition that reduces the chances of success or effectiveness.

Discrete data – Factual information presented in numerical form; the data can only have specific values, e.g. male or female, smoker or non-smoker, those born in 1980, those born in 1981, etc.

Discrimination – The unjust or prejudicial treatment of different categories of people, especially on the grounds of race, age or gender.

Discrimination – Treating some people less well than others because of differences.

Disease incidence – The number of new cases of a specific disease occurring in a population during a specified period of time.

Disease prevalence – The total number of cases of a specific disease in a population during a specified period of time.

Disempowerment – Make a person or group less powerful or confident.

Disengagement – A theory that older people will need to withdraw from social contact with others. Older people will disengage because of reduced physical health and loss of social opportunities.

Distribution of data – An indication of the range or spread between the lowest and highest value of actual measures in a data set measuring the same variable.

Dysfunctional family – A family that is not working well, and not providing all of the support and benefits associated with being in a family.

E

Egalitarian society – A society without hierarchies, where all members are regarded as equal.

Egestion – The process involved in eliminating waste material from the body as faeces.

Ego – The part of the mind whose function it is to moderate the demands of the id and prevent the superego being too harsh. It operates on the reality principle.

Electron microscope – A very powerful type of microscope needed to see inside cells.

Empathy – The ability to develop a deep level of understanding of another person's experience.

Empowerment – Making someone stronger and more confident. This enables a person who uses services to make choices and take control of their own life.

Emulsification – This occurs when an emulsifier causes oil or lipids to be suspended as a large number of tiny globules in water.

Enzymes – These are biological catalysts that alter the rates of chemical reaction (usually speeding them up) but which are themselves unchanged at the end of the reactions.

Equity – The quality of being fair and impartial.

Ethics – Written statements, relating to what is acceptable and unacceptable, that reflect the morals of a society. Morals may be modified over time, so ethical codes tend to evolve to reflect these changes.

Experiment – A test designed specifically to test the validity (truthfulness) of a hypothesis.

Extensors – These carry out extension, which increases the angle between two bones; for example, the triceps (an extensor) straightens the forearm after flexion.

Extract – A section of text taken exactly as written from an existing piece of writing.

F

False consciousness – In Marxist theory, false consciousness is the taking on, by the proletariat, of the views and beliefs of their class enemy, the bourgeoisie. They do not realise that, by working hard, they are serving the interests of the capitalists much more than their own.

Findings – The overall conclusions of an investigation.

First language – The first language that a person learns to speak is often the language that they will think in. Working with later languages can be difficult, as mental translation between languages may be required.

Fit for purpose – A product or object that performs its intended function well.

Flavonoids – The pigments in plants that function as antioxidants.

Flexors – These carry out flexion, which decreases the angle between two bones; for example, the biceps (a flexor) raises the forearm.

Formal care – Care provided by workers who are part of a health or social care service organisation.

Functionalism – A sociological approach that sees the institutions of society as working in harmony with each other, making specific and clear contributions to the smooth running of society.

G

Group values – Group members need to share a common system of beliefs or values in order for the group to communicate and perform effectively. You may be able to identify these values when you watch a group at work.

Growth – An increase in some measured quantity, such as height or weight.

Guideline – A statement of a policy or procedure to help you to follow regulations.

H

Hazard – A hazard is anything that can cause harm, such as a steep staircase.

Health hazards – Incidents leading to illness.

Helplessness – People can give up and become helpless when they learn that they cannot control or influence important personal events. Helpless people can become withdrawn and depressed.

Holistic assessment – An approach to care that addresses the individual's physical, social, emotional and spiritual health, attempting to meet the needs of the 'whole' person.

Holistic development – A person's physical, intellectual, emotional and social development as a whole. Development can be analysed under each of the individual categories to help identify issues but, in life, the categories interact.

Homeostasis – The process of maintaining a constant internal environment despite changing circumstances. For example, the pH, temperature, concentrations of certain chemicals and the water content in the fluid surrounding body cells (the internal environment) must be kept within a narrow range even when you are consuming acids (vinegar, lemon juice), are in a freezing climate, or are doing vigorous exercise.

Homophobia – An extreme and irrational aversion to homosexuality and homosexual people.

Hyperthermia – Increased body temperature above the normal range of values

Hypodermic needles – Needles used to give injections.

Hypothermia – Decreased body temperature below 35°C, which can lead to death.

Hypothesis (plural: hypotheses) – A hypothesis is a statement that predicts an association between two variables.

I

Id – Part of the psyche we are born with. It operates on the pleasure principle.

Impairment – The restrictions on day-to-day activity caused by a physical or mental dysfunction or abnormality, such as the loss of a limb, a sensory impairment or a learning difficulty such as Down's syndrome.

Implementation – The process of actually carrying out the actions identified in a plan.

Incontinence – The inability to control the bladder or bowels.

Independent – Free from control, capable of thinking or acting for oneself.

Independent variable – A variable whose value is not dependent on that of another variable. Time and temperature are common independent variables in scientific experiments.

Inductive reasoning – Arguing logically from the specific to the general.

Infant mortality rate – The number of deaths occurring in infants under one year old per 1000 live births.

Informal care – Care provided by family, friends or neighbours without payment or necessarily involving health or social care providers.

Informed consent – Being provided with all relevant information that may influence the decision to give consent to participate.

Ingestion – The taking in of food, drink and drugs by the mouth.

Interactionism – A sociological approach that focuses on the influence of small groups on our behaviour, rather than the power of large institutions. Interactionists believe that our behaviour is driven by the way we interpret situations in smaller groups, how we see ourselves in relation to other people in the group, how we see other members and how they see us.

Interdependence – Dependent on someone else, depending on each other.

Internalise – This is to do with the way we take in information from the outside world and build it into our sense of self. It then becomes part of our feelings, thoughts and beliefs about who we are and what we expect from the world around us.

Interview – An interaction or conversation between a small number of people for the purpose of eliciting information.

Intolerance – A condition in which a specific food causes unpleasant symptoms such as diarrhoea, bloating and wind. An intolerance is not the same as an allergic reaction.

J

Jargon – Words used by a particular profession or group that are hard for others to understand.

L

Labelling – Assign people to a category, especially inaccurately or restrictively.

Language community – A social community of people that has its own special ways of using language in order to communicate between group members.

Legislation – A law or group of laws.

Liability – Taking responsibility for something.

Life course – a life course is a map of what is expected to happen at the various stages of the human life cycle.

Life expectancy – An estimate of the number of years that a person can expect to live (on average).

Lifestyle – How a person spends their time and money in order to create a 'style' of living.

M

Major injuries – These include fractures (except fingers and toes), dislocations, loss of sight, unconsciousness, poisoning, and any injury resulting in someone requiring resuscitation.

Majority influence – A type of influence exerted by groups that is associated with the individual's desire to be accepted. Behaviour, beliefs and views are changed publicly in order to be in line with the norms of a group, although privately they are unchanged.

Maleficence – Causing harm.

Marginalisation – Treat a person or group as insignificant.

Matrix – Background material in which various types of cells lie.

Maturation – When development is assumed to be due to a genetically programmed sequence of change.

Mean pulse – The mean of a set of numbers is calculated by adding the numbers and dividing by the number of numbers. If an individual's pulse rates were 70, 68 and 64 beats per minute, then the mean would be 70 + 68 + 64 ÷ 3 = 67 (to the nearest whole number). As this calculation has considered three readings, it is more accurate than taking the first reading only.

Metabolism – The metabolism is the sum of all the chemical reactions occurring in human physiology and these involve using or releasing energy from chemical substances.

Minimum standards – These define the minimum standard of practice required.

Mitochondria – Spherical or rod-shaped bodies scattered in the cytoplasm and concerned with energy release.

Modelling – The process of basing behaviour, attitude, style of speech or dress on someone we admire or want to be like.

Morals – The unwritten codes of what a society considers to be acceptable or unacceptable. The morals of a society tend to change over time.

Morbidity rate – This refers to the number of people who have a particular illness during a given period, normally a year.

Morbidly obese – When a person's weight is causing disease, and likely to shorten their life.

Mortality rate – The number of people who have died in the population in a given year. The crude death rate is expressed as the number of deaths in a year per 1000 of the population.

MRSA – Short for methicillin-resistant staphylococcus aureus, sometimes known as a 'superbug' because it is resistant to many antibiotics.

N

Nature – Genetic and biological influences. Those human characteristics that are genetically determined.

Neglect – Fail to care for properly.

Non-participant observer – The individual is an onlooker and not part of the situation being observed.

Norms – The guidelines or rules that govern how we behave in society, or in groups within society.

Nucleus – The central part of the cell, which is usually darker than the rest because it absorbs stain quickly.

Nurture – Social, economic and environmental influences. Those human characteristics that are learned through the process of socialisation.

O

Objective assessment – An assessment that is free from bias and is based on evidence from independent sources.

Observational learning – This occurs when we observe someone behaving in a particular way and we remember this behaviour. We can learn positive and negative behaviours from observing others. For example, we may observe someone going to the aid of a person who collapses.

Organ – A collection of different tissues, such as the heart or the brain, working together to carry out specific functions.

Organelle – A tiny body inside a cell, which carries out its own functions.

Organism – A term for any living thing that can exist independently, including bacteria and viruses.

Osmosis – The passage of water molecules from a region of high concentration (of water molecules) to one of low concentration through a partially permeable membrane such as the cell membranes of simple epithelial cells.

Overnutrition – A condition that results from eating too much, eating too many of the wrong things, or taking too many vitamins or other dietary supplements.

Overt discrimination – Openly discriminatory actions or words.

P

Participant – An individual who contributes information about themselves to a research project; the information may be qualitative or quantitative.

Participant observer – The individual doing the observation is part of the process being observed.

Personal and professional development (PPD) – Learning acquired from experience before qualifying as a professional.

Phenomenon – A term used to describe an event or observation, e.g. the rise in hospital-acquired infections. The plural is phenomena.

Photomicrograph – A photograph taken of an object magnified under a microscope.

Pilot study – An initial, small-scale (perhaps only 10 per cent or the full sample number planned) exercise, in which you use your research tools to see if they are fit for purpose. It is acceptable to make small amendments to improve the reliability and validity of the data gathered in the main, full-scale study.

Policy – A statement of intent and responsibilities in relation to a specific aspect of practice. A document explaining the expected standards.

Power – In the context of interpersonal behaviour, 'power' means the ability to influence and control what other people do.

Prejudice – Preconceived opinion that is not based on reason or actual experience.

Pressure ulcers – These are caused by people sitting, or lying in the same position for a long time, which reduces the oxygen supply to the skin and underlying tissue. In serious cases the tissue dies and turns black.

Primary data – New information generated by observation, interviews, a survey or an experiment.

Primary research – Research that generates new data from sources.

Primary socialisation – The first socialisation of children that normally takes place within the family.

Procedure – A step-by-step description of the processes involved in implementing the policy; instructions about how to carry out a particular task.

Proletariat – In Marxist theory the proletariat are the 'working class', who have only their labour to sell. They work for and are exploited by the bourgeoisie.

Protected mealtimes – A policy whereby patients must not be disturbed from their meals for treatments and tests.

Protoplasm – The word means 'first material'; the protoplasm refers to anything inside the cell boundary. Cell or plasma membrane surrounds the protoplasm.

Provision of services – This refers to health and social care services which are provided, and how they are organised, in communities (e.g. hospitals, care homes, Sure Start centres, etc).

Psyche – The structure of the mind, consisting of three dynamic parts.

Puberty – The developmental process where hormones prepare the body for sexual reproduction.

Q

Qualitative – Data that cannot be 'measured' quantitatively but can only be described using words.

Qualitative information – Information that is described using words and images.

Quantitative – Describes information that is directly measurable; quantitative data usually involves number values and units of measurement, e.g. number of breaths per minute or weight in kg.

Quantitative information – Information that is described using numerical data (e.g. tables, charts and graphs).

R

Racism – Belief that all members of a race possess characteristics that make that race inferior or superior to another race.

Radiotherapy – Treatment for cancer using radiation.

Raw data – Consists of the records of data collected from research in the form they were originally generated.

Reference – An acknowledgement of a source used by someone else to support a specific idea, opinion, quotation, statistic, diagram, flow chart, etc. The reference acknowledges the original author.

Reflection – A conscious process of thinking about a problem in order to understand it.

Reflexes – A rapid automatic response to a stimulus.

Regulation – A principle, rule or law designed to control behaviour.

Reliability – A measure of the quality of the methods used to generate the information. Relates to the extent to which a set of results can be replicated by repeating the test.

Reportable diseases – The reportable diseases most relevant to health and social care include hepatitis, HIV, tuberculosis (TB), and meningitis.

Respondents – The individuals in the selected sample who actually complete the questionnaire and return it to the researchers.

Response frame – The menu of answer options to an individual question provided in a questionnaire.

Response rate – The percentage of respondents from the selected sample. For example, a 30 per cent response rate is good in a survey in which individuals are sent a questionnaire by post.

Responsibility – The duties you are expected to carry out within your job.

Results – Results from research are the data collected and collated into tables, graphs and charts.

Return rate – The number of questionnaires returned, relative to those distributed, expressed as a percentage.

Ribonucleic acid (RNA) – A nucleic acid found in both the cell and the nucleus. RNA is responsible for the manufacture of cell proteins such as pigments, enzymes and hormones.

Risk assessment – Carried out to anticipate danger and plan how to reduce the risk of harm occurring.

Role conflict – This exists when the demands of the social roles that we are expected to perform are not consistent with each other, making it difficult and sometimes impossible to meet all demands.

Role model – An individual who has characteristics that inspire us to copy their behaviour (for example, because they are prestigious, attractive or have high status).

S

Safety hazards – These include incidents leading to personal injury or damage to equipment or buildings.

Sample – In social research, the individuals selected to participate in the research from the sample population.

Sample population – The group of individuals in a population who are targeted for investigation, e.g. older people, college students, etc.

Secondary research – Research in which data is obtained from sources that are already in the public domain, i.e. sources that have been published in journals, books, magazines, etc.

Secondary socialisation – The socialisation that takes place as we move into social settings beyond the family, such as nursery, school and friendship groups.

Secondary sources – Sources of information that have been published by others (e.g. a quotation from an individual that appears in a book or journal).

Security hazards – These include intruders, theft of property or information, and individuals either being abducted or leaving without consent.

Self-actualisation – An innate tendency we all possess as human beings to become the best that we can be in all aspects of personality and intellectual, social and emotional life.

Self-awareness – Being consciously aware of your own strengths and limitations, how others may perceive you and how you may respond to different situations.

Self-concept – The way we see ourselves. In early life this comes from what we are told about ourselves (e.g. 'you're so pretty', 'you're a good footballer', 'what a kind girl you are'). As we grow older, our ability to think about ourselves develops and we begin to incorporate our own judgements (e.g. 'I did well at that test – I'm good at maths', 'I wasn't invited to that party – I must be unpopular').

Self-esteem – How we value or feel about ourselves. The amount of esteem we give to ourselves. Someone with high self-esteem will believe they are loved and lovable and that they are important and valued. By contrast, an individual with low self-esteem may feel themselves to be worthless, of no value to anyone else, unloved and unlovable.

Sensory impairment – Damage to sense organs such as eyes and ears.

Set point – The temperature of the 'hypothalamic thermostat', when autonomic thermo-regulatory mechanisms start to act to reverse the rise or fall and restore normal temperature.

Sexism – Prejudice, stereotyping or discrimination on the basis of gender, typically against women.

Significant – A simple explanation of the term 'significant' in this context would be whether the error was meaningful and likely to distort any conclusions drawn. 'Not significant' means that the error can be ignored.

Skills for Care – One of the sector skills councils for health and social care that set standards for good practice in the UK. The other is Skills for Health.

Slang – Informal words and phrases that are not usually found in standard dictionaries but which are used within specific social groups and communities.

Social control – The strategies used to ensure that people conform to the norms of their society or group.

Social institution – A major building block of society, which functions according to widely accepted customs, rules or regulations. The family, the education system and the legal system are all social institutions.

Social mobility – The process of moving from one social stratum (level) to another. Social mobility can be upward or downward.

Social role – The social expectations associated with holding a particular position or social status in a society or group.

Social stratification – A term (borrowed from geology) describing the hierarchies in society, whereby some groups have more status and prestige than other groups.

Socialisation – The process of learning the usual ways of behaving in a society.

Socio-medical model – An approach to health and illness that focuses on the social and environmental factors that influence our health and well-being, including the impact of poverty, poor housing, diet and pollution.

Stereotyping – Fixed image or idea about a particular type of person or thing.

Superego – Roughly equivalent to a conscience, the superego consists of an internalisation of all the values of right and wrong we have been socialised to believe in. It also contains an image of our ideal self.

Surface tension – The downward pull of water molecules so that the surface of the liquid occupies the smallest possible area.

Survey – A systematic process of gathering information from several people, often using a questionnaire.

T

Target behaviours – Those behaviours that have been defined as being of benefit to the individual's wellbeing.

Transcript – An exact word-for-word written record ('ums' and 'ers' included) of what is said, both by the interviewer and the interviewee, taken from an audio record of the interaction.

U

Uncertain – Where there are many unknowns, where there are considerable gaps in the relevant information, or the strength of different influences could be variable.

Unconditional positive regard – This refers to a totally non-judgemental way of being with and viewing a client. The therapist does not like or approve of the client at some times and disapprove of them at others: they value the client in a positive way with no conditions attached.

Unconditioned response – A response that regularly occurs when an unconditioned stimulus is presented, e.g. the startle response resulting from the thunderclap.

Unconditioned stimulus – A stimulus that regularly and consistently leads to an automatic (not learned) response from, e,g, a clap of thunder.

V

Validity – Relates to the quantity of test results provided to tackle the study in question. 'Valid' means true, sound or well-grounded.

Value consensus – A general agreement as to the values and beliefs of a society.

Values – Principles or standards of behaviour, a person's judgement about what is important in life that we use to guide our thoughts and decisions. They explain what we think of as important or valuable in terms of how we live our lives.

Variable – An entity or factor that can have a range of values that can be measured.

Vegan – A diet that omits all animal products.

Vegetarian – A diet that omits all meat and fish, but includes dairy produce.

Vein – A blood vessel returning blood to the heart from the tissues; the blood has left considerable amounts of oxygen behind to supply the cells and is known as deoxygenated blood.

Venous blood – Blood flowing through veins that are returning blood to the heart from the tissues; the blood has left considerable amounts of oxygen behind to supply the cells and is known as deoxygenated blood.

Voluntarily – Doing something of your own free will, without being forced, or coerced, into doing it.

Vulnerability – Being exposed to harm.

W

Working document – A document that is modified and adapted at the same time as it is being actively used to guide practice.

Index

tube feeding 392
Tuckman's stages of group interaction
   19–20

uncertainty 273
unconditional positive regard 357
unconditioned response 339
unconditioned stimulus 339
unconscious mind, Freud 344–45
undernutrition 370
understanding others 357
unemployment 156, 157
'unfit for human consumption' 102
unpredictable life events 160
unsaturated fats 383
unstructured interviews 433

validity 234, 250–51, 421
value base *see* care value base
value consensus 311
values 26, 56, 157

personal 80–82, 262, 264–65, 281
   see also care value base
variables 434
vegan diet 393
vegetarian 393
veins 192
venous blood 186
ventilation 88–89
Vetting and Barring Scheme 106
visual impairment 165
vitamins 384–85
voluntary sector services 284
vulnerability 56
vulnerable people
   abuse of 119
   and research ethics 420
   safeguarding 105–106

waste disposal 91
water
   dietary consumption of 387

loss of supply 124
websites for research 436–37
weight for height and gender 371–72
well-being, personal 81
work
   effect of shift work 362–63
   ethnic minority disadvantages 57
   in health & social care 293–99
working with others 259–60
working conditions 92–93
working documents 271
working practices
   hazardous 93
   monitoring of 109–10
   see also policies and procedures
written communication 15

x-rays 91–92

zinc 386